Seventh-day Adventist

Attitudes Toward

Roman Catholicism

1844 - 1965

Reinder Bruinsma

Andrews University Press
Berrien Springs, Michigan

This book is a slightly revised version of the Ph.D. dissertation by Reinder Bruinsma titled "A Historical Analysis of Seventh-day Adventist Attitudes Toward Roman Catholicism: 1844-1965," which was submitted to the University of London (Great Britain) and successfully defended in August 1993.

The British spelling has been maintained.

Andrews University Press
Berrien Springs, Michigan 49104-1700
FAX (616) 471-6224

© 1994 by Andrews University Press
All rights reserved. Published 1994
Printed in the United States of America

01 00 99 98 97 96 95 94   7 6 5 4 3 2 1

ISBN 1-883925-04-5
Library of Congress catalog card no. 94-72955

TABLE OF CONTENTS

Chapter 3 SABBATARIAN ADVENTISTS AND CATHOLICS

Chapter 4 ADVENTISTS AND CATHOLICS: 1863-1915

CONCLUSIONS

BIBLIOGRAPHY

ACKNOWLEDGEMENTS

I wish to express my gratitude to all those who have encouraged and supported me while I was working on this project.

A few people ought to be mentioned in particular. My advisor, Dr. Judith F. Champ, Professor of Church History at King's College, University of London, has given me clear guidance, invaluable counsel and sympathetic support. Dr. George Knight, Professor of Church History at Andrews University (Berrien Springs, Mich., USA) read and criticized most of my work. His detailed remarks helped me to avoid a number of errors, while his positive evaluation of an early draft of several chapters gave me the confidence which I needed to finish this project within the time frame I had set myself.

James B. Ford and Sharon J. Cress of the Heritage Room of the James White Library (Andrews University, Berrien Springs, Mich., USA) provided the kind of service every researcher hopes for, while Bert Haloviak, the curator of the Archives of the General Conference of Seventh-day Adventists (Silver Spring, MD, USA), also proved of great assistance.

A considerable part of the research was carried out in 1991. The generosity of the Trans-European Division of the Seventh-day Adventist Church enabled me to devote all my time for almost 10 months to research. I am also most appreciative of the consideration by the board and the Director of the Seventh-day Adventist Institute of World Mission shown to me during 1992 and part of 1993. Their support allowed me to spend a major portion of my time on further research and writing.

I feel a different kind of gratitude toward the four most important people in my life, who, each in her/his own way, have supported me in my academic training in general and the writing of this dissertation in particular. I treasure the memory of my mother, who in the 1950s and 1960s sacrificed to make it possible for me to attend secondary school and college. I owe a great debt to my wife Aafje, who has always been 100 per cent supportive of my academic aspirations, and encouraged me when a few years ago I suggested to register for the external Ph.D. programme at the University of London. Finally, a genuine "thank you" to our daughter Danielle and son Peter, who may not get overly excited about the topic their father was studying, but were most positive in their reactions when he announced that he would join them temporarily in their student status.

ABBREVIATIONS

AH	Adventist Heritage
AHSTR	Advent Herald and Signs of the Times Reporter
AS	American Sentinel
ESH	William Miller, Evidence from Scripture and History of the Second Coming of Christ
GC	Ellen G. White, The Great Controversy
Gen. Conf.	General Conference of Seventh-day Adventists
HOS	J.N. Andrews, History of the Sabbath and the First Day of the Week
MC	Midnight Cry
Lib	Liberty
Min	The Ministry
OFF	Our Firm Foundation
PFOF	Leroy E. Froom, The Prophetic Faith of Our Fathers
PM	Protestant Magazine
PPPA	Pacific Press Publishing Association
PT	Present Truth
RH	Review and Herald
RHPA	Review and Herald Publishing Association
SDA	Seventh-day Adventist(s)
SDABC	The Seventh-day Adventist Bible Commentary
SDAE	The Seventh-day Adventist Encyclopedia
SPA	Southern Publishing Association
SSQ	Sabbath School Quarterly
ST	Signs of the Times
TTM	P.G. Damsteegt, Toward the Theology of Mission of the Seventh-day Adventist Church

INTRODUCTION

The Problem

In an era of increasing interdenominational under-standing and dialogue, not only between various traditions within Protestantism, but also between Protestants and Roman Catholics, the Seventh-day Adventist Church continues to be very reluctant about ecumenical encounters with other Protestants and perseveres in its outright condemnation of Roman Catholicism. This study is an attempt to analyze the factors which have contributed to the unbending anti-Catholic position of Seventh-day Adventists. It will try to establish which external factors played a significant role and will seek to determine which theological and other developments contributed to the persistent anti-Catholic attitude of Seventh-day Adventists.

Nineteenth century and early 20th century American Protestantism in general was characterized by strong anti-Catholic sentiments, but gradually in most deno-minations a more positive assessment of Catholicism replaced the earlier hostility. Why did Adventists scarcely share in this process? That question takes on added meaning when one considers the remarkable change in more recent Adventist attitudes toward other Protestant churches. The earlier negative judgment of contemporary Protestantism as merely "nominal" or even "apostate", has to a considerable extent been replaced by more cordial feelings. Significantly, in the past few decades Adventists have made a decided effort to be recognized by evangelical Protestantism as a genuine part of that tradition. Why has Adventism been able to shift its position with regard to other Protestant churches, but has (at least officially) not been willing to revise its estimate of the Roman Catholic Church?

What have been the major elements in the anti-Catholic position of Adventism? To what extent were they part of the general anti-Catholic climate within 19th century American Protestantism? What did Adventists inherit from the Millerites in this respect and what was unique in the Seventh-day Adventist position? These and related issues this study will address.

Scope and Limitations

Although it was tempting to limit the scope of the investigation to a relatively short period, to the thoughts of a limited number of representative Adventist leaders, or to a restricted geographical environment, a deliberate decision was made to include most of the history of Seventh-day Adventism. A broader analysis of developments over a longer period of time within Adventism seemed preferable, if trends and possible changes were to be recognized. However, three limiting factors have been imposed. The first is, that the study does not go beyond 1965, when the Second Vatican Council ended. This limitation is mainly due to the practical necessity of keeping the investigation within manageable proportions. The second is, that the study is based almost exclusively on American sources. This is not as much of a problem as it might appear at first sight. Although Seventh-day Adventism has spread around the globe, its theology and attitudes have been largely shaped in America, by Americans, or by non-Americans who have accepted the ideas and attitudes of their American brethren. There has only been a very limited degree of adaptation of Adventist views and practices to non-American cultures.[1] Finally, only a limited comparison with other Protestant denominations was possible. Some comparison, however, is made with the development of anti-Catholic sentiments in the Methodist and Baptist traditions, since they shared to a large extent the religious and social context in which Adventism arose.

Methodology and Resources

The first two chapters provide the necessary background. Chapter One outlines how Protestants in Puritan England and in colonial and early republican America viewed Catholicism. It decribes the widespread and deeprooted anti-Roman Catholic sentiments--based on a long tradition of anti-Catholic interpretation of apocalyptic

---

[1] A recent study by Malcolm Bull and Keith Lockhart (Seeking a Sanctuary: Seventh-day Adventists and the American Dream; San Francisco: Harper & Row, 1989) deals in depth with the American character of Adventism. It is their opinion that "to become an Adventist [is] to join an American religion ... Adventism has appropriated and reinterpreted the central themes of American self-understanding" (168).

Bible prophecy--in the United States in general and in the region in which Millerism orginated and briefly flourished in particular.

Chapter Two deals with the Millerite movement, which is seen by Seventh-day Adventists as a prelude to the beginning of their denomination. It describes the views of William Miller and other leaders of the movement, which in a few years developed from an interdenominational revival movement into a separate sect. Miller's system of hermeneutics and the resulting interpretation of the book of Daniel and the book of Revelation, notably where these were applied to Roman Catholicism, receive due attention. The views of Miller and his associates are analyzed against the backdrop of the religious ferment which characterized the New England states and Upstate New York in the 1830s and 1840s, to determine what was unique about them and what was not. The Millerites' interpretations of apocalyptic prophecy and their opinions about Roman Catholics based thereon provided the basis on which Seventh-day Adventists were to build, and are therefore of special importance.

The Millerite movement has in recent years enjoyed considerable interest, resulting in a number of excellent scholarly publications and doctoral disser- tations. These have been extensively used, but for the analysis of Millerite ideas only primary sources have been consulted. A wealth of source material, brought together in the Advent Source Collection (available on microfilm), was easily accessible.

Moving beyond the Millerite movement to Adventism, it seemed advisable to cut the 120-plus year period in a few workable segments:
   a. 1844-1863: the period of Sabbatarian Adventism.
   b. 1863-1915: the formative period of Seventh-day
      Adventism.
   c. 1915-1965: Adventism in its mature stage.
The three main chapters of this dissertation cover these distinct periods. Since b) and c) are relatively long periods, care has been exercised to consult and compare sources from different times within these periods, in order to notice possible developments.

Chapter Three explores how in the formative stages of their denominational history, the Sabbatarian Adventists built on the Millerite heritage. It outlines how they adopted, refined and revised, the Millerite prophetic interpretations, notably those which were applied to Catholicism. But it especially emphasizes how the adoption of the seventh-day Sabbath further, and definitively, shaped the Adventist view of Catholicism: Not only was "Rome" responsible for the substitution of the Sunday for the divinely instituted Sabbath, but the Sabbath-Sunday issue and continued Catholic opposition to the Sabbath and its observers, was accorded enormous eschatological importance. It is further shown how another vital idea was introduced, which would be elaborated upon in later decades: America's "endtime" role in support of Catholicism, and the combined future efforts of a religio-political coalition of Protestants and Catholics, operating on American soil, aimed at the destruction of Sabbath keepers.

In researching this chapter, relevant secondary sources were consulted, but care has been taken to outline the Adventist ideas of this period on the basis of primary evidence. Most of the books and tracts written by the Adventist "pioneers" are extant and available for study. The most important source for this period (and the next: 1863-1915) is the denominational journal, the *Review and Herald*, published weekly since 1850.

Chapter Four covers the period in which Adventism came of age. It follows largely the same pattern as the previous chapter and explores some relevant developments in prophetic interpretation. What makes this period of vital importance is the way in which events on the American religious scene, most notably those directly or indirectly related to Sunday legislation, strengthened Adventists in their conviction of the correctness of their eschatological views, with Catholicism and Protestant America as the persecutors of a Sabbath keeping minority. Once again Adventist reactions to current "Catholic" issues are analyzed and briefly compared to the reactions of some other Protestant denominations. A section of the chapter is devoted to the views of Ellen G. White on Catholicism. Her influence as a "prophet" within Adventism can hardly be overestimated and her views played a significant role in solidifying Adventist anti-Catholic opinion.

What was said about the use of primary and secondary sources in connection with Chapter Three, also applies to Chapter Four.

Chapter Five describes Adventist reactions to issues in or related to Catholicism from 1915 until Vaticanum II, and attempts to determine whether there were changes in attitudes when compared with the earlier periods. It again looks carefully at developments in the Adventist

understanding of the prophetic portions of the Bible
which Adventism has traditionally applied to Roman
Catholicism. The chapter shows how Adventists, while
showing more flexibility in their attitude toward other
Protestant Christians than before, were unwilling to
make a fundamental re-evaluation of their position with
regard to Catholicism.

For this chapter the denominational journal again
provided a considerable amount of material. In this
period, however, a number of publications appeared which
were specifically endorsed by the denomination as
representing current Adventist thinking, and these merit
special attention.

A short concluding chapter summarizes the findings of
this study and re-iterates the main developments in
Adventist thinking regarding Roman Catholicism.

CHAPTER ONE

THE SETTING

I Introductory Remarks

It will not take long before a student of Seventh-day
Adventism is confronted with the anti-Catholic bias
which has characterized much of Adventist literature and
preaching from its very inception. The statement made by
Joseph Bates in 1851, just a few years after Sabbatarian
Adventism had established itself as a group[1] after the
disillusionment of 1844,[2] is typical for the thinking
current during the early stages of the movement.
Commenting on Revelation 13:1-3, he explained:

> We understand it thus: The dragon denotes the
> imperial power of Rome. The beast with seven heads,
> Papal Rome, or Popery.... John saw in vision the
> Papal power of Rome, coming up among the nations of
> Europe in A.D. 538, with the power to continue
> forty-two months [1260 years]. At the expiration of

---

[1] The name Seventh-day Adventists was not adopted
until 1860, hence it is proper to use the term
Sabbatarian Adventism for the period 1844-1860. See Don.
F. Neufeld, ed., <u>Seventh-day Adventist Encyclopedia</u>,
rev. ed. (Washington DC: RHPA, 1976), s.v. "Development
of Organization in SDA Church", 1042-1045. Further
referred to as <u>SDAE</u>.

[2] William Miller had predicted Christ's second
coming on October 22, 1844. When Christ did not come on
that day, the "great disappointment" caused the Millerite movement to disintegrate. A small group of
Advent-believers soon adopted Sabbatarianism and became
the nucleus of what was eventually to become the
Seventh-day Adventist Church. See pp. 75-82.

1

this period "one (the seventh) of his heads is
wounded to death." By adding 1260 years to A.D.
538, we come down to A.D. 1798, at which period the
French nation conquered Rome, and destroyed the
seven-headed power, or Papal Rome....[3]

Ellen G. White, one of the most prolific writers among
Seventh-day Adventists, whose opinions have a special
value to the Adventist Church,[4] left in the fifth volume
of her "Great Conflict" series--which is still in print
and continues to be distributed widely in many languages
--no doubt about her opinion of the Roman Catholic
Church:

> The Roman Church now presents a fair front to the
> world, covering with apologies her record of
> horrible cruelties. She has clothed herself in
> Christlike garments; but she is unchanged. Every
> principle of the papacy that existed in past ages
> exists today....
>   The papacy is just what prophecy declared she
> would be, the apostasy of the latter times. It is
> part of her policy to assume the character which
> will best accomplish her purpose; but beneath the
> variable appearance of the chameleon, she conceals
> the invariable venom of the serpent.[5]

In 1950, in partial fulfillment of the requirements for
his M.A. degree, a student at the Seventh-day Adventist

---

[3] Joseph Bates, "The Beast with Seven Heads," RH
(Aug. 5, 1851), 3.

[4] Ellen G. White is usually referred to as a
"prophet", whose writings are considered to be inspired.
Although officially regarded as "a small light" which
leads to "the greater light" (the Bible), there has
never been complete unanimity among Adventists about the
status of her writings, and there certainly is not
today. That they do have a special place in Adventist
literature is, however, generally accepted. (The oft-
quoted reference to a "lesser light" and the "greater
light" is from E.G. White herself; see E.G. White,
Colporteur Ministry [Mountain View, Cal.: PPPA, 1953],
125).

[5] Ellen G. White, The Great Controversy, (Mountain
View, Cal.: PPPA, 1911), 571. Further ref. to as GC.

Theological Seminary, submitted "A Syllabus and Study
Guide for a Course in Church History". He prefaced his
section "American Catholicism in General: 1789-1900"
with the following paragraph:

> The student of prophecy has little difficulty in
> identifying the course taken by the American
> Catholic Church, for that course is well marked out
> in Biblical prophecy. The student of this unit,
> therefore ... will do well to observe just how
> Roman Catholicism grew to the power it possessed by
> the end of the nineteenth century. The student
> should note her fight against Church and State
> separation; the influence of southern European
> personalities; the attempt to tamper with our free
> press and speech; and her furtherance of corrupt
> politics, particularly in America's larger cities.[6]

He adds the following remark in his section on
"Protestantism in America since 1900":

> By mid-century [i.e. ca. 1950] the ever-increasing
> tempo of Roman Catholic growth was hanging as a
> scythe over the bowed head of a once-powerful and
> proud American Protestantism.[7]

and in his chapter on "Catholicism since 1950":

> ...remember that it will be this potent and
> unscrupulous religious and temporal power which
> will finally unite with a decadent, apostate, and
> once-glorious Protestantism to bring a time of
> great trouble to God's people.[8]

To these few quotations multitudes of others could be
added (and will be added in later chapters). Of course,
many other churches and religious groups have through
the years manifested anti-Catholic sentiments, but few
have sustained these so consistently, even to this very
day, as Seventh-day Adventists have done. Before we turn

---

[6] Stanley R. Peterson, "A Syllabus and Study Guide
for a Survey Course in Church History" (Unpubl. M.A.
thesis, SDA Theol. Sem., 1950), 122.

[7] Ibid., 149.

[8] Ibid., 154.

3

to the history of Adventist attitudes toward Roman
Catholicism we must provide the setting in which
Adventism originated and attention must be paid to the
attitudes toward Catholicism in the Millerite movement
--from which Seventh-day Adventism sprang. Chapter Two
will be devoted to a discussion of Millerite views of
the Roman Catholic Church.

This introductory chapter will proceed to briefly
describe some historical trends which help to explain
the unrelenting anti-Catholic position that characterized Adventism. For this we need to take a good look
at the way Post-Reformation England and 18th and 19th
century American Protestantism have viewed Catholicism.

II England: Post-Reformation Views
on Roman Catholicism

Even before the Reformation dramatically changed the
ecclesiastical picture of England, attempts were made to
limit the power of the Roman Catholic Church, by acts of
Parliament and other political initiatives to counter
the claims of the popes.[9] John Wycliffe (c. 1329-1384)
and his Lollards voiced opposition against a number of
the Catholic doctrines and practices, but remained
relatively ineffective in their efforts to reform the
English church.[10] After King Henry VIII (1509-1547)
established the Church of England and formally
introduced the Reformation in England, but in particular
during the reigns of Edward VI (1547-1553) and Elizabeth
I (1558-1603), anti-Catholic sentiments became more
pronounced. There was increasing concurrence with the
opinion, earlier voiced by men like John Whitgift (c.
1530-1604), John Field (1520-1587), and others, that the
pope was the Antichrist.[11]

This identification of Rome with Antichrist already had

---

[9] J.C. Dickinson, The Later Middle Ages (New York:
Barnes & Noble, 1979), 313-315.

[10] Ibid., 315-335.

[11] Peter Lake, "The Significance of the Elizabethan
Identification of the Pope as Antichrist", Journal of
Ecclesiastical History, vol. 31, no. 2 (April 1980),
161.

a long history in medieval Europe.[12] In equating the "little horn" in Daniel chapter 7, the eschatological culprit *par excellence*, with the Antichrist, the 17th century English expositors followed a long established tradition.[13]

Ball admirably summarizes the background against which these anti-Catholic ideas could develop and prosper:

> "The proximity of this Western Antichrist constituted an ever present threat to Englishmen who were as unwilling as they were unable to forget a thousand years of history. The Spanish Armada, the Gunpowder plot, the Romanizing tendencies of Archbishop Laud and Charles I, and the hazardous course of Continental Protestantism had more recently served to heighten these fore-bodings and explain why, to more modern eyes, the seventeenth

---

[12] Richard Bauckham, <u>Tudor Apocalypse</u> (Oxford: The Sutton Courtenay Press, 1978), 16-37; Christopher Hill, <u>Antichrist in Seventeenth Century England</u>, rev. ed. (London: Verso, 1990), 1-40.

[13] Bryan W. Ball, <u>The Great Expectation: Eschatological Thought in English Protestantism to 1660.</u> Heiko A. Oberman, ed., <u>Studies in the History of Christian Thought</u>, Vol. XII, (Leiden: E.J. Brill, 1975), 132. For a survey of interpretations of apocalyptic prophecy by leading expositors in Post-Reformation times, see Leroy E. Froom, <u>The Prophetic Faith of Our Fathers</u> (Washington, D.C.: RHPA, 1946-1954), vol. II, 783-787. For the views of some famous English expositors in particular, see Leroy E. Froom, Ibid., vol. II, 512-518 (Brightman); 542-549 (Mede); 555 (Forbes). Froom's work is further referred to as <u>PFOF</u>.

Data from Froom's work will be used in this study, notably in chapters 2 and 3, though with caution. His work has received much acclaim for its unusual scope, but its denominational bias and selectivity have been noted by more than one scholar. See comments to that effect, e.g. in A.J.B. Gilsdorf, "The Puritan Apocalypse: New England Eschatology in the Seventeenth Century" (Ph.D. diss., Yale University, 1965), 223; and George Shepperson, "The Comparative Study of Millenarian Movements", chap. in: Sylvia Thrupp, ed., <u>Millennial Dreams in Action</u> (The Hague: Mouton & Co, Publ., 1974), 48.

century appears to have had an almost inordinate pre-occupation with the Papacy.[14]

In Elizabethan times the view that the pope was Antichrist was no longer the idea of a fanatical fringe of the Church of England, but had acquired "theoretical respectability"[15]--although there were some alternative theories about Antichrist's identity[16]--and Roman Catholics were regarded with utmost suspicion.[17] The objections to Catholicism were based on a historicist application of a number of apocalyptic sections from the Bible, and included political enmity against the power of the popes, as well as theological disagreements, notably with regard to the sacerdotal priesthood.[18]

III Puritan Views on Roman Catholicism

It was the Puritan version of English Protestantism which, more than any other brand of the Reformation, left its imprint on the New England States and "Upstate New York" - the famous "Burnt-over District"[19] where the

---

[14] Ibid., 141.

[15] Christopher Hill, Antichrist in Seventeenth Century England, 13.

[16] Ibid., 131-143.

[17] For some interesting examples, see G.F.A. Best, "Popular Protestantism in Victorian Britain," chap. in: R. Robson, ed., Ideas and Institutions of Victorian Britain (New York: Barnes & Noble, Inc., 1967), 115, and Richard Bauckham, Tudor Apocalypse, 91.

[18] G.F.A. Best, "Popular Protestantism," 118, and passim.

[19] The term "Upstate" is used for a region away from and usually north of a big city, especially New York.
The term "Burnt-over District" has been widely used ever since Whitney R. Cross published his book The Burnt-Over District: The Social and Intellectual History of Enthusiastic Religion in Western New York, 1800-1850 (Ithaca, N.Y.: Cornell University Press, 1950).

Millerite movement was to have its base and where the earliest developments of Sabbatarian Adventism were to take place. Since they were to become the chief theologians of 17th century colonial New England, it is important to know how the Puritans developed the anti-Catholic views that were current in 17th century England.[20]

For the Puritans anti-Catholicism was almost "natural." "For them the antichristian nature of popery, summed up in the identification of the pope as Antichrist, provided the central organizing principle for a whole view of the world."[21] In Tudor England the Roman Antichrist was a matter of standard exegesis and a whole genre of books, tracts and sermons were devoted to proving the papacy to be the Antichrist as prophesied in Scripture.[22]

It was this militant anti-Catholic religious tradition, which had flourished since the days when Elizabeth I (1558-1603) was confronted with the threat of Philip of Spain. Now it became even more explicit among the Puritans, and was to be a fundamental factor in American thinking.[23] Thousands of Puritans began to emigrate to New England during the early years of Charles I (1600-1649; reigned from 1625) and soon "scores of illustrious men--strong, independent thinkers who had fled the tyranny of the Old World" (to use some of Froom's emotionally charged language) "were scattered throughout the colonies ... having remarkable unity on

---

[20] Leroy E. Froom, PFOF, vol. III, 22.

[21] Peter Lake, "The Significance of the Elizabethan Identification of the Pope as Antichrist," 161. See also A.J.B. Gilsdorf, "The Puritan Apocalypse," I, II. For the Puritan identification of the papacy with Antichrist, see Christopher Hill, Antichrist in Seventeenth Century England, passim; Bauckham, Tudor Apocalypse, passim; Bryan W. Ball, The English Connection: The Puritan Roots of Seventh-day Adventist Belief (Cambridge: James Clarke, 1981), 209.

[22] Richard Bauckham, Tudor Apocalypse, 99-108.

[23] Sydney E. Ahlstrom, A Religious History of the American People (New Haven and London: Yale University Press, 1972), 556.

the basic principles of prophetic interpretation."[24] The
Puritan divines who arrived in North America (some with
extensive libraries, often graduates from Cambridge or
Oxford), transplanted the Old World historicist hermeneutics and the current prophetic views to their new
fatherland.

Thus, from the outset, apocalyptic prophecy was one of
the most important intellectual traditions in New
England. The works of Joseph Mede (1587-1638) were
extremely popular,[25] as was John Fox's Book of Martyrs
(published in 1563), one of the few books a Puritan
child was allowed to read on Sunday.[26] Men like Thomas
Parker (an English-born pioneer minister in Massachusetts; 1595-1677) and Ephraim Huit (pastor in
Connecticut, also born in England; d. 1644)[27] were soon
ready to write their first commentaries on Daniel and
the Revelation, leaving no doubt about the identity of

---

[24] Leroy E. Froom, PFOF, vol. III, 22.

[25] David D. Hall, World of Wonder, Days of
Judgement: Popular Religious Beliefs in Early New
England (New York: Alfred A. Knopf, 1989), 76-77.

[26] Barbara Welter, "From Maria Monk to Paul
Blanshard: A Century of Protestant Anti-Catholicism",
chap. in: Robert N. Bellah and Frederick E. Greenspahn,
eds., Uncivil Religion: Interreligious Hostility in
America (New York: The Crossroad Publ. Comp., 1987), 45.
See also: Thomas M. Brown, "The Image of the Beast:
Anti-Papal Rhetoric in Colonial America", chap. in:
Richard O. Curry and Thomas M. Brown, eds., The Fear of
Subversion in American History (New York: Holt, Rinehart
and Winston, Inc., 1972), 5.

[27] Ephraim Huit, The Whole Prophecie of Daniel
Explained. By a Paraphrase, Analysis and Briefe Comment:
Wherein the Severall Visions Shewed to a Prophet Are
Clearly Interpreted, and the Application Thereof
Vindicated Against Dissenting Opinions (London: Henry
Overton, 1644); Thomas Parker, The Visions and
Prophecies of Daniel Expounded: Wherein the Mistakes of
Former Interpreters Are Modestly Discovered (London:
Edmund Paxton, 1646). See Leroy E. Froom, PFOF, vol.
III, 60-77.

the dark antichristian power which was therein depicted.[28] And thus, even though in colonial times less than one percent of the American population was Roman Catholic (and most of these were concentrated in the state of Maryland), the anti-Catholic bias became a standard idea of colonial culture.

The Protestant-Catholic antagonism was imported wholesale.[29] In America the Puritans saw the chance to establish a sanctuary where they would be able to construct a church purged of all Romish corruptions. The Puritan roots of the various denominations which came to dominate the American Protestant religious scene in the colonial period--Presbyterians, Congregationalists, Episcopalians, Baptists and later Methodists--ensured that these were, in spite of credal differences, remarkably united in their interpretations of apocalyptic prophecy and their views on "popery."[30]

Not all arguments used by Protestant writers were of a purely theological nature. There was a widespread fear that the papacy was constantly engineering all kinds of conspiracies to undermine the Protestant nations in general, and America in particular--with the Jesuits usually in the key role as secret agents for the papacy and its allies.[31] France and Spain were generally regarded as agents of the papal power. The Spanish attempt to build an empire in the Americas was not merely for Spain's own benefit, but primarily to satisfy the ambitions of the popes.[32] The events in England which led to the Glorious Revolution (1688) continued to remind Protestants in England as well as in America that "a terrible papal plot, seeking to impose arbitrary

---

[28] Thomas H. Olbricht, "Biblical Primitiveness in American Scholarship, 1630-1870", chap. in: Richard T. Hughes, The American Quest for the Primitive Church (Urbano: University of Illinois Press, 1988), 83-86.

[29] Earl Raab, ed., Religious Conflict in America (Garden City, N.Y.: Doubleday and Comp., Inc., 1964), 1.

[30] For a survey of the views of principal American writers on prophecy in the 17th and 18th century, see Leroy E. Froom, PFOF, vol. III, 252-253.

[31] Thomas M. Brown, "The Image of the Beast," 7.

[32] Ibid., 5-6.

government and religious despotism on the English-speaking world had been defeated."[33] In the seven years of the so-called "French and Indian war" (1756-1763) suspicions of a Catholic conspiracy were never far away and resulted in a flood of antipapal rhetoric.[34]

IV America: the 18th and Early 19th Century

Catholicism in the American Republic remained numerically insignificant well into the 19th century. The total number of adherents did not exceed 50,000 by 1800.[35] The era of the Awakening was a difficult time for American Catholics. "Papalism" continued to be denounced by spokesmen for the various churches, which divided the spiritual realm in the steadily increasing number of states of the young republic. The historic Protestant antipathy against Catholicism found expression in the countless sermons, books, pamphlets and periodicals which addressed the issue.[36] Though the Enlightenment had exerted a major influence and had stressed the importance of religious tolerance, Catholicism continued to be seen as a form of superstition and despotism. "Protestants who wrangled among themselves over denominational differences could readily make common cause against the threat of 'popery'."[37] There was widespread concern over the Quebec Act of 1774 as a development which could endanger the future of American

---

[33] Ibid., 12.

[34] Ibid., 15. See also Robert T. Handy, A History of the Churches in the United States and Canada, 2nd ed. (New York: Oxford University Press, 1977), 64; and: Sydney E. Ahlstrom, A Religious History of the American People, 556.

[35] Robert T. Handy, Ibid., 214.

[36] Charles Yrigoyen, jr., "Methodists and Early Catholics in the 19th Century," Methodist History, vol. 28, no. 3 (Apr. 1990), 172.

[37] Robert T. Handy, A History of the Churches in the United States and Canada, 217.

Protestantism.[38]

In the New England states and Upstate New York Baptists and Methodists grew from modest beginnings into the most important religious bodies.[39] Although known for their tolerance for other religious groups, the Baptists published many monographs, pamphlets and periodicals which addressed themselves to "the Catholic question". Some Baptists were actively involved in the editing and publishing of non-Baptist publications of a decidedly anti-Catholic nature or were active in anti-Catholic organizations. Although usually milder in tone than many other Protestants of the 18th and 19th century, Baptists mirrored the intensely anti-Catholic culture of their time.[40]

The Methodists denounced the Catholic Church as Paul's "man of sin" and "Babylon the Great",[41] The ways in which they tried to "expose" and refute Catholic doctrine and papal claims generally included the themes which were characteristic of 19th century Protestant assaults on Catholicism. Methodist writers "addressed the differences between themselves and Catholics as

---

[38] Quebec had been in the French sphere of influence since the early decades of the 17th century. The French had strongly supported the Roman Catholic efforts to evangelize the population in their territories. In Quebec Catholicism became the majority religion.

[39] For statistical information on the development of various religious bodies in America, see Edwin S. Gaustad, Historical Atlas of Religion in America (New York: Harper & Row, Publ., 1962), 43-44.

[40] Terry C. Carter, "Baptist Participation in Anti-Catholic Sentiment and Activities, 1830-1860" (Unpubl. Ph.D. diss., Southwestern Baptist Theol. Sem., Fort Worth, Texas, 1983). The anti-Catholic position of early 19th century Baptist writers is well illustrated in two works on Church History by Baptist authors: John Mockett Cramp, The Reformation in Europe (New York: American Tract Society, c. 1840; and John Dowling, History of Romanism: From the Earliest Corruptions of Christianity to the Present Time (New York: Edward Walker, 1848).

[41] 2 Thessalonians 2:8 and Revelation ch. 18. See Charles Yrigoyen jr., "Methodists and Roman Catholics," 180.

Protestants rather than as Methodists".[42]

V Millenarianism

In this context mention must be made of a related phenomenon which played an increasingly important role in 19th century Britain and America: *millenarianism*.

The term "millenarianist" is derived from the word "millennium", the thousand-year period of Revelation 20. In its stricter sense it refers to those who believe in the reality of a thousand year period, either preceded or followed by the second coming of Christ. But many sociologists, anthropologists, and historians, tend to give the term a much broader meaning and apply it to those who tend to build chronological scenarios for the future and insist that Christ's second coming is near and will be preceded by unparalleled cataclysms.[43]

Millenarianism certainly was not a new phenomenon.[44] But it took on a unique dimension in the New World. It has been said that the whole American experience--the "American dream"--can only be understood within the framework of a basic millenarian philosophy,[45] with

---

[42] Charles Yrigoyen, jr., Ibid., 185-186.

[43] See Ernest Sandeen, "Millennialism", chap. in: Edwin S. Gaustad, ed., The Rise of Adventism: Religion and Society in Mid-Nineteenth Century America (New York: Harper & Row, Publishers, 1974), 104-118.

[44] For a survey of millenarian movements during the Middle Ages, see Norman C. Cohen, The Pursuit of the Millennium, rev. and exp. ed. (New York: Oxford University Press, 1970). Later famous outbursts of millenarianism were to be found in the Anabaptist experiments in Münster (see e.g. George H. Williams, The Radical Reformation [Philadelphia: The Westminster Press, 1962], 362-386), and in the aspirations of the Fifth Monarchy Men (see e.g. B.S. Capp, The Fifth Monarchy Men: A Study in Seventeenth Century Millenarianism [Totowa, N.J.: Rowman and Littlefield, 1972]).

[45] This is argued by H. Richard Niebuhr, The Kingdom of God in America (New York: Harper and Row, Publishers, 1937, Torchbook ed. 1959). He defended the thesis that the expectation of the Kingdom of God on earth must be

religious as well as secular overtones.

During the eighteenth century apocalyptic millenarianism was not as prominent as before but it revived in full force after the French Revolution. "That political cataclysm broke with such force upon Europeans and Americans, that no image but an apocalyptic one seemed to give adequate expression to the drama and the panoramic sweep of those events."[46] The dethronement of the pope by the army of Napoleon in 1798 made sure that "wheels began turning in the heads of biblical scholars".[47] Quite generally, prophetic interpreters turned to the 1260 days of Daniel and the Revelation[48], which they understood to signify 1260 literal year[49] of papal supremacy, beginning in the time of Emperor Justinian and ending with the imprisonment of the pope in 1798.[50]

The French Revolution accelerated the millenarian interests in two ways. It upset the notion of gradual progress which had become rather universal during the eighteenth century Enlightenment, and it suddenly made apocalyptic expectations seem more realistic. The

---

seen as the great common element in American Protestant thought, the underlying constant beneath the immense diversity of American Protestantism.

[46] Ernest Gaustad, "Millennialism," 107-108.

[47] Ibid.

[48] Revelation 11:3; 12:6; also Revelation 11:2; 13:5; 12:14; Daniel 7:25; 12:7.

[49] For a survey of the application of the "year-day principle" from the early church period until the 19th century, see Leroy E. Froom, PFOF, vol. I, 156, 164, 457, 894-897; PFOF, vol.II, 156, 528-531; 784-787; PFOF, vol. III, 743-744; PFOF, vol. IV, 396-401.

[50] C. Mervyn Maxwell provides a considerable amount of information about the ways in which expositors arrived at 538 and 1798 or approximate dates. See his unpubl. M.A.-thesis "An Exegetical and Historical Examination of the Beginning and Ending of the 1260 Days of Prophecy, with Special Attention Given to A.D. 538 and 1798 as Initial and Terminal Dates" (Washington, DC: SDA Theol. Sem., 1951).

interest in the apocalyptic sections of the Bible received a major boost. The most important aspect was not simply "the spiritual reinforcement provided by discovering a prophecy fulfilled, but the fact that one could now make a shrewd guess about the next event."[51]

In Britain numerous millenarian societies sprang up, a great number of books on the subject were published, and "prophetic conferences" were convened, the most famous of which were the Albury Park Conferences of 1829, organized by the banker Henry Drummond. The conclusion of these conferences summarized quite well the beliefs generally held in millenarian circles: 1. the present dispensation will end in cataclysm, bringing judgment and destruction upon the church; 2. the Jews will be restored to Palestine during the period of judgment; 3. after the judgment the millennium will begin; 4. the second coming of Christ will precede the millennium; and 5. the 1260 "years" date from the time of Justinian and end at the time of the French Revolution. Most of the millenarians in Britain at that time expected the next important event in the prophetic calendar to occur somewhere during the years 1843-1848.

British millenarianism gave further impetus to millenarian interests in America, which were more populistic, more democratic, more flamboyant, more revivalist and also more given to extremes.[52] Considerable millenarian parties developed in the Presbyterian and Episcopal churches, but millenarian thinking was, naturally, much more pronounced in revivalist circles, especially among Baptists and Methodists. To what extent William Miller--a Baptist--was directly influenced by

---

[51] Ernest Sandeen, "Millennialism," 108. For a survey of millenarians who subscribed to the view that the 1260 "years" came to a close in the final years of the 18th century, see Leroy E. Froom, PFOF, vol. III, 744.

[52] Cross describes the tendency toward extremes in the "Burnt-over District" with the term "ultraism." This does, of course, imply a rather subjective judgment as to what constitutes "normal" or "extreme" religious belief and behaviour. See David L. Rowe, "A New Perspective on the Burnt-over District: The Millerites in Upstate New York," Church History, vol. 47, no. 4 (Dec. 1978), 408-420.

trends from abroad remains difficult to determine; but he and his movement were part of "this same tradition of biblicism, literal [prophetic] interpretation, and general Christian expectations".[53] An important fact is that in the North-East, where successive waves of revivals had "burnt-over" the entire "district",[54] the receptivity to millenarian speculations was unparalleled. In the midst of the optimism of the Jacksonian era, there more than elsewhere a strong feeling developed on the part of many that dramatic events were just ahead.[55] Too much change in society within a short time contributed to a profound sense of insecurity, while at the same time the churches were unable to provide the answers to the many social problems of the times. Chapter Two will specifically deal with one of the several movements which could originate in this climate: the Millerite movement, with its biblicist and historist approach to the Bible in general and its apocalyptic portions in particular, and its emphasis on predictions about the imminent, premillennial, return of Christ.

VI The General Anti-Catholic Climate of 19th Century America

The widespread--and often bitter and even violent--anti-Catholic feelings in 19th century America were not of a totally religious nature. Intertwined with the religious conviction that the Roman Church was a "false" church, which had to be resisted and against which people had to be warned, were some potent sociological and political factors. And, as is often the case, people at the time did not always recognize the borderline between religious motives and economical and political fears or ethnic xenophobia. As the number of Catholics increased, sociological and political factors became more and more important, though the underlying Protestant view of Catholicism as a danger and

---

[53] Ernest Sandeen, "Millennialism," 110.

[54] The terms have become current after the study of Whitney R. Cross was published. See note 19 on p. 6.

[55] Ernest R. Sandeen, "Millennialism," 114-116.

falsehood, to be combatted at all cost, provided the climate in which anti-Catholicism in its more secular forms could prosper. The words of Thomas More Brown summarize it well: "Over 150 years of reiteration of the master plot of the Antichrist there had been molded a mind that almost instinctively looked behind the turmoil of current politics to discern the manoeuvers of the Devil."[56] From the late 1820s onward, anti-Catholicism became more political, both in action and in ideology.[57]

The enormous influx of Catholic immigrants, first mainly from Germany and Ireland, and later also from southern Europe, contributed to the spectacular growth of American Catholicism. From a mere 50,000 in 1800, the number of Roman Catholic believers had increased to 200,000 by 1820 and 2 million by 1860. Twenty years later the number had again tripled and by the turn of the century the United States of America had 12 million Catholics within its borders.[58] The Irish contingent of immigrants was very significant. Between 1830 and 1860 some 2 million Irish immigrants arrived. Their presence, in particular, was widely resented.[59]

---

[56] Thomas M. Brown, "The Image of the Beast", 20.

[57] Sydney E. Ahlstrom, A Religious History of the American People, 559.

[58] Robert T. Handy, A History of the Churches in the United States and Canada, 214, 312. Among good general works outlining the history of Catholicism in America are: Jay P. Dolan, The American Catholic Experience: A History from Colonial Times to the Present (New York: Doubleday and Co, Inc., 1985); C.E. Eberhardt, A Summary of Catholic History, 2 vols. (St. Louis, MO.: Herder, 1961-1962); John T. Ellis, American Catholicism, 2nd ed. (Chicago: University of Chicago Press, 1969); James J. Hennesey, American Catholics: A History of the Roman Catholic Community in the United States (New York: Oxford University Press, 1981); Thomas T. McAvoy, A History of the Catholic Church in the United States (Notre Dame, Ind.: University of Notre Dame Press, 1969); and Theodore Maynard, The Story of American Catholicism (New York, The MacMillan Co., 1941).

[59] Earl Raab, Religious Conflict in America, 2. The widespread anti-Irish sentiment had carried over from England, where it had a long tradition, dating at least from the time of Cromwell; see Barbara Welter, "From

A major percentage of the new immigrants settled in urban centers, where they competed for jobs with the "native" Americans--a competition often deemed unfair because of their willingness to work for lower wages. A substantial number of new immigrants, however, did not find work at all, and became the objects of charity. The widespread feeling that many countries exported their poorest, and even their criminally inclined, citizens across the Atlantic, had at least some basis in fact.

An important factor in the persistence and intensification of anti-Catholic attitudes was the alleged "un-Americanness" of Roman Catholics: the fear that Catholics were a threat to American democracy. Their first allegiance--through the hierarchy--was suspected to be to a foreign power, whose interests ran contrary to those of the United States and who, in fact, through his agents, had long-term ambitions for himself with regard to America.[60] The rumour that the pope, together with his European allies, was plotting to establish a Roman empire in the southern part of the United States continued to find almost universal acceptance.

The increased organizational strength of the Roman Catholic Church in the United States did not remain unnoticed. Nor did the insistence of the hierarchy on a system of Catholic schools. Its opposition to any idea of sharing authority with the lay members and the establishment of convents and other institutions was also observed. The problem of trusteeism, i.e. whether laymen should have authority over the property of the church, or whether all such temporal authority rested with the hierarchy, led to considerable internal unrest in the Catholic Church, especially in the 1780s in New York and Philadelphia, and in the 1820s in Philadelphia. To non-Catholics it was just one extra proof of the dangerously undemocratic nature of Catholicism.

Maria Monk to Paul Blanshard", 45-46.

[60] The similarity in the prejudices against Mormons, Masons and Roman Catholics has often been noted. All three groups were seen as elements which were "plotting to subvert the American social order" and as the embodiment of traits opposed to the American ideals of democracy. See David Brion, "Some Themes of Counter-subversion: An Analysis of Anti-Masonic, Anti-Catholic and Anti-Mormon Literature", chap. in: Richard O. Curry and Thomas M. Brown, eds., The Fear of Subversion, 61-77.

Not all anti-Catholic opposition--certainly not in
its outbursts of a more political nature in the 1830s
and early 1840s and in the short-lived success of the
"Know-Nothing" party in the mid-1850s--was the work of
the Protestant churches. But the antagonism against the
Catholics may nevertheless be largely characterized as
a "protestant crusade."[61] This crusade was conducted by
men and women of all denominations, in a vast number of
evangelical journals which devoted an increasing amount
of space to anti-Catholic articles. A number of journals
were exclusively dedicated to the defense of Protestant
principles against the threat of the Catholic invasion
of the land. Prominent among these were the *New York
Observer* (founded in 1823), *The Protestant* (founded in
1830) and *The Protestant Vindicator* (founded in 1834).
Anti-Catholic books also found a wide readership. Two
well-known examples were Lyman Beecher's *Plea for the
West* (published in 1835) with 140 pages devoted to the
"Mississippi Conspiracy" by the pope, and Samuel F.B.
Morse's *Foreign Conspiracy against the Liberties of the
United States* (New York, 1841), which deals with the
conspiracy of popes, Jesuits, and the American hierarchy
to subvert the American democracy by promoting large-
scale immigration of Catholics. Some publications
rightly deserved the epithet "horror literature".[62] Other
avenues for disseminating anti-Catholic propaganda were
academic lectures[63], and organizations with a decidedly

------

[61] Cf. the title of the definitive study of anti-
Catholic attitudes on the part of Protestants and of
Protestant anti-Catholic activities in the first half of
the 19th century in the United States: Ray Allen
Billington, The Protestant Crusade, 1800-1860 (New York:
Macmillan Co, 1938).

[62] Most notable in this category are Rebecca Reed's
Six Months in a Convent (Boston: Russel, Odiorne &
Metcalf, 1835) and Maria Monk's Awful Disclosures of the
Hotel Dieu Nunnery of Montreal (New York: Howe & Bates,
1836; repr. New York: Arno Press, 1977). The latter was
the fraudulent product of a group of New York anti-
Catholics, which enjoyed an enormous popularity (latest
reprint 1960); see below, p. 64.

[63] E.g. the annual Dudleyan lectures on Romanism at
Harvard, inaugurated in 1755, which continued without
interruption until 1853. Paul Dudley (1675-1751), a

anti-Catholic slant[64].

VII Conclusion

In our attempts to analyze Seventh-day Adventist attitudes toward Roman Catholicism, we must ever keep the background described above in mind. Three factors stand out:

1. The long tradition of anti-Catholic interpretation of apocalyptic Bible prophecy which Puritanism exported to the New World. Millerites and, later, Adventists were firmly rooted in that tradition.

2. The intense religious ferment in the northeastern part of the United States in the early part of the 19th century, which helps explain the success of the Millerite movement and its ideas.

3. The general anti-Catholic sentiment with its religious, but also sociological and political overtones.

Puritan jurist, left a bequest to Harvard to fund this lecture series. See Leroy E. Froom, PFOF, vol. III, 173-179.

[64] Prominent among these was the American Protective Association, established in 1887; see pp. 132-133.

CHAPTER TWO

MILLERISM AND CATHOLICISM

I Introduction

In May 1850 the Annual Conference of those Adventists who would later adopt the name Advent Christians decided, by unanimous vote, to send a message to Mrs. Lucy Miller, the widow of William Miller, to express sympathy for her and great respect for her late husband, who had died on December 20, 1849. Part of it read:

> We regard him as a man called of God to do a most important work; and as a man greatly blessed in the successful performance of that work.... Through the divine blessing on his teaching, our attention has been directed to a more faithful study of the Scriptures, to clearer, more harmonious and correct views of divine truth...." [1]

But it was not only among this body of Adventists which emerged from the Millerite movement that William Miller continued to be held in high esteem. The Sabbatarian Adventists, who would later organize themselves as the Seventh-day Adventist Church, also regarded Miller as their spiritual father. Not only is a long chapter devoted to him in Ellen G. White's *Great Controversy*, one of the classics of Seventh-day Adventism,[2] but as early as 1875 a 416-page biography of Miller was

---

[1] Albert C. Johnson, <u>Advent Christian History: A Concise Narrative of the Origin and Progress, Doctrine and Work of this Body of Believers</u> (Boston: Advent Christian Publication Society, 1918), 63.

[2] Ellen G. White, <u>GC</u>, chapter XVIII: "An American Reformer", 317-342.

published by the Seventh-day Adventists, which indicates how important it was deemed to keep his memory alive.[3]

Since Seventh-day Adventism is firmly rooted in the Millerite movement, one cannot study Adventist attitudes toward Roman Catholicism without taking a close look at the Millerite movement in general and its attitudes toward the Roman Catholic Church in particular. This we shall do in this chapter. In Chapter Three we will attempt to trace the ideas of the Sabbatarian Adventists with regard to Catholicism and Catholics during the first phase of their (until 1863 rather unorganized) existence, and determine how much influence Millerite ideas on this issue continued to exercise.

II The Millerite Movement

1. General Characterization

The Millerite believers have gone down in much popular history as, at best, a group of simple or deluded people, or, at worst, a community of religious fanatics, who believed in the "prophecies" of "Father Miller" and his associates, that Christ was to return to this world in the very near future. At first dates in 1843 and early 1844 were proposed, but finally "the midnight cry"[4] went out that the Lord would come on October 22, 1844. Stories about large numbers of people becoming insane, about waiting saints dressed in white ascension

---

[3] James White, Sketches of the Christian Life and Public Labors of William Miller (Battle Creek, Mich.: Steam Press of the SDA Publ. Ass., 1875). The book is a re-edited, annotated version of Sylvester Bliss' Memoirs of William Miller, Generally Known as a Lecturer on the Prophecies, and the Second Coming of Christ (Boston: Joshua V. Himes, 1853), which is quoted at length, although some anecdotes from other Millerites are added. The important fact is not, however, the lack of originality, but the strong relationship between Millerism and Adventism it expresses.

[4] A term borrowed from Matthew 25:6. One of the most influential Millerite journals carried that name for a number of years.

robes, and about all sorts of fanaticism, have found widespread acceptance ever since.

One of the most influential books in perpetuating those stories was Clara E. Sears' *Days of Delusion - A Strange Bit of History*. In preparation for the book, the author placed a notice in some leading US newspapers, soliciting responses from readers who had recollections of having heard parents or grandparents tell of the great religious excitement in 1843: "Any anecdotes of that period, or any information however trivial [would] be gratefully received...." Sears' book is based on the 162 personal testimonies which she received between 1920-1923.[5] But modern historians, who have studied the subject, have concluded that most of this and similar accounts of widespread fanaticism and aberrant behaviour are not correct.[6]

In fact, the Millerite movement was much more "normal," i.e. in line with mainline Protestantism of the times, than many other movements, such as Shakerism, Mormonism and various Reform Movements, which originated around the same time in the same part of the United States and flourished especially in the "Burnt-over District" of Upstate New York and surrounding areas.[7] On the one hand, much of its growth and popularity can be explained in the context of the religious ferment which characterized the region, and against the background of the extreme fragmentation of Protestantism and the

---

[5] Clara E. Sears, Days of Delusion - A Strange Bit of History (Boston: Houghton Mifflin Company, 1924).

[6] The definitive refutation of the notion that the Millerite movement was characterized by strange, or even insane, behaviour, is generally recognized to be F.D. Nichol, The Midnight Cry: A Defense of the Character and Conduct of William Miller and the Millerites, who Mistakenly Believed that the Second Coming of Christ would take place in the years 1844 (Washington, DC: RHPA, 1944). Nichol himself was aware of his bias, but his painstaking and detailed research is nevertheless convincing. For a refutation of Sears' Days of Delusion, see pp. 437-447.

[7] See e.g. Winthrop S. Hudson, Religion in America, 4th ed. (New York: Macmillan Publishing Co, 1987), 174-184; Ronald G. Walters, American Reformers, 1815-1860 (New York: Hill and Wang, 1978).

23

revivalist climate of the 1830s,[8] while, on the other hand, its message of doom for the present world profited from the considerable decline of general optimism, which had marked much of the early 1830s, especially after the economic "Panic of 1837.[9].

Excessive attention to the subject of the millennium was not unique to the Millerite movement. Ernest R. Sandeen once said that 19th century America "was drunk on the millennium, ... Whether in support of optimism or pessimism, radicalism or conservatism, Americans seemed unable to avoid--seemed bound to utilize--the vocabulary of Christian eschatology."[10] In the first part of the 19th century Protestants in general accepted prophecy as an integral part of the Christian faith. Its study was "deemed honorable and orthodox". And in spite of all credal and doctrinal differences a great degree of unanimity existed in prophetic exposition and in the belief that the end of history had arrived.[11]

Rowe probably overstates his case when he sees such a close union between the revivalism of the 1830s and Millerism, that "Adventism hardly had an identity of its own."[12] He rightly observes, however, that both Millerism and revivalism crossfertilized each other. Miller kept the revival fires burning, while he in turn received an interdenominational platform for his views.[13] But Millerism did build a definite profile for itself, as

---

[8] David L. Rowe, Thunder and Trumpets: Millerites and Dissenting Religion in Upstate New York, 1800-1850 (Chico, Cal.: Scholars Press, 1985), xi, 24.

[9] Winthrop S. Hudson, Religion in America, 184-187. See also Whitney R. Cross, The Burnt-Over District, 317.

[10] Ernest Sandeen, "Millennialism," 42.

[11] Leroy E.Froom, PFOF, vol. IV, 392-401.

[12] David L.Rowe, Thunder and Trumpets, 24. Miller himself, in the aftermath of the 1844 disillusion, lays stress on the revivalistic aspect of his preaching (Apology and Defence (Boston: J.V. Himes, 1845), 23. One Catholic book refers to Miller as "the famous revivalist" ("A Cosmopolite", Miller Overthrown, or the False Prophet Confounded [Boston: A. Thompkins, 1840], 8, 35).

[13] David L. Rowe, Thunder and Trumpets, 25.

Rowe himself later admits, and was foremost in the "antiformalist rebellion against the formalization of the evangelical pietistic denominations" and was-- compared to other such expressions in contemporary movements--"the most dramatic" one.[14]

Most of Miller's doctrines, however, were not strange by contemporary standards and did not set him apart from his Protestant neighbours.[15] The majority of early 19th century American writers on the subject of prophecy shared the Millerites' historicist pre- suppositions.[16] The famous "day-year principle," which is a key presupposition to the understanding of prophetic periods as spanning the centuries--essential in Miller's 1843-44 calculations--was also quite widely accepted.[17]

Around 1840 N. Southard, the editor of *The Midnight Cry*, gave a synopsis of Millerite views in a contribution to a book about all major religious deno- minations represented at the time in the United States. He pointed out that "Second Advent Believers" only distinguished themselves from other believers in their millennial views and their insistence that the Jews would play no further role in God's plan.[18] Nathan Gordon Thomas agrees, and states that Millerism was one of the "most immediate and dramatic manifestations of a millennial belief which was a common held religious doctrine",[19] even though it should be kept in mind that

---

[14] Ibid., 72.

[15] Ernest Sandeen, "Millennialism", 45, 55.

[16] See Leroy E. Froom, <u>PFOF</u>, vol. IV, 392-401.

[17] See Leroy E. Froom, <u>PFOF</u>, vol. II, 156-157; 542- 549; Hugh I. Dunton, "The Millerite Adventists and other Millenarian Groups in Great Britain, 1830-1860" (Ph.D. diss., London University, 1984), 68.

[18] Rupp, I. Daniel, compiler, <u>HE PASA EKKLESIA: An Original History of the Religious Denominations at present existing in the United States</u> (Philadelphia: J.Y. Humphrey, 1840), 668.

[19] Nathan G. Thomas, "The Second Coming in the Third New England: The Millennial Impulse in Michigan, 1830- 1860" (Ph.D diss., Michigan State University, 1967), ii.

Miller's premillennial views diverged from the more widely held post-millennial theories. He says:

> Miller's chronology had differed but little from many other nineteenth century students of millennialism. His premillennialism was more dramatic, mainly because it was more exact. His preaching was especially effective because he was so positive and forceful in his certainty of Christ's personal coming for judgment at a definite time.[20]

Cross repeatedly makes the same point:

> Little opposition seems to have disturbed [the] rapid spread of the premillennial doctrine. Place after place, begging father Miller to come himself or send a substitute, emphasized the unanimous desire of pastors and flocks of all sects to hear him. The Advent movement's most distinctive feature was in fact its extreme closeness to orthodoxy. Any church might profit from its message, whether or not it chose to follow the letter of the doctrine....[21]

> On every subject but the millennium the Adventists found the same Bible meanings others found and held to them more rigidly than did most.... The only difference between pre- and postmillennialists was a slight degree of literal-mindedness applied to the prophecies of the Second Coming.... Their doctrine was the logical absolute of the fundamentalist orthodoxy ... of revivalism.[22]

If it is correct that Miller and his followers shared in most of the current Protestant ideas of the period--and all evidence points in that direction--we may expect to find the contemporary anti-Catholic attitude of most American Protestants to be reflected in the preaching and publications of the Millerite movement. Indeed, we will find that to be largely the

---

[20] Ibid., 113.

[21] Whitney R. Cross, <u>The Burnt-Over District</u>, 297.

[22] Ibid., 320.

case.[23] But first we must sketch the work of Miller, his most important associates and his movement in some detail as a necessary background for our discussion.

2. William Miller (1782-1849)

a. William Miller's Religious Development

William Miller[24] was born in Pittsfield, Massachusetts, but grew up in Low Hampton, in northern New York, where he lived most of his life. He was largely self-educated, but developed a good basic knowledge of the Bible and of history, and also some skills in writing. After he married Lucy P. Smith, he lived for some time in Poultney, just across the state border in neighbouring Vermont. Though raised as a Baptist, friendship with a number of prominent Poultney citizens brought him into contact with deism, which he soon accepted as more reasonable than the Bible religion of his childhood.

Miller was well accepted in the community, serving it as a constable, justice of the peace, and deputy sheriff. During the War of 1812 (between the United States and Great Britain) Miller served for some time as lieutenant and captain. After his war experience he moved back to Low Hampton, N.Y. to take up farming.

It remains largely a matter of conjecture what caused Miller's renewed interest in religion. The wartime experiences apparently shook his faith in

---

[23] See below, pp. 65-72.

[24] There is no full and critical biography of William Miller. Robert L. Gale, The Urgent Voice (Washington, DC: RHPA, 1975) is almost exclusively based on secondary sources. Miller's own version of his life story is found in his Apology and Defence, 2-36. Most accounts of Miller's life depend on Bliss' Memoirs, which was also largely followed by James White in his Sketches of the Christian Life and Public Labors of William Miller. This is also true of Norman P. Cook, A Brief History of William Miller, the Great Pioneer in Adventual Faith, published in 1915 by The Advent Christian Publication Society. Short overviews of Miller's life are found in Whitney R. Cross, The Burnt-Over District, 288-292; SDAE, s.v. "Miller, William," 889-891, and David L. Rowe, Trumpets and Thunder, 1-30 and passim.

deism.[25] Rowe suggests that Miller's desire for reconciliation with his family, after the death of his father in 1812--with whom he had had severe disagreements about his yearnings for study and education--played at least some part in his return to "the faith of his fathers."[26] He returned to the Baptist Church, where in 1816 he had a conversion experience. Miller remained a Baptist until late 1844, when against his wish the Low Hampton church excluded him from membership.

In 1816 Miller began a two-year systematic study of the Bible, using his Cruden's Concordance as the only other source. Aware of the many disagreements among commentators, he decided to let the Bible be "its own interpreter". Miller's decision "to lay aside all commentaries" implies that he must have read some of them; through these commentaries, no doubt, he was conversant with the "year-day principle".[27] He states in his *Apology and Defence*: "I could only regard the time as symbolical, and as standing each day for a year, in accordance with the opinion of all standard Protestant commentators."[28] Miller was fond of history, and without recourse to history books he could not have constructed his system.[29] Possibly during this period of intensive study he relied on his memory rather than on any active reading of history books. With regard to his prophetic views, there is evidence that Miller had at least read Newton (either Sir Isaac or Bishop Newton) and George S. Faber.[30] In any case, Miller followed most Protestant theologians of his days in his literalistic approach to the Bible. Likewise, his strong interest in the

---

[25] See F.D. Nichol, The Midnight Cry, 17-26.

[26] David L. Rowe, Trumpets and Thunder, 8-9.

[27] Ibid., 12. See also William Miller, Apology and Defence, 6.

[28] William Miller, Apology and Defence, 11.

[29] Hugh I. Dunton, "The Millerite Adventists and other Millenarian Groups in Great Britain," 89.

[30] See N. Southard's editorial, "The Home of Wm. Miller", The Midnight Cry, Oct. 26, 1843, 88; F.D. Nichol, The Midnight Cry, 161-162.

apocalyptic portions of the Scriptures was hardly exceptional. One of his conclusions which would take him on his own independent course, however, was that chronological calculations based on Daniel and the Apocalypse (Daniel 8:14 being the key to this conviction) indicated that Christ would return "about the year 1843". Having completed his systematic study of the Bible, Miller took five years to check his conclusions. While he was occupied with this, and in the years following, he felt an increasing urge to share his views with others. His first public address on his views came when he was invited to speak in the Baptist church of Dresden, N.Y. This was the beginning of his "career" as a (from about 1834 full-time) lecturer on prophecy. A little earlier, in 1832, Miller wrote a series of eight articles for the Baptist newspaper *The Vermont Telegraph*. These were to form the basis of his "course of lectures", which in book-form became the most important manual for the Millerite movement.[31] In 1833

---

[31] The first edition of Miller's printed lectures consists of 16 lectures; the second edition has two more, while the third edition of 1840 and the 1842 edition has a total of 19.

The first edition (William Miller, <u>Evidence from Scirpture</u> [sic] <u>and History of the Second Coming of Christ about the Year 1843: Exhibited in a Course of Lectures</u>) was published by Kemple & Hooper, in Troy, N.Y., 1836.

The second edition in 1838 (William Miller, <u>Evidence from Scripture and History of the Second Coming of Christ about the Year 1843: Exhibited in a Course of Lectures</u>) had a different publisher: Elias Gates, in Troy, N.Y. (1838).

B.B. Mussey in Boston, Mass. printed the third edition in 1840. It contains an interesting note (p. 300) about one particular date related to the Turkish Empire which had proven to be incorrect. The fact that no correction was made indicates a reluctance to make any corrections in these "standard" lectures.

The foremost organizer and publisher of the Millerite movement, Joshua V. Himes, acquired the rights for the next edition, which he published in 1842. It contains the same note referred to above. He added a supplement with a chart of Miller's chronology and prophetic periods. This edition is cited in the present study and will be referred to as <u>ESH</u>.

See also Everett N. Dick, "The Adventist Crisis of 1843-1844" (Ph.D. diss., University of Wisconsin, 1930).

Miller received a Baptist preaching license, which was further upgraded in 1835.

Whitney Cross' description of William Miller is worth quoting:

> William Miller was temperamentally conservative: an ingenious logician with a resourceful mind; not an inspired prophet but a solid, sober student, driven only by the irresistible conclusions of patient research; and withal, an utterly literal-minded soul.[32]

b. Miller's hermeneutical principles

Miller developed a set of clear-cut hermeneutical principles, to which he closely adhered, and which were to be accepted widely by other Millerite preachers and writers.[33]

Miller's basic premise was that much of the message of prophecy is communicated by symbols. For example: "beasts" represent kingdoms, while "water" represents people, and a "woman" represents a church. These "figures" do have a literal and a metaphorical meaning. Thus, literally, a beast would represent a kingdom or an empire, but metaphorically the character of the beast

---

[32] Whitney R. Cross, The Burnt-Over District, 290-291. See further SDAE, s.v. "Miller, William," 890.

[33] These principles are found in a letter by Miller, printed in Signs of the Times, ("Miller's Letter, No. 5 - The Bible its own Interpreter"), May 15, 1840, 25, 26. The "rules" are also found in Joshua V. Himes, ed., Views of the Prophecies and Prophetic Chronology Selected from the Manuscripts of William Miller (Boston, Dow, 1841), 20-24, and in a somewhat adapted form in Apollos Hale, Second Advent Manual (Boston: Joshua V. Himes, 1843), 103-106. For a discussion of Miller's hermeneutical principles, see Gerard P. Damsteegt, Toward the Theology of Mission of the Seventh-day Adventist Church (Grand Rapids, MI.: Wm. B. Eerdmans Publishing Co, 1977), 16-20, (further ref. to as TTM) and Don. F. Neufeld, "Biblical Interpretation in the Advent Movement", chap. in: G. Hyde, ed., A Symposium on Biblical Hermeneutics, (Washington, DC.: GC. of SDA, 1974), 109-125.

would indicate the nature of its rule. The meaning of these figures is found when they are traced through the Scriptures; usually somewhere an explanation is found, which may then be applied elsewhere, since there is complete unity in the Bible.

It was, of course, for historicists like Miller of utmost importance to know how one was to determine which events were fulfillments of specific prophecies. Miller's Rule XIII gives the answer:

> If you find every word of the prophecy (after the figures are understood) is literally fulfilled, then you may know that your history is the true event; but if one word lacks a fulfillment, then you must look for an other event, or wait its future development; for God takes care that history and prophecy shall agree, so that the true believing children of God may never be ashamed. Ps. 22:5; Isa. 45:17-19; 1 Peter 2:6; Rev. 17:17; Acts 3:18.[34]

Miller agreed with the statement by Josiah Litch, which expressed the same sentiment:

> All we profess to do is to state certain texts of Scripture, 'infallibl.e truths', and collate with them certain historical facts and tell the world the impression that collation makes on our minds. If it makes the same on theirs, well and good, we hope they will be benefitted by it; if it does not make the same impression on them that it does on us, we cannot help it...."[35]

David A. Dean, an Advent Christian scholar, offers a critical discussion of Miller's hermeneutical methods.[36] He argues that Miller "tended ... to treat words as lifeless, 'wooden,' linguistic symbols to which

---

[34] Sylvester Bliss, Memoirs, 71.

[35] Josiah Litch, "The Bible its own Interpreter", ST (May 15, 1840), 29.

[36] "Echoes of the Midnight Cry: The Millerite Heritage in the Apologetics of the Advent Christian Denomination, 1860-1960" (Ph.D. diss., Westminster Theol. Sem., 1976), 76-87; 153-188.

single meanings have been assigned arbitrarily".[37] The
extent of this arbitrariness is most obvious in Miller's
"Explanation of Prophetic Figures," where he gives an
alphabetical listing of 139 prophetic terms with their
meaning.[38] Dean's second criticism concerns Miller's
spiritualizing which could reach massive proportions. He
also argues that Miller's approach to the Bible was at
times quite inconsistent, and that he mixed his biblical
principles with a firm dose of the kind of rationalism
he must have retained from his deistic period.[39]

c. Prophetic convictions

Using his hermeneutical principles, Miller's extensive
studies led him to conclude that Christ's second coming
would be pre-millennial, rather than post-millennial.
Also, that the Jews would not play any further role in
God's economy of salvation, as many contemporary
Protestants believed. Miller believed the end to be
near, but refused to give an exact date until a few
weeks before the 1844 disappointment. He at first advocated a time "about 1843," while later he more specifically mentioned the "Jewish year 1843," which would
terminate in the spring of 1844. The October 22, 1844
date was introduced by other Millerite leaders after the
spring-expectation of 1844 did not materialize.[40]

---

[37] Ibid., 84.

[38] Joshua V. Himes, ed., Views of Prophecies and
Prophetic Chronology, 3-32.

[39] David E. Dean, "Echoes of the Midnight Cry," 182-
192. The criticism of one of Miller's opponents seems
quite valid: "Mr. M. does not prove his theories by the
Scriptures. He makes assertions in regard to certain
passages, and then attempts to prove his assertions, by
an appeal to history, with which very few are
acquainted; Rev. Kittredge Haven, The World Reprieved:
Being a Critical Examination of William Miller's Theory
(Woodstock, Vt: Haskell and Palmer, 1839), iv, quoted by
Dean, 180, n. 2.

[40] For a discussion how the various 1843 and 1844
dates were arrived at, see Leroy E. Froom, PFOF, vol.
IV, 789-799. Since this study does not focus on the
Millerite expectations of the imminent coming of Christ,

A number of dates were basic to Miller's chronological framework. The year 677 B.C. (when the "scattering" of God's people, referred to in Leviticus 26:33, began with the captivity enforced by the Assyrian King Essarhaddon and the dethronement of Judah's King Manasseh) was the beginning of a period of 2520 years--the seven times of Leviticus 26:24--which would terminate in A.D. 1843. Artaxerxes' decree of 457 B.C., allowing the Jews to rebuild the walls of Jerusalem, was the starting point not only for the 70 weeks of Daniel 9, but also for the longer period of the 2300 days of Daniel 8:14. The "cleansing" of the sanctuary was to take place in 1843-44, at the end of the period of 2300 literal years, when Christ would come to "cleanse" his church.

A number of other prophetic periods--notably the 1335 days/years of Daniel 12:12--were to terminate at the same time.

The next B.C. date which held special importance for Miller was 158 B.C., when a treaty signed between the Romans and the Jews marked the beginning of the period in which paganism had had the upper hand, and which lasted 666 years (the number of the beast of Revelation 13). This period ended in A.D. 508, when King Clovis of the Franks converted to Christianity.

A.D. 33 was Miller's next most important date: the year in which he believed Christ died.

After the A.D. 508 date, mentioned above, which was seen as the beginning of the 1290 days/years of Daniel 12:11, the year A.D. 538 played a pre-eminent role. The 1260 days/years of Revelation 12:6 and 11:3 (identified with the "time, times and half a time" of Daniel 7:25; Revelation 12:14 and the 42 months of Revelation 11:2) began, Miller stated, in A.D 538, after the Arian threat had been removed from Rome, when Emperor Justinian's decree--which acknowledged the pope as the head of Christendom--took effect. The 1260 years of papal supremacy lasted from A.D. 538 to A.D. 1798, when the French general Louis Berthier took Pope Pius VI captive. This event played a pivotal role in Miller's scheme, only second to the event expected some 45 years later,

---

we will not distinguish between the phase in which an 1843 or early 1844 date was generally accepted and the latter phase, during which Oct. 22, 1844 was emphasized, but will simply refer to the *1843-44* expectation.

IMPORTANT DATES IN MILLER'S PROPHETIC SCHEME

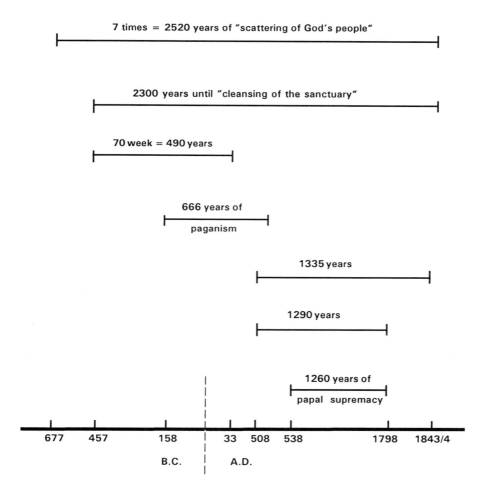

7 times = 2520 years of "scattering of God's people"

2300 years until "cleansing of the sanctuary"

70 week = 490 years

666 years of
paganism

1335 years

1290 years

1260 years of
papal supremacy

677 457   158 | 33 508 538   1798 1843/4

B.C. | A.D.

when the time of the end would expire with Christ's coming.[41]

Miller had no doubt that the prophecies of the Bible, especially those of Daniel and the Revelation, permitted the Bible reader to view history from God's perspective and to identify many of the powers and individuals which had led in the affairs of the world during the previous twenty-five centuries: Babylon, Medo-Persia, Greece, Rome, the nations of Central and Western Europe (notably France in Napoleonic times), etc. The Turkish Empire was thought to be of special importance, as some important aspects of the prophecies of the Revelation (the 5th and 6th trumpets of chapter 9) which were applied to the Saracens and the Turks, were expected to find their fulfillment around the year 1840. The severe reduction in Turkish power in 1840 was seen by the Millerites as convincing proof of the correctness of their method of prophetic interpretation and strengthened their conviction that their 1843-44 prediction would also come true.

With many others, William Miller believed that the most important power referred to under various symbols in the prophetic portions of the Bible, was the Roman Catholic Church, (or the Papacy, Popery, Romanism – to mention some of the terms more commonly used by 19th century American Protestants, Millerites included). This antichristian power, it was argued, had its roots in the paganism of the beginning of the Christian era; it rose to prominence in the 6th century; it reigned supreme for over twelve centuries, while the true Christians were hiding to escape annihilation. In 1798, however, the Catholic power had been spectacularly reduced, never again to regain its former glory until it would be rightfully judged at Christ's imminent coming. But before we can return to these Millerite convictions, some paragraphs must be devoted to the scope of the Millerite movement and its relationship to the Protestant churches.

---

[41] For the most detailed exposition of Miller's view, see Miller's ESH. See especially the supplement in the 1842 edition (Exposition of Miller's Chart of the Chronology of the World, and of the Prophetic Periods). A summary of his ideas may be found in the 64-page Synopsis of Miller's Views (Boston: Joshua V. Himes, 1842). See also P.G. Damsteegt, TTM, 21-46, and Leroy E. Froom, PFOF, vol. IV, 461-475; 478-482; 719-737.

3. From Ecumenical Movement to Sect

a. Interdenominational appeal

From 1838 onward a number of influential ministers of different persuasions not only accepted Miller's views, but joined him as lecturers and authors. Foremost among these was Joshua V. Himes, most noted for his organizational talent and his editorial contributions. He published many Adventist publications, written by Miller and other Millerite preachers, including himself. He also initiated the two parent-journals of the Millerite movement: *The Midnight Cry* (1842-1844)[42] and the *Signs of the Times* (1840-1844).[43] Other prominent leaders included Josiah Litch, Charles Fitch, Henry Jones, Apollos Hale, Sylvester Bliss, and the prominent Episcopalian clergyman Dr. Henry Dana Ward. Hundreds of ministers eventually joined the movement. Some estimates of the number of clergymen who openly aligned themselves with Miller ran as high as 800[44] or even 1500-2000.[45] Miller himself stated that some two hundred ministers "embraced [his] views."[46]

Scores of journals echoed Miller's views.[47] All the

---

[42] Further referred to as <u>MC</u>, later continued as <u>Morning Watch.</u>

[43] Further referred to as <u>ST</u>; from February 1844 continued as <u>Advent Herald and Signs of the Times Reporter</u> (further referred to as <u>AHSTR</u>).

[44] See Leroy E. Froom, <u>PFOF</u>, vol. IV, 86.

[45] Lorenzo D. Fleming, "A Chapter on Popery," <u>MC</u>, March 21, 1844, 282.

[46] William Miller, <u>Apology and Defence</u>, 22.

[47] For a complete listing of all known Millerite periodicals, see Vern Carner, Sakae Kubo, and Kurt Rice, "Bibliographical Essay," chap. in: Edwin S. Gaustad, <u>The Rise of Adventism</u> (New York: Harper & Row, 1974), 303-317. For a similar, annotated, list, see Everett N. Dick, "The Adventist Crisis of 1843-1844," 101-119. For the scope of Millerite publishing activities, see David T. Arthur, "Joshua V. Himes and the Cause of Adventism: 1839-1845" (M.A. thesis, University of Chicago, 1961),

available revivalist communication techniques--lecture series, campmeetings, tent crusades, publications and "prophetic charts"--were used.[48] As a result, Millerism became a movement with a very considerable following, to be counted in the tens or even hundreds of thousands. Again, Miller himself was quite modest in his estimates. In his *Apology and Defence*[49] he speaks of "about one thousand Adventist congregations, some 50,000 people." He may have referred to the loyal core which stayed with him after the disappointments of 1843 and the spring of 1844. When the Millerite fervour was at its peak, the number of adherents may have been much larger. Some sources even mention one million.[50]

The Millerite movement drew its supporters from many different Protestant denominations. Miller, himself a Baptist, preached not only within the confines of his own denomination, but accepted many invitations to lecture for Congregationalist, Christian, Methodist and Presbyterian audiences.

Miller's closest associates were of a wide variety of persuasions. Some prominent Millerite ministers were Baptists or Methodists, while others were Reformed, Congregationalists, Presbyterians, Methodist Episcopa-

---

103-104; Nathan O. Hatch, The Democratization of American Christianity (New Haven: Yale University Press, 1989), 141-142.

[48] Several such charts which gave a bird's eye view of the prophetic periods, with symbols, dates, and some explanatory remarks were developed by the Millerites. The "1843-Chart", developed in 1842 by Charles Fitch with the assistance of Apollos Hale, became the standard chart until early 1844. It represents the mature Millerite position. Leroy E. Froom provides an in-depth analysis of the various prophetic charts and shows how they reflect the Millerite understanding of some key prophecies (PFOF, vol. IV, 719-737).

[49] William Miller, Apology and Defence, 22.

[50] John Bach McMaster, A History of the People of the United States, From the Revolution to the Civil War (New York: D. Appleton and Company, 1883-1913), vol. VII, 136. See Leroy E. Froom, PFOF, vol. IV, 686.

lians, or belonged to the Christian Connection.[51] Among
the Millerite following the diversity was even greater.
The Advent Shield and Review, the most sophisticated
Millerite journal, enumerates some 17 denominations from
which the Millerites drew adherents.[52] A major percentage
of the Millerite following were Methodists, Free-will
Baptists or members of the Christian Connection.
Catholics were sometimes invited to join, but apparently
few responded.[53]

In the earlier stages of their movement the Advent
believers had no intention of organizing a separate
church. In fact, they were very outspoken against such
an idea--Miller even more so than some of the other
leaders:

> In all my labors I had never had the desire, or
> thought to establish any separate interest from
> that of existing denominations; or to benefit one
> at the expense of another. I thought to benefit
> all.... I did not conceive there would ever be any
> necessity for separate meetings.... The great
> majority of those who were converted under my
> labors united with the various existing churches.
> When individuals came to me to enquire respecting
> their duty, I always told them to go where they
> would feel at home: and I never favored any one
> denomination in my advice to such.[54]

---

[51] David T. Arthur, "Come out of Babylon: A Study of
Millerite Separatism and Denominationalism," (Ph.D.
diss., The University of Rochester, 1970), 14.

[52] "The Rise and Progress of Adventism," Advent
Shield and Review, May, 1844, 90.

[53] In the "Address of the Conference on the Second
Advent of the Lord, convened at Boston, Mass., October
14, 1840" it was stated: "... nor do we refuse any of
these, or others of diverse faith, *whether Roman or
Protestant*, who receive and heartily embrace the
doctrine of the Lord's coming in his kingdom...."
Printed in Report of the General Conference of
Christians expecting the advent of our Lord Jesus
Christ, held in Boston, Oct. 14, 15, 1840 (Boston: J.V.
Himes, 1841), 23.

[54] William Miller, Apology and Defence, 23.

38

Just prior to the October 22, 1844 disappointment Miller, for some time, had some doubt whether staying in their churches was a realistic option for his followers.[55] In December of that year, however, any such doubt had again disappeared. Looking back Miller once more described what had been his consistent policy:

> For years after I began to proclaim this blessed truth of Christ at the door, I never, if possible to avoid it, even alluded to sectarian principles; and the first objection my Baptist brethren brought against me, was, that I mixed with, and preached unto, all denominations....[56]

The Millerite leaders emphasized their bond with Christians of different ecclesiastical traditions:

> Again we are agreed and harmonize with the published creed of the Episcopal, Dutch Reformed, Presbyterian and Methodist churches ... and the Lutheran and *the Roman Catholic churches*, in maintaining that Christ's second and only coming now will be 'to judge the world at the last day.'[57] (*Emphasis supplied.*)

Sectarianism was, in fact, seen as one of the signs of the times.[58] In journals, such as the *Signs of the Times*, a certain amount of diversity of opinion was accepted, as an editorial pointed out:

> Our fellow laborers are among the choicest of the faithful in Christ from among all denominations. We know no sect or party as such, while we respect all; and wish them to have an equal privilege to our columns, to address the people and diffuse our views on the near advent.[59]

---

[55] See below, pp. 43-44, n. 73.

[56] "Letter from Bro. Miller", AHSTR (Dec. 18, 1844), 142; quoted in Sylvester Bliss, Memoirs, 283.

[57] Report of the General Conference, 22.

[58] William Miller, ESH, 294.

[59] "Our Course," ST (Nov. 15, 1840), 126.

Plurality of opinion was welcome, as long as there was agreement on the one fundamental truth of the imminence of Christ's coming:

> Some men are Roman Catholics, some are Protestants: let them be Catholics or Protestants, only looking for the coming of the Lord according to his word. Some expect the natural Jews to return in this life; others expect the Jews to return in the resurrection of the just; let it be, while both expect the Lord will first come. Some look for the end of all things within a few months especially: others look for it continually without regard to a particular year....[60]

b. Opposition to Millerism

The situation did, however, change drastically. In the last phase of the movement Millerism met with increasing opposition from the Protestant world. Those who persevered in their allegiance to the Advent movement were often disfellowshipped by their churches. Some drastic moves on the part of a few Millerite leaders in the spring and summer of 1844 precipitated the irreversible parting of the ways, but a number of earlier factors greatly contributed to the process.

As early as October 1840, when the first of a series of "general conferences" was held, the outlines of a simple, rudimentary organization" were visible.[61] The very fact that such a general conference was held indicates that the Millerites had established a sense of identity, and were beginning to act as an identifiable group. During the first conference a number of committees were appointed and a statement of essential beliefs was issued. At least as important was the fact that the Adventist leaders operated their own publishing outreach.

The second general conference (June 1841) outlined some of the duties of the Advent believers. In

---

[60] Dana Ward, "To the Conference of Christians," ST (Jan. 1, 1842), 146-147.

[61] David T. Arthur, "Millerism," chap. in: Edwin S. Gaustad, ed., The Rise of Adventism: Religion and Society in Mid-Nineteenth Century America (New York: Harper and Row, Publ., 1974), 156.

proclaiming their views they were to go beyond the utilization of normal church channels. The fourth general conference established unequivocally the leadership of Miller, Himes, Litch, Jones and Ward.

The emergence of "Second Advent associations" was another important step toward separation. Even though most of the members of these associations, which were established in a number of cities, continued to worship in their own churches, they met separately on Sunday afternoon for fellowship with other Advent believers and study of the prophecies.

From 1842 onward the aspect of the time of Christ's second coming received more and more emphasis. A resolution passed during a general conference in May 1842 regarding 1843 as the year of Christ's return, alienated some of the leaders (notably Jones and Ward), and further precise time-predictions during 1843 and 1844 (and subsequent disillusions) caused the movement to lose much of its credibility and led to increased opposition from the various denominations, and to the publication of a number of books against Miller and his views.[62] As the Millerites became more aggressive in their preaching, with greater emphasis on a specific date for Christ's return, the churches began to close to Miller and his fellow-lecturers. Some pro-Miller ministers were defrocked, many were ridiculed and abused, while members were disfellowshipped in growing numbers. David T. Arthur aptly summarizes the situation in these words:

---

[62] Among the most important anti-Miller publications were: "A Cosmopolite" (pseudonym of a Catholic author), Miller Overthrown, or the False Prophet Confounded; this Catholic attack became almost the "standard text" for Protestant antagonists of Miller; Otis A. Skinner (a Universalist), Miller's Theory Utterly Exploded (Boston: T. Whittemore, 1840); Dr. John Dowling, An Exposition of the Prophecies Supposed by William Miller to Predict the Second Coming of Christ in 1843, With a Supplementary Chapter Upon the True Scriptural Doctrine of a Millennium Prior to the Judgment (New York: J.R. Bigelow, 1842); Prof. Moses Stuart, Hints on the Interpretation of Prophecy (Andover: Allen, Morrill & Wardwell, 1842); Dr. George Bush, Reasons for Rejecting Mr. Miller's Views on the Advent; with Mr. Miller's Reply (Boston: Joshua V. Himes, 1844).

...the Millerites were the initiators, the aggressors. It was they who were propagating, indeed trying to force acceptance of, new views. They had expressed these vigorously in their churches and public meetings and had questioned their ministers before congregations. They had established their own meetings, presses, associations, conferences, campmeetings, despite their assertions that they were not trying to disrupt or divide the churches or to establish a new one.... While believing themselves to have laid aside sectarian views, they had in truth established their own. All that remained was the call for a final break....[63]

c. Separation from "Babylon"

The call for a final break did indeed come. In July 1843 Charles Fitch preached his famous "Come out of Babylon!" sermon,[64] based on Revelation 18:4, which was to become "the most widely read and influential statement of Millerite separatism and sectarianism."[65] So far, the most common view had been to equate "Babylon"--the apocalyptic term for the ultimate opposition against God --with Roman Catholicism.[66] Like others, Fitch applied the statements in the Revelation about Babylon to the Catholic Church, without seeing any need for supporting arguments for that application:

No Protestant would think this language too strong to express the true state of things in the Catholic church at the present time; and the Catholics in

---

[63] David T. Arthur, "Millerism," 162.

[64] Charles Fitch, Come Out of Her, My People, A Sermon (Rochester, N.Y.: J.V. Himes), 1843. Quotes are from this edition. The sermon was first printed in Fitch's journal Second Advent of Christ (July 26, 1843), and in The Midnight Cry (Sept. 21, 1843), 33-36). Part of it was printed in Signs of the Times ("What is it for God's People to Come out of Babylon?" Sept. 13, 1843, 27).

[65] David T. Arthur, "Come out of Babylon", 60.

[66] See also below, pp. 61-62.

turn would say the same things of the Protestants. *We need not stop to show how the language applies to Catholicism. The justice of the application is sufficiently obvious.*[67] (Emphasis supplied.)

Fitch had some rather harsh words for the Catholics, who, while claiming to be the church of God, had always sought the support of secular power, and hence are rightfully accused by the Apocalypse of "fornication" and of being "the great whore" (Revelation 18:3; 17:5).[68] But his prime target were the sects of Protestantism which were as much part of Babylon as the papists.

Equating the terms "Babylon" and "Antichrist," Fitch took his cue from 1 John 4:2 and 2 John:7, where the Gnostic denial of the reality of Christ's coming "in the flesh" is depicted as the essence of Antichrist. Referring to passages such as Acts 2:29-34, Fitch extended the argument to a denial of the "personal reign of Christ over this world on David's throne." One may admit that Christ has come in the flesh, but at the same time be opposed to "the object for which he came"--and thus belong to Antichrist!

The entire Roman Catholic Church, Fitch maintained, must thus be classified as Antichrist and Babylon.[69] The primitive church in the first centuries believed in the personal reign of Christ, and looked and longed for it. This, however, changed drastically:

... when the papacy came into power, they concluded to have Christ reign, not personally, but spiritually, and hence the Pope entered in to the stead of Christ, and undertook to rule the world for him--claiming to be God's viceregent on earth. Inasmuch, therefore, as the Papists wish to retain their power, we find them all opposed to Christ's coming to establish a personal reign. They are willing that Christ should reign spiritually, provided they can be his acknowledged agents, and thus bring the world to bow down wholly to their dictation, and use God's authority for their own aggrandizement. But to the idea of Christ's coming

---

[67] Charles Fitch, <u>Come out of Her, My People</u>, 16.

[68] Ibid., 10.

[69] Ibid., 8-9.

43

to establish a personal reign, they are decidedly and bitterly hostile.... Hence they are Antichrist."[70]

This was not only true of the Catholic Church, but also of the Protestant denominations, which led the people astray with their post-millennial heresy, and denied the biblical truth of Christ's imminent premillennial coming. Among all the sects into which the Protestant church was divided Fitch could not find one that "is not decidedly hostile to the Bible truth that Christ has been raised up to sit personally on David's throne."[71] And, according to Fitch, this could only lead to one conclusion: "Inasmuch as these multiplied sects are opposed to the plain Bible truth of Christ's personal reign on earth, THEY ARE ANTICHRIST."[72]

Thus, for Fitch, and for those who soon supported his new "cry"--like e.g. George Storrs, Joseph Marsh, David Plumb, and (after considerable hesitation) Joshua V. Himes, and eventually (just weeks before October 22) even William Miller himself--the only option for true Christians would be to heed the call "Come out of her, my people" (Revelation 18:4), and, in separating from Babylon, to escape the divine judgments.[73] Fitch and his

---

[70] Ibid., 9-10.

[71] Ibid., 10.

[72] Ibid., 13.

[73] The application of "Babylon" to at least part of Protestantism did not originate with Charles Fitch. See Leroy E. Froom, PFOF, vol. IV, 767-770; P.G. Damsteegt, TTM, 48, n. 249. Henry Jones, for example, in his Principles of Interpreting the Prophecies; briefly illustrated and Applied with Notes (Andover and New York: Gould and Newman, 1837) had argued that Babylon was "not just popery, but the whole kingdom of Antichrist" (20-26).

At least on one occasion Miller, when addressing a conference in Boston at the beginning of 1844, referred to the Protestant churches as the "daughters" of the "mother of harlots" (Catholicism), who "partake of the spirit of the old mother" ("To the Conference", AHSTR [Feb. 10, 1844], 9); see also David T. Arthur, "Come out of Babylon", 48. This does, however, not represent Miller's almost consistent position that Advent

"Come-Outers" were in fact saying that in order to be a Christian, it is necessary to become an Adventist.[74]

The appeal to "come out" and be separate was the climax of the growing separation between Millerism and the Protestant churches, but it was part of a process--from an interdenominational movement into a separate sect--which had been in the making for some of years. David Arthur comments:

> It can be said that Millerism had become separatist in spite of itself. The honesty of the leaders in stating that they had no intention of forming a new church need not be questioned. But the hope was a vain one. Their exclusive emphasis upon a single group of doctrines and their growing exclusiveness in spirit and fellowship made separation certain.[75]

III Catholicism in the Millerite Chronological Scheme

The Millerite prophetic interpretations in which the Roman Catholic Church figured prominently were largely based on the traditional scheme developed by Protestant historicist interpreters and supported by historical evidence from Protestant historians with a definite anti-Catholic bias. In his preface to the 1833 edition of his *Evidences from Scripture and History* Miller denied his intention to claim "the title of Theologist, nor of infallibility." He only wanted to present himself "in common with other writers on the same, or other subjects of like import, to be tried by the infallible touchstone of Divine Truth...."[76]

Contemporary non-Millerites with similar prophetic views were often cited at length in Millerite journals. A prominent example was Professor Gaussen's discourse to theological students in Geneva about the role of Roman Catholicism, which was printed in the two most important

---

believers were to stay in their churches until they were no longer tolerated.

[74] Charles Fitch, <u>Come out of Her, My People</u>, 19; David T. Arthur, "Come out of Babylon," 64.

[75] David T. Arthur, "Come Out of Babylon," 76.

[76] William Miller, <u>EHS</u>, 3.

Millerite journals and published a few weeks later by
Joshua Himes as a separate pamphlet.[77]
    Millerites largely agreed with other Protestants in
their perception of Roman Catholicism as the great
apostate power, with a long history of persecution, lust
for power, and immorality, which, though weaker since
the French Revolution, still needed to be feared. The
fact that around 1840-1844 Catholics in the United
States still formed a small minority, did not make their
threat any less real.[78] Catholics were Catholics, and
given a chance, they would do in America what they had
done to medieval Europe! This basic conviction shaped
the Millerites' opinion toward Catholics and most Protestants alike.
    Apart from the apostle Paul's statement about the
"man of sin" (2 Thessalonians 2:7,8),[79] the Bible

---

[77] "Popery, an Argument for the Truth, by its
Fulfillment of Scripture Prophecies, AHSTR (July 3,
1844), 169-171; (July 10, 1844), 177-178; "A Voice from
Geneva," MC (July 11, 1844), 409-411; Professor Gaussen
of Geneva, The German Rebuke of American Neology, A
Discourse by Prof. Gaussen, of Geneva, To the Theological Students at the Opening of the Course in October
last, entitled: Popery, an Argument for the Truth, by
its fulfillment of Scripture Prophecies (Boston: J.V.
Himes, 1844).

[78] Detailed statistics of the strength of the Roman
Catholic Church are available from annually published
"almanacs." According to The Metropolitan Catholic
Almanac and Laity's Directory for the year 1844
(Baltimore: Fielding Lucas, jr., ca. 1845), the church
in 1844 counted 1.3 million members, in 21 dioceses,
with 17 bishops, 8 bishops elect and 634 priests (58,
167). Protestants did not implicitly trust the figures
provided by the Catholic clergy, but believed them to be
much higher. This mistrust is for example reflected in
Joshua V. Himes' book about the threat of Catholicism:
Statement of Facts Demonstrating the Rapid and Universal
Spread and Triumph of Roman Catholicism (Boston: J.V.
Himes, 1847), passim.

[79] In numerous instances in Millerite writings
Paul's "man of sin" (2 Thessalonians 2:3-8) is
identified as the papacy. For some examples, see William
Miller, EHS, 98; William Miller, Dissertations on the
True Inheritance of the Saints, and the Twelve Hundred

portions applied to Roman Catholicism were found in Daniel (chapters 7-9, 11, 12) and in John's Apocalypse (chapters 2, 3, 5, 6, 11, 12-14, 16-19), where figures such as the "little horn," the "beast," the "harlot" and "Babylon" were seen as key concepts in an understanding of the true nature of Catholicism.

1. Catholicism in the Prophecies of Daniel

a. Daniel 7

Miller and his associates saw Daniel 7 as a close parallel of Daniel 2, which relates the story of Nebuchadnezzar's dream of the metallic image. The gold, silver, bronze, and iron were taken as symbols for the Neo-Babylonian, Medo-Persian, Greek-Macedonian and Roman empires. The four beasts of chapter 7 were explained in the same manner: The eagle-winged lion was believed to represent Babylon; the voracious bear, Medo-Persia; the four-headed leopard, Alexander the Great's empire and its four subsequent divisions; and the "terrible beast" with the iron teeth, Rome. The ten horns of this beast were the "kingdoms" which "replaced" the Roman Empire in Western and Central Europe, although Millerite expositors could not always fully agree on the exact list.[80] Three of these horns were "plucked out" to make room for a "little horn." This power had "eyes like the eyes of a man" and blasphemed God; it made "war with the saints and prevailed against them;" it thought "to change times and laws," but would only be permitted to do so "until a time, and times and a dividing of time".

---

and Sixty Days of Daniel and John, with an Address to the Conference of Believers in the Near Advent (Boston: Joshua V. Himes, 1842), 30-31; Josiah Litch, An Address to the Public and Especially the Clergy on the Near Approach of the Glorious, Everlasting Kingdom of God on Earth, as Indicated by the Word of God, the History of the World, and Signs of the Present Times (Boston: J.V. Himes, 1842), 58; "The Glory of God in the Earth," MC (Nov. 28, 1842), 4; George Storrs, "Exposition of Daniel 7th Chapter," MC (May 4, 1843), 34; "Reasons for Believing the Second Coming of Christ in 1843," MC (Nov. 23, 1842), 3-4.

[80] P.G. Damsteegt, TTM, 23.

It would eventually see its power curtailed until it would be utterly destroyed (vs. 8, 20, 21, 24-26).

In identifying Roman Catholicism with the little horn, the Millerites were treading familiar ground. The author of "A Chapter on Popery," an article in *The Midnight Cry*, pointed out how unnecessary it was to explain the reasons for this identification:

> It is doubtless quite unnecessary for us to consume time, by here going to work to prove to our readers that this little Horn is the representation of the Papal power: as it would only be proving what they all admit.[81]

The three horns which were "plucked up by the roots" (vs. 8) were generally identified as the three Arian powers whose downfall facilitated the emergence of the papacy as an important power.[82] This process was completed, it was argued, in 538, from which date the period of "a time, times and a dividing of times"--or the 1260 years during which the little horn harassed "the saints of the most High" (vs. 25)--extended to 1798. The length of this period of "a time, times, and a dividing of time" (also mentioned in Daniel 12:7; Revelation 12:14) was determined by assuming that these "times", just as the 1260 days (= years) of Revelation 11:3; 12:6 and the 42 months (of 30 days/years) of Revelation 11:2; 13:5 referred to the 538-1798 time period. Its 538 date was determined by the *terminus ad quem*: 1798, when the "dominion" of the little horn was taken away.[83] The events of the French Revolution, resulting in 1798 in the removal of the pope from Rome-- an event which seriously curtailed the influence of Catholicism--were fresh in America's collective memory. This date stood out as a clear mark of an irreversible

---

[81] Lorenzo D. Fleming, "A Chapter on Popery," MC (March 21, 1844), 276.

[82] Most Millerite preachers identified these powers as the Heruli, the Vandals and the Ostrogoths, but Miller held them to be Lombardy, Rome, and Ravenna. See William Miller, ESH, 46.

[83] See e.g. "The Fall of Popery, Events of 1798," MC (Nov. 25, 1842), 2.

loss of influence.[84] Said Litch in "An Address to the Public and Especially the Clergy":

> This point is so evident and so fully before the community, that it is needless to present evidence on the point. Popery is the mere shadow of what it once was; nor can it by any artifice ever again resume its former vigor and power. It is a plant of darkness; it cannot live and flourish under the flood of light and liberty which irradiates almost every point of our earth. Protestants are now tolerated in every Papal kingdom on the continent of Europe.[85]

Calculating backwards from 1798, the beginning of the 1260 years had to be in 538. By checking historical sources it was found that in 538 Belisarius, a general of the Byzantine emperor Justinian (527-565) subjugated the enemies of the papacy in Rome. This development made effective the decree of Justinian, issued March 15, 533, by which Pope John II was recognized as "the head of all churches"[86]

---

[84] For a review of the history of the Roman Catholic Church in the late 18th and early 19th century, see e.g. A. Latreille, L'Eglise Catholique et la Révolution Française, 2 vols. (Paris: Les Editions du Cerf, 1970); J.B. Bury, History of the Papacy in the 19th Century, augmented ed. (New York: Schocken Books, 1964); Fernand Mourret, A History of the Catholic Church; vol. VII: Period of the French Revolution - 1775-1823 (St. Louis, MO: B. Herder Book Co, 1955); and vol. VIII: Period of the Early Nineteenth Century - 1823-1878 (St. Louis, MO: B. Herder Book Co, 1957); Thomas S. Bokenkotter, A Concise History of the Catholic Church (Garden City: Doubleday & Company, 1977), 257-310; E.E.Y. Hales, The Catholic Church in The Modern World (Garden City: Hannover House, 1958), 17-146; Owen Chadwick, The Popes and the European Revolution (Oxford: Clarendon Press, 1981).

[85] Josiah Litch, An Address, 66.

[86] Various authors were cited in support of these dates, notably: Croly, The Apocalypse of St. John (Philadelphia: E. Littell, 1827), 113-117; Gerard T. Noel, A brief Enquiry into the Prospects of the Church, in Connexion with the Second Advent of our Lord Jesus

Miller was positive in his assertion that the description of the little horn in Daniel 7:8 could only refer to the Church of Rome. There was ample evidence of the blasphemous "speaking of great things" (vs. 8, 20):

... the blasphemies against God, in the pretensions of the Roman clergy to divine power, working of miracles, canonizing departed votaries, changing ordinances and laws of God's house, worshipping saints and images, performing rites and ceremonies too foolish and ridiculous to be for a moment indulged in, and which an unprejudiced mind cannot for a moment believe to be warranted by divine rule, or example of Christ or his apostles.[87]

When dealing with the prophecies of Revelation 12, the Millerite expositors usually went into greater detail about the religious persecutions carried out by the Roman Catholic Church or with its approval, than they did in the context of Daniel 7. One of the aspects in Daniel 7 which received constant attention was the relative strength of Catholicism after 1798. Here the tension between the "taking away of the dominion" (vs. 26) and this power's "prevailing against the saints" (vs. 21) was not always successfully resolved. On the one hand, it was continually emphasized how effectively the papacy's "dominion" had been reduced to almost nil. It was affirmed that the power of the pope was no more, as the prophecy had predicted. "His holiness, now, is of little more consequence to the church, than that of a degraded priest granting absolutions to the crimes of

Christ, (Philadelphia: Orrin Rogers, 1840), 100; William Cunninghame, The Political Destiny of the Earth, as Revealed in the Bible (Philadelphia: Orrin Rogers, 1840), 28; Edward King, Remarks on the Signs of the Times (Philadelphia: Jas. Humphreys, 1800). See also Sylvester Bliss, Memoirs, 197.

Edward Gibbon, The History of the Decline and Fall of the Roman Empire, 5 vols. (London: W. Strahan and T. Cadell, 1776-1788; many later editions) is also mentioned at times in support of the 538-1798 dates; e.g. "Daniel's Vision of the Four Beasts," MC (Aug. 10, 1843), 196.

[87] William Miller, ESH, 47-48. See also "Daniel's Vision of the Four Beasts," MC (Aug. 10, 1843), 196.

France."[88] Proof that the temporal power of the pope had been "taken away" was found in the instruction of Pius VII in 1805 to his nuncio in Vienna, in which the pope complained that he could not even exercise his rights of "deposing heretics from their principalities and declaring them deprived of their property."

> To be sure, we are fallen into such calamitous times, that it IS NOT POSSIBLE for the spouse of Jesus Christ TO PRACTICE, nor even expedient for her to recall HER HOLY MAXIMS OF JUST RIGOR against the enemies of the faith....[89]

Another Millerite author made the same point by quoting from the encyclical letter "Probe Nostis" of Gregory XVI of September 1840, in which the pope admitted his lack of authority, "Are we not compelled to see the most crafty ENEMIES of the TRUTH ranging, far and wide, with impunity?" The author emphasized how the time was past when the occupant of the chair of St. Peter could directly interfere in the affairs of states.[90]

In 1842 Miller stated that the pope of Rome had "lived out his day" and was now being "consumed" by the gospel light, "and only awaits the glorious coming of the Son of Man to be utterly destroyed."[91] Storrs agreed: Against those who maintain that the civil power of the papacy is not completely taken away in 1798, he is willing to admit that a new pope was chosen, "and that he may have some civil power in Italy is not denied." However, the picture had drastically changed from what it was before. Storrs maintained "... that he has power

---

[88] Quoted from Josiah Sutcliffe, <u>An Introduction to Christianity</u> (1817), 151 in: "Has the Pope's Dominion Been Taken Away?" <u>MC</u> (Nov. 9, 1842), 2-3.

[89] "The Fall of Popery, Events of 1798," <u>MC</u> (Nov. 25, 1842), 2.

[90] "Popery," <u>MC</u> (Nov. 22, 1842), 3. For a recent edition of the text and translation of this encyclical, see Claudia Carlen, ed., <u>The Papal Encyclicals: 1740-1878</u> (Wilmington, N.C.: McGrath Pub. Co., 1981), 259-261.

[91] William Miller, <u>Dissertations</u>, 57.

to depose kings and to put to death the saints now, is denied."[92]

At the same time, however, while laying stress on the demise of the power of Catholicism, the Millerite preachers--somewhat paradoxically--untiringly warned about the increasing danger of Catholicism. The little horn is still "prevailing" in many ways, notably in the United States. The arrival of great numbers of Catholic immigrants kindled great fears in the minds of Protestant America[93] and the Millerites were not immune to that anxiety:

> The dark wing of papal influence is rapidly beskirting our American horizon ... It is acquiring an influence that has given it an audaciousness unprecedented. It is fully justifying all that the spirit of prophecy has authorized us to expect...[94]

Numerous articles in *The Midnight Cry*, and, even more so, in the *Signs of the Times*, present examples of the "prevailing" of Catholicism. The Jesuits are singled out as the worst culprits, comprising, it is said, one third of the annual increase of some 200,000 Catholics.[95]

---

[92] George Storrs, "Exposition of Daniel 7th Chapter," MC (May 4, 1843), 36. The article contains an extensive quote from Gregory XVI's Encyclical letter.

[93] See Ray Allen Billington, The Protestant Crusade, 32-237 for a review of the anti-Catholicism of the period; esp. pp. 127-128 on the perceived danger of Catholic immigration.

[94] L.D. Fleming, "A Chapter on Popery," MC (March 21, 1844), 276.

[95] According to the vehemently anti-Catholic journal New York Observer of February 16, 1843, quoted in ST, "The Little Horn Prevailing," (Apr. 26, 1843), 62. The same ST article quotes from Dr. William C. Brownlee's book Historical Sketch of the Jesuits in support of its thesis that "the Romish church" continues to exert "an overwhelming influence" through the Jesuit order. (Dr. Brownlee, a Dutch Reformed clergyman--who in the words of Billington "showed himself incapable of moderation"-- was one of the most prominent anti-Catholic leaders of the time.) Fear for the Jesuits was also expressed in:

Incidents are repeatedly mentioned as evidence of the rapid increase of Catholic influence and power. We shall return to that aspect later in our discussion.

b. Daniel 8 and 9

As indicated above[96] chapters 8 and 9 of the Book of Daniel were essential for the Millerite calculations concerning the Second Coming in 1843-44. But chapter 8 described another aspect which is more relevant to our present study: another little horn, growing out of a power which is identified as the Seleucid kingdom, one of the divisions of the Greek-Macedonian Empire. Few contemporary Protestant expositors of prophecy identified the little horn of Daniel 7 as the Seleucid king Antiochus Epiphanes (175-164 B.C.), one of the fiercest enemies of the Jews in the second century B.C.. This Antiochus Epiphanes was, however, quite commonly seen as the little horn of Daniel 8.[97] His desecration of the Jerusalem temple in 168 B.C. seemed to fit in exactly with texts such as Daniel 8:11, where the little horn is reported as taking away "the daily sacrifice."

The Millerite leaders rejected the Antiochus Epiphanes application, as well as the attempts of some to bring the Turks into the picture. Their main argument against the Antiochus interpretation was that this Seleucid king did not "wax great," certainly not when compared to the other powers mentioned earlier in the chapter (portrayed as a two-horned ram, and a powerful "he-goat" with "a notable horn between his eyes," and subsequently replaced by four other "notable horns"), which were believed to be the Medo-Persian Empire, the empire of Alexander the Great, and the fourfold division of Alexander's empire after Alexander's death. Following

---

"The Little Horn - the Pope," ST (Feb. 15, 1841), 169-171; and "Triumph of the Jesuits in New York," ST (Apr. 20, 1842), 21. News items which reflected negatively on the Jesuits were often taken from other journals, e.g. ST (Apr. 20, 1842), 22-24; TS (Apr. 27, 1842), 26-27. A filler in AHSTR (Aug. 7, 1844), characterized the Jesuits as men "who lengthened the Creed, and shortened the Decalogue" (7).

[96] See p. 32.

[97] See LeRoy E. Froom, PFOF, vol. IV, 392-393.

the same sequence they believed to be present in chapter 2 as well as in chapter 7, they could only conclude that the great power following the Greeks was Rome.

Miller insisted that the details of the description of the little horn of Daniel 8 could not be made to fit the career of Antiochus Epiphanes, but did harmonize perfectly with the history of Rome.[98] Litch rejected the Antiochus hypothesis, and denied the possibility that the little horn could refer to "mohammedism[sic]," since this power did not originate in Syria, but in Arabia.[99] Other Millerites voiced the same opinion.[100]

When applying the symbol of the little horn of Daniel 8 to Rome, the Catholic Church was seen as an extension of imperial Rome. This two-phase interpretation of "pagan" and "papal" Rome also allowed for a dual significance of the sanctuary: the Jewish sanctuary which was "trodden under foot" by the Romans, while in the second phase the people of God, symbolized by the sanctuary, were "trodden under foot" by the Roman church.[101]

A critical part of the Millerite understanding of Daniel 8 centered around the meaning of "the daily sacrifice" of vs. 11, 13 and "the transgression of desolation" of vs. 13. It was emphasized that the word *sacrifice* was supplied by the translators and was not present in the Hebrew text. What then was this "daily" which was removed by the little horn in its second--papal--phase? The answer to that question was: Paganism!

---

[98] William Miller, EHS, 50; also Silvester Bliss, Memoirs, 188.

[99] Josiah Litch, An Address, 78.

[100] "Is Antioch Epiphanes the hero of Daniel's Prophecy?", ST (Dec. 28, 1842), 113-114; George Storrs, "Exposition of Daniel 8th Chapter," MC (May 4, 1843), 37-44; "Daniel's Vision of the Four Beasts," MC (Aug. 10, 1843), 196; S. Hawley, "The Doctrine of the Second Advent sustained by the Voice of the Church - Extract of a Sermon preached at the Dedication of the Tabernacle, May 4th, 1843, by Rev. S. Hawley", ST (June 7, 1843), 110.

[101] William Miller, ESH, 48-56; Josiah Litch, An Address, 78-80; George Storrs, "Exposition of Daniel 8th Chapter," MC (May 4, 1843), 37-44. See also P.G. Damsteegt, TTM, 32-33.

... although the empire was nominally Christian most of the time from the days of Constantine, yet Paganism continued to maintain itself in Rome, and Pagan sacrifices were offered there until the conversion of the Ostrogoths to Christianity, about A.D. 508, since which time we have no account of any public Pagan sacrifices being offered in the city of Rome ...[102]

The "transgression of desolation" follows the "daily" of paganism: it represents the consistent effort of the Catholic Church to destroy true Christianity.[103] Satan was, of course, the real instigator. The pagan abominations were not enough for him. When God set up his "gospel kingdom" in the world, Satan changed his policies:

Therefore, in order to carry the war into the Christian camp, he suffers the daily sacrifice abomination to be taken out of the way, and sets up papacy, which is more congenial to the Christian mode of worship in its outside forms and ceremonies, but retaining all the hateful qualities of the former. He persuades them to erect images to some or all of the dear apostles; and even to Christ, and Mary, the "Mother of God." He then flatters them that the church is infallible. (Here was a strong cord by which he could punish all disputers.) He likewise gives them the keys of heaven, (or Peter, as they call it.) This will secure all authority. He then clothes them with power to make laws, and to dispense with those which God had made. This capped the climax. In this

---

[102] Josiah Litch, An Address, 81; William Miller, ESH, 94-96; "The Vision of the Ram and the He-Goat," MC (Aug. 10, 1843), 196-198. For the date A.D. 508, see pp. 33-34.

[103] For the dual "abomination-motif" with the "desolation of transgressions" following the "daily", see also "Reasons for believing the Second Coming of Christ in 1843", MC (Nov. 23, 1842), 3-4; Elon Galusha, Address of Elder Elon Galusha, with Reasons for Believing Christ's Second Coming at hand (Rochester, N.Y., 1844), 11-13; Apollos Hale, Second Advent Manual, 59-81.

he would fasten many thousands who might protest against some of the vile abominations; yet habit and custom might secure them a willing obedience to his laws, and to a neglect of the laws of God. This was Satan's masterpiece....[104]

The Catholic Church, Litch assured his audience, fulfills all details of the prophecy. "An host was given against the daily ..." (vs. 12) indicates how all the energies of the church "were to be directed by the aspiring pontiffs against pagan institutions, and to bring the pagans over to the Christian faith."[105] But, lest too favourable an impression of Catholicism be created, Litch quickly added his interpretation of the second part of vs. 12 ("it cast down the truth to the ground; and it practiced and prospered"). The papal power, he explained, trampled on God's Word, corrupting the doctrines of the gospel, and "imposed on men's consciences burdens, heavy and intolerable to be borne; [it] persecuted to death all who would not submit to the yoke."[106]

c. Daniel 11 and 12

The interpretation of Daniel 11 and 12 presented considerable problems for Miller and his associates. Most of chapter 11 was seen as referring to Greek and Roman history, but from verse 36 onward they saw the introduction of another power: the papacy, symbolized by the fierce "king of the North," with verses 40-45 dealing specifically with the Napoleontic period.[107] The

---

[104] William Miller, ESH, 55.

[105] Josiah Litch, An Address, 81.

[106] Ibid., 81-82.

[107] William Miller (ESH, 97-98) affirms that this king is the same as the little horn of Daniel, the "man of sin" and "mystical Babylon." For his interpretation of Daniel 11:36-45, see ESH, 98-113. Verse 37 is seen to contain a reference to forced celibacy and to the claims of the pope to be God's viceregent; vs. 38 refers to the papal obsession with wealth, while "the strange god" of vs. 39 is interpreted as "the patron saints, which the pope divided among the several nations of the earth."

most important link with Daniel 8 was, however, found in chapter 12:11-12, where the prophetic periods of the 1290 days and 1335 days are introduced. Here a time element related to the ta•.ing away of "the daily" is mentioned, which is absent in Daniel 8! The 1290 and 1335 days are, as would be expected, interpreted as 1290 and 1335 years respectively, which were then, rather pragmatically, tied in with the 1260 years and the 2300 years. If the 1260 years and the 1290 years were both to end in 1798, as was assumed, the 1290 years had to begin in A.D. 508, and if the 1335 years were to begin at the same time as the 1290 years, they would have to end with the 2300 years in 1843-44.

What then happened in A.D. 508? Answer: The taking away of the (pagan) "daily"! What historical event corresponded to this? Paganism was effectively terminated when most of the territory of the former Roman Empire converted to Christianity. The most significant moment in that long chain of events was the conversion of King Clovis of the Franks in A.D. 508.[108] It set the stage for the further advance of the Catholic Church, which received another, even more important, boost, when Justinian's decree gave formal recognition to papal power. And thus its period of supremacy could begin, and could last until it would face the opposition of Bonaparte in "the time of the end" (Daniel 11:40).

2. The Catholic Church in the Book of Revelation

a. Revelation 2 and 3

Although much attention focused on the "papal beast" of chapter 13 and on "Babylon" in chapters 17-19, a number of paragraphs in earlier chapters in the book of

---

See also Josiah Litch, An Address, 95-104; "A Paraphrase on the 11th chapter of Daniel," MC (Aug. 10, 1843), 198-199.

[108] William Miller, ESH, 95; William Miller, "A Dissertation on Prophetic Chronology," in Report of the General Conference, 90-92; "Reasons for Believing the Second Coming of Christ in 1843," MC (Nov. 23, 1842), 3-4; Apollos Hale, Second Advent Manual, 59-81; Elon Galusha, Address of Elder Elon Galusha, 10-13.

Revelation were also seen as referring to Catholicism. The letters to the seven churches in Asia Minor (chapters 2 and 3) were understood as characterizations of seven periods in the history of the church.[109]

The third church, Pergamos, symbolized the worldly church of the period 312-538. It was in this fateful era that the church received "that monster, the man of sin, the son of perdition, into her bosom, which stung the church with the poison of asps, and filled the temple of God with image worship, and the church with idolatry, selfishness, avarice and pride."[110] It was the time when numerous pagan rites and ideas were assimilated into the church.[111]

Thyatira, the fourth church, represented the church "after she is driven into the wilderness by the anti-Christian beast"; it had to deal with "the woman Jezebel," who was identical with the woman on the scarlet-coloured beast of Revelation 17. The Thyatira period extended, Miller suggested, from 538 till the 10th century, and was a time of despair for the true church of God.[112]

b. Revelation 6-8

In a manner similar to the seven churches of chaps. 2 and 3 the seven seals were understood as portraying periods of history from a particular perspective (chps. 6-8). The fourth seal (6:7, 8) has to do with "the bloody and persecuting reign of the papal church," beginning in 538 A.D., and extending until "the beginning of the 18th century, A.D. 1700, when the bloody persecutions against Protestants ceased, and the nations of the world began to enjoy religious freedom."[113]

---

[109] Miller's 9th and 10th lectures were devoted to this subject: ESH, 107-144. Other Millerite leaders paid little attention to this theme.

[110] Ibid., 137.

[111] Ibid., 139-140.

[112] Ibid., 144.

[113] Ibid., 182-183.

In his treatment of the seven trumpets (chapters 8,
9, 11:15-19), Miller paid most attention to the last
three, which, he said, are "descriptions of the
judgments that God has sent and will send on this Papal
beast, the abomination of the whole earth."[114] The fifth
trumpet (9:1-12) "alludes to the rise of the Turkish
Empire under Ottoman, at the downfall of the Saracens,"
which became a powerful "barrier to the spread of the
Papal doctrine and power in the eastern world."[115] The
sixth trumpet portrays the expansion of the Turkish
Empire into the territory of the Byzantine Empire and
covered a period of "an hour, and a day, and a month,
and a year," which by means of the day-year-principle
translates into 391 years and 15 days, and would extend
from ca. 1450 to the very time of the Millerite
movement. The advance of the Islamic Turks, of course,
further curtailed the power of the Church of Rome in an
extensive geographical area.

c. Revelation 11, 12

Revelation 11:1-14 tells us that the holy city will be
"trodden underfoot" for a period of 42 months, and then
presents the reader with two witnesses, "clothed in
sackcloth" during--once again--1260 days. The 1260 days
equal the 42 months and extend from 538 to 1798. The two
witnesses were interpreted as the Bible--the Old and the
New Testament--which could not let their light shine
(symbolized by the covering with sackcloth) during the
1260 years of papal supremacy. Miller did not mince
words when describing this period during which "the word
of God was darkened by monkish superstition, bigotry,
and ignorance in its sacred principles."[116] He continues:

It did not give its true light, because the laws,
doctrines and ordinances were changed by the laws
of the Latin church; its doctrine was perverted by
the introduction of the doctrine of devils and the
anti-Christian abominations: its ordinances were so
altered as to suit the convenience of carnal men;
and it was obscured, because the common people were

---

[114] Ibid., 116.

[115] Ibid.

[116] Ibid., 194.

forbidden to read it, or even to have it in their houses, by the Papal authority.[117]

Revelation 11:7-14 continues with the career of the witnesses after the 1260 day/year period. Miller and his associates believed that this section referred to the French Revolution and its efforts to do away with the Bible and Christianity.

In Revelation 12 the focus is on a pure woman, who is forced to hide in "the wilderness" during a period of 1260 days. The standard explanation was that this symbol referred to the true church--suffering, and often (as in the case of the Waldenses) in hiding, in fear of papal persecution.

d. The beast of Revelation 13

The "beast from the sea"--presented in Revelation 13:1-10--together with the little horn of Daniel 7, provided the Millerites with their most popular and potent images of Catholicism. Even though some uncertainty and disagreement remained with regard to some details of the description of this monster, the similarities between the little horn of Daniel 7 and the beast of Revelation 13 seemed so obvious that there could not be any doubt as to the identity of the power symbolized by the beast: "Romanism." It should be noticed, however, that verses 1-3 of Revelation 13 were often applied to the Roman Empire, which gave way to the papacy after it had received a deadly wound, with the papacy being introduced from vs. 3b onwards. This was the theory to which Miller himself subscribed.[118]

---

[117] Ibid. The opposition of the Catholic Church to the reading of the Bible by the laity was often mentioned; see e.g. "Popery vs. the Bible," MC (May 8, 1844), 343; "The Pope and the Bible," MC (July 18, 1844), 6-7; "The Pope and the Bible," AHSTR, (July 31, 1844), 201-202.

[118] The ten horns (vs. 2) were interpreted as the European powers which came to prominence after Rome's demise, while the seven heads were seen as the seven forms of government of Rome from its very beginning to the present (senatorial, tribunate, consular, decemvir,

Miller gave some attention to "the mark of the beast," which he explained as relating to the difficulties in buying or selling or pursuing a lawful trade for those who did not obey the papacy, in those times and lands where the papacy held supreme power.[119] But he was more intrigued, it seems, with "the number of the beast" (Revelation 13:18). He was aware of the various attempts to explain the meaning of the cryptic number 666:

> This text [Rev. 13:18] has caused as much speculation as any text in the whole Bible; rivers of ink have been shed to explain its meaning, brains have been addled in trying to find some great mystery which the wisdom of this world, as was supposed, could not discover...."[120]

He disagreed with Greek and Latin scholars who had found a multitude of names with a numerical value of 666,[121] and proposed "to present the Scripture on the point, and then leave you to judge whether we have light or not."[122] Miller linked the number 666 with the imperial Roman beast of vs. 1-3 and suggested that

---

triumvirate, imperial, papal). See William Miller, ESH, 78-81.

[119] William Miller, Remarks on Revelation Thirteenth, Seventeenth and Eighteenth (Boston: J.V. Himes, 1844), 14-16. Others saw the mark of the beast as a sharing in the character of the beast; see e.g. "The Mark of the Beast," MC (Oct. 26, 1843), 84-85.

[120] William Miller, ESH, 76.

[121] Ibid.
Litch, following Clark's Commentary, proposed H BASILEIA LATINE as a possible solution, but admitted that he was not sure (An Address, 72). The New York Observer suggested that the Greek value of the letters of "Captain Miller" would also give 666 (see "The New York Observer," MC [March 10, 1843], 45; and in "Scoffing in High Places," ST [March 8, 1843], 5).

[122] William Miller, ESH, 77.

reference was to a period of 666 years of pagan dominance, from 158 B.C. to A.D. 508.[123]

e. Revelation 16-18

Rather than interpreting the seven plagues of Revelation 16 as part of God's final judgment, Miller saw the first six as already fulfilled in divine judgments meted out to the beast. The first plague with the sores, afflicting those who had the mark of the beast, "was sent on the Romish church about the year A.D. 1529, under the preaching of Luther, Calvin, and others who opposed and exposed the corruptions [the sores] of the church of Rome."[124] Other events were connected with each of the following plagues, the rise of Islam being linked to the sixth plague and the last plague being expected in the immediate future--creating the unparalleled chaos which was to precede the Second Coming of Christ.[125]

The Millerites' view on the identity of the "mother of harlots" in Revelation 17 paralleled the current Protestant conviction. In flowery language Miller affirmed the common knowledge that "the false church" of Rome corresponds in minute detail to the characteristics of the "whore" of the Revelation:

---

[123] Predictably, Miller tried to establish a period which would end in A.D. 508, when his 1290 and 1335 day/year periods began. Calculating backwards he arrived at the year 158 B.C., when, according to Miller, paganism received a major boost fromy a treaty concluded between the Romans and the Jews. See William Miller, ESH, 83; also William Miller, Remarks, 14-16.

Miller's view with regard to the number 666 was not generally accepted by his associates. Indicative of the lack of acceptance is the fact that the 666-year period was no longer included in the 1843 prophetic chart. See Leroy E. Froom, PFOF, vol. IV, 736.

[124] William Miller, ESH, 221.

[125] Ibid., 221-229. Although Miller thought he had used "a fair and scriptural explanation of the figures and metaphors used" in Revelation 16 (229), his interpretation of the plagues did not figure very prominently in Millerite preaching.

The rainment [sic] and splendor, with the riches of
this false Church, is literally fulfilled in the
dress and pomp and show of the Pope, Cardinals,
Bishops, Legates and Priests of the Roman Catholic
Church. The golden cup in her hand, is the
political bait she holds out to all nations. In a
republic she can be a great republican; and in a
kingdom a flaming royalist. Her golden cup is held
out to all sorts of governments, so that if
possible by false pretenses, plighted faith and
broken vows, she may obtain her object--power over
all.[126]

The same is true with respect to Babylon, which
contemporary Protestants, almost without exception, saw
as the apostate Roman Catholic Church. It can,
therefore, hardly surprise us that few, if any, efforts
were made to prove a point which was so obvious to most
of the Millerite audience. The remarkable aspect of the
Millerite views on the "whore" and Babylon was rather
the growing inclination to tie nominal Protestantism in
with the apostate "Romish" system. As early as 1837,
before he had aligned himself with Miller, Henry Jones
wrote that the traditional idea of "the New Testament
Babylon as a type of popery" was no longer adequate. "We
live in the latter days, and see popery under different
circumstances," he writes, before he continues to
explain how the "Mother of Harlots" will soon combine
with "all the other powers of wickedness" and then the
great apocalyptic Babylon will be truly constituted.[127]
Babylon is not restricted to Roman Catholicism, even
though she remains its nucleus: it "embraces everything
which is Anti-christian in its tendencies."[128] How the
Millerites, particularly during the last phase of the
movement, came to focus on the Protestant churches as
"daughters of the harlot" and part of "Babylon," has
already been discussed.[129]

---

[126] William Miller, Remarks, 18.

[127] Henry Jones, Principles of Interpreting the
Prophecies, 26-27.

[128] [Sylvester Bliss], "The Downfall of Great
Babylon," Advent Shield (May 1844), 116.

[129] See above, pp. 42-46.

63

IV Millerism and the Catholic Threat

1. Anti-Catholic Sentiments in the 1830s and 1840s

In America the late thirties and early forties of 19th century were characterized by constantly increasing anti-Catholic sentiments. As the Catholics became more numerous—through immigration and territorial additions to the United States—suspicions increased. There was widespread fear that Catholics would not be able to accept true democracy and were propagating "un-American" values. Economic factors, such as native workers being forced out of work by less demanding new Catholic arrivals, did not help to allay anti-Catholic feelings. Ugly incidents, as the burning of the Ursuline convent and a girls' school near Charleston in 1834, and serious riots in Philadelphia and New York in 1844, left a lasting impression.[130]

Anti-Catholic sentiments were not limited to one or two Protestant denominations. Billington provides convincing evidence that "by the middle of the 1840s the American churches were able to present a virtually united front against Catholicism."[131] The Presbyterians, of course, had a heritage of strong antagonism with Rome. Internal conflict in the mid 1830s—between the Old School and the New School—deflected their attention from anti-popery matters for a number of years, but after 1841 they were again ready to pay full attention to the problem of Catholicism. The Methodists were so involved in internal conflicts regarding the slavery issue, that the Catholic threat was for a while somewhat relegated to the background. Congregationalists, the "low church" part of the Episcopal Church, Baptists,

---

[130] Robert T. Handy, A History of the Churches in the United States and Canada, 214-218. See also Sydney E. Ahlstrom, A Religious History of the American People, 558-563; Michael Feldberg, The Philadelphia Riots of 1844: A Study of Ethnic Conflict (Westport, Conn.: Greenwood, 1975); Ray Allen Billington, The Protestant Crusade, 53-84; 220-237; Gustavus Myers, History of Bigotry in the United States (New York: Capricorn Books, 1960), 129-128.

[131] Ray Allen Billington, The Protestant Crusade, 181.

Dutch Reformed and Lutherans were all quite vocal in their anti-Catholicism.[132] A number of interdenominational agencies--such as the American Tract Society, the American Education Society and the American Bible Society--also exerted a strong anti-Catholic influence.

Protestant journals allotted an increasing amount of space to anti-Catholic articles, while some journals and associations were exclusively devoted to the Protestant crusade against the threat of Catholicism.[133] Even though Catholic reactions could at times be bitter, harsh or vehement, Protestants by far outranked them in verbal violence and "hate-" or "horror-literature." The most sordid example of this type of anti-Catholic propaganda was no doubt Maria Monk's *Awful Disclosures of the Hotel Dieu Nunnery of Montreal*[134], which even surpassed Rebecca Theresa Reed's *Six Months in a Convent.*[135]

Anti-Catholicism found political expression in the early 1840s in the nativistic American Party. This political party (which was increasingly anti-Irish and by 1843 strongly anti-Catholic) campaigned for the exclusion of all foreigners from public office and a 21-year period of residency before any possibility of naturalization. It was for a while quite successful in some major cities, and exploited the anti-Catholic sentiments resulting from Archbishops Hughes' attempts in New York to procure public funds for Catholic education.[136]

---

[132] Ibid., 166-185.

[133] Sydney E. Ahlstrom, <u>A Religious History of the American People</u>, 558-563. For a detailed of account anti-Catholic agitation in this period, see Ray Allen Billington, <u>The Protestant Crusade</u>, 53-237.

[134] In the period before the Civil War as many as 300,000 copies were sold; it went through many later editions, one as recent as 1960. See Ray Allen Billington, <u>The Protestant Crusade</u>, 99-104.

[135] The book was so popular that 200,000 copies sold within a month. See Ray Allen Billington, <u>The Protestant Crusade</u>, 90.

[136] Gustavus Myers, <u>History of Bigotry</u>, 110-128.

2. Anti-Catholicism in Millerite Journals

Millerites joined in the Protestant accusations against the Catholic Church, even though usually they were more restrained in their verbal assaults than many contemporary vehemently anti-Catholic preachers and writers. The main reason for this difference, no doubt, lay in the fact that the primary burden of Miller and his associates was the proclamation of the imminent second coming of Christ; their anti-Catholicism was only subservient to this. In the general anti-Catholic climate of the day it was almost natural to see Catholicism as the one great enemy of true Christianity and to build on current anti-Catholic prophetic views. Their main purpose in their lectures, books and journals, however, was not to expose Catholicism, but to use such arguments and to point to such events as would strengthen their main thesis concerning the prophetic certainty of Christ's soon coming. As a consequence we find in the Millerite publications no systematic treatment of Protestant objections against Roman Catholicism, but they are referred to whenever this would support their specific views.

The closest parallel to the "horror-literature" of the period may well be Miller's account of "A Scene of the Last Day," printed in 1842 by Joshua V. Himes, although Miller had not intended it for publication. In his "supposed reflections of a sinner, witnessing the solemn events which immediately precede, and follow, the second advent of our Lord Jesus Christ, and the conflagration of the world," Miller saw ... the cloisters of the Roman monks, and the dark cells of the nuns, which long had kept from view the secret crimes and midnight revels of their murderous, cruel, lustful inmates; I saw the dark-walled chamber of the inquisition, filled with its means of torture, that had in ages past drenched all its walls in blood, now hung in solemn mockery, with images of Christ, with likenesses of angels, and pictures of the Virgin Mary, blasphemously called 'the mother of God;'--all were consumed by this pervading flame.[137]

---

[137] William Miller, A Familiar Exposition of the Twenty-Fourth Chapter of Matthew and the Fifth and Sixth Chapters of Hosea. To which are Added an Address to the General Conference on the Advent, and A Scene of the Last Day (Boston: Joshua V. Himes, 1842), 99-115.

The Millerite journals felt the need to inform their readers about dark conspiracies which were supposed "to render the Catholic religion predominant in the United States."[138] Such fears were at times fanned by rather tactless Catholic claims about the growth of their church. Protestant journals, Millerite included, were apt to print remarks like those made in a speech by the chaplain to the legislative assembly of Wisconsin:

> Popery is here--with a sharp look-out. It is passing up all our navigable streams, surveying the borders of our lakes, travelling through the country on all our public routes, and planting its standard at every important point from Mackinaw to Balize. It has seized upon the fairest portions of our territory; and be assured no pains will be spared and no means wanting, in the power of the Vatican, to subject this whole land to papal dominion. It is the avowed object of the Church of Rome to get the ascendancy here, and to obtain possession of this country.[139]

And Millerite journals would eagerly report rumours foreign correspondents might pick up. "An intelligent Papal priest" had remarked to a Berlin correspondent of an American newspaper

> that the news they were daily receiving, especially from America and England, fully justified the expectations that in less than two generations, the Catholics ... would so outflank and divide the Protestants, that Protestantism would be obliged to hide itself in a few obscure corners like Norway and Lapland, if indeed it continued to vegetate at all...."[140]

When somewhere a Bible-burning incident was reported, the Millerite journals would include an

---

[138] See e.g. "Catholic Schemes," an article quoted *in extenso* from the "Newark Daily" in MC (Nov. 25, 1842), 1.

[139] Extract from the "Catholic Herald" in MC (Aug. 3, 1843), 191.

[140] "Papal Expectations," ST (June 15, 1842), 95.

extract of such a report in their next issue.[141] The Protestant perception of Catholic enmity against the Bible was confirmed by a bull of Gregory XVI which was highly critical of Bible Society activities and Bible translations in the vernacular. Before quoting from the bull, the *Advent Herald and Signs of the Times Reporter* commented on this "new specimen of deceivableness of Popery." While the Pope "pretends an earnest desire to have the Bible known and understood by the people ... he furnishes renewed and abundant evidence of his horror at the free circulation of the word of God."[142]

Several times the Millerite journals refer to the issue of trusteeism--the disagreement, and often confrontation, between the American Catholic hierarchy and the laity about the authority over real estate and other property.[143] Millerite sympathy was squarely with the Catholic laity. When difficulties over this problem arose in New Orleans in 1844, the Catholic laity was praised for its courageous opposition to "the oppressive exactions of the bishops" and for stating "many truths which Catholic bishops are not accustomed to hear."[144] The same problem caused "a large French and German Catholic church in Buffalo" to suffer "oppression from bishop Hughes."[145]

Some Protestants who had sent their children to Catholic schools, as a consequence found them "trapped in Catholicism."[146] Other school-related issues were the

---

[141] E.g.: "Roman Catholic Protracted Meeting," MC (Dec. 6, 1842), 1, about Catholics burning 200-300 Protestant Bibles in Carbo, N.Y.

[142] "The Pope and the Bible", AHSTR (July 31, 1844), 201-202.

[143] For a discussion of the issue of trusteeism, see Jay P. Dolan, The American Catholic Experience, 164-169; James Hennesey, American Catholics, 77-78.

[144] N.Y. Evan, "The Catholics in New Orleans, AHSTR (May 15, 1844), 118-119.

[145] "Popish Tyranny in America," MC (July 18, 1844), 4.

[146] "Popish Falsehood", MC (July 4, 1844), 406; "Popery Prevailing by Craft," MC, (July 11, 1844), 414.

use of public money for Catholic schools and the resistance against the use of the King James' version of the Bible in public schools.[147] Referring to a bill passed in New York City in 1842, which gave "Romanists part of public school money" and assured "the exclusion from the schools of such books as are of a sectarian nature," a *Signs of the Times* article signalled a matter a great concern:

> ... for if one has a right to object to a book, another may; and the atheist has as good a right to the censorship of the press as any one else, and thus all reference to God, eternal life, and a coming judgment, must be kept away from the forming minds of the children the chief part of six days in the week ... A tide of moral pollution is rolling over the land, as fatal to the soul as carbonic acid gas to the body.[148]

The 1844 Philadelphia riots[149] received ample attention in the Millerite journals. Their aggressive and consistent anti-Catholic propaganda made the Protestants at least partly guilty of the outbreak of violence, but the two major Millerite journals, as a matter of course, sympathized with the Protestant party. The underlying cause was clear: "The Native Americans of Philadelphia have endeavored, as in New York, to rescue that city, from the undue influence which the Catholic Irish have obtained for the last few years."[150] No mention was made of the anti-Catholic debates and other propaganda which did much to arouse anti-Catholic sentiments, but the *Signs of the Times* did mention the preaching of Dr. Moriarty, "a distinguished Catholic Divine," who succeeded in converting 300 persons to Catholicism and in doing so contributed to the outbreak

---

[147] For a discussion of the development of the Catholic parocial school system and related problems, see Jay P. Dolan, The American Catholic Experience, 262–293; James Hennesey, American Catholics, 108–109.

[148] "The Little Horn Prevailing", ST (Aug. 2, 1843), 174.

[149] See Ray Allen Billington, The Protestant Crusade, 220–237.

[150] "Riots in Philadelphia," MC (May 16, 1844), 348.

of the "religious war."[151] When a meeting of Native Americans was disturbed by Catholic Irishmen, "this ... exasperated the Americans that they would fain crush all the Irish in the city,"[152] but it was admitted that the Protestant soldiers overreacted and "acted more like drunken men than anything else,"[153] causing a "fearful combat" in which "blood has been poured out like water."[154] To the Millerites it was just one more additional proof of the imminent end of the world:

> There seems to be an unnatural recklessness, a feverish, yet determined power at work, like a deep undercurrent, which threatens mutual extermination. It is a spirit in accordance with the whirlwind impetuosity of the times, whose impetus accelerates each moment, as all near the grand vortex of a world's crisis....
>
> ... Many who have been opposed to our views, now begin to consider whether indeed these things are not so; even some of our Catholic neighbors have said,--'Well this looks as if what the Miller people say, is coming to pass.'[155]

3. Millerite Perception of the Catholic Threat

The remaining question is, to what extent the Millerites perceived the Catholics as a threat. They shared the Protestant fears of Catholicism's triumph in America,[156] and they were thoroughly convinced that, given the chance, the Roman Catholic Church would again persecute the true followers of Christ. After quoting *in extenso*

---

[151] "Religious Excitement in Philadelphia," ST (Apr. 1, 1841), 7.

[152] "Riots in Philadephia," MC (May 16, 1844), 348.

[153] "Philadelphia Riots," MC (July 11, 1844), 413.

[154] According to a somewhat exaggerated account by C.S.M., "Philadelphia Riots," AHSTR (May 29, 1844), 133.

[155] Ibid.

[156] See pp. 64-65.

from an article in the *Baptist Recorder*, in which the author attempted to show that "Popery ... is marching forward with giant strides in this country," the *Signs of the Times* quotes the appeal made by the Baptist journal with apparent approval: "Fellow citizens and Christian brethren! What are we doing to check these invaders of our civil and religious liberties?"[157]

Citing a number of anti-Protestant incidents in Canada, Italy, South America, and Madeira, Himes assures his readers that "... the old gory enemy of 'them that keep the commandments of God, and the testimony of Jesus Christ', was at the bottom of that fearful exhibition of persecuting vengeance!"[158]

But the Catholic Church also used more subtle methods to gain dominance! The Oxford Movement with its "Romanizing" tendencies reached the peak of its influence in Britain around 1841. While John H. Newman (1801-1880) and several other prominent figures in the Movement decided to become Roman Catholic, Edward B. Pusey (1800-1882), another prominent leader, remained in the Anglican Church, which he saw as a bridge between Catholicism and Protestantism. "Puseyism" was denounced by the American anti-Catholic crusaders, and the Millerites regularly quoted from their articles against this English phenomenon, which was also believed to be making definite inroads in America, especially among Episcopalians.[159] Not only were the papists in England "multiplying churches and proselytes," but "the Oxford divines are throwing abroad, the seeds of popery, under another name."[160] And the same danger was threatening America.[161]

---

[157] "Progress of Popery," ST (Oct. 25, 1843), 77-78.

[158] Joshua V. Himes, "Operations of Popery," ST (Nov. 1, 1843), 81-83.

[159] [D. Millard], "The Inquisition in America," MC (Oct. 19, 1843), 80.

[160] "Collisions of Protestantism and Popery," ST (March 1, 1841), 182; see also ST (March 8, 1843), 5

[161] "The Last Form of Papacy," ST (June 8, 1842), 76; "Popery," MC (Aug. 3, 1843), 191; "Puseyism, a Sign of the Times," MC (Jan. 25, 1844), 215; "Puseyism and Neology," ST (Aug. 23, 1843), 4, 6.

However, according to the Millerites, imitation of "popery" by Protestantism was not limited to Puseyism. In an article in the non-Millerite journal *Disciple*, quoted at length by *The Midnight Cry*, "popery" is defined as "the existence and the exercise of the worst passions of human depravity, under the name of religion." "Why do we manifest such horror," it is asked, "when this is manifested under the cloak of popery, if the same things also happen under the name of Protestantism?"[162]

Numerous news items are quoted by the Millerites, especially during 1843 and 1844, which reflect the fear of a growing Catholic influence.[163] This fear was not unfounded, they maintained: The papacy "is becoming more and more powerful" in Europe as well as in America.[164] "...The Mother of Harlots has thrown her arms around the world; she leads a host to listen to her siren song, and to drink from her cup of abominations...."[165] But all this is but a short prelude to the final judgments which will come in the very near future. And, though warning their followers about the new power of Roman Catholicism, the Millerite preachers assured their audiences that the Roman game was over.[166] With approval

---

[162] "The Pope in America," MC (May 4, 1843), 63, quoted from Disciple; see also H.J., "Popery, Where Unsuspected," MC (Aug. 22, 1844), 50-51.

[163] One issue of MC (Feb. 8, 1844) contained as many as six news items about Catholicism: the "Roman Catholic Aggression"; the activities of Belgian missionaries in Oregon; Catholic activities in Hongkong, membership growth in Asia; the power of the Jesuits in France; and a news item about Catholics in Rome (228).

[164] "Will Papacy Have Dominion Again?" MC (Oct. 19, 1843), 79; "The Little Horn Prevailing," ST (Oct. 11, 1843), 61.

[165] "The Little Horn Prevailing," cont., ST (Apr. 26, 1843), 63.

[166] When in September 1839 a number of their missionaries were killed in Korea, the Roman Catholics did not retaliate. Rather than praising them, however, for their non-violent reactions, their restraint was interpreted as weakness. Formerly, nations, as well as individuals, were punished by the Roman Catholics. "Now,

The Midnight Cry printed a statement, written in 1798, which expressed a fundamental Millerite conviction:

> We will not be so rude as to say the Whore of Babylon, but the poor old lady, call her by what name you please, is literally upon her last legs, and the staggering blows she has lately had, from her own unnatural sons, will certainly lay her flat as a flounder. And then farewell to future Bulls, Indulgences, Dispensations, Benedictions, Anathemas, and the holy commodities of the Holy See, when the holy sons of the Church shall exclaim with holy sorrow, that the title of his holiness is gone forever.[167]

A few words from George Storrs summarized the fundamental Millerite position in a succint way: "If the Papacy has a second rise, it is not to power, but to go into perdition.[168]

V Conclusion

The Millerites remain best known for their calculations of specific dates for Christ's return to this earth in 1843-44. These were, however, part of a system of prophetic interpretation that to a large extent shared its presuppositions and hermeneutical methods with expositors in many of the American Protestant denominations. Attributing a role to Roman Catholicism, and more specifically to the papacy, in the prophetic scheme, was the rule rather than the exception in contemporary American Protestant circles.

---

the successor of those who have claimed the rightful jurisdiction over all nations, has no power to punish those who may even put large numbers of his adherents to death" ("The Signs of the Times," MC [Nov. 30, 1843], 132-133).

[167] "An Interesting Relic," MC (Aug. 10, 1843), 193, quoting from an unidentified English paper, which in turn had copied it from The Oracle of Dauphin, and Harrisburgh Advertiser (Jan. 18, 1798).

[168] "Will Papacy Have Dominion Again?" MC (Oct. 19, 1843), 79.

The generally accepted anti-Catholic views (such as the identification of the little horn of Daniel 7, the beast of Revelation 13, Babylon, and the whore of Revelation 17 with Roman Catholicism) were creatively embedded in Miller's overall chronological scheme, with some embellishments which apparently neither shocked nor excited his contemporary listeners and readers too much.

Miller and his associates were not criticized by other Protestants because of their anti-Catholic sentiments. In fact, many of Miller's critics were far more anti-Catholic than he or his associates ever were. Moreover, many Millerite statements critical of Catholicism, were quoted--often verbatim and at length --from other Protestants publications.

In two major aspects the Millerite views differed substantially from those of most contemporary Protestants: the belief in the imminent end of Catholicism (a logical implication of their views on Christ's Second Coming and the judgment He would bring), and their extension of one of the symbols which was traditionally applied to Catholicism only (Babylon), to contemporary Protestantism--a truly remarkable development for a movement which earlier took great pains to underline its non-sectarian interdenominational character. This critical view of Protestantism was to be retained by the Sabbatarian Adventists of the post-1844 period and has remained the official position of the Seventh-day Adventist Church.

When viewed against the background of the anti-Catholic sentiments of the 1830s and 1840s among American Protestants in general, the anti-Catholicism manifested by the Millerites was certainly not excessive. The Millerite criticism of Catholicism resembled that of their fellow-Protestants in its emphasis on the power structure of the papacy, as manifested in past history, and as an increasing threat in their contemporary world, notably in North America. Criticism of Catholic doctrine was not totally absent, but was accorded far less prominence. Millerite fears of a resurgence of Catholic power and a "Romanist" conquest of America were, naturally, mitigated by their pre-occupation with an imminent Second Coming.

CHAPTER 3

SABBATARIAN ADVENTISM
AND CATHOLICS

I Developments in Sabbatarian Adventism

The Sabbatarian Adventists regarded themselves as the
true successors of the Millerite movement, "as retaining
and carrying on to completion the main principles of
Millerite doctrine and correcting and clarifying the
misunderstanding that has caused the disappointment" of
1844.[1] But at first they were by no means the largest
group to emerge from the Millerite heritage.[2]

In the immediate post-disappointment period--
characterized not only by new date setting for the
Second Advent, but also by bitter debate on various
points of doctrine and a number of "extreme" practices.

---

[1] SDAE, s.v. "Millerite Movement," 898.

[2] For an early account of the history of Adventism
during the aftermath of the 1844 disappointment and the
emergence of Sabbatarian Adventism, see J.N.
Loughborough, Rise and Progress of Seventh-day Adventists (Battle Creek: Gen. Conf. of the SDA, 1892), 88-
260. Among later histories of Adventism the following
deserve to be mentioned for their wealth of detail, in
spite of their hagiographic tendencies: M.E. Olsen,
Origin and Progress of Seventh-day Adventists (Washington, D.C.: RHPA, 1925), 177-253; Arthur W. Spalding,
Origin and History of Seventh-day Adventists, vol. 1
(Washington, D.C: RHPA, 1961), 97-311. Recent, more
objective, works include: R.W. Schwarz, Light Bearers to
the Remnant (Boise, ID: PPPA, 1979), 53-103; Godfrey T.
Anderson "Sectarianism and Organization - 1846-1864,"
chap. in: Gary Land, ed., Adventism in America, 36-65;
and Jonathan M. Butler, "Adventism and the American
Experience," chap. in: Edwin S. Gaustad, ed., The Rise
of Adventism, 173-206.

Some continued to defend the imminent Advent, but
believed that there had been an error in the Millerite
calculations; others, in retrospect, rejected the
movement which had focused on October 22, 1844 as a
Satanic influence; still others believed that the
emphasis on a specific date had been divinely ordained,
but tried to re-interpret what had actually happened on
October 22, 1844.[3] For this latter group the parable of
the ten virgins in Matthew 25:1-13 provided the key: The
door had been shut when the Bridegroom had gone to the
wedding (vs. 10). This had occurred on October 22, 1844.
Now just a short period would remain until Christ would
"return from the wedding."[4]

A conference in Albany, N.Y. (April 29, 1845) tried
to deal with the threat of complete disintegration of
the Second Advent movement and to come to some doctrinal
consensus. From a later Seventh-day Adventist viewpoint
the meeting was not primarily important for the little
it did achieve--which was certainly not the unity the
leaders had hoped for--but for its rejection of
"extreme" standpoints as the practice of footwashing,
and, especially, the keeping of the seventh-day
Sabbath.[5]

The Second Advent movement did, however, survive.
A number of fairly coherent Adventist groups existed by
1852. Adventists in the Boston area looked to Himes,
Bliss and Hale for leadership. They, eventually,
organized the Evangelical Adventist Conference, but
moved more and more toward the mainline churches. The
"Age-to-Come" Adventists, with their belief in a second
period of probation during a future millennium, were

---

[3] Andrew G. Mustard, James White and SDA
Organization: Historical Development, 1844-1881 (Berrien
Springs, MI: Andrews Univ. Press, 1987), 69-91.

[4] For the classic exposition of this "shut-door-
theology," see Apollos Hale and Joseph Turner, "Has Not
the Savior Come as the Bridegroom? Advent Mirror (Jan.
1845), 1-4. Miller himself held the shut-door position
until early 1845. Himes and some other key-leaders
opposed the concept almost immediately. See Andrew G.
Mustard, James White and SDA Organization, 75-77; R.W.
Schwarz, Light Bearers to the Remnant, 54-55.

[5] Andrew G. Mustard, James White and Organization,
86; R.W. Schwarz, Light Bearers to the Remnant, 56-58.

concentrated around Rochester, N.Y. and rallied around Joseph Marsh's periodicals *Advent Harbinger* and *Bible Advocate*. They remained opposed to any form of organization. The Second Advent believers in the Hartfort, Conn./New York area clustered around Joseph Turner. Himes later joined them. They accepted Storrs' theory of the soul sleep and the annihilation of the wicked, and eventually formed the Advent Christian Church.[6]

The seventh-day Sabbath had received some limited attention prior to the disappointment. Early 1844 Frederick Wheeler and his small New Hampshire church of Advent believers, probably challenged by Rachel Oakes (a Seventh-day Baptist), began to keep the Sabbath. But it was only after the disappointment that the Sabbath became an issue on a wider scale. Various small Sabbath-keeping groups emerged across Maine, New Hampshire, Massachusetts and western New York. Even though the members of these groups were former Millerites, none of the leaders of these "Sabbath and Shut-door brethren" had had any significant leadership status in the Millerite movement, except former sea-captain Joseph Bates.[7] These small groups became the nucleus of what was to become Seventh-day Adventism, although they "did not become identifiable as a distinct group until several closely related themes were integrated with the Sabbath."[8]

An article on the Sabbath by T.M. Preble in *Hope of*

---

[6] R.W. Schwarz, Ibid., 57; Godfrey T. Anderson, "Sectarianism and Organization," 36; P.G. Damsteegt, TTM, 114-115. For accounts written from the Advent Christian perspective, see D.T. Arthur, "Come Out of Babylon," 84-379; Albert C. Johnson, <u>Advent Christian History</u>, 84-379; Isaac Wellcome, <u>History of the Second Advent Message and Mission, Doctrine and People</u> (Yarmouth: by the author), 335-650.

[7] R.W. Schwarz, <u>Lights Bearers to the Remnant</u>, 58. For more information on Joseph Bates, see his biography by Godfrey T. Anderson, <u>Outrider of the Apocalypse: Life and Times of Joseph Bates</u> (Mountain View, Cal.: PPPA, 1972).

[8] Andrew G. Mustard, <u>James White and Organization</u>, 92. For a more detailed study of the development of Adventist doctrines in the immediate post-1844 period, see P.G. Damsteegt, TTM, 103-164.

Israel convinced Bates of the validity of the seventh-day Sabbath.[9] A tract written by Bates on the same subject in turn persuaded others, most notably James and Ellen White, who with Bates may well be termed "co-founders" of the Seventh-day Adventist Church.[10]

In their attempts to deal with the 1844 disappointment, the "shut-door" view--the conviction that conversions were no longer possible--in one form or another, continued to play an important role until the early 1850s.[11] Of more lasting influence, however, was the sanctuary doctrine, first introduced by Hiram Edson, F.B. Hahn and O.R.L. Crozier[12] and subsequently refined by others. This doctrine posited the existence of a sanctuary in heaven, the "cleansing" of which had begun on October 22, 1844, at the end of Daniel's 2,300 days/years. This "cleansing" was the antitype of the Day of Atonement in the Old Testament sanctuary ritual. The Millerite 1844-calculation of the 2,300 day/year prophecy of Daniel 8:14 had been correct, but, it was argued, there had been an error in the event which the Advent believers expected. At the prophesied date, Christ did not return to this earth, but He began a new and final phase of his heavenly high priestly ministry. The relationship between the Ten Commandment law and the Old Testament sanctuary provided the rationale for a

-----

[9] The article was shortly afterwards printed as a tract: T.M. Preble, Tract, Showing that the Seventh Day Should Be Observed as the Sabbath, Instead of the First Day; "According to the Commandment (Nashua: Printed by Murray & Kimhall, 1845).

[10] Joseph Bates, The Seventh Day Sabbath, a Perpetual Sign, From the Beginning, to the Entering into the Gates of the Holy City, According to the Commandment (New Bedford: Press of Benjamin Lindsey, 1846).

[11] See Ingemar Lindén, 1844 and the Shut Door Problem, vol. 35 in "Acta Universitatis Upsaliensis", 1982; P.G. Damsteegt, TTM, 42-44; 149-164; 281-280. For an other recent study on the subject, see Rolf J. Poehler, "And the door was shut: Seventh-day Adventists and the shut-door doctrine in the decade after the Great Disappointment," (Unpubl. paper, Andrews Univ., SDA Theol. Sem., 1978).

[12] O.R.L. Crozier, "The Law of Moses," The Day-Star Extra (Feb. 7, 1846), 37-44.

strong emphasis on the intimate relationship between the Sabbath and the sanctuary doctrine.[13]

During 1848 a number of "Sabbath Conferences" were organized by the leaders of the growing Sabbatarian groups, which contributed greatly to establishing some doctrinal unity. Much discussion centered around the Sabbath and the sanctuary. By 1850 the major distinctive Sabbatarian Adventist doctrines had taken shape. Building on the Millerite heritage of prophetic interpretation, and continuing to stress the imminent personal Advent of Christ, they now also underlined the immutability of God's law (including the seventh-day Sabbath), the conditional immortality of the soul, and Christ's ministry in heaven. The message of "the third angel" of Revelation 14:9-11 was singled out as having utmost importance, being understood as a direct reference to the work of Sabbath-keeping Adventists in proclaiming the Sabbath and the Second Coming. Furthermore they agreed on baptism by immersion, footwashing, and the Lord's Supper.[14]

The leadership in these groups at the Sabbatarian fringe of Adventism was provided by a few men--such as Joseph Bates and Hiram Edson--who had been actively involved with the Millerite movement, but increasingly by a small group of younger persons. Most prominent among these was James White, author, publisher and organizer.[15] In 1852 he was joined by John N. Andrews, theologian, author and pioneer missionary,[16] and a few

---

[13] For a survey of the development of the sanctuary doctrine among Sabbatarian Adventists, see Frank B. Holbrook, ed., <u>Doctrine of the Sanctuary - A Historical Survey</u> (Silver Spring: Bibl. Research Inst., Gen. Conf. of SDA, 1989); P.G. Damsteegt, <u>TTM</u>, 139-140, 165-177.

[14] Godfrey T. Anderson, "Sectarianism and Organization - 1844-1864," 40-41.

[15] For a popular account of James White's life, see Virgil Robinson, <u>James White</u> (Washington, D.C.: RHPA, 1976). For a scholarly account of his initiatives in organizing early Adventism, see Andrew G. Mustard's dissertation: <u>James White and SDA Organization</u>.

[16] Detailed information about J.N. Andrews is found in Harry Leonard, ed., <u>J.N. Andrews - the Man and the Mission</u> (Berrien Springs, MI: Andrews Univ. Press, 1985).

years later by Uriah Smith, editor, author and
theologian, and some leaders of lesser importance (J.N.
Loughborough, S.N. Haskell and others).[17] Ellen G. White
had a unique, and increasingly influential role as the
prophetic voice of the movement.[18] Practically all of
these "pioneers" were prolific (and some even
accomplished) writers. The role of their publications
and notably of the *Second Advent Review and Sabbath
Herald*, the journal which was to be become the official
organ of the Seventh-day Adventist Church, can hardly be
overestimated.[19]

---

[17] Eugene F. Durand, Yours in the Blessed Hope
(Washington, D.C.: RHPA, 1980).

[18] Books about Mrs. E.G. White are almost as
numerous as her own literary output of over 60 books and
thousands of letters and articles. The six-volume
biography by her grandson, Arthur L. White, Ellen G.
White, (Washington, D.C.: RHPA, 1982-1986) is unsur-
passed in its richness of detail, but is hagiographic in
nature. This is also true of the apologetic work by F.D.
Nichol: Ellen G. White and Her Critics, (Washington,
D.C: RHPA, 1951). Nichol's work contains a chronological, annotated bibliography of Ellen G. White's
books (except compilations published after 1950): 691-
703. Ronald L. Numbers in his Prophetess of Health: A
Study of Ellen G. White (New York: Harper & Row, 1976)
offers a sharp but sympathetic analysis of Ellen White
against the backdrop of the reform movements of 19th
century America.

[19] James White published 11 issues of a journal
entitled Present Truth between July 1849 and Nov. 1850,
and 5 issues of The Advent Review (so named, because it
reprinted and reviewed materials from the pre-
disappointment period) between Aug. and Nov. 1850. These
two parent-journals were replaced by the Second Advent
Review and Sabbath Herald, the first issue of which
appeared Nov. 18, 1850. In 1851 the name was changed
into The Advent Review and Sabbath Herald, while in 1961
this was further abbreviated to Review and Herald. In
1971 the original name Advent Review and Sabbath Herald
was restored. The current name Adventist Review has been
in use since Jan. 5, 1978. The early places of publication were Paris (Maine), Saratoga Springs (N.Y.) and
Rochester (N.Y.). It was published in Battle Creek from
1855 to 1903 and in Washington, D.C. from 1903 until

During the period under review in this chapter Uriah Smith emerged as the most authoritative Adventist expositor of Bible prophecy. It has long been recognized, however, that he was heavily dependent upon others. He conducted a weekly Bible study group in his home church in Battle Creek which discussed the Apocalypse verse-by-verse during 1862/63, the results of which were reported in a series of articles in the *Review and Herald* (first by James White, but from chapter 10 onward by Uriah Smith). These articles became the basis for Smith's later commentary in book form. But he also freely used published materials from others--so freely that he has at times been charged with plagiarism.[20] His views--original or not--were shaped and refined during the phase of Sabbatarian Adventism. They received their definite form in a two-volume book which remained the standard Seventh-day Adventist interpretation well into the twentieth century.[21]

The early Sabbatarian Adventists were extremely reluctant to accept any organizational structure.[22] Some argued that even the most simple form of organization would automatically classify them as "Babylon." But practical concerns led to a gradual development of an

---

1983. Presently it is published in Hagerstown, MD. The journal will in this study be referred to as Review and Herald (abbreviated as RH).

[20] For a discussion of the background of Smith's commentary on Daniel and the Revelation and his literary dependency, see Uriah Smith, "Thoughts on Revelation," RH (June 3, 1862), 4-5; Arthur L. White, "Thoughts on Daniel and the Revelation," Min, vol. 18, no. 1 (Jan. 1945), 11-14; and Mervin R. Thurber, "Uriah Smith and the Charge of Plagiarism," Min, vol. 18, no. 7 (June 1945), 15-16.

[21] Uriah Smith, Thoughts Critical and Practical on the Revelation (Battle Creek: Steam Press of the SDA Publ. Ass., 1865) and Uriah Smith, Thoughts Critical and Practical on the Book of Daniel (Battle Creek: Steam Press of the SDA Publ. Ass., 1873).

[22] See Godfrey T. Anderson, "Sectarianism and Organization," 46-65; Andrew G. Mustard, James White and SDA Organization, 116-162; and R.W. Schwarz, Light Bearers to the Remnant, 86-103.

organizational infrastructure. By 1851 a rudimentary organizational form for individual congre-gations existed. Two years later a system of issuing credentials to ministers was initiated. When in the 1850s the Sabbath-keeping Adventists followed the westerly migration to better homesteads in southern Michigan, the publishing enterprise was relocated and moved to Battle Creek, where in 1861, on the insistence of James White, who still functioned as the legal owner, the publishing and printing institution became a stock company. In the meantime (1860) the Parkville church in Michigan became the first church to organize itself as a legal society which could hold property in a legal manner. The name "Seventh-day Adventists" was, not without long debate, adopted as the official name for the group which was about to establish itself as a distinct denomination. The process was completed when, in 1861, a number of local congregations united in the Michigan Conference, and when, in May 1863, the General Conference was organized.

One important aspect should, however, not be lost sight of: the small beginnings of Seventh-day Adventism. The number of Seventh-day Adventist congregations in 1863 did not exceed 125, with a total membership of at most 3,500. This fact must be kept in mind as one tries to understand the attitude of Seventh-day Adventists toward Roman Catholicism during these formative years.[23]

II Catholicism and its Opponents

Nineteenth Century American Christianity, in the aftermath of the Second Great Awakening and as the result of continued revivalism, became increasingly pluralistic.[24] The traditional mainline churches saw much of their terrain lost to a host of new denominations, while much of their energy was sapped by internal strife and the challenges posed by Universalists and Trans-

---

[23] Jonathan M. Butler, "Adventism and the American Experience," 180.

[24] For a general survey of American Christianity during the first half of the 19th century, see Robert T. Handy, A History of the Churches in the United States and Canada, 162-227; Sydney E. Ahlstrom, A Religious History of the American People, 415-697; Winthrop S. Hudson, Religion in America, 415-697.

cendentalists. Baptists and Methodists--divided into
many different groups--were especially successful in
their attempts to win converts in the constantly
expanding frontier territories. In New England, and
particularly in upstate New York's "Burnt-over
District," a number of millenarian movements captured
the imagination of the people. A colourful palette of
voluntary societies campaigning for all sorts of
reforms, missionary societies and an avalanche of
religious newspapers, journals and books, further
crowded the religious scene.

One of the most significant facets of American
church history of this period is, however, the rapid
growth of the Roman Catholic Church, from a small group
of no more than 50,000 in 1800 to over 2 million in
1860.[25]

As indicated in Chapter One, Protestant fears of a
rapidly growing Catholicism gave rise to various waves
of nativism. After the nativistic explosions of the mid
1840s, anti-Catholic tempers cooled considerably during
the 1845-1850 period of the Mexican War,[26] but gained a
new momentum in the 1850s, when nativistic concerns
about Catholicism's growing power and the vast numbers
of Catholic immigrants found political expression in the
short-lived success of the Know-Nothing party,[27] while
anti-Catholic publications continued to flood the

---

[25] Robert T. Handy, A History of the Churches in the
United States and Canada, 214.

[26] See Sydney E. Ahlstrom, Religious History of the
American People, 564-568; but especially Ray Allen
Billington, The Protestant Crusade, 290-344; 380-436.

[27] The American Party, more popularly called the
Know-Nothing Party, represented a major nativistic
political movement, which for a short time (ca. 1850 -
ca. 1860) achieved some national prominence. It was
strongly Anglo-Saxon Protestant and just as strongly
anti-Irish and anti-Catholic. Many of its adherents at
first worked through "secret societies," on election
days clandestinely throwing their support to candidates
sympathetic to their views. When asked about their
activities, their standard answer was that they did not
know anything. Hence the name: "Know Nothings"!

market.[28] The anti-Catholic atmosphere in which Sabbatarian Adventism originated has been admirably
captured by Billington in the following words:

> The average Protestant American of the 1850s had
> been trained to hate Catholicism; his juvenile
> literature and school books had breathed a spirit
> of intolerance; ... his religious and even secular
> newspapers had warned him of the dangers of Popery;
> and he had read novels, poems, gift books,
> histories, travel accounts, and theological
> arguments which confirmed these beliefs. Only the
> unusually critical reader could distinguish between
> truth and fiction in this mass of calumny....[29]

III Crystallizing of Prophetic Views

The Sabbatarian interpretations of Bible prophecies, and
especially of the apocalyptic books of Daniel and the
Revelation show a remarkable continuity with those of
the Millerites, particularly those of Miller himself,
but also of others, notably Litch. But though the basic,
historicist, approach remained largely the same and the
main thrust of Millerite prophetic exposition was maintained, modifications were made and emphases shifted.[30]
The role attributed to Roman Catholicism remained in
essence the same, but here also modifications and shifts
in emphasis occurred. The most significant modifications
concerned:
   1. A shift in the interpretation of the 5th and 6th
trumpet in Revelation 9; the reduction in papal power

---

[28] On the 19th century anti-Catholic literature, see
Ray Allen Billington, The Protestant Crusade, 345-379,
and his bibliography, 445-504.

[29] Ray Allen Billington, Ibid., 345. For a study of
the anti-Catholic bias in schoolbooks, see Marie Leono
Fell, The Foundations of Nativism in American Textbooks,
1783-1860 (Washington, D.C., 1941).

[30] Don. F. Neufeld, "Biblical Interpretation in the
Advent Movement," in Gordon Hyde, ed., Symposium on
Biblical Hermeneutics, 113-114. Two prominent "prophetic
charts, of 1850 and 1863 respectively, provide a bird's
eye view of developments in prophetic interpretation.
See Leroy E. Froom, PFOF, vol. IV, 1070-1082.

received less emphasis in this context.

2. A greater clarity about the recovery of the deadly wound of the beast of Revelation 13;

3. A reinterpretation of the opposition of the little horn of Daniel 8 against the sanctuary, which was now identified as the heavenly sanctuary;

4. The development of the view that the second beast in Revelation 13 symbolized the United States, which in the (imminent) final events of earth's history would align itself with the Catholic Church;

5. A strong emphasis on the historical role of "Rome" in the promotion of Sunday worship and its opposition to the true Sabbath of the fourth commandment, and its eschatological implications.

1. The Prophecies of Daniel

The title of a 95 page tract, *The Prophecy of Daniel: the Four Kingdoms, the Sanctuary, and the Twenty-three Hundred Days*, is indicative of the focus of Adventist expositors of *Daniel* on chapters 2, 7, 8 and 9.[31] In this tract--one of several on the subject written by him--Uriah Smith outlined what had become the standard Adventist exegesis.

The little horn of Daniel 7--identical with Paul's "man of sin" was beyond any shadow of doubt a symbolic representation of Roman Catholicism, more specifically the papacy, which reigned supreme for 1260 years (538-1798).[32] The symbol of the little horn of Daniel 8 was applied to Rome in its pagan and papal phases. The possibility that it might refer to Antiochus Epiphanes was said to have been invented "by the Papists to save their church from any share in the fulfilment of the prophecy" and was forcibly rejected.

Numerous are the tracts and articles in the *Review and Herald* which follow this same pattern.[33] Three

---

[31] By Uriah Smith, published in Battle Creek (Steam Press of the SDA Publ. Ass., 1863).

[32] Ibid., 22, 26.

[33] See e.g. Josiah Litch, "The Four Beasts of Daniel VII," RH (June 20, 1854), 161-163; "Daniel Chapters VIII and IX," RH (Nov. 21, 1854), 116-117; George Storrs, "Exposition of Daniel 7th Chapter, Or, The Vision of the Four Beasts," RH (Feb. 3, 1853, 150-151; Feb. 17, 1853),

features about the little horn in chapter 7 receive most
attention: its blasphemous speaking (vs. 8, 25), its
attempts to change "times and laws" (vs. 25) and "the
taking away of its power" (vs. 26). The blasphemies
uttered by this power are clearly identified as the
papal claims to universal authority and the titles
assumed by the pope, such as "Most Holy Lord"[34] and many
others (Universal Father, Holy Father, His Holiness,
Vicar of Christ, etc.).[35]

Repeatedly, reference is made to the Encyclical
"Probe Nostis" of Gregory XVI which expresses the pope's
recognition that his power had been limited--a clear
proof that his former "dominion" had been taken away
since the 1260 years had ended.[36] Selective quotes from
this encyclical repeatedly suggest the pope's
exasperation about Bible distribution in the vernacular
and the flood of publications from the Protestant enemy,
especially aimed at uneducated and young Catholics,
"which spread everywhere unpunished."[37]

The emphasis on Daniel 7:25b--the attempt to change

153-154; also two later somewhat amplified versions of
this article: "Exposition of Daniel VII, Or, The Vision
of the Four Beasts, RH (Nov. 14, 1854), 108-110;
"Exposition of Daniel VII: Or, The Vision of the Four
Beasts," RH (Apr. 23, 1857), 194-196.

[34] George Storrs, "Exposition of Daniel 7th
Chapter," RH (Feb. 17, 1853), 113-114; see also later
versions of the same article.

[35] [Uriah Smith], "The Little Horn" in the series
"Synopsis of Present Truth," RH (Dec. 24, 1857), 52.

[36] Uriah Smith, Ibid., 53.

[37] Taken as a whole, however, the encyclical does
not manifest the desperate tone the selective quotes
intend to convey, but does also strongly emphasize the
many recent victories of the Catholic Church and the
success of the Society for the Propagation of the Faith
and other mission organizations. For a recent edition
(text and translation) see "Probe Nostis" - Encyclical
of Pope Gregory XVI on the Propagation of the Faith -
September 18, 1840, in Claudia Carlen, The Papal
Encyclicals: 1740-1878 (Wilmington, N.C.: McGrath Publ.
Co., 1981), 259-261.

"times and laws"--is directly related to the "rediscovery" of the seventh-day Sabbath. "Rome's" attempts to change the Ten Commandment law by substituting the Sunday for the seventh-day Sabbath was seen as the precise fulfilment of this aspect of the prophecy:

> The papal power evidently fulfills this prophecy perfectly. The pope has exalted himself above God; has taken his place; has garbled the law of God, and torn from it the second commandment. To supply this deficiency in the number of commandments he has divided the tenth command, making two of it. And last, though not least, he has changed the fourth commandment from the seventh to the first day of the week.[38]

The deliberate tampering with God's law by the little horn became one of the two foci of attention in Daniel's prophecies for the early Sabbatarian Adventists.[39] The other focus of attention was directly related to an other "new" doctrine: the sanctuary. Once that doctrine had been developed, the activities against the sanctuary, as mentioned in Daniel 8, could be placed in a new perspective and the role played by "Rome" could be more clearly established.[40]

2. The Prophecies of Revelation

Most conclusions about the role of "Rome" in the prophecies of the Revelation were likewise carried over from the Millerite movement into early Sabbatarian Adventism. The seven churches of chapters 2 and 3 continued to be interpreted as seven periods in the history of the church, but the sixth (Philadelphia) was no longer viewed as applying to the period from the Reformation to 1798, with the Laodicea-period extending from 1798 to 1843/4, as Miller and his associates had

---

[38] B.F. Snook, "The Holy Sabbath of the Lord," RH (June 19, 1860), 34.

[39] See below, pp. 99ff.

[40] See below, p. 111. See also P.G. Damsteegt, "Among Sabbatarian Adventists (1845-1850)", in: Frank B. Holbrook, ed., Doctrine of the Sanctuary, 31, 62-63.

maintained,[41] but as ending in 1844, with Laodicea extending from that time until the end. Emphasis was usually placed on Thyatira, the fourth church, symbolizing the 1260 years of papal supremacy from 538 to 1798.[42]

The seven seals of chapters 6-8 continued likewise to be interpreted as descriptions of seven eras in church history. Again Roman Catholicism featured as the main culprit, especially in the fourth seal, which was thought to coincide with the period of the church of Thyatira, noted for its persecution of religious dissidents:

> ... what language could better illustrate the dreadful cruelties of the Papal power on the Church of Jesus Christ ... Christians were killed with the sword. They were imprisoned and stoned to death. The most cruel and bloody means of torture were invented to inflict death in every possible shape that men and devils could invent. Tens of thousands suffered death under the most excruciating torments that the Inquisition could devise. And after the Papal bloodhounds had glutted their thirst for blood, thousands were thrown to ferocious beasts....[43]

Uriah Smith limited the period of the fourth seal from 538 to the time when the Reformers "commenced their work of exposing the corruptions of the Papal system." He dates the fifth seal from the time of the Reformation to ca. 1798. The crying "souls under the altar" (pictured under the fifth seal) were interpreted as a symbolic representation of the martyrs executed by papal Rome: "Luther and his associates were imbued with the spirit of this cry which went up from the earth that had drunk

---

[41] William Miller, EHS, 148-151. See also P.G. Damsteegt, TTM, 47-48; 244-248.

[42] James White, "The Seven Churches," RH (Oct. 16, 1856), 188-189, 192; James White, "The Seven Churches, Seven Seals, and Four Beasts," RH (Feb. 12, 1857), 116-117; J.N. Loughborough, "A Letter to a Friend on the Seven Churches," RH (March 19, 1857), 153-155.

[43] James White, "The Seven Churches, Seven Seals, and Four Beasts," RH (Feb. 12, 1857), 117.

the blood of millions of the martyrs of Jesus...."[44]

Litch's position on the seven trumpets, emphasizing the role of the Saracens and Turks under the fifth and sixth trumpet, became and remained the standard interpretation.[45]

Apart from the sections dealing with the great whore and Babylon in chapters 17-19, which continued to be viewed as referring to Roman Catholicism--with the term Babylon receiving the wider application which had become current in the last phase of the Millerite movement[46]--chapters 13 and 14 were deemed to be the most explicit about the deceptive work of the papal church in past, present and future. J.N. Andrews provided the first extensive Sabbatarian Adventist exposition of these chapters, which largely followed what had become traditional teaching.[47]

The first beast of Revelation 13 continued to be interpreted as the papacy.[48] It was seen to be clearly identical with the little horn of Daniel 7, both in its characteristics and in the period of the uncontested exercise of its brutal power, but includes the pagan phase which preceded Rome's papal phase. The seven heads were the seven forms of the Roman government since the

---

[44] Uriah Smith, "Thoughts on Revelation," RH (July 8, 1862), 44.

[45] "The Sounding of the Seven Trumpets," RH (July 8, 1858), 57-59; (July 15, 1858), 65-67; (July 22, 1858), 73-75; (July 29, 1858), 82-84; (Aug. 5, 1858), 89-90. See also James White, The Sounding of the Seven Trumpets of Rev. 8 and 9 (Battle Creek, MI: Steam Press of the Review and Herald Office, 1859).

[46] Cf. pp. 42-46, 62-63.

[47] J.N. Andrews, "Thoughts on Revelation XIII and XIV," RH (May 19, 1851), 81-86.

[48] One of the most succinct explanations of the first beast is found in article no. 25 of a series of 28 articles (from Nov. 12, 1857 to June 10, 1858), outlining all basic Adventist beliefs, entitled "Synopsis of Present Truth": [Uriah Smith], "The Message from the Sanctuary," RH (May 20, 1858), 4.

Roman power originated. When John was writing his Apocalypse, he lived under the sixth (the imperial) form; the seventh--the papal phase--was yet to come.[49] The blasphemies uttered by the "papal beast" consisted in "applying those titles to mortal men which belong exclusively to God," such as "His Holiness," or "the Lord God the Pope."[50] But they also included a blaspheming of those "that dwell in heaven":

> The beast, in causing men to confess to priests on earth, to gain their intercession on their behalf, has blasphemed the Minister of the Sanctuary in heaven .... Is not the doctrine that the spirits of the dead are our guardian spirits, blaspheming against the true ministering spirits...? The Catholics pray to Mary and the 'saints,'.... as being our guardian spirits....[51]

3. Prophecy and the Resurgence of the Papacy

The papal beast claimed the authority to punish and correct heretics. But it could no longer exercise that power when, in 1798, the 1260 days/years ended and it received its deadly wound (Revelation 13:3). The view of the Millerites that the Roman Empire was the recipient of this deadly wound had now given place to a consensus that this wound was inflicted on the papacy in 1798. A passing of time and a diminished emphasis on an immediate date for Christ's coming did now allow for a more pronounced possibility of a recovery of this deadly wound, as alluded to in the prophecy (13:3)[52] The extent of the recovery of papal power to be expected remained, however, a debated issue. Some already saw clear evidence of a resurgence of Catholic power. O. Nichols

---

[49] J.N. Andrews, "The Three Angels of Revelation XIV:6-12," cont., RH (March 20, 1855), 194; "Revelation XII and XIII," RH (May 29, 1860), 4; Uriah Smith, "Thoughts on Revelation," RH (Nov. 4, 1862), 188.

[50] R.F. Cottrell, "Blasphemy," RH (Jan. 31, 1854), 13.

[51] Ibid., 14.

[52] J.N. Andrews, "Thoughts on Revelation XIII and XIV," RH (May 19, 1851), 82.

states that the pope has begun "to speak great words again."[53] Andrews confirms this belief that the deadly wound is in the process of being healed.[54] Bates sees in the political situation in Europe around 1815, with the pope "being once more reinstated in its ancient domain," a beginning of the healing of the deadly wound.[55] J.M. Stephenson considers the healing to be in the near future.[56]

Others, however, continue to emphasize the great reduction in papal influence. In the early 1860s the *Review and Herald* repeatedly quotes from articles in other journals which stress "the peculiar circumstances of perplexity and affliction in which the Holy Father is placed"[57] and report Pope Pius IX's admission that "the noble devotedness" of his supporters "is now useless, for all is finished."[58] Other articles with extensive quotations from both Protestant and Catholic sources corroborate the same opinion.[59]

With the adoption of the seventh-day Sabbath and its identification as the ultimate seal of divine authority, the "mark of the beast" could become the opposite: "a rival sabbath," "a mark by which the Papal church

---

[53] See his article "The Dragon, the Beast, and the False Prophet," RH (March 2, 1852), 99.

[54] "The Three Angels of Revelation XIV:6-12," cont., RH (March 20, 1855), 195.

[55] Joseph Bates, "The Beast with Seven Heads," RH (Aug. 5, 1851), 4.

[56] J.M. Stephenson, "The Scarlet-colored Beast," RH (Jan. 31, 1854), 14-15.

[57] See e.g. "The Pope's Perplexity," RH (July 23, 1861), 59, quoting from Cardinal Wiseman's Pastoral Letter in The Catholic of June 1, 1861.

[58] "Facts for Everybody," RH (Sept. 10, 1861), 115, quoting from the journal Ami de la Religion.

[59] "The Popedom," RH (July 29, 1862), 67; "The Pope's Troubles," RH (Aug. 26, 1862), 99. See also Uriah Smith, "The Little Horn," RH (Dec. 24, 1857), 53.

maintains her authority"[60]:

> In place of God's seal or mark, we have Sunday
> attached to the law. It does not point out the
> living God, but claims to be instituted on
> authority of the Papal church. Yea, it points to
> the Pope. It is "the mark of the beast".[61]

Sunday worship, contrary to the divine command to
keep the "Holy Sabbath, which is the sign and memorial
of God, and of his right to rule," is "the token, or
sign," by which the pope shows "that he is God, and able
to change the times and the laws of God."[62] We shall
return to the role attributed to Roman Catholicism in
the change of Sabbath to Sunday.[63]

The opinion of some Millerites that the number 666--the
"number of the beast"--referred to the number of "sects"
in Protestantism,[64] continued to be held by some

---

[60] R.F. Cottrell, "Mark of the Beast," RH (Aug. 6,
1857), 109.

[61] J.N. Loughborough, "The Two-Horned Beast," RH
(March 28, 1854), 75.

[62] H. Edson, "The Two Laws," RH (Oct. 7, 1851), 39.
See also H. Edson, "The Commandments of God, and the
Mark of the Beast brought to view by the Third Angel of
Rev. XIV, considered in connection with the Angel of
Chap. VII, having the Seal of the Living God," RH (Sept.
2, 1852), 65-67; (Sept. 16, 1852), 73-75; (Sept. 30,
1852), 81-84; J.N. Andrews, The Three Angels of Rev.
14:6-12: particularly, The Third Angel's Message, and
Two-Horned Beast (Rochester, N.Y.: Advent Review Office,
1855), 110; and R.F. Cottrell, "Mark of the Beast and
Seal of the Living God, RH (July 28, 1859), 77-78.

[63] See pp. 99-106.

[64] J.M. Stephenson, "The Number of the Beast," RH
(Nov. 29, 1853), 166. J.N. Loughborough refers to this
article in "The Two-Horned Beast," concl., RH (March 28,
1854), 73, and also in his tract The Two-Horned Beast
(Rochester, N.Y., ca. 1854), 47-48. See also M.E.
Cornell, "They will Make an Image to the Beast," RH
(Sept. 19, 1854), 43; and J.N. Loughborough, "The Two-
Horned Beast of Rev. 13, a Symbol of the United States,"

Sabbatarian Adventists, but others were apparently not so sure.[65]

4. The USA in Prophecy

The second, "two-horned", beast of Revelation 13:11-15 with both lamb-like and dragon-like features, which would make an "image" to the first beast and enforce its worship, had been the subject of some speculation among Millerites, but had generally received little attention.[66] Litch at one time applied the symbol to Napoleon, but later admitted he simply did not understand its meaning.[67] The Sabbatarian Adventists adopted the almost exclusive position that the two-horned beast of Revelation 13 symbolized the United States of America, with its lamb-like features dominating from the 1780s through the 1830s and the dragon-like characteristics increasingly prominent since the 1840s and 1850s.[68] Already in 1851 Bates presented the outline of what was to become one of Seventh-day Adventism's rather unique aspects of prophetic interpretation:

> Will not our better judgment decide at once that the location of this power is in America, and that the civil power of one horn is the government of the Republic, and the religious power of the other horn Protestantism; and that Republicanism and Protestantism united will make itself an image to the

---

cont., RH (June 25, 1857), 75.

[65] Uriah Smith in his remarks on chapter 13 in his series "Thoughts on Revelation" made no attempt to explain the number 666 - RH (Nov. 11, 1862), 188.

[66] Miller believed it was another symbol for ecclesiastical Rome, while some of his associates thought France was intended. See William Miller, EHS, (1836 ed.), 78; Leroy E. Froom, PFOF, vol. IV, 850.

[67] See J.N. Andrews, The Three Angels of Rev. 14:6-12, 77; J.N. Andrews, "The Angels of Revelation 14," no. 4, RH (Dec. 23, 1851), 69.

[68] Jonathan M. Butler, "Adventism and the American Experience," 180-181.

seven-headed beast, and thus become united...?[69]

Other prominent writers--Andrews,[70] Smith,[71] Cornell,[72] Cottrell[73] and notably Loughborough--developed this view further.[74] Their comments usually included references to the dragon-like behaviour of Protestant America with regard to the slavery issue. In our present context, of course, its (mainly future) blurring of the lines between church and state, its (again, mainly future) close relationship with Roman Catholicism, culminating in its (ultimate) enforcing of the mark of the beast are of special interest. All of these elements are dealt with by the writers mentioned above. Although the concern about Sunday "blue laws" in the United States became more pronounced among Seventh-day Adventists in later years, any Sunday legislation was

---

[69] Joseph Bates, "The Beast with Seven Heads," RH (Aug. 5, 1851), 4.

[70] See e.g. The Three Angels of Rev. 14:6-12, 90-108; "The Three Angels of Rev. 14:6-12," 195.

[71] E.g. "The Present State of the World," RH (June 20, 1854), 164-165; "Thoughts on Revelation," RH (Nov. 11, 1862), 188.

[72] "They Will Make an Image to the Beast," RH (Sept. 19, 1854), 43; Facts for the Times - Extracts from the Writings of Eminent Authors, Ancient and Modern (Battle Creek: by the author, 1858), 51-76.

[73] "What Will Cause the Image?" RH (Nov. 14, 1854), 110; "Speaking of the Image," RH (Dec. 12, 1854), 134.

[74] See his tracts The Two-Horned Beast (Rochester, N.Y, ca. 1854) and The Two-Horned Beast of Rev. 13, a Symbol of the United States (Battle Creek: The Review and Herald Office, 1857); also his series of articles in 1854 and 1857: "The Two-Horned Beast," RH (March 21, 1854), 65-67; (March 28, 1854), 73-75, 79; "The Two-Horned Beast of Rev. 13, a Symbol of the United States," RH (June 25, 1857), 57-60; (July 2, 1857), 65-68; (July 9, 1857), 73-75. These tracts and articles all contain basically the same arguments.

viewed with the utmost suspicion.[75] Sabbatarian Adventists were already developing an apocalyptic outlook that saw Sunday observance as about to be enforced nationwide, with civil and religious liberty being trampled into the dust in the process.[76] Referring to state Sunday laws already enacted, Loughborough believed that "all that remains undone for an image to the first beast, is a universal law on Sunday keeping."[77]

5. Babylon

"Babylon" is a theme which probably received more attention during the period under review than any other aspect of apocalyptic prophecy. The notion, introduced by Charles Fitch and others in the Millerite movement, that Babylon is not limited to "popery," was retained and further developed.[78]

The term Babylon could not just refer to the Roman Church, it is argued, because Babylon was said to have "fallen" (Revelation 14:8; 18:2) and this could not just apply to Rome:

> The fact that she has always been corrupt, and about as low as she possibly could be, forbids the application of this moral change, or fall, to that

---

[75] See e.g. J.N. Loughborough, "The Image of the Beast," RH (Sept. 20, 1853), 85; J.N. Loughborough, "The Two-Horned Beast," concl., RH (March 28, 1854), 79; N.G. Sanders, "Facts vs. Unbelief," RH (Sept. 30, 1858), 150; R.F. Cottrell, "Breaking the Law of the Land," RH (Feb. 9, 1860), 92-93.

[76] Godfrey T. Anderson, "Sectarianism and Organization - 1846-1864," 46.

[77] J.N. Loughborough, "The Two-Horned Beast of Rev. 13, a Symbol of the United States," RH (June 25, 1857), 74.

[78] The application of "Babylon" to parts of Protestantism had some precedents. See Leroy E. Froom, PFOF, vol. IV, 767-770, and M.E. Cornell, Facts for the Times, 18-23. But to some early Sabbatarian Adventists "it has been a trial that any should call the Protestant churches Babylon"--Letter by E.P. Butler to James and Ellen G. White, RH (Jan. 1851), 30.

corrupt church. Again, Babylon, signifying "confusion, or mixture," cannot be applied to the Roman Church, she being a unit.[79]

Added confirmation for the correctness of interpreting the Protestant denominations as (the most important) part of Babylon was found in the fact that the apostate woman of Revelation 17--unanimously understood as a symbol for Catholicism--is said to have "daughters": a clear indication of the intimate relationship between the Catholic "mother church" and the churches to which she gave birth: the Protestant denominations.[80]

The apostate woman was seen as a striking symbol of the papacy. Even her clothing of purple and scarlet corresponded with the robes of popes and cardinals. And from the golden cup in her hand have come forth "only abominations, and wine of her fornication, [a] fit symbol of her abominable doctrines and still more abominable practices."[81]

Sometimes Babylon was given an all-inclusive meaning. Andrews defined it as comprising "all the corrupt religious bodies which have ever existed, or which exist at the present time, united to the world, and sustained by the civil power." He specifically mentioned "the Jewish church" which killed Jesus; "the corrupt papal and Greek churches;" "the great body of Protestant churches;" Calvin (who had Servetus executed); the Church of England (which persecuted dissenters); and the New England Puritans (who persecuted Quakers and

---

[79] James White, "Babylon," RH (June 10, 1852), 21; James White, The Signs of the Times, showing that the Second Coming of Christ is at the Doors. Spirit Manifestations, a Foretold Sign that the Day of God's Wrath Hasteth Greatly (Rochester, N.Y.: The Review Office, 1853), 82.

[80] "Come out of Babylon," (extracted from "The Voice of Truth" of September 1844), RH (Dec. 9, 1851), 58-59; James White, "The one hundred and forty-four thousand," RH (May 9, 1854), 123-124.

[81] Uriah Smith, "Thoughts on Revelation," RH (Dec. 9, 1862), 12.

Baptists).[82] James White proposed a more limited application: Babylon is where God's people are, since they must be called out of Babylon! The question then was: "Where are the people of God of this generation? Are they in the Roman Catholic Church?" The answer must be negative. "They have been, and many still are, in the Protestant sects."[83] In his view the "fall" of Babylon dated from 1844 when nominal Protestantism rejected the Advent message.[84] But that does not mean that every individual remaining in these churches after that date is forthwith condemned: "That God has ministers and people in Babylon who are striving for heaven amid the moral darkness that envelopes her, we fully believe...."[85]

Andrews gave a detailed description of the "fall" of Babylon.[86] It was a *moral* fall: love for the world manifested in worldliness of dress, the erection of opulent church buildings, the acquisition of wealth and the use of titles such as "reverend."[87] In these respects Protestants were worse than Catholics, "the Babylon of

---

[82] J.N. Andrews, "What is Babylon?" RH (Feb. 21, 1854), 37. See also J.N. Andrews, "The Angels of Revelation 14," cont., RH (Sept. 2, 1851), 21; J.N. Andrews, "The Three Angels of Rev. 14:6-12," RH (Feb. 20, 1855), 177-178; J.N. Andrews, The Three Angels of Rev. 14:6-12, 46-51.

[83] James White, "Babylon," RH (March 10, 1859), 122.

[84] James White, "Signs of the Times", RH (Sept. 8, 1853), 71.

[85] James White, The Signs of the Times, 47; James White, "Signs of the Times," RH (Sept. 8, 1853), 71.

[86] The Three Angels of Rev. 14:6-12, 46-68. See also his series of articles under the same title (RH, Jan. 23, 1855, 161-163; Feb. 6, 1855, 169-171; Feb. 20, 1855, 177-178; March 6, 1855, 185-187; March 20, 1855, 193-196; Apr. 3, 1855, 201-205; Apr. 17, 1855, 209-212; May 1, 1855, 217-218) which formed the basis for this tract.

[87] J.N. Andrews, The Three Angels of Rev. 14:6-12, 46-51; J.N. Andrews, "What is Babylon?", RH (Febr. 21, 1854), 36; Uriah Smith, "Thoughts on Revelation," RH (Dec. 16, 1862), 20.

old":[88]

> Thousands on thousands are expended in gay and
> costly ornamentals to gratify pride, and a wicked
> ambition, that might go to redeem the perishing
> millions! ... These splendid monuments of popish
> pride, upon which millions are squandered in our
> cities, virtually exclude the poor ... No wonder
> God withholds his influence....[89]

Living in the northern states, most Sabbatarian
Adventists, though little involved in actual politics,
tended to be radical republicans and abolitionists.[90]
This helps to explain why slavery was seen as possibly
the worst sin of Protestant America. The "professed
church," Andrews said, was "to a fearful extent the
right arm of the slave power."[91]

But the underlying cause of Babylon's fall was doctrinal: the rejection of "the vivifying truth of ... the
great advent proclamation."[92] The European churches had
lost "the purity and piety they once possessed" and the
American churches were "fast following in the wake of
the theology of the old world" and have made "many sad
departures" from "the faith once delivered to the

---

[88] Even where the issue of infallibility is
concerned, the Protestants are no better than the
"Romanists". Protestants pretend they do not believe in
infallibility, but in fact they claim it for their
credal statements. See J.N. Andrews, The Three Angels
of Rev. 14:6-12, 49.

[89] Editorial note, quoting from Golden Rule, RH
(Dec. 18, 1856), 53.

[90] Jonathan M. Butler, "Adventism and the American
Experience," 182-188.

[91] J.N. Andrews, "The Three Angels of Revelation
14:6-12," cont., RH (March 6, 1855), 186. See also J.N.
Andrews, "What is Babylon?", RH (febr. 21, 1854), 36.

[92] Uriah Smith, "Thoughts on the Revelation," RH
(Nov. 18, 1862), 197.

saints."[93] These corruptions not only concerned the seventh-day Sabbath (see below) and heresies concerning the Second Advent and the millennium. They also had to do with the teachings of Universalism[94] and with the doctrine of baptism. Doctrinal corruption was further apparent in the doctrine of the Trinity, which "destroys the personality of God, and his Son Jesus Christ our Lord,"[95] and "the doctrine of the natural immortality of the soul," which "was derived from pagan mythology" and introduced into the church by former pagans and now formed "the foundation of modern Spiritualism."[96] Protestantism had opened its doors to Spiritualism, thus fulfilling Revelation 14:6-8 and making Babylon a "habitation of devils."[97]

IV Rome and Sunday Observance

1. Catholicism Responsible for Sabbath-Sunday Change

In the late 1840s and early 1850s the Sabbath and its history soon became an important topic in Adventist publications. A tract written in 1850 by J.W. Morton,

---

[93] "The Downward Tendency of Man," RH (Feb. 21, 1854), 35.

[94] Universalists believe in the ultimate reconciliation and salvation of all. An important formative element in liberal American Protestantism, Universalism was widespread in later colonial times and in the Revolutionary period, reaching its peak in 1830-1860. See Sydney E. Ahlstrom, A Religious History of the American People, 481-483; Robert T. Handy, A History of the Churches in the United States and Canada, 336-337; Winthrop S. Hudson, Religion in America, 154.

[95] J.N. Andrews, The Three Angels of Rev. 14:6-12, 54-55.

[96] Ibid., 54. See also pp. 112-113.

[97] J.H. Waggoner, The Nature and Tendency of Modern Spiritualism (Battle Creek: Steam Press of the Review and Herald Office, 1860), 123-138. See also James White, "The Third Angel's Message," RH (Aug. 14, 1856), 116.

who, while working as a missionary for the Reformed Presbyterian Church in Haiti, had become convinced of the Sabbath, apparently circulated among Sabbatarian Adventists. It was reprinted (in part) in the columns of the *Review and Herald*.[98] The tract continued to be read by Sabbatarian Adventists and was later reprinted by the Adventist publishing house.[99]

T.M. Prebble's tract which appeared a few years earlier (1845), and Joseph Bates' first publication on the topic, which was published in 1846, have already been referred to.[100] For a number of years Bates was the foremost defender of the seventh-day Sabbath among post-disappointment Adventists.[101] In his first pamphlet, *The Seventh Day Sabbath, a Perpetual Sign*, he set out to convince his readers that the Sabbath was established in paradise, for all of mankind. Just as marriage, it was "coeval and co-extensive with the world."[102] It was not a Jewish institution and was not to be confused with the temporal ceremonial Sabbaths. Nor was there any indication that Christ or the apostles ever abolished the biblical Sabbath. In a short paragraph--which makes reference to Daniel 7:25--Bates lays the blame for the change from Sabbath to Sunday with Constantine the Great and Pope Gregory the Great.[103]

In the second, enlarged, edition of this pamphlet,

---

[98] J.W. Morton, "Narrative of Recent Events," RH (Nov. 1, 1853), 129-131. Andrews quotes from Morton's tract in: "The First Day of the Week not the Sabbath of the Lord," Tract no. 1 of Advent and Sabbath Tracts (Rochester, N.Y., 1854), 12.

[99] J.W. Morton, Vindication of the True Sabbath; in Two Parts (Battle Creek: Steam Press of the SDA Publ. Ass., 1876).

[100] See pp. 77-78.

[101] See C. Mervyn Maxwell, "Joseph Bates and Seventh-day Adventist Sabbath Theology," chap. in: Kenneth A. Strand, ed., The Sabbath in Scripture and History (Washington, DC: RHPA, 1982), 352-363; P.G. Damsteegt, TTM, 138-146.

[102] Joseph Bates, The Sabbath, a Perpetual Sign, 9.

[103] Ibid., 41-42.

Bates extended his argument by focusing on those "who keep the commandments of Jesus" (Revelation 14:12) as the last-day saints, who would be distinguished by their loyalty to all the commandments, including the seventh-day Sabbath.[104] They received the divine seal by leaving Babylon and by embracing the true Sabbath. Eventually these faithful would constitute the 144,000.[105] These he contrasted with the majority who possessed the "mark of the beast," which he identified as the keeping of the first day of the week.[106]

However, as author on the Sabbath and related issues Bates would soon be eclipsed by the much younger John N. Andrews, who was to be responsible for the most scholarly Adventist publication during the 1844-1863 period, *History of the Sabbath and the First Day of the Week*, published in 1862.[107] Andrews has justly been called "the foremost Adventist intellectual of the 19th

---

[104] Joseph Bates, The Seventh Day Sabbath, a Perpetual Sign, from the Beginning, to the Entering into the Gates of the Holy City, according to the Commandment. Revised and enlarged ed. (New Bedford: Press of Benjamin Lindsey, 1846), 58; see also Joseph Bates, Second Advent Way Marks and High Heaps, or a Connected View, of the Fulfillment of Prophecy, by God's Peculiar People, From the Year 1840 to 1847 (New Bedford: Press of Benjamin Lindsey, 1947), 68-79.

[105] Joseph Bates, A Seal of the Living God. A Hundred Forty-Four Thousand of the Servants of God Being Sealed (New Bedford: Press of Benjamin Lindsey, 1849), 37, 62.

[106] Joseph Bates, The Seventh Day Sabbath, a Perpetual Sign (Revised and enlarged ed., 1846), 58.

[107] The full title is: History of the Sabbath and the First Day of the Week, Showing the Bible Record of the Sabbath, also the Manner in which it has been Supplanted by the Heathen Festival of the Sun (Battle Creek: Steam Press of the SDA Publ. Ass., 1862). This work will be referred to as HOS (1862). In the second edition of 1873 the second, historical, part of the book was significantly enlarged. Posthumous editions appeared in 1887 and 1912. The 1912 edition was translated into German, with important changes, by L.R. Conradi. See p. 153, note 102.

century"[108] and "the architect of Adventist doctrines."[109] Although he lacked a formal education beyond a few grades of elementary school, Andrews developed into a first-class scholar with considerable linguistic skills: he had a knowledge of at least seven languages.

In 1846, as a 17 year old youth, Andrews accepted the validity of the Sabbath. Towards the end of 1850 and throughout 1851 his articles began appearing in the *Review and Herald*.[110] During the 1850s he wrote several tracts[111] and a number of series of articles in the *Review and Herald* on the Sabbath.[112] These publications dealt (a) with a Biblical defense of the validity of the Sabbath and the unscripturalness of the Sunday and (b) with the history of the Sabbath-Sunday controversy. Especially in this second area he continued to expand his horizon.

In his early years Andrews relied heavily on Seventh-day Baptist sources.[113] But as time went on he

---

[108] Joseph G. Smoot, "Andrews' Role in Seventh-day Adventist History," chap. in Harry Leonard, ed., J.N. Andrews, 10.

[109] F.K. Mueller, "The Architect of Adventist Doctrines," chap. in Harry Leonard, ed., J.N. Andrews, 75.

[110] For a complete bibliography of Andrews' writings, see Gordon Balharrie, "A Study of the Contributions Made to the Seventh-day Adventist Movement by John Nevins Andrews" (MA-thesis: SDA Theol. Sem., 1949).

[111] Advent and Sabbath Tracts, No. 1-4 (Rochester, N.Y., n.d.).

[112] Andrews published several series of articles dealing with the "History of the Sabbath." In these (from the series from April 14 - May 12, 1853 to the much longer series which ran from Dec. 3, 1861 to May 27, 1862, with several series in between) Andrews gradually developed the material which he published in his book History of the Sabbath.

[113] A source frequently cited by Seventh-day Baptists and Andrews and other Sabbatarian writers is Peter Heylyn, The History of the Sabbath, in Two Books

was able to consult an ever widening array of historical sources, which resulted in significant additions in later editions of his *magnum opus: The History of the Sabbath and the First Day of the Week.*[114] The first edition (1862), however, represents his findings during the period under review in this chapter. In the second part of the book, entitled "Secular History," Andrews has much to say about the role of the Catholic Church, but his language is always restrained and is very different from the violent "anti-popery" language of so many of his contemporaries.

After having shown in the first part of the book that there is no biblical justification for keeping Sunday as a day of worship and/or rest, Andrews proceeds in the second part to prove that the first trace of the counterfeit Sabbath--the Sunday as a Christian festival--is found in the church of Rome.[115] The Roman church is probably very old, and may even date from apostolic times. But that, Andrews argues, does not make it apostolic in character. The New Testament (Acts 20:29,30; 2 Thessalonians 2:3-8; 2 Timothy 4:2-4) indi-

---

(London, 1636). Heylyn, though not a Sabbatarian himself, provided them with many historical arguments in support of their thesis.

[114] A historical note accompanying the publication of Andrews' <u>History of the Sabbath</u> refers to his "studious and arduous researches upon the subject, as he had opportunity for the last ten years"--[J.N. Andrews], "History of the Sabbath," <u>RH</u> (Oct. 22, 1861), 168. Studies in libraries on the East coast of the US resulted in significant additions in the 1873 edition. Convinced of the importance of Andrews' research, James White tried to raise money to equip Andrews with the necessary books. He aimed for small amounts in 1854 and 1855, but asked for as much as $ 2000 in 1870. See ed. note, <u>RH</u> (March 7, 1854), 56; "The Office," <u>RH</u> (Feb. 20, 1855), 182-183; "Two Hundred Men Wanted," <u>RH</u> (Sept. 20, 1870), 112.

[115] J.N. Andrews, <u>HOS (1962)</u>, 233. See below (p. 105) for comment on Justin Martyr's statement which links Rome to the origins of Sunday observance. This emphasis on the "Rome-connection" does not appear in Andrews' earlier <u>Advent and Sabbath Tracts</u> and is less pronounced in his earliest series of articles on the history of Sabbath and Sunday.

cates that apostasy already appeared in the first century.[116] The fundamental apostasy of the church in Rome was "the Romanist Rule" which adds tradition to Scripture, instead of basing its faith on the Bible alone, as the "Rule of the man of God" requires.[117]

Andrews further maintained that the frequently cited statements from early second century sources, which supposedly support an early transition from Sabbath to Sunday, carry little weight. The reference in the Epistle of Barnabas (15:9) to "observing the eighth day with gladness" must be discounted, as most authorities refuse to accept this document as genuine.[118] The statement in the Epistle of Pliny (Book X, 96) about "a stated day" on which Christians assemble before sunrise, refers more likely to the Sabbath than to the Sunday.[119] The statement about the non-observance of sabbaths, but a keeping of the Lord's day, in the Epistle of Ignatius of Antioch to the Magnesians (3:3-5) must also be discarded. According to many authorities the letter is spurious. Those who do accept it, say the text is corrupt. In any case: the word "day" is supplied by the translators; a more probable reading would be "life" instead of "day."[120]

---

[116] Ibid., 194-195.

[117] Ibid., 202. See also J.N. Andrews, "Is the First Day of the Week the Sabbath?" RH (March 31, 1853), 180; J.N. Andrews, "Tradition," RH (Oct. 10, 1854), 69-70.

[118] J.N. Andrews, HOS (1862), 206-210. For an English text of the Letter of Barnabas, see Edgar J. Goodspeed, The Apostolic Fathers (London: Independent Press, Ltd, 1950), 23-45.

[119] J.N. Andrews, HOS (1862), 210-211. For a recent English translation of the Letter of Pliny, see Betty Radice, ed., The Letters of the Younger Pliny (Harmondsworth: Penguin Books, 1975 ed.), 293-295. Later attempts to prove that Pliny's "stated day" was the Sunday referred to an ancient document, "Acta Martyrum." Andrews was confident that this work did not exist and the reference constituted a fraud perpetrated by "some doctors of divinity." See his HOS (1862), 217-223.

[120] J.N. Andrews, HOS (1862), 211-216. For an English text of Ignatius' Letter to the Magnesians, see Edgar J. Goodspeed, The Apostolic Fathers, 213-217.

"The earliest testimony on behalf of first-day observance that has *any* claim to be regarded as genuine is that of Justin Martyr," in his First Apology, written about A.D. 140[121] in which he mentions a church assembly on Sunday (chap. 67). Andrews says,

> This passage, if genuine, furnishes the earliest reference to the observance of Sunday as a religious festival in the Christian church. It should be remembered that this language was written at Rome, and addressed directly to the emperor. It shows therefore, what was the practice of the church in that city and vicinity, but does not determine how extensive this observance was.[122]

Two factors are singled out in the efforts of the Roman church to replace the Sabbath by the Sunday: Bishop Victor's attempts to enforce a Sunday Passover in opposition to the practice of the Eastern churches[123] and, subsequently, the turning of the Sabbath into a day of fasting.[124]

From remote antiquity Sunday was a heathen festival, generally observed by the Gentiles. By adopting it as the Christian day of worship, the church hoped to facilitate the conversion of the Gentiles.[125] Constantine's Sunday law (321) "could not fail to strengthen the current already strongly set in favor of Sunday, and greatly to weaken the influence of the

---

[121] J.N. Andrews, <u>HOS (1862)</u>, 229. For an English text of Justin Martyr's First Apology, see Alexander Roberts and James Donaldson, <u>The Ante-Nicene Fathers</u>, vol. 1 (Edinburgh: T&T Clark; Grand Rapids, MI: Wm. B. Eerdmans, 1989 reprint), 163-187.

[122] J.N. Andrews, <u>HOS (1862)</u>, 231.

[123] J.N. Andrews, <u>HOS (1862)</u>, 236-238; these so-called Quartodecimans celebrated Easter on the 14th of the Jewish month Nissan (the date for the Jewish Passover), whatever the day of the week.

[124] J.N. Andrews, <u>HOS (1862)</u>, 242.

[125] Ibid., 224-229.

Sabbath."[126] After that "it was the part of popery" to transform the Sunday into a Christian institution, which it did in the fourth and fifth century through the decisions of various councils and measures against Sabbath keepers.[127] Numerous testimonies from the 4th and 5th century, notably those of historians Sozomen (early 5th century) and Socrates (ca. 380-450), however, indicate that Sabbath-keeping was far from obliterated,[128] and the concluding chapter of Andrews' book lists instances of continued Sabbath observance in many areas throughout the Middle Ages and until the 19th century:[129]

> The Church of Rome was indeed able to exterminate the Sabbath from its own communion, but it was retained by the true people of God who were measurably hidden from the papacy in the wilds of Central Europe; while those African and Indian churches that were never within the limits of the pope's dominion, have steadfastly retained the Sabbath to the present day.[130]

2. Protestants Following Catholic Traditions

The clinching argument of the Sabbatarian Adventists against Protestant Sunday-keepers was invariably to point at Catholic catechetical or apologetical works which defended the validity of Roman Catholic tradition by referring to the fact that even Protestants ignored biblical commands such as footwashing and Sabbath observance in defiance of clear scriptural injunctions.[131] These Catholic works reminded Sunday-

---

[126] Ibid., 252-259.

[127] Ibid., 259-264.

[128] Ibid., 267-270.

[129] Ibid., 313-340.

[130] Ibid., 313.

[131] For a description of these catechetical and apologetical works, which were available in the United States in the mid-19th century, see Charles J. Carmody,

keepers that strict obedience to Scripture alone would require a return to Sabbath observance. In quoting from these sources, Andrews as well as other Sabbatarian writers followed the Seventh-day Baptist example.[132] The standard quotations were collected in a small tract *"Who Changed the Sabbath?"*[133]

The following quote from Henry Tuberville's catechesis became immensely popular among Adventist writers:

Q. Why was the *Jewish* Sabbath changed into *Sunday*?
A. Because Christ was born upon a *Sunday*, rose from the dead upon a *Sunday*, and sent down the Holy Ghost on a *Sunday*: works not inferior to the creation of the world.
Q. By whom was it changed?
A. By the Governors of the Church, the Apostles who also kept it; for St. John was in the Spirit on the Lord's Day, (which was Sunday). Apoc. 1:10.
Q. How prove you that the Church hath power to command feasts and holydays?
A. By the very act of changing the Sabbath into *Sunday*, which Protestants allow of; and therefore they fondly contradict themselves, by keeping *Sunday* strictly, and breaking most other feasts commanded by the same Church.
Q. How prove you that?
A. Because by keeping *Sunday*, they acknowledge the Church's power to ordain feasts, and to command them under sin: and by not keeping the rest by her commanded, they again deny, in fact, the same

---

"The Roman Catholic Catecheses in the United States 1784-1930: A Study of its Theory, Development and Materials" (Ph.D. diss., Loyola Univ. of Chicago, 1975), especially 42-93, 437, 438, 454, 456, 463-464.

[132] See e.g. George Carlow, <u>A Defense of the Sabbath</u> (New York: Publ. by Paul Stillman, for the American Sabbath Tract Society, 1847), 159-160. This book was originally printed by the English Seventh-day Baptists in 1724.

[133] <u>Who Changed the Sabbath?</u> (Battle Creek, ca. 1854). An expanded version appeared in August 1854: <u>Why don't you keep the Sabbath?</u> (Rochester, N.Y.: The Advent Review Office, 1854).

power.[134]

Another popular statement constantly referred to as proof for Catholic responsibility for the change from Sabbath to Sunday was found in Stephen Keenan's *Doctrinal Catechism*:

> Q. *Have you any other proofs that they* [the Protestants] *are not guided by the Scripture?*
> A. Yes; so many, that we cannot admit more than a mere specimen in this small work....
> Q. Give some examples....
> A. They should, if the Scripture were there only rule, wash the feet of one another, according to the command of Christ, in the 13th chap. of St. John; - they should keep, not the Sunday, but the Saturday, according to the commandment, "Remember thou keep holy the SABBATH-day"; for this commandment has not, *in Scripture*, been changed or abrogated....[135]

Similar statements were also found in James Butler's *Catholic Catechism of Christian Religion*,[136]

---

[134] Henry Tuberville, <u>Douay Catechism or An Abridgment of the Christian Doctrine. With Proof for Points Controverted by Way of Question and Answer. Composed in 1649 by Rev. Henry Tuberville of the English College of Douay. Now Approved and Recommended for His Diocese by the Right Rev. Benedict [Fenwick], Bishop of Boston</u> (New York: P.J. Kennedy, Excelsior Publishing House, 1833), 58.

[135] Stephen Keenan, <u>A Doctrinal Catechism; wherein divers points of Catholic Faith and Practice Assailed by Modern Heretics are Sustained by an Appeal to the Holy Scriptures, the Testimonies of the Ancient Fathers, and the Dictates of Reason on the Basis of Scheffmacher's Catechism.</u> (New York: P.J. Kennedy and Sons, 1846(?), 3rd American ed.), 101; another oft-quoted statement is found on pp. 351-354.

[136] Dr. James Butler's Catechism was widely used in the USA and served as a source for many other, later, catecheses. The edition probably used by the Sabbatarian Adventists was: <u>The Most Rev. Dr. James Butler's Catechism, Revised, Enlarged, Approved, and Recommended by the Four Roman Catholic Archbishops of Ireland as a</u>

Challoner's *The Christian Catholic Instructed*,[137] the *Treatise of Thirty Controversies*,[138] and a Catholic tract *A Question for all Bible Christians*. An other frequently quoted source was Milner's *The End of Religious Controversy*,[139] an extremely popular and influential attack on Protestantism.[140] Reference to one or several of these works became standard Sabbatarian Adventist procedure.[141]

General Catechism for the Kingdom. To Which is Added the Scriptural Catechesis of Rt. Rev. Dr. Milner. This catechesis went through many editions, by many American publishers, from 1827 onward.

[137] Rt. Rev. Dr. Richard Challoner, The Catholic Christian Instructed in the Sacraments, Sacrifice, Ceremonies, and Observances of the Church. By Way of Question and Answer. This work was first published in the USA in 1786 and went through many editions.

[138] Sylvester Norris, An Antidote or Treatise of Thirty Controversies: With a large Discourse of the Church, in which the Souvereigne Truth of Catholike doctrine, is faythfully deliuevered: against the pestiferous writings of all English Sectaryes ..., 1622. Reprinted in D.M. Rogers, ed., English Recusant Literature: 1558-1640, vol. 185 (London: The Scholars Press, 1974). See part 1, p. 50.

[139] John Milner, D.D., The End of Religious Controversy, in a Friendly Correspondence between a Religious Society of Protestants and a Roman Catholic Divine (New York: P.J. Kennedy, Catholic Publishing House, 1802).

[140] Robert Gorman, Catholic Apologetical Literature in the United States - 1784-1858 (Washington, DC: The Catholic Univ. Press, 1939), 53-54.

[141] For some of the many instances see J.N. Andrews, "Things to be Considered," RH (Jan. 31, 1854), 9; J.N. Andrews, The Three Angels of Revelation 14:6-12, 112; J.N. Andrews, "History of the Sabbath and the First Day of the Week," RH, (Aug. 4, 1859), 83-84; J.N. Andrews, HOS (1862), 203; Joseph Bates, "Church Order," RH (Aug. 29, 1854), 22-23; R.F. Cottrell, "Mark of the Beast," RH (Aug. 6, 1857), 109; R.F. Cottrell, Mark of the Beast,

V Other "Popish Errors"

Although the criticism of Sabbatarian Adventists focused in a special way on the Catholic role in the substitution of the Sunday for the Sabbath, Roman Catholic tradition was blamed for a long list of "damnable heresy ... which she proves by those same fathers."[142] Among the "popish errors" listed, with the dates of their alleged origin, were the use of holy water (120), penance (158), "monkery" (328), Latin Mass (394), purgatory (558), invocation of Mary and the saints (594), image worship (715), canonizing saints (993), transubstantiation (1000), celibacy (1015), indulgences (1190), elevation of the host (1222) and the immaculate conception (1854).[143] Catholics were, however, not the only ones to be blamed for believing heresy. Cornell remarks that "Protestants and Catholics are so nearly united in sentiment, that it is not difficult to conceive how Protestants may make an image to the Beast":

> The mass of Protestants believe with Catholics in the Trinity, immortality of the soul, consciousness of the dead, rewards and punishments at death, the endless torture of the wicked, inheritance of the saints beyond the skies, sprinkling for baptism,

---

and Seal of the Living God (Battle Creek, n.d.), 11-14; R.F. Cottrell, "Mark of the Beast, and Seal of the Living God," RH (July 28, 1859), 78; "A Cutting Reproof; Extracts from Milner's End of Controversy, a Catholic work; pages 89, 90," RH (Jan. 20, 1853), 139; J.N. Loughborough, "The Two-Horned Beast," concl., RH (March 28, 1854), 73; J.N. Loughborough, The Two-Horned Beast (Rochester, N.Y., ca. 1854), 26, 29; J.N. Loughborough, "The Two-Horned Beast of Rev. 13, a Symbol of the United States," cont., RH (July 9, 1857), 74-75; Uriah Smith, "Don't Break the Sabbath," concl., RH (Oct. 24, 1854), 86; B.F. Snook, "The Holy Sabbath of the Lord," RH (June 19, 1860), 34; James White, "The Sabbath," RH (Oct. 30, 1856), 204.

[142] J.N. Andrews, "Things to be Considered," RH (Jan. 31, 1854), 10.

[143] "Origin of Popish Errors," RH (Sept. 11, 1856), 147.

and the PAGAN SUNDAY for the Sabbath; all of which is contrary to the spirit and letter of the new testament. Surely there is between the mother and daughters a striking family resemblance.[144]

As already mentioned,[145] the Roman Catholic Church was criticized for its refusal to honour the true, heavenly sanctuary as it came to be understood by the Sabbatarian Adventists. The Pope had "trodden underfoot"--the reference is to Daniel 8:13--the temple of God, by turning the worship of mankind to his own sanctuary in Rome. And he had "trodden underfoot" Jesus Christ "by exalting himself above all that is called God, and assuming to be the head of the church in the place of Jesus Christ."[146] Uriah Smith summarized this papal abomination in the following words:

> After the typical sanctuary of the first covenant had given place to the true sanctuary of God, Satan baptized his Pagan sanctuary and rites, calling them Christianity. Thenceforward he had at Rome a "temple of God," and in that temple a being exalted above all that is called God, or that is worshipped. 2 Thess. 2:4. And this Papal abomination has trodden under foot the holy city, Rev. 11:2; 21:2, by persuading a large portion of the human family that Rome, the place of this counterfeit temple of God, was "the holy city" or "the eternal city"....
> ... [And he blasphemed] God's sanctuary by calling his own sanctuary the temple of God; blasphemed Christ by making the pope head of the church.[147]

The sprinkling of infants was regarded as yet another example of the corruption of Bible truth. The biblical

---

[144] M.E. Cornell, Facts for the Times, 76.

[145] See p. 85.

[146] Uriah Smith, "The Sanctuary," cont., RH (March 21, 1854), 78. See also J.N. Andrews, "The Sanctuary," RH (Jan. 6, 1853), 129; J.N. Andrews, "The Sanctuary," cont., RH (Feb. 3, 1853), 145.

[147] Uriah Smith, The Prophecy of Daniel: the Four Kingdoms, the Sanctuary, and the Twenty-three Hundred Days, 74.

mode of baptism by immersion as "the divinely authorized
memorial of our Lord's burial and resurrection" had been
changed to "sprinkling, or pouring, the fitting memorial
of but one thing, viz., the folly and presumption of
man."[148] Again, the origin of this change from biblical
practice to a man-made counterfeit was traced to the
Catholic Church.[149]

More important even was the role of Catholicism in
the introduction of the doctrine of the immortality of
the soul. Even though the idea of conditional immortality and the soul sleep had not been adopted by most
Millerites, it was soon generally accepted by those
Adventist groups which would become the nucleus of the
Advent Christian denomination and by the Sabbatarian
Adventists.[150] Before long the doctrine of the immortality of the soul came to be seen as at the root of
most of what is wrong with Roman Catholicism.[151] Moses
Hull argued that Roman Catholicism shared this fundamental error of the immortality of the soul with Protestants who believe in an eternal hell or adhere to Universalism, and with Spiritualists.[152]

Uriah Smith greeted any protest against the
doctrine of the immortal soul with whole-hearted approval:

Men are growing suspicious of the truth of a
declaration, first uttered by a doubtful character
in Eden, perpetuated thence through heathenism, and
at last through the medium of the Mother of

---

[148] J.N. Andrews, "The Three Angels of Rev. 14:6-
12," cont., RH (March 6, 1855), 185.

[149] B.F. Snook, The Nature, Subject and Design of
Christian Baptism (Battle Creek, MI: Steam Press of the
Review and Herald Office, 1861), 44-45.

[150] C.F.X. Rubencamp, "Immortality and Seventh-day
Adventist Eschatology" (Ph.D. diss., The Catholic Univ.
of America, 1968), 108-117.

[151] Ibid., 233.

[152] Moses Hull, The Transgressor's Fate, or A Short
Argument on the First and Second Deaths (Battle Creek:
Steam Press of the Review and Herald Office, 1861), 19.

harlots, disseminated through all the veins and channels of Orthodoxy.[153]

The Roman doctrine of purgatory was regarded as of direct pagan origin, while the unscriptural Protestant notion of an eternal hell was traced from "a misconception of some passages of Scripture," through the Roman Catholic doctrine of the hell, to "the Pagan notion of the immortality of the soul."[154] Moreover, the false teaching of the immortality of the soul served as the foundation for Spiritualism, which in 1848 experienced its American rebirth with the rappings in the home of the Fox sisters in Rochester, N.Y.[155]

Most of the Sabbatarian leaders of the early period (and some for some time afterward) were anti-Trinitarians. Several of them had come from the "Christian Connection," a rather loosely connected persuasion, which originated on the New England frontier as a result of the preaching of Abner Jones and Elias Smith. Advocating a return to the "primitive gospel," this group was revivalistic, strongly anti-Calvinist and anti-Trinitarian,[156] and, in general, strongly opposed to

---

[153] Uriah Smith, Which? Mortal or Immortal? or An Inquiry into the Present Constitution and Future Condition of Man (Battle Creek: Steam Press of the Review and Herald Office, 1859), 124.

[154] "Destruction of the Wicked," extracted from "Bible vs. Tradition," RH (Oct. 24, 1854), 82-83.

[155] J.N. Andrews, "The Three Angels of Rev. 14:6-12," cont., RH (March 6, 1855), 185. See also D.P. Hall, Man not Immortal, the Only Shield against the Seductions of Modern Spiritualists (Rochester, N.Y.: Advent Review Office, 1855).

[156] Godfrey T. Anderson, "Sectarianism and Organization," 43-44. For a recent study which gives considerable attention to Jones and Smith and their movement, see Nathan O. Hatch, The Democratization of American Christianity, 42, 57, 68-70, 129. For the anti-Trinitarian views in the Christian Connection, see: Thomas H. Olbricht, "Christian Connection and Unitarian Relations," Restoration Quarterly, vol. 9, no 3 (3rd quarter 1966), 160-161, 167-174, 184-185. For the considerable influx of members of the Christian Connec-

the formulation of creeds.[157]

With this background of aversion against the sophisticated theology of a professional clergy, these Sabbatarian Adventists were quite ready to see pronouncements of church councils as Romish manipulation of biblical truth, including those of the important Council of Nicea in 325, in which Emperor Constantine played such a significant role. This explains the opposition of some to the Nicene view of the nature of Christ as a doctrine which can be traced back "no further than to the origin of the 'Man of Sin'"[158] and to the doctrine of the Trinity. For this doctrine, which by "infamous measures" was forced upon the church, destroyed the personality of God and of his Son.[159]

VI Limited Interest in Current Issues in Catholicism

What has been said so far in this chapter might lead some to think that in the eyes of Sabbatarian Adventism Roman Catholicism was by far the most important danger. A careful analysis of all the available sources, however, points in a somewhat different direction. When surveying all the negative statements about the historical role of the papacy, it is evident that most of these referred either to the past or to the future. With regard to the present, the Babylonian state of Pro-

---

tion into the Millerite Movement, see Milo T. Morrill, A History of the Christian Denomination in America (Dayton: The Christian Publishing Association, 1912), 175.

[157] R.W. Schwarz, Light Bearers to the Remnant, 166.

[158] D.W. Hull, "Bible Doctrine of the Divinity of Christ," RH (Nov. 10, 1859), 193.

[159] J.N. Andrews, "The Three Angels of Rev. 14:6-12," cont., RH (March 6, 1855), 185. See also: M.E. Cornell, Facts for the Times, 76. For a detailed study of anti-Trinitarian beliefs in early Adventism, see E.R. Gane, "The Arian or Anti-Trinitarian Views Presented in Seventh-day Adventist Literature and the Ellen G. White Answer" (Unpubl. M.A. thesis, Andrews Univ., 1963).

testantism and the threat of "modern" Spiritualism, received far more emphasis.

Among the signs of the times the moral fall since the mid-1840s of "professed Christianity," which is "divided up into about 600 sects," is the most startling.[160] 2 Timothy 3:1-7 offers "an inspired portrait of the popular church."[161] Series of quotations from denominational journals of various persuasions are regularly cited to illustrate the "melancholy picture of the state of religion in our country."[162] Slavery is singled out as the "most grievous sin of Babylon." A major section of Hastings' book on the "signs of the times" deals with the slavery issue.[163] Protestant America had authorized an unparalleled "commerce in human flesh,"[164] and church organizations themselves allegedly owned no less than 600,000 slaves.[165]

Spiritualism is another significant sign of the times. This phenomenon, together with apostate Protestantism, is the most important sign that the coming of Christ is at the door.[166] Hundreds and possibly thousands of warnings against Spiritualism are scattered throughout the pages of the *Review and Herald* of the 1850s.

---

[160] M.E. Cornell, "Meetings in Chesaning, Mich.," RH (Feb. 26, 1861), 117. See also H.L. Hastings, The Signs of the Times; or, a Glance at Christendom as it is (Boston: H.L. Hastings, 1862), passim.

[161] G.W. A., "Evidences of the End," RH (Nov. 20, 1860), 5-6; J.H. Waggoner, "Babylon is Fallen," RH (Sept. 5, 1854), 29.

[162] E.g. "Religion in the United States," extracted from "London Christian Times," RH (Feb. 14, 1856), 159.

[163] H.L. Hastings, The Signs of the Times; or a Glance at Christendom as it is, 28-46.

[164] "The Dragon Voice," RH (Feb. 5, 1857), 106.

[165] G.W. A., "Evidences of the End," RH (Nov. 20, 1860), 5-6.

[166] James White, The Signs of the Times, Showing that the Second Coming of Christ is at the Doors, 25-64.

In striking contrast with the space allotted to apostate
Protestantism and Spiritualism is the limited attention
paid to current issues involving the Catholic Church,
both in the ecclesiastical as well as in the political
arena. The eagerness of the Millerite journals to report
incidents of an anti-Catholic nature is almost totally
absent. Even an event like the official promulgation of
the doctrine of the "Immaculate Conception of the
Blessed Virgin Mary" is no occasion for a flood of anti-
Catholic articles and tracts.[167]

The political interest of Sabbatarian Adventism seems to
have been largely absorbed by the slavery issue and the
future of the Union, leaving very little attention, or
sympathy, for nativistic forces such as the Know-Nothing
Party. A statement--one of the few on this subject--by
R.F. Cottrell is revealing: It would do no good to vote
Catholics out of office, because that would only
strengthen the Protestant position![168] An editorial in
the *Review and Herald* urged its readers not to get
involved in politics: prophecy indicated that no
betterment of the situation is to be expected. And
Catholicism was only part of the problem: "The great
antagonistic principles of Temperance and Intemperance,
Protestantism and Catholicism, Freedom and Slavery,
Republicanism and Tyranny, are all at work!"[169] And
rather than speaking of the Know-Nothing movement as an
ally in the struggle against a Catholic threat, it is
viewed as a sign of the times, from which "the cause of
truth and of humanity has little to hope."[170]
   None among the numerous tracts and books published
by James White and his associates in Rochester, and
later in Battle Creek, were dedicated to revealing the
depravity of convents and clergy, which many Protestants

---

[167] There is not a single reference to this event in
the 1854 and 1855 issues of the Review and Herald.

[168] R.F. Cottrell, "How Shall I Vote?" RH (Oct. 30,
1856), 205. See also Jonathan M. Butler, "Adventism and
the American Experience," 182.

[169] [Uriah Smith], "Politics," RH (Sept. 11, 1856),
152. See also Uriah Smith, "The Present State of the
World," RH (June 20, 1854), 164.

[170] J.N. Andrews, The Three Angels of Revelation
14:6-12, 108.

supposed to exist. The only exception is a book by M.B. Czechowski, published by himself.[171]

A Pole by birth, Czechowski was educated for the priesthood by the Franciscans in Cracow. Having been forced to flee his native land, and after wandering around Europe--a visit to Rome and an audience with pope Gregory XVI included--he became disillusioned with the Catholic Church, married, emigrated to America and became a Protestant. After attending an Adventist evangelistic meeting, and having become convinced of the correctness of the Adventist position, he worked for some time as an itinerant preacher among French speaking people in Canada, and across the border in the USA, before he returned to Europe.[172]

In his book Czechowski relates some shocking incidents of immorality in the convents in which he had lived and among the clergy he had encountered,[173] but one may agree with the preface that, certainly when compared

---

[171] M.B. Czechowski, Thrilling and Instructive Developments: an Experience of Fifteen Years as Roman Clergyman and Priest (Boston: published by the author, 1862).

[172] The Adventist leaders were not prepared to honour his request that he be sent as a missionary to Europe. An other (Sunday-keeping) Adventist group subsequently (in 1864) enabled him to go. Though not supported by Sabbath-keeping Adventists, he nevertheless preached the Sabbath in Italy, Switzerland and Romania and formed the first Seventh-day Adventist groups in Europe. For information on his life, see Rajmund L. Dabrowski, "M.B. Czechowski - his Early Life until 1851," chap. in: Rajmund L. Dabrowski and B.B. Beach, eds., Michael Belina Czechowski 1818-1876 - Results of the Historical Symposium about his Life and Work, held in Warsaw, Poland, May 17-23, 1976, Commemorating the Hundredth Anniversary of his Death (Warsaw: Znaki Czasu Publishing House, 1979), 78-99; and Rajmund L. Dabrowski, "The Sojourn of M.B. Czechowski on the American Continent," chap. in: Rajmund L. Dabrowski and B.B. Beach, eds., Michael Belina Czechowski 1818-1876, 100-159.

[173] See e.g. M.B. Czechowski, Thrilling and Instructive Developments, 24, 154, 169-170.

to many other 19th century writings on the subject, "the narrator does not indulge either in vituperation, or in the rancor which the proselyte to a new faith frequently shows toward those of his abandoned creed."[174] Though not published by the office of the *Review and Herald*, the book was advertised in the journal. Sales, however, remained disappointing.[175]

Czechowki's book about his experiences in the Roman Catholic Church was not typical of the publications of the Sabbatarian Adventists. Even Ellen G. White's first book on the "great controversy between Christ and Satan," which would eventually develop into "The Great Controversy" is quite moderate in tone when dealing with the history of Catholicism.[176] It does argue that Satan corrupted the pure Christian doctrine by persuading the believers to worship images of saints, of Mary, and even of Christ.[177] But the direct references to Roman Catholicism are remarkably few.[178] Also when describing the Reformation, Ellen G. White uses moderate language. Luther is said to have "raised his voice against the errors and sins of the Papal church," but this and other occasions are not seized upon to describe horrible incidents of apostasy.[179] And in the endtime scenario worldly Protestantism and Spiritualism, rather than Roman Catholicism are seen as the major players.[180] This early Ellen G. White book resembles very closely many other Sabbatarian Adventist publications in devoting more of its criticism to "nominal Protestantism" than to

---

[174] Ibid., iv.

[175] "Book Notice," RH (May 6, 1862), 184. See Rajmund L. Dabrowski, "The Sojourn of M.B. Czechowski on the American Continent," 120.

[176] Ellen G. White, <u>Spiritual Gifts</u>, vol 1: The Great Controversy (Battle Creek: James White, 1858).

[177] Ibid., 104-105.

[178] Ibid., 108-113.

[179] Ibid., 119-124.

[180] Ibid., 189-193.

Roman Catholicism.[181] Only occasionally antagonism from Catholics is reported.[182] And where one would expect a lengthy tirade against "popish corruptions" many tracts and books show remarkable restraint. This is true of the first little tract published jointly by the founders of the Adventist Church,[183] but also of more sophisticated and larger publications from the 1850s and early 1860s[184] and important series of articles in the *Review and Herald*.[185]

---

[181] Criticism of mainline Protestantism was certainly no invention of Millerites or Sabbatarian Adventists, but was shared by many fringe movements and populist preachers. For a fascinating study of this aspect of American Christianity in the 19th century, see Nathan O. Hatch, <u>The Democratization of American Christianity</u>, 162-189.

[182] M.E. Cornell, "Meetings in Anamosa, Iowa," <u>RH</u> (Feb. 23, 1860), 109; M.E. Cornell, "The Cause in Marion, Iowa," <u>RH</u> (May 10, 1860), 193; "French Mission," <u>RH</u> (May 5, 1859), 189.

[183] James White, <u>A Word to the Little Flock</u> (May 1847). On page 7 mention is made of the brightness of Christ's coming to destroy the "man of sin," but no further identification of this "man of sin" is given and neither are his evil deeds described.

[184] Among books which fail to mention Roman Catholicism or give very little emphasis to it, while the subject matter would have suggested some strong anti-Catholic statements, see H.L. Hastings, <u>The Signs of the Times</u>; Cornell, M.E., <u>Facts for the Times</u>; B.F. Snook, <u>The Nature, Subjects and Design of Christian Baptism</u>; Moses Hull, <u>The Transgressor's Fate</u>; Moses Hull, <u>The Bible from Heaven: or a Dissertation on the Evidences of Christianity</u> (Battle Creek: Steam Press of the SDA Publ. Ass., 1863).

[185] See e.g. Andrews' repeated series "History of the Sabbath and the First Day of the Week," (cf. note 112) which show great restraint in its accusations against Catholicism and refrain from using strong language when dealing with subjects as the little horn, etc.

VII Conclusion

The Sabbatarian Adventists inherited, with the hermeneutical methods of the Millerites, most of their prophetic views. Emphases shifted after the "great disappointment" and time calculations became somewhat less prominent. But the key chapters in Daniel and the Revelation where the Millerites--and many other Protestants--had found the prophecies regarding the papacy, continued to be interpreted by Sabbatarian Adventists in much the same way as Miller and his associates had done. Although there was still some uncertainty about Rome's possible future role, it was now generally accepted that Catholicism received its deadly wound in 1798, but was in the process of being healed, and would play a significant role in the endtime drama. In the interpretations of the prophecies which were applied to the Roman Catholic Church, the special focus was on the papacy's role in the gradual substitution of the Sunday for the Sabbath as a day of worship and/or rest. J.N. Andrews did seminal work in focusing on Rome as the primary locus where this substitution was first realized and forcibly promoted. Protestant Sunday worship was seen as unmistakable proof that Protestants were willing to put a Catholic tradition above the clear teaching of the Bible. As the sanctuary doctrine was further developed, Rome's alleged animosity towards the heavenly sanctuary and its priesthood could also become a standard criticism against Roman Catholicism.

A further significant aspect of this period (1844-1863) is the rather limited attention paid to current issues in the Catholic-Protestant debate of the 1850s and 1860s (such as the promulgation of the Doctrine of the Immaculate Conception; the diplomatic relations between the USA and the Vatican, the sojourn of Cardinal Bedini in the USA, and--most of all--the political aspirations of nativists, culminating in the Know-Nothing movement). The Adventist approach to apocalyptic Bible prophecy fostered an intense interest in history. This, undoubtedly, led Adventists to focus primarily on the role of the papacy in the past. In the 1840s to 1860s their attitudes toward the papacy were not so much shaped by contemporary incidents on the American scene, but rather by historical data which were eagerly collected to undergird their convictions about the role of the papacy in history.

The Sabbatarian Adventists of this period were certainly not more anti-Catholic in their attitudes than most other Protestant denominations and often showed a greater restraint in expressing anti-Catholic sentiments, and certainly in taking part in anti-Catholic activities, than was current in many quarters of 19th century American Protestantism.[186] A contributing factor to this was undoubtedly the still extremely limited numerical strength of Sabbatarian Adventism, which prohibited involvement on too many different fronts at the same time. But the emphasis on the imminent second coming of Christ and the conviction that his kingdom was about to be ushered in, also inevitably discouraged political involvement,[187] and helps to explain the Adventist refusal to get actively involved in anti-nativistic (and thus strongly anti-Catholic) political activities. In fact, as Adventists in the 1850s began to contemplate their obligation toward the world, they tended to see the large influx of immigrants to the United Stated as providential: it enabled them to preach their message "to all nations" without having to go abroad.[188]

The key concepts that were to determine the eschatological endtime scenario in which both Protestantism and Roman Catholicism would play a prominent role and in which the issue of an enforced Sunday-worship, combined with a persecution of a Sabbath-keeping minority, would figure prominently, were being worked out during the phase of Sabbatarian Adventism, ready for use in the decades to follow.

In this context it is important to notice how the Protestant churches, which had failed to heed the Advent message, received considerably more criticism for their moral and doctrinal corruption than Roman Catholicism.

---

[186] For an overview of Methodist attitudes towards Roman Catholicism in the 19th century, see Charles Yrigoyen, Jr., "Methodists and Roman Catholics in 19th Century America," Methodist History, vol. 28, no. 3 (Apr. 1990), 172-186. For a study of Baptist attitudes toward Roman Catholicism – which strongly supports the suggestion that other Protestants were more vehemently anti-Catholic during this period than Sabbatarian Adventists - see Terry C. Carter, "Baptist Participation in Anti-Catholic Sentiment and Activities, 1830-1860," (Ph.D. diss., Southwestern Baptist Theol. Sem., 1983).

[187] See e.g. James White, "Politics," RH (Aug. 21, 1860), 108.

[188] See P.G. Damsteegt, TTM, 281-282.

The "fallen" Protestant churches and the "modern" resurgence of Spiritualism during this period clearly eclipsed Catholicism as the main, immediate threat. But knowing what they did about the historic role of the papacy, Adventists found it easy to imagine what might happen in the United States, once a sufficiently strong Catholicism joined hands with the Protestants in their final opposition to God's loyal remnant.

CHAPTER FOUR

ADVENTISTS AND CATHOLICS: 1863-1915

I The Formative Period of Seventh-day Adventism

The organization of the General Conference of Seventh-day Adventists in 1863 seems an obvious and valid line of demarcation between the distinct periods of Sabbatarian Adventism and Seventh-day Adventism. The choice of 1915 as the *terminus ad quem* for this chapter would appear somewhat more arbitrary. But it is defensible for a number of reasons. It is practical: this study focuses on Adventist attitudes toward Roman Catholicism from the time the Seventh-day Adventist Church was officially organized until the Second Vatican Council (1962-1965); ending this chapter in 1915 cuts the century-long period neatly in half. But there are other, and better, justifications. By the beginning of the 20th century the formative stages of the Adventist Church were clearly ending. Adventist theology had been largely defined; and the infrastructure--a network of institutions and a re-organized system of church governance--that would facilitate a much more rapid growth than had been possible in the 19th century, was now in place. Some historians of Adventism have preferred 1901 as a line of demarcation, emphasizing the fundamental changes in the organizational structure which were decided upon during that year's "general conference." A few important facts do, however, warrant the choice of 1915 as a dividing line between more or less distinct epochs: the organizational restructuring of 1901 was not complete until some years later; many of the issues of the 1890s spilled over into the first decade of the next century; Ellen G. White's death in 1915 certainly was the end of an era in Adventist history; and in American society at large the involvement of the United States in the First World War was significant in many ways--one of them being a temporary lull in anti-Catholic attitudes, which represents a factor of importance in the context of this study.

1. Growth and Organizational Development

Seventh-day Adventism experienced modest but continuous membership growth between 1863 and 1915. From a mere 3,500 in 1863, it climbed to 29,711 by 1890, 67,131 by 1900, 90,736 by 1910, and 136,807 by 1915.[1] Throughout that period the majority of Seventh-day Adventists continued to be found in North America. The geographical expansion followed largely the patterns of western settlement into the Great Plains, California and the North-West, "by appealing to people uprooted from home, family and church,"[2] while Battle Creek in Michigan remained the center of all activities until the turn of the century. The South largely escaped Adventist evangelistic attention until the 1890s.

Increasingly, however, Adventists came to see the world as their parish and gradually developed a "theology of mission," which, based on their self-understanding as the "remnant" entrusted with a warning message, led to the sending of missionaries to areas outside of North America.[3] The first official missionary left the United States for Switzerland in 1874. Soon others followed to Scandinavia, England and Australia. In the late 1880s and 1890s an Adventist presence was established in several other European countries, Russia, the Near East, India, the Pacific Islands, and in several countries of Africa, the Far East, and Central and South America.[4]

---

[1] Membership statistics must be compiled from a number of sources. For 1870-1879: RH; for 1885-1890: Seventh-day Adventist Yearbook; for 1895-1900: General Conference Bulletin; and for 1905 to the present: General Conference of Seventh-day Adventists Annual Statistical Reports.

[2] Emmet K. VandeVere, "Years of Expansion: 1865-1885," chap. in: Gary Land, ed., Adventism in America, 66.

[3] P.G. Damsteegt, TTM, 298; for the Adventist self-understanding of being the "remnant," see TTM, 243-244.

[4] R.W. Schwarz, Light Bearers to the Remnant, 142-150; 214-231; a valuable survey of the early Adventist mission advance remains William A. Spicer, Our Story of Missions (Mountain View, Cal.: PPPA, 1921).

Considering the limited membership the development of a network of major institutions is remarkable. It gave the church a strong presence in many areas, but it carried a sometimes burdensome price tag, financially and otherwise. To the first college in Battle Creek several others were soon added in other parts of the USA, with also one established in Australia (1897).[5] The Western Health Reform Institute, which first opened its doors in 1867, grew into the mammoth Battle Creek Sanitarium, which, under the leadership of the talented, but strong-willed, John Harvey Kellogg would eventually employ more than 1,000 people, and would cause the struggling infant church considerable frustrations. But is was only one in a series of medical institutions, of which the Loma Linda Sanitarium in California was, after the Battle Creek "San," to be the most well-known.[6] Another area of institutional emphasis was publishing. The Review and Herald Publishing Association in Battle Creek remained the main "printing office," but the Pacific Press Publishing Association in California (1875), the Southern Publishing Association in Tennessee (1900) and institutions outside North America also had an increasingly important part in the printing and distributing of magazines (some with surprisingly large editions of hundreds of thousands), pamphlets and books. The introduction of "literature evangelism," a door-to-door sales system employing full-time and part-time self-supporting men and women, was an important factor

---

[5] For the development of the Adventist educational system, see E.M. Cadwallader, A History of Seventh-day Adventist Education (Lincoln, Nebr.: Union College Press, 1958) and E.C. Walter, "A History of Seventh-day Adventist Higher Education in the United States" (Ed.D. diss., Univ. of California, Berkeley, 1966).

[6] For a history of the establishment of early Adventist medical institutions, see Dores E. Robinson, The Story of Our Health Message: The Origin, Character and Development of Health Education in the Seventh-day Adventist Church (Nashville, Tenn.: SPA, 1955); for a study of the relationship between early Adventist health concepts and those of contemporary health innovators in the USA, see Ronald L. Numbers, Prophetess of Health: A Study of Ellen G. White. A scholarly biography of John H. Kellogg is R.W. Schwarz, "John Harvey Kellogg: American Health Reformer" (Ph.D. diss., Univ. of Michigan, 1964).

in the success of the Adventist publishing endeavour.

Two other "institutions" contributed enormously to the strengthening of the Adventist witness. The first was the concept of "systematic benevolence"--first suggested in 1859 and soon quite generally accepted--which demanded from the members regular contributions in proportion to their financial strength. In the 1870s "tithing" gradually superseded "systematic benevolence." The second was the development of the Sabbath School, both for children and adults, inspired by contemporary Sunday School models. This institution greatly assisted in indoctrinating church members in Adventist viewpoints and became an important avenue for collecting funds for foreign missions.

2. Theological Developments

The doctrinal basis of Adventism had been laid in the pre-1863 period. The prophecies of Daniel and the Revelation, Christ's pre-millennial second coming, the Sabbath and the sanctuary remained the key-elements of the "present truth."[7] Uriah Smith's commentary on Daniel and the Revelation[8] was so popular--among church members and as well as colporteurs--that it became the virtually undisputed authority on the subject, with the unfortunate result that it "tended to retard further elucidation of the prophetic topics that inspired Seventh-day Adventists."[9]

Andrews continued to dominate the discussion on the Sabbath, especially its historical aspects. Both Smith and Andrews wrote on the sanctuary and related topics. Other important Adventist opinion leaders--apart from Ellen G. White--who published extensively in journals and books, were James White, J.H. Waggoner,

---

[7] For a summary of the Adventist doctrinal position in this period, see Uriah Smith, Synopsis of the Present Truth: A Brief Exposition of the Views of S.D. Adventists (Battle Creek, MI: SDA Publ. Ass., 1884).

[8] See pp. 133-134.

[9] Emmet K. VandeVere, "Years of Expansion: 1865-1885," 92.

D.M. Canright[10], and later E.J. Waggoner, A.T. Jones and the German Louis R. Conradi.

Besides the key-topics mentioned above, the question as to whether the atonement was accomplished on the cross or rather during a pre-Advent "investigative judgment," in progress in the heavenly sanctuary since 1844, was heavily debated. The subject of conditional immortality and related themes also received considerable attention. An interesting development was the growing conviction about the close relationship between health and religion, which resulted in a rejection of "unclean" foods and stimulants like tobacco and alcohol, and made Adventists staunch "health reformers" and "temperance" promoters. Baptism by immersion was never an issue and was practiced righs from the beginning.

Over the years the strong anti-Trinitarianism and Arianism, which had characterized Sabbatarian Adventism, was gradually eroded and by 1900 the views on the godhead and the person of Christ had in general--not in the least as the result of the publications of Ellen G. White--moved quite close to the orthodox Christian position.[11] Although Adventists refused to formulate any credal statements, they issued a short summary of beliefs in 1872 which succinctly formulated the main Adventist doctrines as understood at that time.[12]

The Adventist church had to deal, however, with a number of serious doctrinal conflicts, especially toward the end of the century. The acrimonious debates of the 1888 General Conference in Minneapolis about such non-essentials as the law in Galatians and the identity of the ten kings in Daniel 2, but also about the heart of

---

[10] After severing his ties with Adventism in 1887, Dudley M. Canright became the church's most important critic. His 413-page book Seventh-day Adventism Renounced (New York: F.H. Revell, 1889) "quickly became the chief weapon in evangelical Protestantism's anti-Adventist arsenal." See R.W. Schwarz, Light Bearers to the Remnant, 469.

[11] See E.R. Gane, "The Arian or Anti-Trinitarian Views...", passim.

[12] A Declaration of the Fundamental Principles Taught and Practiced by the Seventh-day Adventists (Battle Creek, MI: SDA Publ. Ass., 1872); repr. in P.G. Damsteegt, TTM, 303-305.

the Christian gospel--legalism versus righteousness by faith alone--continue toreverberate even in present-day Adventism.[13] Only after a painful decade of controversy did the church align itself with the gospel emphasis of A.T. Jones and E.J. Waggoner, who enjoyed the support of Ellen G. White.

The controversy over Kellogg's alleged pantheism, centering on his book *The Living Temple*,[14] was as much a power struggle between the clergy of the denomination and "the doctor" whose growing "empire" met with great suspicion, as a theological disagreement. Other conflicts centered around persons who (in addition to Ellen G. White) were claiming the prophetic gift, most notably Anna Phillips in the 1890s in Battle Creek. And it can hardly be surprising that in a time of widespread emphasis on perfection and holiness, during which modern Pentecostalism emerged, Adventism had its own charismatic experiments, such as the Holy Flesh movement in Indiana (ca. 1901).

3. Major Problems

Two major challenges facing the church remain to be briefly discussed. The first one was of an organizational nature: the concentration of power in the hands of a few men in Battle Creek, responsible for leading the increasingly complex, increasingly international, and highly institutionalized church structure. After more than a decade of fierce struggle, in which vested interests played a major role, the General Conference of 1901 succeeded in establishing a much more

---

[13] There is a wealth of publications about this key event in Adventist history, both of a more popular and of a more scholarly nature. A recent, very readable and well researched, treatment is George R. Knight, Angry Saints (Hagerstown: RHPA, 1989). About the role of one of the most important players in the Minneapolis drama, see George R. Knight, From 1888 to Apostasy - The Case of A.T. Jones (Hagerstown: RHPA, 1987), esp. 23-74. Less objective but valuable are: A.V. Olsen, Through Crisis to Victory, 1888-1901 (Washington, DC: RHPA, 1966) and Leroy E. Froom, Movement of Destiny (Washington, DC: RHPA, 1971), 148-374; 518-540; 673-686.

[14] J.H. Kellogg, The Living Temple (Battle Creek, MI: Good Health Publishing Company, 1903).

efficient organizational model with considerable power sharing at different levels. Unfortunately, it would cost a few additional years of bitter strife to bring the medical branch also under denominational control.[15] Related to the organizational changes was the dispersion of Adventist institutions from Battle Creek. Both the Review and Herald Publishing Association and the church's headquarters were moved to Washington, DC, in 1903.

The second challenge was presented by the American *milieu* of the late 1880s to the late 1890s. A more positive attitude on the part of many denominations toward cooperation, especially with regard to social issues, even between Protestants and Roman Catholics; the emergence and growing influence of such movements as the National Reform Movement, aspiring to make America into a "Christian nation"; some major initiatives to introduce Sunday legislation on the state and federal level; the apparent bias in the enforcement of Sunday laws by some states when dealing with Seventh-day Adventists; the powerful temperance movement, to which Adventists were basically sympathetic, which, however, tended to join forces with the pro-Sunday lobby; these and other related factors convinced the Adventists of those days that the eschatological moment was not far distant when large-scale persecution of God's Sabbath keeping remnant would be the immediate prelude to Christ's second coming. These events not only confirmed the Adventist believers in the correctness of their prophetic views, but also motivated them--often quite aggressively--to launch a counter-offensive by organizing an association for the promotion of religious liberty and by flooding the market with journals, pamphlets and books dealing with these issues. We will return to this in more detail later in this chapter, since this cluster of events was a major factor in shaping Adventist views on Catholicism.[16]

---

[15] R.W. Schwarz, Light Bearer to the Remnant, 267-313. See also Barry David Oliver, "Principles for Reorganization of the Seventh-day Adventist Administrative Structure, 1888-1903: Indications for an International Church" (Ph.D. diss., SDA Theol. Sem., Andrews Univ., 1989).

[16] A seminal study about the history of Seventh-day Adventist attitudes toward religious liberty, which deals at some length with this period of late 19th

During the 1863-1915 period one voice was not only constantly heard, but became increasingly influential: that of Ellen G. White. Although not all Adventist leaders were always inclined to listen to her "testimonies," and although she had a more direct influence on decisions of an organizational and practical nature than on the settling of fine points of doctrinal dispute or prophetic exegesis, she would determine to a large extent the "flavour" of the Adventism of her times and beyond. We shall also return to her later in this chapter.

II Developments in Catholicism

In spite of major external and internal problems the Roman Catholic Church ended the nineteenth century much stronger than it had been just after the French Revolution. The gradual loss of the Papal States, though continuously lamented, did not mean the demise of papal power, but was more than compensated for by the growing spiritual power and prestige of the papacy. Pius IX (1846-1878), who regarded himself a prisoner in the Vatican, after Rome had been occupied by Italian forces (1870), vigorously opposed the liberalism of the times, as was most clearly demonstrated by his *Syllabus Errorum* of 1864. A convinced ultramontanist, Pius IX succeeded in having the First Vatican Council officially confirm the concept of papal infallibility (1870). During his pontificate (which was the longest in history) the church registered considerable growth and in many ways experienced a significant revitalization.

Pope Leo XIII (1878-1903) continued the process of centralization, but differed in many ways from his predecessor. He attempted to bring the church to terms with the modern world and responded in his encyclical *Rerum Novarum* to the many problems regarding labour and

---

century Sunday agitation in the United States, is Eric D. Syme, <u>A History of S.D.A. Church-State Relationships in the United States</u> (Mountain View, Cal.: PPPA, 1973), which is based on his earlier dissertation on the subject (Eric D. Syme, "Seventh-day Adventist Concepts of Church and State," Ph.D. diss., American University, 1969). See also Dennis Pettibone, "The Sunday Law Movement," chap. in: Gary Land, ed., <u>The World of Ellen G. White</u> (Washington: RHPA, 1987), 113-128; George R. Knight, <u>From 1888 to Apostasy</u>, 75-88; 117-131; and R.W Schwarz, <u>Light Bearers to the Remnant</u>, 250-256.

capital. Leo XIII was a skilful diplomat, who successfully mediated in a number of European political crises.
The Church saw strong growth during his pontifical
reign, most notably in the United States.

With Pius X (1903-1914) the Roman Catholic Church
elected a "religious" rather than a "political" pope. He
strongly resisted "modernistic" tendencies and was extremely concerned lest the Catholic Church in America
should develop its own ways and traditions.

The Roman Catholic Church in the United States
experienced a phenomenal growth in this period.[17] In 1860
the total population of the United States stood at 31.4
million, while the Catholic Church had, according to one
Catholic source, about 3.4 million members. By 1900
there were 13.5 million Catholics, with a population of
76 million. And by 1910 there were 18.5 million
Catholics, while the population had increased to 91.9
million.[18]

The phenomenal growth of the Catholic Church was
largely due to the flood of Catholic immigrants, first
from Ireland and Germany, and after 1890 notably from
Italy and Eastern Europe.

Blessed by a number of strong and capable leaders
(John England, Francis Patrick Kenrick, Martin Spalding,
John Hughes, James Gibbons and others), and fortified by
a rapidly expanding infrastructure and a solid
educational system, the church took full advantage of
the opportunities of American freedom and democracy.

That is not to say that the Catholic Church did
not face many difficulties: Like any religious organization, the Roman Catholic Church had its factions (often
along ethnic lines, such as Germans against Irish), its
disagreements over strategies (e.g. in the controversy
of parochial vs. public schools and related issues),

---

[17] For a review of the history of the Roman Catholic
Church during the second part of the 19th and the early
20th century, see Winthrop S. Hudson, Religion in
America, 224-244; James Hennesey, American Catholics,
158-203; Jay P. Dolan, The American Catholic Experience,
127-346; Thomas T. McAvoy, History of the Catholic
Church in the United States, 163-352.

[18] J.F. Regis Canevin, An Examination Historical and
Statistical into Losses and Gains of the Catholic Church
in the United States from 1790-1910 (Pittsburgh, PA,
1912), 8-12.

problems concerning the formulation of proper responses
to the social, political and economic problems of the
time, and its rivalries between more "conservative" and
more "liberal" leaders and thinkers.

Anti-Catholic sentiments on the part of many Protestants
continued to play an important role. Although not all
nativism was anti-Catholic, much of it was.[19] During the
Reconstruction, following the Civil War, earlier anti-
Catholic feelings receded into the background. But
Protestant misgivings about the Catholic insistence on
a separate Catholic school system, the Catholic attempts
to secure tax support for their institutions and the
success of Catholics in being elected to public office,
became increasingly strong in the 1870s and 1880s. The
presidential campaign of 1884 fuelled anti-Catholic
feelings, not only because the Republican candidate,
James G. Blaine, had a Catholic mother, but also because
one of the candidate's supporters labeled the Democrats
a party of "rum, Romanism and rebellion."
    A considerable amount of anti-Catholic propaganda
continued during the 1880s and 1890s, with the American
Protective Association (organized in 1887) as its most
vivid expression. When, during the "panic of 1893"
economic prospects were dim, the A.P.A. was able to
convince a large segment of the American population of
the advisability of placing limits on immigration. The
A.P.A. protested loudly against the arrival of apostolic
delegate Monsignor Satolli in 1893, believing that this
meant the beginning of full diplomatic ties with Rome.
After 1897 the A.P.A faded into near oblivion.[20]
    During the first decade of the 20th century, anti-
Catholicism remained largely dormant, to be revived
again after 1908 as an important element in a general
resurgence of nativism. Immigrants--among them hundreds
of thousands of Catholic Italians--were, after a relatively "quiet" period, once again arriving in record
numbers. This, of course, strengthened xenophobic re-
sentments. The significant increase in anti-Catholic
feelings must at least partly be explained in the con-

---

[19] See John Higham, <u>Strangers in the Land: Patterns
of American Nativism, 1860-1925</u> (New Brunswick, N.J.:
Rutgers Univ. Press, 1955), passim.

[20] Donald L. Kinzer, <u>An Episode in Anti-Catholicism:
The American Protective Association</u> (Seattle: Univ. of
Washington Press, 1964).

text of widespread fears that the foreign-born stood in the way of social improvements and as an outlet for frustrations of unfulfilled expectations about social and economic reform.[21] In part it was, no doubt, also a reaction against the publicity surrounding the first American Catholic Missionary Congress, held in 1908 in Chicago and the appointment of two additional American cardinals.[22] When the economy slid into recession in 1914, this inevitably strengthened anti-foreign, and thus also anti-Catholic, tendencies. But throughout the pre-war period and the war years the "no-Popery" tradition, though not lacking in propaganda outlets, never had the type of organization it acquired in the A.P.A. years.

III Continued Prophetic Interest

The groundwork for the Seventh-day Adventist interpretation of the prophecies of Daniel and the Revelation had been laid in the pre-1863 period. This was especially true for those prophecies which were seen as related to the past, present and future of Roman Catholicism and the apocalyptic *finale* of earth's history in which Catholicism, Protestantism and Spiritualism would form a tripartite, antichristian front against the Sabbath keeping remnant.

As indicated earlier, Uriah Smith not only had a decisive role in the development of Adventist prophetic interpretation in the early years of Sabbatarian Adventism, but became the unrivalled architect of Seventh-day Adventist views on prophecy. His *Thoughts, Critical and Practical on the Book of Daniel* and *Thoughts, Critical and Practical on the Book of Revelation* have been studied and distributed by Adventists from the moment they came off the press, and have remained in print even to the present day.[23] Some,

---

[21] John Higham, <u>Strangers in the Land</u>, 175-193.

[22] Clifton E. Olmstead, <u>History of Religion in the United States</u> (Englewood Cliffs, N.J.: Prentice Hall, 1960), 434-435.

[23] The first edition of <u>Thoughts, Critical and Practical, on the Revelation</u> was published in 1865 (Battle Creek, MI: Steam Press of the SDA Publ. Ass.).

at times, understood the strong endorsement of the prophet, Ellen G. White, as indication of a quasi-inspired status of this Adventist classic.[24] Such a view was not general, but another factor was clearly at work: in spite of the negative attitude among Adventists toward the development of a creed, there was the undeniable tendency to codify existing views. These soon acquired a certain aura of sacredness, that in turn hindered the development of a new and deepened understanding of various Bible subjects.[25]

1. Earlier Interpretations Re-affirmed

Seventh-day Adventists continued to operate with basically the same hermeneutical principles as had been employed by the Millerites and Sabbatarian Adventists. As a result the application of various prophecies in Daniel (chapters 7, 8, and 11) and the Revelation (chapters 12-14; 17-19) to the Roman Catholic Church remained virtually unchanged: the little horn of Daniel 7, the little horn of Daniel 8, the beast of Revelation

---

For some background to the origin of this book, see p. 81. Thoughts, Critical and Practical on the Book of Daniel followed in 1873 (Battle Creek, MI: Steam Press of the SDA Church), with a second, enlarged and revised edition in 1881. Soon afterwards the two books were bound together and became the first colporteur book among Adventists. The last edition which was revised by Smith himself appeared in 1897: Daniel and the Revelation; The Response of History to the Voice of Prophecy (Battle Creek, MI: Review and Herald Publ. Company). A major posthumous updating of the book occurred in 1912, without, however, altering any of the main theses of the book. For the history of the book, see Eugene F. Durand, Yours in the Blessed Hope, 215-224; and Ulf L. Gustavsson, "Aspects of the Development of Prophetic Interpretation within the Seventh-day Adventist Church," (Unpubl. M.A. thesis, Andrews Univ., 1981), 25-35. See also pp. 213-214.

[24] See Arthur L. White, "Thoughts on Daniel and the Revelation," mimeographed document publ. by the Ellen G. White Estate (Washington, DC, n.d.).

[25] Ulf Gustavsson, "Aspects of the Development of Prophetic Interpretation," 71.

13 and the whore of Revelation 17 were applied, as before, to the papacy.

Daniel's time prophecies of the 2300 days/years and the related sanctuary doctrine, and of the 1260 days/years of papal supremacy received prime attention, but those of the 1290 and 1335 days/years played an increasingly minor role.[26] Opinions differed as to what extent Rome was referred to in Daniel 11, but that chapter was not as vital to Adventist views as were chapters 2, 7, 8 and 9. The only real change in the interpretation of Daniel's prophecies were the allusions to recent events as added proofs of the correctness of earlier espoused views regarding the identification of the papacy as the antichristian power.[27]

More substantial are the developments in Smith's treatment of Revelation 13:11-17 which describes the actions of the two-horned beast. From 1851 onwards this power had been identified as the United States,[28] but events unfolding in the 1880s and 1890s gave this aspect of the study of the Revelation an enormous extra impulse.[29] In general, later treatments of the prophecies

---

[26] For a synthesis of Adventist prophetic views in the early 1860s, see Key to the Prophetic Chart (Battle Creek: Steam Press of the SDA Publ. Ass., 1864), which provided a brief explanation to the prophetic chart in use at that time by Adventist preachers.

[27] After 1870, the dogma of papal infallibility, became one of the startling examples of the "great words" of the little horn. See Uriah Smith, Thoughts on Daniel, 1873 ed., 146-147. More debate was occasioned by the "Eastern Question," which concerned the role of the Turks in the prophecies of the Revelation.

[28] R.F. Cottrell, "The Approaching Conflict," RH (July 15, 1884), 497. See pp. 129-131.

[29] In the later editions of Daniel and the Revelation the space allotted to the discussion of this passage grew from just a few pages to over one hundred. Smith also wrote a book dealing specifically with this subject: The United States in the Light of Prophecy, or, An Exposition of Revelation 13:11-17 (Battle Creek, MI: Steam Press of the SDA Publ. Ass., 1876), which, updated and enlarged, appeared subsequently as The Marvel of Nations - Our Country: Its Past, Present, and Future, and What the Scriptures Say of It (Battle Creek, MI:

of Daniel and the Revelation, though differing in
emphasis and tone, followed Smith's basic pattern.[30] That
is also true of the work of Louis R. Conradi, the first
important non-American Adventist author, though he
attempted to cite more European historical sources to
support his arguments.[31]

That the study of these prophecies remained a very
important aspect of Adventism can be seen from the
amount of space allotted to it in some publications
which tried to give an overview of all denominational
teachings,[32] and from the contents of the Sabbath School

Review and Herald Publ. Co., 1886). Uriah Smith's son,
Leon A. Smith (1863-1958), revised and again updated his
father's book and republished it under the title The
United States in Prophecy; Our Country: Its Past,
Present, and Future, and What the Scriptures Say of It
(Nashville, Tenn.: SPA, 1914). See also Uriah Smith,
"Rome and the United States," RH (Sept. 22, 1896), 605-
606.

[30] See e.g. W.H. Littlejohn, Rome in Prophecy
(Battle Creek: Review and Herald Publ. Co., 1898).
Littlejohn deviated from Smith in his interpretation of
the seven heads of Rev. 13:1 (27-41); S.N. Haskell, The
Story of Daniel the Prophet (Nashville, Tenn: SPA,
1903), which used much milder language than Smith in
referring to the Catholic Church; E.J. Waggoner,
Prophetic Lights: Some of the Prominent Prophecies of
the Old and New Testaments, Interpreted by the Bible and
History (Oakland, Cal.: PPPA, 1888).

[31] L.R. Conradi, Die Weissagung Daniels (Hamburg:
Internationale Traktatgesellschaft, 1901); L.R. Conradi,
Die Offenbarung Jesu Christi (Hamburg: Internationale
Traktatgesellschaft, 1903); L.R. Conradi, Der Seher von
Patmos (Hamburg: Internationale Traktatgesellschaft,
1906) - a revision of Die Offenbarung Jesu Christi.

[32] See Uriah Smith, Synopsis of the Present Truth,
which fails to mention such fundamental themes as the
Godhead, the nature of Christ, the atonement, etc., but
gives extensive attention to Daniel 7 and 8 and
Revelation 12, 13, 14, 17, 18, 20. Also Bible Readings
for the Home Circle (Battle Creek, MI: Review and Herald
Publ. Co., 1891). The first edition, which sold over
1.25 million copies, starts with a major section on
Daniel and has other sections on the implications of key

lessons which were studied by the members. Godloe H. Bell's *Progressive Bible Lessons* served as the main study guide until, in 1889, the Pacific Press Publishing Company began to print quarterly lesson pamphlets. Bell's study guide contains 195 lesson outlines, 74 of which are related to Daniel 7 and 8 and Revelation 12-14, 17 and 18.[33] Several of the quarterly lesson pamphlets after 1889 were exclusively devoted to the study of Daniel and the Revelation.[34]

2. The Healing of the Deadly Wound

Some details of the prophecies of John's Apocalypse which were seen as applying to Roman Catholicism continued to be debated. Opinion shifted as to the time of the healing of the deadly wound of the "papal beast" of Revelation 13. We noted in the previous chapter the tendency among Sabbatarian Adventists to emphasize the reduction in papal power. They agreed on the time when the wound was inflicted--1798, when the pope was taken prisoner--but remained uncertain about the time and the extent of the recovery--the healing--of the papacy.

A perusal of the *Review and Herald* in the period under review in the present chapter indicates that this uncertainty about a strong recovery of the papal power continues for about twenty more years. From time to time

---

prophecies, such as a full chapter on the National Reform Movement. After the 1914 revision (Bible Readings for the Home Circle, Washington, DC: RHPA, 1914) the topics in the book were arranged in a more logical order, with all prophetic material in one block, after the fundamentals of the gospel had been dealt with.

[33] Godloe H. Bell, Progressive Bible Lessons for Youth; to be Used in Sabbath Schools, Bible Classes, and Families (Battle Creek: Steam Press of the SDA Publ. Ass., 1877).

[34] The 2nd quarter of 1895 dealt with the book of Daniel. The theme for the fourth quarter of 1895 was religious liberty; these lessons made extensive use of the Revelation. The first quarter 1896 lesson pamphlet dealt with "the great threefold message of Revelation fourteen". The first and the third quarter of 1904 respectively were devoted to a study of the book of Daniel and a study of the Revelation.

reference was still made to the 1840 encyclical "Probe Nostis" as proof of the pope's realization of the curtailment of his influence.[35]

Numerous articles and short news items (usually clippings from other journals, both European and American) were devoted to the political upheavals in Italy, detailing the support of Napoleon III for the pope in his efforts to retain at least part of the Papal States and the Italian process of unification which at last resulted in the pope's loss of Rome and his self-inflicted imprisonment in the Vatican. "His [the pope's] race is run, his end is at hand," writes D.M. Canright, before quoting with clear satisfaction from a Catholic journal: "[He is] deserted by all the great powers of the earth, robbed of the patrimony of St. Peter...."[36] Shortly afterwards the church's official journal quoted from another source which described the pope as having become "a mere curiosity.... The pope and his phantom is being tolerated, and quietly stultified by being tolerated."[37]

It was clear to Adventist opinion leaders of the time--with their narrow focus on the loss of temporal power--that the pope was "in extremis."[38] Confirmation of that was seen in Pius IX's encyclical of October 17, 1867, in which he speaks of his "calamities and sorrows."[39] When reporting the success of Bible distribution in Rome, it was remarked that "surely something has happened to the pope's power" when such a thing can take place.[40] In several European countries, notably Italy and

---

[35] See e.g. James White, "Our Faith and Hope; or, Reasons why we Believe as we Do," RH (Feb. 8, 1870), 51.

[36] D. M. Canright, "Men and Things," RH (Feb. 27, 1872), 85.

[37] "The Pope and Europe," RH (Apr. 9, 1872), 133.

[38] "The Pope in Extremis," RH (Sept. 6, 1870), 91. The words were quoted from a Baptist journal.

[39] "The Pope's Lamentations," RH (Nov. 26, 1867), 382. For a text of the encyclical "Levate," see Claudia Carlen, The Papal Encyclicals: 1740-1878, 389-391.

[40] "The Bible in Rome," RH (Jan. 31, 1871), 49; "The Bible in Rome," RH (Sept. 26, 1871), 115.

Austria, but also in Bismarck's Prussia and in Spain, papal power was eroding fast.[41]

But in the 1880s a significant change in the Adventist estimation of papal strength (or the lack thereof) was taking place. Although an 1885 editorial in the *Review and Herald* pointed to the election of a new pope (Pius VII), in 1800, as the precise moment of the "healing of the deadly wound,"[42] majority opinion seemed to favour the concept of a gradual healing which was now becoming visible. The most conspicuous proof of this healing process was the numerical increase of Catholics in the United States, where by now one in six citizens was a Catholic.[43] And although in Adventist perception Leo XIII's bull proclaiming a Holy Year and Jubilee from Christmas 1889 to Christmas 1890 offered little more than an encouragement to lament the present state of the papacy and to long for "the restoration of the civil power, the lack of which the papacy unceasingly bewails," the "present growth of papal prestige,"[44] both

---

[41] "The Pope and the Roman Catholic Monarchs," RH (Nov. 5, 1867), 326; "Temporal Power of the Pope," RH (July 28, 1868), 94; "The Pope's Troubles," RH (Nov. 10, 1868), 238-239; "Another Blow at the Papacy," RH (Dec. 1, 1868), 262-262; "Decline of the Romish Church in Europe," RH (June 6, 1871), 198; "Bismarck and the Pope," RH (March 10, 1874), 99; J.N. Loughborough, "Temporal Power of the Papacy--Italian and other Testimony," RH (March 24, 1874), 118-119.

[42] "The Deadly Wound--When was it Healed?" RH (June 30, 1885), 408. A. Smith, "The Ten-Horned Beast of Revelation 13:1-10," RH (Jan. 24, 1888), 51, quotes Dr Clarke's words [no exact source given] about the healing of the deadly wound in 1800, "which now appears to be healed, but it is skinned over, and a dreadful ciatrice remains."

[43] W.C. Gage, "His Deadly Wound Was Healed," RH (Dec. 5, 1882), 762. See also Stephen N. Haskell, The Story of the Seer of Patmos (Nashville, Tenn.: SPA, 1905; 1977 facs. reprod.), 240-241.

[44] L.A. Smith, "Growth of Papal Prestige," RH (Sept. 18, 1888), 601.

in the United States[45] as in Europe,[46] "tended to
strengthen the feeling that Rome would again have spiritual dominion over the whole world," even though "the
hour of Rome's triumph will mark the time of her
overthrow."[47]

At times the *Review and Herald* editor would
continue to utter his delight that the pope no longer
"could hurl his anathemas over Europe and bring down the
proudest monarch in abject servility," and suggest that
"the wails that have been issuing with such delightful
frequency of late from the Vatican are the best commentary on the fulfillment of prophecy."[48] But such an
occasional low estimate of papal authority was by far
outweighed by reports of increasing strength of Catholicism.[49] R.F. Cottrell summarized Adventist feelings
regarding the resurgence of Catholic power as follows:

---

[45] For the growing influence of Catholicism in the
United States, see pp. 131-133; 166-174.

[46] L.A. Smith, "Growth of Papal Prestige," RH (Sept.
18, 1888), 601; J.H. Durland, "The Coming Struggle for
Supremacy," RH (Dec. 14, 1886), 770; (Dec. 21, 1886),
786; H.P. Holser, "Papists and Protestants in Europe,"
RH (Sept. 2, 1890), 533; J.H. Durland, "England and
Catholicism," RH (Jan. 21, 1890), 34; (Jan. 28, 1890),
50; (Feb. 4, 1890), 67; L.A. Smith, "Increasing Power of
the Papacy," RH (March 24, 1903), 5. The most perceptive
account of underlying (ultramontane) trends is probably
John Vuilleumier, "The Coming Crisis in Europe," RH
(July 16, 1889), 450-451; (July 23, 1889), 467-468.

[47] W.W. Prescott, "Roman Optimism," RH (Feb. 8,
1912), 8.

[48] "Not As It Once Was," RH (Nov. 17, 1891), 712.

[49] Repeatedly articles in the RH refer to the
splendour surrounding the papal jubilee in 1887; see
e.g. L.A. Smith, "The Pope's Jubilee," RH (May 24,
1887), 336; and L.A. Smith, "The Pope's Jubilee," RH
(June 7, 1887), 368. The same point was stressed in
connection with the 1910 prestigious 21st International
Eucharistic Congress, held in Montreal, Canada, to which
the Review and Herald sent a special reporter; see C.M.
Snow, "The Roman Catholic International Eucharistic
Congress," RH (Sept. 29, 1910), 12-14; (Oct. 6, 1910),
6-8.

Almost every week presents new features of the
fulfillment of the prophecy of Revelation 13, "All
the world wondered after the beast," and
"worshipped the beast."[50]

W.W. Prescott, in 1912, echoed the same sentiment:

The student of prophecy recognizes that the
rehabilitation of the Papacy in the last
generation is one of the signs indicating the
nearness of the coming of Him whose right it is to
reign, and foreshadowing the utter overthrow of
the kingdom of the Antichrist.[51]

3. Babylon

A few paragraphs must again be devoted to the concept of
Babylon. The traditional view, held by the Millerites
and their Sabbatarian successors, continued to be
underlined: Babylon consisted of "the Roman Catholic
Church and the apostate Protestant churches which have
descended from her, as so many daughters from a common
mother."[52] The "great sisterhood of the churches" had, as
Butler expressed it in 1887, been "properly represented
by the name Babylon."[53] The mere existence of several
hundred denominations in the land, all professing to

---

[50] R.F. Cottrell, "Keep Your Eyes Turned Toward
Rome!" RH (July 23, 1895), 472.

[51] W.W. Prescott, "The Empty Boast of the Roman
Catholic Church," RH (Jan. 25, 1912), 10. The same
sentiment is found in L.R. Conradi, Die Offenbarung Jesu
Christi, 329-332; and Conradi, Der Seher von Patmos,
337-345.

[52] R.M. Kilgore, "Babylon," RH (Sept. 17, 1895),
595. See also J.N. Andrews, The Three Messages of
Revelation XIV, 6-12 (Battle Creek, MI: Steam Press of
the SDA Publ. Ass., 1864), 46-60; and various later
editions; L.R. Conradi, Der Seher von Patmos, 435-438;
George I. Butler, "Babylon and Its Fall," RH (Feb. 11,
1909), 9-10; Stephen N. Haskell, The Story of the Seer
of Patmos, 300-309.

[53] George I. Butler, "Fall of Babylon," RH, extra
issue (Nov. 22, 1887), 9.

take the Bible as the foundation of their faith, yet each one condemning all the rest, shows a state of Babylonian confusion. In view of such confusion "it can be truthfully said, 'Babylon is fallen.'"[54]

The Protestant failure in the 1840s to accept the Millerite message of an imminent pre-millennial Advent was still viewed as the deciding moment in Babylon's fall,[55] but that fall was clearly progressive, with such trends as Darwinism, "modern spiritualism", and the departure into the realm of politics--to promote a union of church and state and further Sunday legislation--added to earlier apostate beliefs and practices.[56] The fall of Babylon not only showed clear parallels with the apostasy of "the Jewish church" at the time of the first Advent, when it rejected the "present truth" of that time,[57] but the flirtations of Protestantism with Spiritualism, infidelity, socialism, free-love, trade union activities, and even communism, also presented striking similarities with trends that led to the French Revolution. And these same causes would, it was believed, soon lead to similar results and "culminate in a state of anarchy, and a reign of terror much more

---

[54] SSQ, 2nd quarter, 1893, 32.

[55] George I. Butler, "Has There Been a Moral Fall of the Churches?" RH (Dec. 15, 1891), 776; George I. Butler, "The Causes Which Led to the Fall of Babylon," RH (March 4, 1909), 9-10.

[56] George I. Butler, "Interesting Facts Concerning Babylon's Fall," RH (Apr. 1, 1909), 9-10. In an earlier article, Butler noted that "A fall is a downward process. There is a beginning and an ending to it always. That process is accelerated the longer it continues. It becomes more and more marked," with an increased openness toward Rome as one of the factors giving the downward process a gathering momentum - George I. Butler, "Has There Been a Moral Fall of the Churches?" cont., RH (Dec. 22, 1891), 792.

[57] D. Hildreth, "Babylon is Fallen," RH (June 30, 1863), 35; George I. Butler, "Has There Been a Moral Fall of the Churches?" RH (Dec. 15, 1891), 777. SSQ, 1st quarter 1896, 35.

frightful than the French Revolution."[58] Yet, at the same time, some care was exercised not to be too strong in condemning all Protestants. The complete fulfillment of the prophecy of Babylon's fall was still future: It "will be reached through some movement which will draw the world into the Babylonian church, until every mark of distinction between it and the world shall be obliterated."[59] Such a situation had not yet been reached. The churches were still doing positive things in foreign missions, Bible translation and distribution, temperance promotion and charitable works.[60] The trend of Protestantism, however, was "away from God's truth toward worldliness, pride, etc." Nevertheless, Babylon's fall was not to be interpreted as "the total rejection" by God of every person who is a member of such churches, so that none belonging to them can be saved."[61] There were "multitudes of excellent, devoted, noble-hearted Christians among them who are living up to all the light they have, and are mourning over the sad state of the churches in the various communions of the Protestant world...."[62]

4. The Number of the Beast

Toward the end of the 1860s Adventists began to feel more sure about the meaning of the enigmatic number 666, which Revelation 13:18 affixes to the beast. In 1866 the editor of the *Review and Herald*, instead of trying to provide some explanation for this cryptic verse of Scripture, stated as his opinion that it was still unclear what is meant, but that future developments

----

[58] Uriah Smith, <u>The United States in the Light of Prophecy</u>, 108-109.

[59] L.A. Smith, "Babylon's Fall; and the Church's Purification," <u>RH</u> (Nov. 12, 1901), 737.

[60] George I. Butler, "Has There Been a Moral Fall of the Churches?" <u>RH</u> (Dec. 15, 1891), 776

[61] Ibid.

[62] George I. Butler, "Fall of Babylon," <u>RH</u> (Nov. 22, 1887), 10.

would no doubt clear this issue up.[63] Just a few years later, however, Uriah Smith tentatively suggested an explanation which soon became the standard Adventist view on the matter. Commenting on the views of H.E. Carver, another writer on the prophecies of the Revelation, Smith rejected the suggestion that the supposed (Greek) numerical value of the word "Lateinos" (an epithet given by some commentators to the Roman Catholic Church) of 666, is the true solution. He then stated that "the most plausible" term with a numerical value of 666--which provides an added identification of the beast as the papacy--is one of the titles of the pope: "Vicarius Filii Dei."[64] As supporting evidence for this statement he referred to a book published in 1832, of which he furnished the title ("The Reformation"), but not the author. This book allegedly reported someone's visit to Rome during which that visitor saw this title on the front of the pope's mitre.[65]

Smith continued to express himself somewhat guardedly on the subject. He wrote in 1872 that "the pope wears upon his pontifical crown in jeweled letters, this title; 'Vicarius Filii Dei,' 'Vicegerent of the Son of God'; the numerical value of which title is just six hundred and sixty six." Smith found it "the most plausible supposition we have ever seen on this point," that "we here find the number in question."[66] In another article on the subject he employed the word "probably"

---

[63] "The Visions--Objections Answered," RH (July 31, 1866), 65.

[64] There are a few earlier non-Adventist applications of the number 666 to "Vicarius Filii Dei" in: Prophetic Conjectures on the French Revolution (anonymous), originally published in 1747 and reprinted in part in Philadelphia (William Young, 1794); Amzi Armstrong, A Syllabus of Lectures on the Visions of the Revelation (Morris-town, N.J.: P.A. Johnson, 1815); Richard Shimeall, Age of the World (New York: Swords, Stanford & Co, 1842). See Leroy E. Froom, PFOF, vol. IV, 112, 197, 372.

[65] Uriah Smith, "The Two-Horned Beast--A Review of H.E. Carver," RH (Nov. 20, 1868), 196.

[66] Uriah Smith, "The United States in the Light of Prophecy," RH (Feb. 13, 1872), 68.

when tying "Vicarius Filii Dei" to the 666 number.[67]

In his column "In the Question Chair" Uriah Smith repeatedly answered questions about the validity of what was becoming the standard view on 666. He continued to refer to the 1832 work "The Reformation" as his source and quoted from it as follows:

> The following extract on this point is from the work entitled "The Reformation," bearing the date of 1832:-
> 'Mrs. A., said Miss. Emmons, I saw a very curious fact the other day; I have dwelt upon it much and I will mention it. A person, lately, was witnessing a ceremony of the Romish church. As the Pope passed him in the procession, splendidly dressed in his pontifical robes, the gentleman's eye rested on these full, blazing letters in front of his miter: "VICARIOUS [sic] FILII DEI," the Vicar of the Son of God." His thoughts with the rapidity of lightning, reverted to Rev. xiii:18. Will you turn to it? said Mrs. A. Alice opened the New Testament and read: 'Let him that hath understanding count the number of the beast; for it is the number of a man; and his number is six hundred three score and six.' She paused, and Miss Emmons said, He took out his pencil, and, marking the numerical letters of the inscription on his tablet, it stood 666.[68]

Smith asserted he had no reason to doubt the accuracy of the information given in that work, but admitted that it may have been a particular pope who at a particular occasion wore a crown with the "Vicarius Filii Dei" title. He argued, however, that this was not

---

[67] Uriah Smith, "Vicarius Filii Dei," RH (May 13, 1875), 157. Cf. his Thoughts on Revelation (1875), 240, where he uses the words "most plausible" in this connection. In his book on the United States in prophecy of 1876 and its later expanded version of 1886, he affirms again that this view is "the most plausible supposition we have ever seen on this point." See Uriah Smith, The United States in the Light of Prophecy, 198; and Uriah Smith, The Marvel of Nations, 266-267; cf. L.A. Smith, The United States in Prophecy, 294.

[68] Uriah Smith, Thoughts on Revelation, 1865 ed., 225-226.

the most important thing: what counted was the well-established fact that the pope does claim to be the Vicar of Christ, and translated into Latin the term Vicarius Filii Dei--which has a numerical value of exactly 666--is a faithful rendering.[69]

J.N. Andrews, in his exposition on "the three angels of Revelation 14:6-12," remained silent on the meaning of the number of the beast until 1877. In the revised edition which appeared in that year a few lines referred to the title of "Vicar of the Son of God ... which the pope had caused to be inscribed upon his mitre." When written in Latin, Andrews added, "the numerical letters employed make the sum of 666."[70] Some other Adventist writers concurred with that conclusion.[71]

There are indications of some uneasiness regarding the scanty witness upon which the assumption of the presence of this title upon the papal tiara rested. This might possibly be the reason why the popular and voluminous *Bible Readings for the Home Circle*, which contained large sections on the denomination's prophetic views, remained completely silent on the subject of 666.

In their quest for more information on the words on the papal crown, two contributors to the *Review and Herald*, writing in 1905 and 1906 respectively, came to rather different conclusions. Chas. T. Everson, who was writing from Rome, informed the readers about his attempts to get a close look at the papal tiara and about his secret arrangements with personnel of the Vatican to see the crown for himself and to acquire photographs (at the request of W.W. Prescott, at that time the editor of the *Review and Herald*[72]). He

---

[69] Uriah Smith, "In the Question Chair," RH (Jan. 19, 1897), 42; Uriah Smith, "In the Question Chair," RH (March 2, 1897), 135; Uriah Smith, "In the Question Chair: Motto on the Pope's Tiara," RH (July 23, 1901), 475.

[70] J.N. Andrews, The Three Messages of Revelation XIV, 6-12, 109.

[71] E.g. A. Delos Westcott, "What Sunday-Keeping Really Means," AS (Sept. 21, 1894), 301.

[72] "The Triple Crown," PM, vol. 2, no. 1 (1st quarter 1910), 3; G.M. Valentine, "William Warren Prescott: Seventh-day Adventist Educator" (Ph.D. diss., Andrews Univ., 1982), 601. See also below, pp. 226-231.

succeeded, but to his disappointment found no such inscription. He remarked that it is unknown whether earlier tiaras had the words "Vicarius Filii Dei" on them, since they were taken by Napoleon, but he was convinced that the one worn since 1836 did not have the inscription. He believed that the Adventist application of 666 was nevertheless valid, because the pope, after all, does claim to be the Vicar of Christ, "but to be perfectly correct in our statements, we cannot say that there is an inscription of this nature on the tiara at present."[73] D.E. Scoles, on the contrary, claimed he had met two persons who had actually seen the words "Vicarius Filii Dei" on the papal crown. A former Catholic priest, who had become a Sabbath keeper, repeatedly saw the tiara in the Vatican Museum and remembered the arrangement of the phrase with the word "Dei" made of diamonds. A Presbyterian minister, who at one time studied for the priesthood in Rome, provided a written affidavit, stating that in 1845 during an Easter service he had seen Gregory XVI wearing a triple crown with the words "Vicarius Filii Dei."[74]

In spite of the historical uncertainty surrounding the issue, the "Vicarius Filii Dei"-666 connection became a popular feature in Adventist lectures and popular literature about the antichristian nature of Catholicism.[75] Even the 1912 edition of the more scholarly work of J.N. Andrews, *History of the Sabbath*, mentioned it without any documentary evidence.[76]

---

[73] Chas. T. Everson, "The Inscription on the Pope's Tiara," RH (July 27, 1905), 10-11.

[74] D.E. Scoles, "The Pope's Crown," RH (Dec. 20, 1906), 10.

[75] See e.g. J.J. Kennedy, Catholic Doctrine: How I Found the Faith (Oakland, Cal.: Pacific Press Publishing Co., 1902), 7; L.R. Conradi, Die Offenbarung Jesus Christi, 401-402; L.R. Conradi, Der Seher von Patmos, 409-411; Stephen N. Haskell, The Story of the Seer of Patmos, 243-244.

[76] This addition was the work of L. R. Conradi, the editor of the 1912 posthumous edition. See J.N. Andrews and L.R. Conradi, History of the Sabbath and First Day of the Week (Washington, DC: RHPA, 1912), 801.

5. Catholic Doctrine: Paganism in Disguise

Adventist writers of the period under review were more interested in the temporal power of the Catholic Church in the past and its political designs for the present and the future than in a careful analysis of Catholic doctrine. But a number of doctrinal aspects did receive regular attention.

Underlying the Adventist assessment of Catholic faith and practice was the assumption that Catholicism was "simply paganism re-christened and called Christian," and that all the leading features of the Roman Catholic ritual were "copied pure and simple from the forms of ancient heathen worship."[77] This made it quite understandable that Rev. Alexander Hislop's book, *The Two Babylons*, in which the author "sets forth the similarity of [sic] Papal Worship and that which was instituted by Nimrod and his wife," was advertised in the Adventist church paper.[78]

The antiquity of the Roman Church was far from a guarantee for purity of doctrine. One author found at least 36 major deviations from authentic apostolic belief.[79] The early church fathers

> ... were at best but half Christian, whatever their intentions may have been, for they drank from the muddy pool of the heathen philosophy instead of a pure fountain of divine revelation;

---

[77] Uriah Smith, "Catholic Ceremonies of Heathen Origin," RH (Apr. 3, 1888), 216; see also J.N. Loughborough, "Similarity of Paganism and Papacy," RH (Apr. 14, 1874), 142-143.

[78] RH (June 19, 1900), 303. See Alexander Hislop, The Two Babylons, or the Papal Worship Proved to Be the Worship of Nimrod and his Wife, (first published in 1858; recent photostatic edition: Neptune, N.J.: Loizeau Brothers, Inc., 1959).

[79] T.R. Williamson, "The First Church - Can the Roman Catholic Church Rightfully Claim that Designation?" RH (Nov. 29, 1887), 743.

and their effort was to assimilate Christianity and pagan philosophy.[80]

The veil of sanctity which had been thrown over the early church, needed to be removed, in order that the origins of the papacy might be laid bare, "which was built on the foundation of the so-called Fathers."[81]

Catholics were accused of great superstition;[82] of exploiting the credulity of the masses by plain deception;[83] and of gross commercialism in their practice of saying Mass for the departed.[84] The Catholic Church was further criticized for its provisions for doing penance[85] and selling indulgences;[86] its veneration of

---

[80] E.J. Waggoner, Prophetic Lights, 95. For some time the doctrine of the Trinity continued to be viewed as an amalgamation of Bible truth and pagan philosophy. See e.g. R.F. Cottrell, "The Doctrine of the Trinity," RH (June 1, 1869), 180-181. The anti-Trinitarian views would gradually disappear as the century wore on. See below, p. 205.

[81] E.J. Waggoner, Fathers of the Catholic Church: A Brief Examination of the "Falling Away" of the Church in the First three Centuries (Oakland, Cal.: Pacific Press Publishing Company, 1888), iii; see esp. 57-73; 242-346.

[82] Ibid., passim.

[83] Such as hiding a small water reservoir in a statue that was supposed to shed miraculous tears – "Miracle of the Romish Church," RH (Nov. 20, 1868), 199.

[84] Uriah Smith, "A Timely Truth," RH (Jan. 2, 1894), 8; J.N. Loughborough, "Purgatory and Mass," RH (May 26, 1874), 191; (June 2, 1874), 199; M.E. Kellogg, "Salvation by Works," RH (June 8, 1897), 361-362.

[85] S.N. Haskell, "Penance," RH (Aug. 20, 1895), 538.

[86] E.J. Waggoner, Prophetic Lights, 96-97; M.E. Kellogg, "Prayers and Purgatory," RH (May 2, 1893), 279; "Catholic Total Abstinence Union," RH (June 14, 1887), 384.

saints[87] and relics;[88] its image worship;[89] and its management of pilgrim resorts like Lourdes.[90] Charges of Mariolatry[91] and of putting tradition above the Bible were also regularly made,[92] while Catholic claims about the Mass "were blasphemous arrogant assumptions."[93] To suggest that an other sacrifice than Calvary is necessary, is in fact a repudiation of Christ's sacrifice and overturns the entire plan of redemption.[94]

6. The Immortality of the Soul

The themes which continued to receive most criticism, however, were the doctrine of the immortality of the soul, the change from Sabbath to Sunday, and, after

---

[87] J.N. Loughborough, "Invocation of the Saints and Exaltation of Mary," RH (May 12, 1874), 175.

[88] A. Kuntz, "Roman Catholic Pilgrim Resort," RH (Sept. 1, 1891), 551.

[89] See a series of articles by A.T. Jones on "The Keeping of the Commandments--The Second Commandment," RH (Apr. 2, 1990), 216; (Apr. 9, 1890), 223; (Apr. 16, 1890), 249-250; (Apr. 23, 1890), 265-266. See also "Ancient and Modern Idolatry," RH (Oct. 21, 1902), 24; ed. note, RH (Oct. 17, 1907), 6.

[90] A. Kuntz, "Roman Catholic Pilgrim Resort," RH (Sept. 1, 1891), 551.

[91] "The Worship of the Virgin," RH (Feb. 28, 1871), 81; "Papal Infallibility and Mariolatry," RH (Aug. 29, 1871), 82; Uriah Smith, "A Timely Truth," RH (Jan. 2, 1894), 8; L.D. Santee, "The Worship of the Virgin Mary," RH (June 29, 1897), 403; M.E. Kellogg, "Idolatry," RH (June 11, 1901), 377.

[92] J.N. Loughborough, "Papal and Protestant Bible," RH (Apr. 28, 1874), 159.

[93] "The Mystery of Iniquity," RH (May 24, 1870), 182.

[94] C.M. Snow, "Rome's Substitute for Christ," PM, vol. 1, no. 1 (2nd quarter 1909), 36-41.

1870, the claim of papal infallibility.

The Roman Church, it was maintained, had received the doctrine of the immortality of the soul, with the related concepts of purgatory and eternal misery, from the Greeks, as "is evident from the perfect similarity between the two systems."[95] This may be traced back even further: The idea of an immortal soul was first found in Egypt, from where it was brought by Greek philosophers (Anaxagoras, Socrates, and Plato) into Europe. Through the Alexandrian school of philosophy it was introduced in Rome, and via Neoplatonism it found its way into the church.[96]

The Apostolic Fathers and other early authorities were completely silent on the issue of the immortal soul.[97] It was the emergence of Origen's allegorical method of Bible interpretation which helped to reconcile this pagan philosophy with the Bible. The end result was, that from about the close of the third century, "the work of apostasy had become so far advanced, that the doctrine of the immortality of the soul was generally entertained in Christendom, and so remained till the great reformation of the sixteenth century."[98]

Acceptance of the concept of the immortality of the soul led to "all that host of heathen superstitions, holydays, feasts, ceremonies, &tc., &tc., which now

---

[95] Dudley M. Canright, "Origin of the Doctrine of the Immortality of the Soul and Eternal Misery," RH (Dec. 8, 1863), 9.

[96] Dudley M. Canright, History of the Doctrine of the Immortality of the Soul (Battle Creek, MI: Steam Press of the SDA Publ. Ass., 1871), passim.

[97] Uriah Smith, Here and Hereafter (Battle Creek, MI: RHPA, 1897), 322. D.M. Canright makes the same point, but apparently recognizes the inconsistency of appealing to the early fathers when they seem to support a particular Adventist viewpoint, while questioning or even denying their authenticity when they show support for early Christian Sunday worship. In a footnote he acknowledges that some doubt the value of these sources, so that their silence on the topic must be taken for what it is worth (History of the Doctrine of the Immortality of the Soul, 122).

[98] Uriah Smith, Here and Hereafter, 322-323.

exist in the Roman Catholic Church."[99] And, most notably, it prepared the way for Spiritualism.[100]

7. Sabbath vs. Sunday

The Adventist understanding of the Roman Church as the decisive agent in the change from Sabbath to Sunday, as suggested by Joseph Bates and developed by J.N. Andrews in his articles in the 1850s and early 1860s and in the 1862 ed. edition of his *History of the Sabbath and First Day of the Week*, remained the unchallenged position throughout the period under review in this chapter.[101] One significant change may, however, be noted in the 1912 edition of Andrews' work by his revisor Louis R. Conradi, who placed strong emphasis on the role of Gnosticism as an early factor in the antinomian spirit in the Roman Church, which contributed to the growing

---

[99] D.M. Canright, "Origin of the Doctrine of the Immortality of the Soul and Eternal Misery," concl., RH (Dec. 15, 1863), 21.

[100] Ibid., 22. See also Uriah Smith, "A Timely Truth," RH (Jan. 2, 1894), 8; A.T. Jones, "Which is the More So?" RH (Oct. 12, 1897), 647.
See also the chapter "The Adventists and the Roman Catholic Church" in C.F.X. Rubencamp, "Immortality and Seventh-day Adventist Eschatology," pp. 232-243. Cf. above, p. 112.

[101] Andrews summarized his position in "Causes Which Elevated the Sunday," RH (Feb. 3, 1874), 60. He continued to improve his main work on the Sabbath; see J.N. Andrews, History of the Sabbath and First Day of the Week (Battle Creek, MI: Steam Press of the SDA Publ. Ass., 1873); J.N. Andrews, History of the Sabbath and First Day of the Week (Battle Creek, MI: Review and Herald Publ. Ass., 1887). The relevant patristic evidence was published as a separate publication: J.N. Andrews, The Complete Testimony of the Fathers of the First Three Centuries Concerning the Sabbath and First Day (Battle Creek, MI: Steam Press of the SDA Publ. Ass., 1876). For a discussion of Andrews' views, see pp. 101-106.

disrespect for the Sabbath.[102] Other authors who contributed articles or wrote tracts on the subject basically followed the established pattern.[103]

The sources to which Adventist authors appealed in the pre-1863 era as proof that Rome accepted the responsibility for introducing the Sunday and discontinuing Sabbath observance, remained popular elements in Adventist apologetics. They continued to quote Butler's *Catholic Catechism of Christian Religion*, Tuberville's *Abridgment of Catholic Doctrine*, Challoner's *The Catholic Christian Instructed*, Keenan's *Doctrinal Catechism*, Millner's *The End of Religious Controversy*, and the *Treatise of Thirty Controversies*, even though most of these were written or introduced into the United States early in the 19th century. An additional, frequently quoted, source in which the same point of Rome's initiative in the Sabbath-Sunday change was made, was an article by W. Lockart of Oxford, Toronto in the journal *Mirror*.[104] It was only later that

---

[102] J.N. Andrews and L.R. Conradi, The History of the sabbath and First Day of the Week (Washington, DC: RHPA, 1912), 226-233; 452-472. This emphasis on the role of Gnosticism is not yet present in Conradi's earlier adaptation of the book in German: J.N. Andrews and L.R. Conradi, Die Geschichte des Sabbats und des Ersten Wochentages (Basel: Internationale Tratat-Gesellschaft, 1891).

[103] See e.g. Uriah Smith, "Sunday Keeping--Is it of Rome?" RH (Sept. 22, 1874), 108, which declared the Sunday to be "wholly a Romish institution"; D.T. Bourdeau, "How the Sabbath was Changed," RH (June 10, 1873), 201-202 (he acknowledged in a footnote his direct dependence on Andrews for his historical facts); W.H. Littlejohn, The Coming Conflict: Or, The United States Becoming a Persecuting Power, 307-310.

[104] For bibliographical details for these various sources, see. pp. 108-109. Precise bibliographical information on the article by Lockart is not available.
For some occasions where these sources are referred to, see Moses Hull, "The Mark of the Beast, and the Seal of the Living God," RH (Sept. 29, 1863), 137-138; Albert Stone, "Authority for Sunday-Keeping," RH (March 10, 1874), 99; Godloe H. Bell, Progressive Bible Lessons, 271-273; U. Smith, Thoughts on Revelation, 1865 ed., 273; Littlejohn, W.H., The Coming Conflict, 307-

a similar statement from Cardinal Gibbons' popular *Faith of Our Fathers*, though already published in 1876, was added to the stock quotations on the Sabbath-Sunday change:[105]

> Is not the observance of this law [to sanctify Sunday] among the most prominent of our sacred duties? But you may read the Bible from Genesis to Revelation, and you will not find a single line authorizing the sanctification of Sunday. The Scriptures enforce the religious observance of Saturday, a day which we never sanctify.[106]

Later in the chapter we shall discuss how toward the end of the century the Adventist emphasis on Rome's involvement with the beginnings of the Sabbath-Sunday controversy began, at least partly, to be eclipsed by a concern about Rome's present and future role in universal Sunday legislation.

310; George I. Butler, <u>The Change of the Sabbath: Was It by Divine or Human Authority?</u> (Battle Creek, MI: Review and Herald Publ. Co., 1889), 166-173; E.J. Waggoner, <u>Prophetic Lights</u>, 93; <u>Bible Readings for the Home Circle</u>, 1891 ed., 49, 63, 130, 241, 403; 1914 ed., 441, 449-450; Uriah Smith, <u>The United States in Prophecy</u>, 145-147; L.A. Smith, <u>The United States in Prophecy</u>, 218-222.

Rubencamp aptly commented on the tendency, still present in contemporary Adventism, to use a limited number of selective quotes from old sources, when criticizing Catholicism; see his dissertation "Immortality and Seventh-day Adventist Eschatology," 236-237.

[105] For example: The 1914 edition <u>Bible Readings</u> referred to Gibbons' book, whereas the 1891 edition did not. See <u>Bible Readings</u>, 1914 ed., 441. The 1912 ed. of <u>HOS</u> for the first time included the particular statement (245).

[106] Gibbons' <u>Faith of Our Fathers</u> went through numerous editions. For this study the 1885 and 1896 editions (both published in Baltimore by John Murphy & Company) were consulted. In both editions the statement is found on p. 111.

8. Papal Infallibility

The events surrounding the proclamation of the teaching of papal infallibility during Vaticanum I were keenly followed. Adventist publications were certainly not alone in condemning the ultramontane tendencies of the papacy and in their severe criticism of the Dogmatic Constitution on the Church of Christ, promulgated during Vaticanum I, in which the concept of papal infallibility was embedded.[107] In fact, much of their reporting of the Council and their commenting on its significance was in the form of lengthy quotations from other journals. One such *Review and Herald* article underlined the prevailing opinion that Vaticanum I was the "greatest and most notable of all ... remarkable events" of the decade: "... very great and important results are destined to flow from this gathering of Catholic dignitaries-- results affecting the status and welfare of millions, and closely related to the near coming of our Lord...."[108]

As early as 1867 the pope's intentions of convening a general council were known and viewed with the utmost suspicion.[109] When the council was under way and the matter of infallibility was discussed, the minority position of the opponents of papal infal-

---

[107] See J. Ryan Beiser, The Vatican Council and the American Secular Newspapers, 1869-70 (Washington, DC: The Catholic Univ. of America Press, 1941), passim, but esp. 12, 17, 298, 299.

For a detailed account of the proceedings at the First Vatican Council from an American Catholic perspective, see James Hennesey, The First Council of the Vatican: The American Experience (New York: Herder and Herder, 1963).

For the text of the First Dogmatic Constitution, "Pastor aeternus," on the Church of Christ, see John F. Broderick, Documents of the Vatican Council I, 1869-1870 (Collegeville, Minn.: The Liturgical Press, 1971), 53-63.

[108] "Remarkable Events During the Past Nine Years," RH (Feb. 15, 1870), 63.

[109] "Convocation of a General Council at Rome," RH (Jan. 2, 1867), 81. "The General Councils of the Romish Church," RH (Oct. 1, 1867), 246-247.

libility naturally received greater attention than that of the supporting majority.[110] G. Strossmayer, the bishop of Bosnia, and I. Dollinger, a professor from Munich, were the heroes of the story, because of their strong opposition against the intended proclamation of papal infallibility.[111] The reporting of the public announcement of the disputed dogma was not without a sense for the dramatic:

> He [the pope] had so arranged the time and the throne on which he was to sit that the sun at that particular moment would shine through a concealed window, throwing its rays on his head, thus leading the people to believe that Heaven approved the doctrine, but lo! when the vast congregation assembled, and the hour had arrived for the annunciation dark clouds obscured the sun, loud thunders rolled above the Vatican, the rain fell in torrents, and a vivid flash of lightning struck and shattered to pieces the very window through which the divine light was expected to stream ....[112]

Looking back on the events of 1870, S.N. Haskell in his book *The Story of Daniel the Prophet*--which on the whole is very low-key in its accusations addressed at Rome--in commenting on the "great words" spoken by the little horn of Daniel 7, states what by then had become a firm conviction of Adventist prophetic interpreters: "The greatest words ever spoken against God was the decree of infallibility issued by the ecumenical council in 1870."[113] This decree sealed Rome's fate:

---

[110] This was also true in the American press in general; see Beiser, 12.

[111] D.M. Canright, "Are the Roman Catholics United?" RH (May 31, 1870), 189; "The Great Speech in the Vatican," RH (June 13, 1871), 202-203; "The Great Speech in the Vatican," RH (June 27, 1871), 10. "Papal Infallibility and Mariolatry," RH (Aug. 29, 1871), 82.

[112] "Papal Infallibility and Mariolatry," RH (Aug. 29, 1871), 82.

[113] S.N. Haskell, The Story of Daniel the Prophet, 102.

When the dogma of infallibility was proclaimed in 1870, and the Roman Church was thus rendered irreformable, the utter destruction of that body, as a whole, was just as certainly decreed as was the destruction of Jerusalem, when the Jewish hierarchy refused the offers of divine mercy and finally rejected the Messiah....[114]

Like most contemporary Protestant publications in America, Adventists gave a rather imprecise interpretation to the idea of papal infallibility[115], without due recognition of the limitations as defined in the Constitution of the Church, which states that the pope is infallible only when speaking *ex cathedra* in matters of faith and morals.[116] By accepting papal infallibility, it was believed, the Catholic Church had locked itself into the position, that it now had to affirm the continued validity of all previous papal pronouncements, such as the *Syllabus Errorum*[117]--which condemned a number of things that touched the very essence of Protestantism. Moreover, all previous popes--even the 31 popes of the tenth century, whose reigns were mostly short and dishonourable, and among whom was Pope Sergius III who had a son with a prostitute ("those vile, degraded and beastly men")--were in the light of Vaticanum I to be regarded as part of "an unbroken line of infallible vicars of Jesus Christ."[118]

---

[114] W.W. Prescott, "The Empty Boast of the Roman Catholic Church," RH (Jan. 25, 1912), 10.

[115] For one of the few exceptions, see "The Infallibility of the Pope," PM, vol. 5, no. 9 (Sept. 1913), 401.

[116] See chapter IV of "Pastor Aeternus" in John F. Broderick, Documents of Vatican Council I, 63.

[117] L.A. Smith, "Pope Leo's Encyclical," RH (June 30, 1891), 416; L.R. Conradi, "The World Turning Toward Rome," RH (Feb. 11, 1896), 89. For the text of the "Syllabus Errorum," see H. Denzinger, Enchiridion Symbolorum Definitionum et Declarationum de Rebus Fidei et Morum (Freiburg i.Br., 1952), 465-473.

[118] R.F. Cottrell, "The Popes of the Tenth Century," RH (Feb. 27, 1872), 87.

Prophetically induced wishful thinking did, however, discern one bright aspect:

> We are coming to think that the infallibility dogma is a good thing.... He designed it to show himself infallible; but his course in this question is simply proving the prophetic scripture infallible; for it is alienating all his national supporters, and giving new impetus to the decadence of his influence, which the Scriptures foretold should take place in the last days....[119]

IV Emphasis on History

From the beginning Adventists were students of history. Their approach to prophecy mandated a search for past trends and events which could be construed as fulfillments of prophecy. Both Smith's and Andrews' major works, as well as the writings of other prominent Adventists, showed a strong emphasis on history. The search for historical clues had a number a specific foci: the Sabbath-Sunday controversy through the ages; the history of Babylon, Medo-Persia,[120] the Macedonian-Greek Empire of Alexander and its subsequent divisions; the Roman Empire, especially its decline and break-up; the French Revolution and subsequent developments; and Middle East events relating to Egypt, and in more recent times to the Saracens and the Turks. But the history of the papacy remained the historical interest *par excellence*.[121]

---

[119] "Papal Infallibility," RH (March 12, 1872), 100.

[120] With special attention for the dating of Cyrus' "command" to the Jews to return to their land, which was relevant to the dating of the 2300 day/year period.

[121] In 1867 a "historical department" was created in the Review and Herald. This weekly "department", which was continued as a regular feature until mid-1868, contained rather lengthy articles--often chapters taken from historical books--usually about aspects of Catholic history. One of the first articles in the series was entitled "The Inquisition" and was taken from Anthony L. Gavin's book The Great Red Dragon; or the Master-key to Popery (Boston: Samuel Jones, 1854), which was quite popular at the time (RH, March 19, 1867, 172). Some

The attention directed towards the last days of the Roman Empire centered mainly on the exploits of the three Arian powers, the Vandals, the Ostrogoths and the Heruli, which sealed the end of the Roman power in the West and paved the way for the papal supremacy. Gibbon remained the main source from which this argument, which undergirded the dating of the 1260 days/years, was deduced.[122]

Popular sources among Adventists for the history of Catholicism, especially during the Reformation era, were Dowling's *History of Romanism*; Bower's *History of Popes*; Mosheim's *Ecclesiastical History*, Wylie's *History of Protestantism*, and, most of all, D'Aubigné's *History of the Reformation*.[123] The report of a study committee on

---

weeks later four contributions consisting of sections from Bower's History of the Popes followed ("Ending of the 1260 Years," RH, June 18, 1867, 6-7; June 25, 1867, 22,23; July 2, 1867, 38-39; July 9, 1867, 54-55); the next contribution was a reprint of an article about blasphemous titles of the pope, which had appeared in a journal "Advent Herald" ("Decretalia," RH, July 9, 1867, 55). In August an article entitled "Bower's Escape from Inquisition", taken from a Methodist journal, was printed in two consecutive issues (RH, Aug. 13, 1867, 134-135; Aug. 20, 1867, 150-151); the Sept. 18 issue again included an article about Catholicism: "Methods of the Romish Church" (198). Other such articles in the series were: "General Councils of the Romish Church", RH (Oct. 1, 1867), 246-247; "Primitive Christianity in England--An Incident of Romish Aggression," RH (Oct. 15, 1867), 278; and "Persecution," RH (Jan. 7, 1868), 54-55.

[122] See Edward Gibbon, The History of the Fall and Decline of the Roman Empire, chapters 37-41, in Encyclopaedia Britannica ed.: vol I, 593-671; vol. II, 1-31; For Smith's use of Gibbon, see e.g. Thoughts on Daniel, 1881 ed., 147-162. See also L.R. Conradi, Die Offenbarung Jesu, 341.

[123] John Dowling, The History of Romanism: From the Earliest Corruptions of Christianity to the Present Time (New York: Edwin Walker, 1845); Johann L. Mosheim, Institutiones Historiae Ecclesiasticae Antiquae et Recentioris (6 vols., 1755; an English translation, An Ecclesiastical History, Ancient and Modern, from the Birth of Christ to the Beginning of the Eighteenth Century, 6 vols., first appeared in 1819); J.A. Wylie,

continuous education for Seventh-day Adventist ministers in 1870 listed both Mosheim's and D'Aubigné's book as among the seven books ministers were to study for the reading course![124]

The subject of the inquisition was an ever-recurring theme.[125] The total number of victims of persecutions by the Roman Catholic Church was usually put at 50 million,[126] although at times it was estimated as possibly as high as 100 million.[127] The campaigns against the Waldenses and Albigenses were regularly mentioned in much detail,[128] as were the infamous St. Bartholomew's Day of August 24, 1572[129] and the terrible persecution in

---

The History of Protestantism, 3 vols. (London: Cassel Peter & Galpin, n.d.); Merle d'Aubigné, Histoire de la Réformation du seizième siècle, 5 vols., 1835-1853 (first published in English as History of the Great Reformation of the Sixteenth Century, 1838-1841).
     Ellen G. White used both Wylie and D'Aubigné extensively for her Great Controversy; see below n. 251.

[124] "Course of Study for Ministers," RH (May 10, 1870), 164. W.H. Littlejohn gave a favourable review of D'Aubigné's work in "D'Aubigné's History of the Reformation," RH (July 18, 1871), 33.

[125] See e.g. Uriah Smith, "The Little Season of Rev. 6:11," RH (Dec. 23, 1873), 9. J.N. Loughborough, "Inquisition and Papal Intolerance," RH (Sept. 22, 1874), 105-106; (Sept. 29, 1874), 115. Uriah Smith, Thoughts on Daniel, 162-167.

[126] See e.g. Bible Readings, 1891 ed., 31; W.H. Littlejohn, "The Temple in Heaven," RH (March 24, 1885), 167-168; ed. note, RH (Apr. 27, 1891), 224; L.R. Conradi, Die Weissagung Daniels, 130.

[127] Uriah Smith, Synopsis of the Present Truth, 14.

[128] E.J. Waggoner, Prophetic Lights, 91; C.P. Bollman, Papacy and Persecution, or Did the Roman Catholic Church Ever Persecute? (Battle Creek, MI: IRLA, 1895), 6-9.

[129] E.J. Waggoner, Prophetic Lights, 92; A. Smith, "Drunken with the Blood of the Saints," RH (Apr. 3, 1894), 214.

the Low Countries.[130] Attempts by Roman Catholic authorities to distance themselves from the persecutions by their church in past centuries, such as Cardinal Gibbons' remarks in his *The Faith of Our Fathers*, were vehemently rejected as insincere.[131] Nor was any distinction accepted between a supposedly rather mild ecclesiastical inquisition and a cruel Spanish inquisition, which had been a state affair.[132] Complaints about cruelties suffered by Catholics in colonial days were regarded as the "unbecoming selfpity" of an organization which itself "has been the direst persecutor the world has ever seen."[133] And not only had the Roman Church persecuted millions of "heretics," it had also wilfully kept whole nations in the grossest ignorance.[134]

Although it is true, as Henry S. Commager asserts, that by the 1880s "the conviction that every village priest was undermining the foundations of the Republic and that every nunnery and monastery housed strange and fascinating iniquities" was largely a thing of the past,[135] Adventist journals from time to time printed

---

[130] "Roman Catholic Inquisition," RH (May 2, 1871), 159.

[131] C.M. Snow, "Roman Purpose and American Liberties," RH (June 23, 1910), 10-11.

[132] Uriah Smith, "A Voice from the Dark Ages," RH (Sept. 8, 1896), 569; C.P. Bollman, Papacy and Persecution, 10.

[133] W.A. Colcord, "Unbecoming Selfpity," RH (Dec. 3, 1889), 768.

[134] "Protestant and Romish Nations," RH (June 30, 1863), 34; M.E. Kellogg, "The Cause of a Nation's Decadence," RH (Jan. 2, 1894), 5-6; Uriah Smith, "Thrives on Ignorance," RH (Jan. 23, 1897), 121; Uriah Smith, "A Sly Word for America," RH (Apr. 23, 1895), 266.

[135] Henry S. Commager, The American Mind - An Interpretation of American Thought and Character Since the 1880's (New Haven: Yale Univ. Press, 1950), 191.

stories, usually clipped from other papers, about excesses in Catholic convents.[136] It troubled the editor of the *Review and Herald* that American authorities did not have the authority to inspect convents on American soil:

> What a world of suffering and crime would be revealed could all, or any, of the nunneries of even America, reveal the secret tale of what transpires within their walls. The conditions of the unhappy victims of their closed chambers is that of the most terrible slavery....[137]

A report of the discovery during renovations of a secret prison between the garret and the roof of the Sistine Chapel--which in the past allegedly was used "to confine recalcitrant cardinals"--elicited an immediate warning: If such a prison exists in the Vatican, it should not come as a surprise if it were to be found that in churches and cathedrals around the world such "secret recesses" exist, "which, in the future, will be used for the imprisonment and punishment of those who are regarded by the popes as heretics and offenders."[138]

---

[136] R.M. Kilgore reports the case of a girl in a convent in Cincinnati who on hospitalization was found to have numerous pins and needles in her body as a result of doing penance - "Paying Penance," RH (Sept. 4, 1895), 612. Another news item reported a raid on a nunnery in Naples, Italy, where sixteen nuns were found "in a condition closely bordering on insanity. They were scantily covered with rags, and their surroundings were filthy in the extreme" - "Inside the Nunnery," RH (Nov. 4, 1890), 679.

[137] "Works of Darkness," RH (July 11, 1893), 448.

[138] W.A. Colcord, "The 'Secret Recesses' of Rome," RH (Aug. 23, 1906), 19-20. Years earlier M.E. Kellogg, commenting on the inability of American authorities to inspect convents, declared that this situation strikingly reminded him of the words of Ellen G. White in Spirit of Prophecy, vol. IV, 397: "Throughout the land, she [Rome] is piling up her lofty and massive structures, in the secret recesses of which her former persecutions will be repeated" - M.E. Kellogg, "Romish Secrets," RH (Feb. 14, 1893), 105-106. See also Uriah Smith, "The Spirit of Rome," RH (June 12, 1888), 376.

V Adventist Reactions to Current Issues
Regarding Catholicism

There was hardly any systematic treatment of Catholic doctrine and theology in Adventist publications, and likewise there was no methodical way of commenting on issues in the Catholic Church in general and in the American Catholic Church in particular. But some trends, events and papal pronouncements did receive some attention.

As already indicated, the political events in Europe which contributed to the decline of the temporal power of the pope received regular coverage in the *Review and Herald*, as did the First Vatican Council, which underlined the vitality of the papacy, in spite of the dismantling of the Papal States.[139] Apart from these two aspects a few encyclicals received some attention as far as international Catholic events were concerned.

Pius IX's Encyclical "Quanta Cura" of December 8, 1864 was as much decried by Protestants in general as by Adventists, mainly because of the attached "Syllabus Errorum."[140] The Encyclical "Etsi Multa," of November 21, 1873, in which Pius IX complained about his "burden of distress," was referred to as proof that the papacy was still suffering the after-effects of the deadly wound.[141]

The difference between the more doctrinally interested Pius IX and "the political and philanthropic pontificate" of Leo XIII was duly noted, but Leo's social concerns were largely viewed as clever politics.[142] L.A. Smith in his comments on Leo XIII's famous encyclical "Rerum Novarum," of May 15, 1891, was extremely negative. With approval he cited a remark also

---

[139] See pp. 155-158.

[140] J.H. Waggoner, "Policy of Romanism," RH (Oct. 7, 1875), 109; "The Papal Syllabus of Errors," PM, vol. 4, no. 1 (1st quarter 1911), 35-63. For the text of "Quanta Cura," see Claudia Carlen, The Papal Encyclicals: 1740-1878, 381-386.

[141] Uriah Smith, "The Pope's Lament," RH (March 24, 1874), 120. For the text of "Etsi Multa", see Claudia Carlen, The Papal Encyclicals: 1740-1878, 427-434.

[142] John Vuilleumier, "The Coming Crisis in Europe," RH (July 16, 1889), 450-451; (July 23, 1889), 467-468.

reiterated by others: "If length be not a merit, it hath no other." He was convinced that the pope merely tried to control and guide a process which he could no longer repress.[143] The next encyclical of any interest to Adventists was Leo XIII's "Longinqua," of January 6, 1895, which was especially addressed to American Catholics.[144] The main point of criticism was the pope's statement that the American democratic ways, though they had helped the advance of the Catholic Church, should not be taken as the most ideal arrangement, to be followed as a blueprint elsewhere.[145]

"Pervading the entire letter," G.C. Tenney writes, "is a paternal solicitude for America and its interests which remind us of the earnest care exercised by the fable spider for the comfort and happiness of the poor little fly."[146]

The encyclical letter "Praeclara," of June 20, 1894, in which Leo pleaded for a return of the Orthodox and the Protestants to Rome, was regarded as "an able plea for the supremacy of the pope," and a fulfillment of the prophecy which indicated a resurgence of Catholicism before the world's end.[147] His encyclical letter "Ad Anglos," of April 14, 1895, which revealed a special concern for the conversion of England, received

---

[143] L.A. Smith, "Pope Leo's Encyclical," RH (June 30, 1891), 416. For the text of "Rerum Novarum", see Claudia Carlen, The Papal Encyclicals: 1878-1903, The Pierian Press, 1990), 214-261.

[144] For the text, see Claudia Carlen, The Papal Encyclicals: 1878-1903, 363-370.

[145] Ibid., 364-365. See also C.P. Bollman, Papacy and Persecution, 11; M.E. Kellogg, "Comments on the Papal Encyclical," RH (Feb. 19, 1895), 122-123.

[146] G.C. Tenney, "The Papal Encyclical," RH (Feb. 5, 1895), 86.

[147] M.E. Kellogg, "The Pope's Encyclical," RH (July 31, 1894), 486. For the text of "Praeclara," see John J. Wynne, ed., The Great Encyclical Letters of Pope Leo XIII (New York: Benziger Brothers, 1903), 303-319.

similar comment.[148]

The insistence on the development of a parochial school
system and the use of public funds for Catholic schools
were among the issues occupying the attention of the
Catholic Church in the United States, and were discussed
from time to time in Adventist publications.[149] Adventist
sympathy was solidly with Edward McGlynn, a New York
priest, who because of his opposition to the parochial
school system was temporarily suspended.[150] The role of
Francesco Satolli, who after an earlier assignment in
the United States in 1889, came to represent the pope
during the Chicago World Fair and the Catholic
Congresses of 1893, and then stayed on as the apostolic
delegate, was seen as one of "a second pope in our
midst."[151] His special authority, conferred upon him by
the pope, was yet another ominous detail in the
threatening picture of the early 1890s, to which we will
shortly turn.[152]

---

[148] M.E. Kellogg, "A Reunion of Christendom," RH
(July 21, 1896), 453. For the text of the apostolic
letter, see John J. Wynne, The Great Encyclical Letters
of Pope Leo XIII, 336-349.

[149] See e.g. "Popery and the Schools," RH (July 7,
1885), 421-422; Uriah Smith, "The Spirit of Rome," RH
(June 12, 1888), 376; R.W. Roberson, "The Catholic Party,"
RH (Oct. 3, 1893), 619; M.E. Kellogg, "The Cause of the
Nation's Decadence," cont., RH, (Jan. 9, 1894), 21-22.

[150] W. Penniman, "What Romanism is Doing," RH (May
20, 1880), 322. Uriah Smith, "Showing Her Colors," RH
(May 3, 1887), 280; Uriah Smith, "The Vatican and the
White House," RH (July 12, 1887), 441; L.A. Smith, Dr.
McGlynn Excommunicated," RH (July 19, 1887), 454; Uriah
Smith, "Romanism and Progress," RH (Feb. 8, 1887), 89.

[151] M.E. Cornell, "The Power of Satolli, RH (May 9,
1893), 295; L.A. Smith, "Popery in Washington," RH (Feb.
21, 1893), 119; M.E. Kellogg, "The Cause of the Nation's
Decadence," cont., RH, (Jan. 9, 1894), 21-22.

[152] "Roman Catholic Claims," RH (Apr. 10, 1894),
240; "The Pope Speaks Again," RH (July 23, 1895), 471;
M.E. Kellogg, "The Meaning of Satolli," RH (Apr. 25,
1893), 263.

VI Adventist Fears for the Immediate Future

1. Roman Catholic Plans for America

Like their Sabbatarian predecessors in the pre-1863 period, Seventh-day Adventists were not immune to the waves of nativistic, anti-Catholic sentiments which regularly swept through much of Protestant America. This is quite evident from an editorial by Uriah Smith in the *Review and Herald*:

> We hail with pleasure every indication that some are awakening to the dangers that threaten us.... We bid the noble men who are lifting a standard among these [Catholic] influences which are arising to overthrow our most precious institutions, Godspeed in their work.[153]

Adventists were, however, opposed to the tactics of aggressive anti-Catholic organizations such as the American Protective Association, which had its heyday in the early 1890s, because they believed these showed the same kind of intolerance of which they accused the Catholics and were fighting "Catholics as such, more than the principles underlying their faith."[154] Later F.M. Wilcox expressed his appreciation for the earnestness of much anti-Catholic activity, but registered his regret for "the intense partisan spirit" which many anti-Catholic journals manifested, which was so much different from the "fearless, dignified spirit" of Adventist journals devoted to religious liberty issues![155] The *American Sentinel* lamented the circulation of a fake encyclical by the "anti-Catholic press"--which called upon the Catholic faithful to exterminate all "heretics" in the United States--as a "stupid forgery."[156]

---

[153] Uriah Smith, "A Good Contest Begun," RH (Jan. 1, 1889), 8.

[154] M.E. Cornell, "Ye Know Not What Manner of Spirit Ye Are Of," RH (Jan. 2, 1894), 7.

[155] F.M. Wilcox, "The Roman Catholic Peril," RH (May 9, 1912), 9.

[156] "The So-called Encyclical," AS (June 29, 1893), 206.

The proposal of the A.P.A. that Catholics be restricted in their freedom of speech could not count on Adventist support. Adventist were "not endorsing some of the methods of the A.P.A." and insisted that Catholics, "with all other citizens of the United States, are entitled to the right of free speech."[157]

But the Adventist assessment of the ever strengthening Catholic presence[158] was at times expressed in just as negative, and unfriendly, terms as was found in many other quarters of American Protestantism. The following quotation from Uriah Smith's pen is one of many examples that could be cited:

> Creeping upon us from the darkness of the Dark Ages, a hideous monster is intently watching to seize the throat of liberty in our land. It thrusts itself upon the noonday of the nineteenth century, not that it may be benefitted by its light and freedom, but that it may suppress and obscure them. The name of this monster is Popery; and it has fixed its rapacious and bloodthirsty eyes on this land, determined to make it its helpless prey....[159]

As the century progressed, the success and strength of American Catholicism became more and more apparent and its sometimes audacious statements about

---

[157] J.O. Beard, "The Last Move," RH (May 1, 1894), 278. See also M.E. Kellogg, "The Catholic Church and the A.P.A.," RH (Feb. 19, 1895), 119; C.P. Bollman, "The A.P.A. and the Papists," AS (Sept. 28, 1893), 299; A.T. Jones, editorial, AS (March 15, 1894), 81-82.

[158] George B. Starr noted that official Catholic statistics were untrustworthy and that American Catholicism was growing much more rapidly than Catholics were claiming. However, even by their own figures, the American population had since 1790 increased by factor 15, while the Roman Catholic Church had increased by factor 189 - "Rome's Hold Upon the United States," RH (Feb. 18, 1890), 103. M.E. Kellogg complained that the prevailing religion in many places in New England was now Catholic in stead of Puritan -"Catholicism in New England," RH (June 13, 1893), 375.

[159] Uriah Smith, The United States in the Light of Prophecy, or, An Exposition of Revelation 13:11-17, 107.

even more success in the future did little to abate the
fears of many Protestants, in whose collective memory
still lingered the era of Catholic enmity against the
"protesting" reformers. The unassailable unity of the
Catholics, their centralized control and discipline,
their elaborate organization, their clear-cut programme
and comprehensive and rigid control of the education of
their children contrasted sharply with the "indivi-
dualism, liberalism, provincialism and fragmentation of
Protestantism" and together they go far to explain the
perception of Catholicism as a potential dangerous
power.[160] Adventists shared the quite common fear that
the Roman Catholic Church had one major ambition: to
make America Catholic.

In the immediate post-bellum period Adventist
fears of the growing Catholic influence in America
thrived on rumours of Catholic strategies to gain a
strong foothold in the Mississippi valley,[161] or in
Georgia,[162] and to exploit "the ignorances of the
freedmen" which "makes them easy subjects for the
shrewdness of the Catholic priesthood."[163] But at times
the Catholic plans were seen as even more ambitious:

> Next to the great enemy of all righteousness, we
> know of no power which labors with more patient
> persistence, reaching forward, planning,
> constantly striving, and ever holding itself to
> the one object of carrying its own purposes, than
> this power. The one aim of Romanism in this
> country is to secure political ascendancy.[164]

---

[160] See Henry Steel Commager, The American Mind,
190-194.

[161] "Methods of the Romish Church," RH (Sept. 18,
1867), 198.

[162] Uriah Smith, "Disturbing Voices," RH (Sept. 4,
1888), 568; see also editorial note, RH (June 5, 1888),
368.

[163] "Plans of the Catholics," RH (Jan. 21, 1868),
90.

[164] "Efforts and Aims of Romanism," RH (July 26,
1870), 48.

Articles such as the one in the *Catholic Mirror* of November 16, 1889, only confirmed the suspicions. Under the title "Making America Catholic" it presented the great challenge to its readers:

> Our work is to make America Catholic. If we love America, if we love the church, to mention the work suffices. Our cry shall be 'God wills it,' and our hearts shall leap with Crusader enthusiasm.[165]

Small wonder this elicited sharp comment:

> Like the rider on the pale horse, the Catholic Church is never satisfied. She has laid her withering and relentless hand on every country that it has been within her power to do. And from an early date she has had her eye fixed with covetous desire upon this fair land.[166]

And when "a high dignitary of the Church of Rome in America" declared that "what Rome has done for other countries she will do for the United States," this was not easily forgotten, but continued to evoke images of backwardness, ignorance, and superstition in the traditionally Catholic countries of Europe.[167] Such a statement was "full of terrible suggestions of evil"

> ... to any one who knows the true, unvarnished history of Rome, and what her influence and power

---

[165] Quoted by W.A. Colcord, "Making America Catholic," RH (Nov. 26, 1889), 752. This particular statement would be referred to repeatedly in Adventist publications of the 1880s and 1890s. See e.g. H.F. Phelps, "The Present State of Protestantism," RH (Jan. 2, 1900), 2. In 1911 W.W. Prescott quoted a similar statement from the "official record" of a National Conference of Catholic missionaries to non-Catholics: "We come not to conquer, but to win. Our purpose is to make America dominantly Catholic." See W.W. Prescott, "The Roman Catholic Program," RH (Nov. 2, 1911), 7.

[166] W.A. Colcord, "Making America Catholic," RH (Nov. 26, 1889), 752.

[167] M.E. Kellogg, "The Cause of a Nation's Decadence," RH (Jan. 2, 1894), 5-6.

have been to dwarf the spiritual life and retard the material progress of every country where she has been a dominating influence....[168]

This was "presuming upon the ignorance or indifference of Americans to a degree that is marvelous to behold."[169] A "Catholic America! That is the hope of the papacy."[170]
And this was precisely the fear of the true Protestant, "that the man wearing the tiara, ... sitting by the Tiber with two hundred million of people to obey his nod, says, 'America is the hope of Rome.'"[171] But those who studied the Scriptures, would understand what God has foretold in his Word: "Every degree of power gained by this religio-political monstrosity on American soil will be used to persecute the truth and the people of God."[172]

Adventist sources hardly mention the issue of the large numbers of immigrants--an aspect which was given much attention in nativistic circles in general. Though sharing in the general fear of the flood of immigrants, Adventists at the same time welcomed the arrival of people from so many countries as a divinely ordained opportunity of preaching their message to people from all nations. But they voiced their concern about the lack of democratic sentiment among Catholics: Knowing that the foundations of the United States rest on Puritanism, the Catholic can never "heartily become a

---

[168] Ibid., 5.

[169] Uriah Smith, "Thrives on Ignorance," RH (Feb. 23, 1897), 121.

[170] W.W. Prescott, "The Program of the Papacy," RH (Nov. 30, 1905), 5; see also "The Plans of the Papacy," AS (March 28, 1895), 97-98; "Is America to Become Roman Catholic?" PM, vol. 4, no. 2 (2nd quarter 1912), 112-114; "The Land of Promise," PM, vol. 5, no. 10 (Oct. 1913), 438-447.

[171] Dr. [?] Goodman, "Possessing the Land," RH (Aug. 30, 1881), 148.

[172] G.C. Tenney, "The Papal Encyclical," RH (Feb. 5, 1895), 87.

citizen of the republic...."[173] And that is especially
true of the Irish immigrant, who feels "an instinctive,
ineradicable consciousness of alienation between him and
the laws, institutions, religion and customs of this
country."[174] As a result, "... we have in our midst a
large and powerful class of hereditary, traditional,
civil and religious enemies of our free Protestant
institutions."[175] But that was not the only concern!
Catholics were beginning to use their political
influence. They already decided elections in some large
cities.[176] In some departments of the Washington
bureaucracy Roman Catholics were now in the majority.[177]
New York was becoming more Roman Catholic than Rome
itself.[178] Corrupt politicians, it was feared, would not
hesitate to manipulate "the Catholic vote."[179] And if
"normal" strategies would not work, the Roman Church
could always rely on the "vigilance and skill" of the
Jesuits, who would accomplish "by fraud, stratagem, or
an underhanded policy, what they could not do in any
other way."[180] And as a result, "the Roman Catholic
Church has more influence with the Protestant President

---

[173] Uriah Smith, "Pope or President," RH (Dec. 1, 1863), 1.

[174] Ibid.

[175] Ibid.

[176] "Plans of the Catholics," RH (Jan. 21, 1868), 90; Uriah Smith, "Rome Rules in New York," RH (Jan. 8, 1889), 26.

[177] L.A. Smith, "Washington in the Lap of Rome," RH (June 5, 1888), 368.

[178] W.W. Prescott, Seventh-day Adventists and the Roman Peril (Washington, DC: Religious Liberty Association, 1912), 4.

[179] Uriah Smith, The United States in the Light of Prophecy, 107.

[180] W. Penniman, "What Romanism is Doing," RH (May 20, 1880), 322. About the alleged activities of Jesuits, see also Dr. [?] Goodman, "Possessing the Land," RH (Aug. 30, 1881), 148.

and the Secretary of State than the Protestant churches have."[181]

An added dimension to the danger of Roman Catholic dominance in the political arena was seen in the attempts in the late 1890s to form a federation of Catholic societies, which would be able to exert considerable political pressure. The *Review and Herald* sounded early warnings about the preliminary steps, which would lead to a federation representing some 1.5 million Catholics.[182] Once it was officially formed (1901), news about the federation was followed with keen interest. It was regarded as an indirect meddling by the Catholic Church in politics,[183] with the aim of securing legislation favourable to the church, and of appropriating more public funds for Catholic schools, and having more influence in issues regarding the relationship of capital and labour. Ultimately, of course, its purpose was "having the laws and the institutions of the nation patterned after the ideals of the church."[184] Its millions of members represented a "compact mass of Catholic voters" which could be manipulated at any time to further the interests of the Catholic hierarchy."[185]

In reality the federation was far less powerful than it seemed in Adventist eyes. It always remained a

---

[181] L.A. Smith, commenting on the homage paid by American political figures at Cardinal Gibbons' Jubilee in 1911 - The United States in Prophecy, 182-183.

[182] A.T. Jones, "Catholic Federation," RH (Dec. 18, 1900), 808.

[183] L.A. Smith, "Note and Comment," RH (May 20, 1902), 6.

[184] L.A. Smith, "The Catholic National Federation," RH (June 30, 1904), 5. See also L.A. Smith, The United States in Prophecy, 153; W.W. Prescott, "Federation Among Catholics," RH (Aug. 23, 1906), 3-4; John S. Wightman, "A Significant Movement--Federation Among the Catholics," RH (Aug. 23, 1906), 9-12; C.M. Snow, "The American Federation of Catholic Societies, RH (Sept. 12, 1912), 6-8.

[185] C.M. Snow, "American Federation of Catholic Societies," Lib, vol. 6, no. 4 (4th quarter 1911), 25.

loose federation, careful not to frustrate the autonomy of member societies, and never had central headquarters. Work between mostly annual conventions was carried out by two men who found it difficult to work together, and was greatly hampered by lack of funds. The federation gradually disintegrated and ceased to exist in 1919.[186]

The concern about increasing Catholic strength and related issues (notably the Sabbath-Sunday agitation of the 1880s and 1890s) led in 1889 to the organizing of a National Religious Liberty Organization, which, during the first decade of its existence, was probably more active than it has ever been since.

Some of the positions advocated by the leaders in the religious liberty field were clearly not shared by other Adventist leaders and were considered extreme.[187] But the fear for the ever-increasing influence of the American Catholic Church kept the Adventist interest in religious liberty issues very much alive. This situation led to a flood of publications on religious liberty related issues, in the form of books, brochures and journals. Most prominent of these was the journal *The American Sentinel* (1886-1900), succeeded by *The Sentinel of Liberty* (1901-1904), and in 1906 by *Liberty*. E.J. Waggoner, A.T. Jones and C.P. Bollman were the most prominent editors and contributors. Throughout its first decade, Sunday legislation was the most important theme in *The American Sentinel*, but the threat of Catholicism to freedom and democracy was also a constantly recurring topic, especially during 1894 and a few years afterwards. An editorial note in the first issue of 1895 stated that every forthcoming issue would contain matter useful "in combating Romanism." *The American Sentinel* claimed to be the "only paper in the United States wholly devoted to combating Romanism, and its image in

---

[186] Sister M. Adele Francis Gorman, "Federation of Catholic Societies in the United States - 1870-1920," Ph.D. diss., Notre Dame, Ind., 1962.

[187] George R. Knight, From 1888 to Apostasy: The Case of A.T. Jones, deals at some length with some of the more extreme views of A.T. Jones, "who had risen to an undisputed leadership in that area," which were opposed by other leaders, such as Uriah Smith, and especially by Ellen G. White, who often took a much more pragmatic view of things (42, 48, 117-131).

apostate Protestantism.[188]

A more sophisticated journal, also devoted to the history and teachings of Catholicism and its threat for America--*The Protestant Magazine*--was published from 1909 to 1915, at first quarterly, but monthly from October 1912.[189] It was felt that *Liberty* magazine was inadequate to deal with Catholic aggressiveness. *The Protestant Magazine* was to remind Protestants of their duty to protest and to warn them not to depart from the original principles of Protestantism.[190] Banners on the cover summed up the journal's raison d'être: "Advocating Primitive Christianity" and "Protesting against Apostasy." The content mainly consisted of articles about the history of the papacy and key Catholic doctrines. But these were balanced by positive presentations on justification by faith, the mediation of Christ and discussions of prophecies. Each issue had a section of comments on current developments in Catholicism. The journal was predominantly dignified in tone (certainly in comparison to other contemporary anti-Catholic journals), but the editors could not totally resist the temptation to add some sensational material.[191] In spite of concerted efforts to promote the journal, its number of regular subscribers remained disappointing--23,000 at its peak in March 1915--and it continued to lose money. For this and other reasons it was discontinued in the fall of 1915.[192]

---

[188] Editorial note, <u>AS</u> (Jan. 3, 1895), 1.

[189] For further details about the history of <u>The Protestant Magazine</u>, see G.M. Valentine, "William Warren Prescott: Seventh-day Adventist Educator," 451-464.

[190] Editorial, <u>PM</u>, vol. 1, no. 1 (2nd quarter 1909), 1.

[191] E.g. the four-part series "A Convent Tragedy", about a young girl concealed from her parents in a convent, with lengthy extracts from official court records about immoral priests and lesbian nuns - <u>PM</u>, vol. 5, no. 3 (March 1913), 102-111; vol. 5, no. 4 (Apr. 1913), 150-163; vol. 5, no. 5 (May 1913), 203-217; vol. 5, no. 6 (June 1913), 258-266.

[192] G.M. Valentine, "William Warren Prescott: Seventh-day Adventist Educator," 460-461; See pp. 242-243.

2. *Protestant Initiatives toward Religious Legislation*

Seventh-day Adventists were concerned about what they saw on the Roman Catholic front, but they were just as much troubled by developments in Protestantism. In their criticism of the Babylonian confusion which they felt was rampant in the fragmented and apostate Protestantism of their days, they were also increasingly worried by tendencies towards interdenominational cooperation and a growing desire on the part of many even to join forces with Roman Catholics on a number of issues.[193] The end result, they believed, would be the creation of an image to the beast--a situation in which the state would be subservient to the wishes of the apostate churches--and a persecution of the remnant, those who were sealed by the Sabbath truth, carried out by those who had the mark of the beast.

Church members studying their Sabbath School lessons during the first quarter of 1896 were reminded how "the present state of things" had rapidly come about. There had been a succession of seven events which were clearly the preliminaries to the final crisis:

1. The activities of the National Reform Association, "which has been working for a union of church and state ever since 1863. The literature and lectures of this organization have leavened the minds of men in all the various denominations."

2. The adoption of the same principles by the Woman's Christian Temperance Union (1886).

3. The commitment of the Prohibition Party to the same principles (1887).

4. The founding of the American Sabbath Union (1888), "one object of which is to obtain and secure the

---

[193] For a discussion of growing emphasis among American denominations on cooperation during the 1860-1890 period, see Robert T. Handy, A Christian America: Protestant Hopes and Historical Realities (New York: Oxford University Press, 2nd ed., 1984), 82-84; see also Philip D. Jordan, The Evangelical Alliance for the United States of America, 1847-1900: Ecumenism, Identity and the Religion of the Republic (New York: The Edwin Mellen Press, 1982), 99-196. For a detailed account of the origin and early history of the Federal Council of Churches, from ca. 1895 to 1916, see Elias B. Sanford, Origin and History of the Federal Council of the Churches of Christ in America (Hartford, Conn.: The S.S. Scranton Company, 1916).

enforcement of religious legislation."

5. The Trinity Church decision of the Supreme Court of the United States (February 29, 1892), which declared that 'this is a Christian nation.'"[194]

6. "The decision by both houses of Congress in the same year of a religious controversy, the Sabbath question, and the endorsement of the same by the President, thus committing the legislative and executives branches to religious legislation." (This rather nebulous description refers to the Sunday-closing controversy of the 1893 Chicago World Fair.)

7. "The enforcement of religious [Sunday] laws in various states, thus bringing persecution upon men for conscience's sake.[195]

The author of these lessons was absolutely sure that "the fulfillment of the prophecy of Revelation 13 [was] no longer a matter of prophecy"; it was fulfilling before their very eyes.[196]

The incarnation of Adventist fears of what might happen when the "fallen" Protestant churches would seek to impose restrictions on Sabbath keeping was the National Reform Association, with its journal *The Christian Statesman*. The movement had its origin during the crisis years of the Civil War. When early in the war things were not going well for the Union, a number of clergymen, representing 11 Protestant denominations, met at Xena, Ohio (February 4, 1863), seeking ways to appease a God who was allowing the defeats of the North as a manifestation of his wrath.[197] The way to avert the divine judgments on America would be to acknowledge Christ's Lordship over the affairs of the state and to ensure that God's moral law would be the basis for all

---

[194] William A. Blakely, American State Papers on Freedom in Religion, 325-338. For the strong protest of the (Adventist) International Religious Liberty Association, see A.T. Jones, Appeal from the U.S. Supreme Court Decision Making this "a Christian Nation" (Battle Creek, MI: IRLA, 1893).

[195] SSQ, 1st quarter 1896, 39.

[196] Ibid. See also Godloe H. Bell, Progressive Bible Lessons, 277-283.

[197] Dennis Pettibone, "The Sunday Law Movement," 120.

legislation. The first item on the agenda of the National Reform Association was a religious amendment to the Constitution that would make the USA a Christian nation.[198] But from 1879 onward much of the attention of the National Reform Association was focused on a national Sunday law.[199] For A.T. Jones the activities of the Association amounted to a "great conspiracy."[200] Together with The Woman's Christian Temperance Union,[201] the Prohibition Party,[202] and the American Sabbath

------

[198] Anson Phelps Stokes and Leo Pfeffer, Church and State in the United States (Westport, Con: Greenwood Press Publishers, 1975), 565-570. The proposal for a religious amendment was taken seriously enough to be examined by Congress in 1874. Similar proposals have often been made since. The present leading movement for such a proposal is the Christian Amendment Movement. See also William A. Blakely, American State Papers, 149-157.

[199] W.H. Littlejohn, The Coming Conflict: Or The United States to Become a persecuting Power (Battle Creek: Review and Herald Publishing House, 1883), v-l.

[200] As reads the title of a chapter on the subject in A.T. Jones, The Two Republics: Rome and the United States of America (Battle Creek, MI: Review and Herald Publ. Co., 1891), 699-752. See also L.A. Smith, The United States in Prophecy, 230-295, which to a large degree builds on Uriah Smith, The Marvel of Nations, 190-266; and a series of articles by W.L. Littlejohn, "The Constitutional Amendment: Or the Sunday, the Sabbath, the Change, and the Restitution," RH (Oct. 22, 1872), 145-146; (Oct. 29, 1872), 159; (Nov. 5, 1872), 163.

[201] An organization of Christian women, founded in 1874 for the protection of the home. Its main goal was the abolition of liquor traffic. See Ruth B. Anderson, Women and Temperance (Philadelphia: Temple Univ. Press, 1981); Jack S. Blocker, jr., American Temperance Movements: Cycles of Reform (Boston: Twayne Publishers, 1989, 61-94).

[202] The Prohibition Party was founded in 1869. Though it never received more than a few percent of the votes, the party contested every presidential election. See Jack S. Blocker Jr, American Temperance Movements, 84-89; 99-102; for an Adventist critique of the Pro-

Union,[203] the National Reform Association formed

> ... a colossal religious combination to effect
> political purposes, the chief purpose being to
> change the form of the United States government,
> to turn it into a new 'kingdom of God,' a new
> theocracy, in which the civil power shall be but
> the tool of the religious.[204]

Adventists had, for years, been looking for "a
religious power to rise to a position where it can
dominate the civil, and employ the state where it can
forward its design." That power had arrived in the form
the National Reform Association.[205] A new Adventist
journal *The American Sentinel*, already referred to
above,[206] was started to oppose the sinister National
Reform plans.[207] Its first few volumes were devoted
almost exclusively to this issue.

3. Catholics Working Together with Protestants

Adventist leaders were alarmed but not really surprised
about the eagerness of the "Reformers" to co-operate

---

hibtion Party, see C.P. Bollman, <u>The Prohibition Party
and Freedom of Conscience</u> (Oakland, Cal.: Pacific Press
Publishing Co., 1891).

[203] The American Sabbath Union, an interdenominational organization to promote Sunday legislation, was the brainchild of Wilbur F. Crafts, a Presbyterian minister whose ideas were very similar to those
of the National Reform Association. See Dennis
Pettibone, "The Sunday Law Movement," 121.

[204] A.T. Jones, <u>The Two Republics</u>, 749-750.

[205] <u>Bible Readings for the Home Circle</u>, 1891 ed.,
235. Cf. the 1914 ed., which gave even more attention to
the Nat. Ref. Ass. (271-279). See also R.F. Cottrell, "A
Prophecy Being Fulfilled," <u>RH</u> (June 11, 1889), 370.

[206] See pp. 173-174.

[207] J.H. Waggoner, "The American Sentinel," <u>AS</u> (Jan.
1886), 1-2.

with Catholic organizations. For in spite of all their
differences, Protestants and Catholics, they believed,
had one fundamental desire in common: a union between
church and state. Instead of working under its own name,
"Romanism"--"as crafty, as cruel, as bitterly opposed to
our free institutions as [she] is"--was expected to be
more than content to hide under the National Reformers'
umbrella.[208] An overture to that effect in *The Christian
Statesman* of December 11, 1884, did not remain
unnoticed. For years Adventist authors would repeat the
ominous words: "Whenever they [the Roman Catholics] are
willing to cooperate in resisting the progress of
political atheism, *we will gladly join hands with
them.*"[209] And statements expressing a Catholic willingness to work with Protestant Christians on social issues
and to promote Sunday holiness were seen as fitting into
the same framework.[210]

While anti-Catholic organizations were still active and
"Romanism" continued to be regarded by many as one of
the great perils threatening America,[211] the attitudes of

---

[208] A.T. Jones, <u>The American Papacy - The Outcome of
National Reform Religion</u> (Oakland, Cal.: Pacific Press
Publishing Co., 1889), 5.

[209] See e.g. A.T. Jones, <u>The Two Republics</u>, 727;
<u>Bible Readings</u>, 1891 ed., 236; A.T. Jones, <u>The American
Papacy</u>, 5; H.F. Phelps, "Catholics and Protestants to
Elevate the American Sunday," <u>AS</u> (Sept. 7, 1893), 276-
277.

[210] A Mr. Manly B. Tello, editor of a Catholic
journal, read a paper during a Laymen's Congress in
1889, which celebrated the 100th anniversary of the
establishment of the American hierarchy, in which he
expressed such a desire. See A.T. Jones, <u>The Two
Republics</u>, 756; "Rome Takes a New Departure," <u>RH</u> (Jan.
7, 1890), 7; Uriah Smith, "A Good Contest Begun," <u>RH</u>
(Jan. 1, 1889), 8; George E. Fifield, "Sad Apostasy," <u>RH</u>
(Jan. 21, 1890), 35; C.M. Snow, "American Federation of
Catholic Societies," <u>Lib</u>, vol. 6, no. 4 (4th quarter,
1911), 24.

[211] So described by Josiah Strong, the general
secretary of the Evangelical Alliance in the USA, in his
influential book <u>Our Country: Its Possible Future and
its Present Crisis</u> (New York: The Baker & Taylor Co.,

Protestants in general toward Rome were changing. The *Review and Herald* regularly reported these ecumenical "signs of the times," whether they took the form of local initiatives,[212] or rapprochements between denominations.[213] In many quarters the atmosphere in Protestant-Catholic relations was changing. Protestants were beginning "to smile graciously on Rome and Romish doctrines" and even sought audiences with the pope.[214] They were willing to sing hymns composed by Catholics,[215] and to make all sorts of other concessions to the Roman Church.[216] Many Protestants called priests "father," wealthy Protestants often sent their daughters to convent schools, and newspapers published portraits and eulogies of Catholic clergy.[217] Some Protestants no longer wanted to hear the apocalyptic terminology applied to the Catholic Church. "The people of this country," writes M.E. Kellogg, "is [sic] becoming so enamored of the 'beast' that it is considered almost sacrilege to say, even what the Scriptures teach of Rome, her character and her final fate."[218] The general anti-Catholicism of "a few years ago" was in striking

---

1885), 46-49. With immigration, and Mormonism, "Romanism" headed the list of perils facing the American nation. Adventist writers often quoted from this book which went through large printings.

[212] "Protestantism and Catholicism Joining Hands," RH (May 16, 1871), 171.

[213] E.g. D.M. Canright, "Episcopalians Returning to Rome," RH (Nov. 17, 1874), 165; M.E. Kellogg, "A Reunion of Christendom," RH (July 21, 1896), 453.

[214] M.E. Kellogg, "Patting Rome on the Back," RH (Dec. 22, 1891), 800.

[215] "Charity Run Wild," RH (Apr. 22, 1880), 265.

[216] "Something About Catholics," RH (Feb. 10, 1874), 67.

[217] B.E. Tefft, "Toward Rome," RH (May 24, 1887), 327.

[218] M.E. Kellogg, "Rome's Character, Fate and Company," RH (Feb. 20, 1894), 121.

contrast with "the marked indifference which prevails today" in regard to the "increasing strength and arrogance of Roman Catholicism."[219]

All this corresponded perfectly to Adventist eschatological expectations:

> The movement which is to fulfill ... the prophecy, is to be looked for in the popular churches of our land. First, a union must be effected between these churches, with some degree of coalition between these churches, with some degree of coalition also between these bodies and the beast power, or Roman Catholicism, and secondly, steps must be taken to bring the law of the land to the support of the Sunday Sabbath.[220]

When that stage was reached, it was believed that Sabbath keepers would be at the mercy of the Catholics:

> Then, when the time comes for the enforcement of the laws which they now demand, what is to hinder the Catholics from assisting in the work, and that, too, in the Catholic way? Every priest in the United States is sworn to root out heresy.... And when, by Constitutional Amendment, the refusal to observe the Sunday becomes heresy that can be reached by law, what then is to hinder the Catholics from acting a prominent part in rooting out the heresy? ...
>
> The success of the National Reform movement will be the success of Rome. Therefore, to support the National Reform movement is to support Rome....[221]

---

[219] "Significant," RH (Feb. 14, 1888), 112.

[220] Uriah Smith, The United States in the Light of Prophecy, 155.

[221] A.T. Jones, The American Papacy, 11-12, 14; see also A.T. Jones, "The American Papacy, AS (Dec. 1886), 93-94; A.T. Jones, "An Image of the Papacy," AS (March 1887), 19-20.

4. Fears Realized in Current Events

In the days of Sabbatarian Adventism and in the 1860s and 1870s the Review and Herald repeatedly reported about new state Sunday laws and emphasized how these all pointed in the direction of a final conflict in which Sabbath keepers would be fiercely persecuted by a religio-political power, which drew its strength from both Catholics and Protestants.[222] Sunday "blue" laws[223] had existed in America since colonial days.[224] But it was not until the late 1880s and early 1890s that a more widespread agitation on the Sunday issue occurred.[225] During that period 17 of the 48 states with Sunday laws were actually using them to prosecute Sabbath observers. Arkansas and Tennessee were the worst.[226] During 1895 and

---

[222] Cf. the title of W.H. Littlejohn's book: <u>The Coming Conflict: Or the United States to Become a Persecuting Power</u>.

[223] There is difference of opinion about the origin of the term "blue" laws. Some say the "blue" refers to the colour of the paper upon which the code of laws of the New Haven colony was printed in 1665. Others maintain that "blue" refers to the strictness with which laws were observed by Puritans. Blue was the colour of constancy and fidelity. At the court of Charles II "true blue" was a term of reproach, reserved, among others, for Puritans. See David N. Labland and Deborah H. Heinbuc, <u>Blue Laws: The History, Economics, and Politics of Sunday-Closing Laws</u> (Lexington, Mass.: Lexington Books, 1987), 8.

[224] A Seventh-day Baptist source which provides a wealth of detail is: Abraham H. Lewis, <u>A Critical History of Sunday Legislation from 321 to 1888 A.D.</u> (New York: D. Appleton and Company, 1888).

[225] See Warren L. Johns, <u>Dateline Sunday, U.S.A. - The Story of Three and a Half Centuries of Sunday-law Battles in America</u> (Mountain View: PPPA, 1967); and also Eric D. Syme, "Seventh-day Adventist Concepts of Church and State," 88-111.

[226] William A. Blakely, <u>American State Papers</u>, 654-672; 672-717; B.O. Flower, <u>Religious Intolerance in the Republic: Christians Persecuting Christians in Tennessee</u> (Battle Creek, MI: IRLA, 1892); "Where Sunday Laws Hit,"

1896 no less than 76 Adventists were prosecuted in the United States and Canada under existing Sunday laws. Of these, 28 served terms of various length in jails, chain-gang, etc., aggregating 1,144 days. Others were fined, while a few were acquitted.[227] And it had not remained unnoticed several European countries had also initiated further Sunday legislation.[228]

The strong lobby of Protestant organizations, which, with the increasing support of the Catholic Church,[229] campaigned for a stricter Sabbath (Sunday) observance, created a climate which Adventists perceived as more and more threatening. They expected national Sunday laws to be passed, and large-scale persecution to follow. This was what their prophetic views had predicted all along. Now truly the end was near!

Three events in particular heightened the tension.[230] In 1888, Senator H.W. Blair introduced a law, which, although dressed in secular language, was seen as an attempt at religious enforcement of the Sunday as a day of rest.[231] Vigorous opposition by Jews, Seventh-day

---

AS (Apr. 17, 1889), 100-101.

[227] William A. Blakely, American State Papers, 726; C.P. Bollman, "Seventh-day Adventists in the Chain-Gang," AS (Aug. 18, 1892), 251.

[228] Uriah Smith, The Marvel of Nations, 219-221.

[229] In 1889 Cardinal Gibbons wrote a letter expressing his support for the Protestant initiative. His backing was interpreted as a pledge of support on behalf of all 7.2 million Catholics. See A.T. Jones, The American Papacy - The Outcome of National Reform Religion, 10; also Eric D Syme, "Seventh-day Adventist Concepts on Church and State," 111.

[230] Eric D. Syme, "Seventh-day Adventist Concepts on Church and State," 111-132; Dennis Pettibone, "The Sunday Law Movement," 112-128.

[231] "The National Sunday Bill, AS (Oct. 1888), 73-74; L.A. Smith, "The Blair Sunday Bill in Secular Dress," RH (Jan. 7, 1890), 8-9. See also A.T. Jones, The Two Republics, 820-826; E.J. Waggoner, The Blair Sunday-Rest Bill. Its Nature and History (Oakland, Cal.: Pacific Press Publishing Co., 1889).

Baptists and Seventh-day Adventists and other groups contributed to the defeat of the 1888 proposal and its 1889 amended version.[232]

A new attempt was made in 1890, when Senator W.C.P. Breckinridge introduced a Sunday bill for the District of Columbia. Breckinridge included in his proposal an exemption clause for those who conscientiously believed in and observed another day of the week than Sunday. The Seventh-day Baptists were satisfied with that provision, but Seventh-day Adventists insisted that any kind of Sunday legislation was a wrongful meddling by the state in religious affairs.[233] After considerable controversy, in which Adventists once again played a major role, this proposal was also defeated.

A third battle between Sunday keeping forces and Sabbath keepers followed in 1892-1893, when preparations were made for the 1893 World's Columbian Exposition in Chicago. In January 1892 a bill was introduced in the House of Representatives requiring that "no exposition or exhibition for which appropriation is made by Congress shall be open on Sunday." This and another bill provided for financial assistance on condition that the World Fair would remain closed on Sundays. The bills passed, in a modified form, in both the House and the Senate. Only after extensive legal battles--and after the fair had already been open for a number of weeks-- did the organizers obtain permission from the court to be also open on Sundays.[234] Again Adventists, led by A.T. Jones, were active in opposing this breach in the wall of separation between church and state.[235]

---

[232] A.T. Jones, "The New Blair Sunday Law," AS (Jan. 9, 1890), 9-11.

[233] L.A. Smith, "The Breckinridge Sunday Bill for the District of Columbia," RH (Jan. 21, 1890), 3; A.T. Jones, "The Breckinridge Sunday Bill," AS (Jan. 23, 1890), 25-27; A.T. Jones, The Two Republics, 829-860.

[234] L.A. Smith, "The Sabbath and the World's Fair," RH (Sept. 23, 1890), 585.

[235] For an account of the Adventist activities to oppose the Sunday closing, see Ben McArthur, "The 1893 Chicago World's Fair: An Early Test for Adventist Religious Liberty," AH, vol. 2, no. 2 (Winter 1975), 23-32.

Roman Catholics presented a high profile before and during the Chicago World Fair. Opponents of the plans for a Sunday closing of the fair noted that the supporters of Sunday closing appealed to the Roman Catholics for help.[236] But the Catholics also took advantage of the vast number of people coming to Chicago, "to hold a series of congresses of more than national interest" and to prepare an "Educational Exhibit." The Catholic Congress was a resounding success; it was a "Mecca, from day to day, of vast crowds of the faithful, and was honored by such an attendance of our prelates and clergy as were never before present at an assembly of the kind...."[237] Catholics were also spectacularly in the forefront during another widely publicized congress held at the time of the World Fair, the Parliament of Religions.[238]

Of special significance in this context was a series of four articles in *The Catholic Mirror* (a prominent Catholic weekly, published in Baltimore),

---

See also A.T. Jones, <u>The Captivity of the Republic: A Report of Hearing by the House Committee on the Columbian Exposition, January 10-13, 1893, and the Present Status and Effect of the Legislation on Sunday Closing of the World's Fair</u> (Washington, DC: IRLA, 1893), and vol. 8 of the <u>American Sentinel</u> (1893), which carried numerous articles on the subject.

[236] Abraham H. Lewis, <u>The Catholization of Protestantism on the Sabbath Question or Sunday-Observance Non-Protestant</u> (Plainfield, N.J.: American Sabbath Tract Society, 1897), 27.

[237] See <u>Progress of the Catholic Church in America and the Great Columbian Catholic Congress of 1893</u> (Chicago: J.S. Hyland & Company, 1897), 9; and <u>The World's Columbian Catholic Congresses and Educational Exhibit</u>, vols. I and II (New York: Arno Press, 1978).

[238] See G.T. Wilson, "The Keys of the Future – Or, the Meaning of the Chicago Catholic Congress and the World's Parliament of Religion," chap. in: Walter R. Houghton, ed., <u>The Parliament of Religions and Religious Congresses at the World's Columbian Exposition</u> (Chicago: F.T. Neely, 1893), 326-327.

which defended the position of the Sabbath keepers as scriptural against the main body of Protestants.[239] Soon these articles were reprinted as a pamphlet by the Seventh-day Baptists.[240] The Seventh-day Adventists published the text of these articles in their religious liberty journal *The American Sentinel*,[241] and also reprinted them as a pamphlet.[242] The preface of this pamphlet claims that the articles appeared after the *Mirror* editors had studied Adventist religious liberty publications.[243] An appendix emphasized the prestige of the *Mirror* as the semi-official mouthpiece of the cardinal and the Catholic Church of America and argued that the arguments of its four articles were unanswerable.[244]

While Catholics were seen to get more involved in the Sabbath-Sunday issue,[245] they also joined the forces of temperance reform, as part of a concerted effort to strengthen their influence. Adventists were extremely skeptical regarding Catholic sincerity about temperance. As "a notable intemperate people"[246] they would need time

---

[239] "The Christian Sabbath," The Catholic Mirror (Sept. 2, 1893), 8; (Sept. 9, 1893), 8; (Sept. 16, 1893), 8; (Sept. 23, 1893), 8-9.

[240] Abraham H. Lewis, The Sabbath Question from the Roman Catholic Standpoint as Stated by the "Catholic Mirror," together with Introduction and Remarks (New York: American Sabbath Tract Society, 1894).

[241] "The Christian Sabbath," AS (Sept. 21, 1893), 291; (Sept. 28, 1893), 298-299; (Oct. 5, 1893), 308-309; (Oct. 12, 1893), 316-317.

[242] Rome's Challenge: Why Do Protestants Keep Sunday? (Battle Creek, MI: IRLA, n.d.), 4-30. This pamphlet has been reprinted numerous times and continues to be available even at present [1993]).

[243] Ibid., 3.

[244] Ibid., 32.

[245] See p. 179.

[246] A. Weeks, "The Catholics Preparing," RH (Apr. 29, 1884), 274.

to effect reform of such a radical character, and, therefore, "the probability that Catholics will within a short time confine themselves to milk and water for drinking purposes seems ... to be very remote."[247] The problem was, however, that the temperance cause, "which is a righteous one," was "inseparably yoked with Sunday laws [e.g. Sunday closing of saloons], which are altogether wrong." The Catholic Church "joins its mighty influence to the cause that presents a fair name to the world" as an alibi to its devious efforts on behalf of Sunday laws.[248]

VII Ellen G. White's views on Catholicism

Around 1883 Ellen White began to write in a systematic way about the history of the Christian church. In her "Introduction" to *The Great Controversy* she claimed that "the illumination of the Holy Spirit" permitted her to see scenes of the past and the future,[249] while at the same time acknowledging her dependence on historical sources and other Adventist writers, who she often paraphrased.[250] The writer who most influenced her was no doubt D'Aubigné,[251] with Wylie as a close second.

---

[247] M.E. Kellogg, "Catholics and the Liquor Business," RH (Aug. 21, 1894), 535.

[248] G.C. Tenney, "Rome is Waking Up," RH (Aug. 27, 1895), 549. That danger was earlier noted in: "Catholic Total Abstinence Union," RH (June 14, 1887), 384.

[249] GC, 1911 ed., x, xi.

[250] Ibid., xi, xii. In the 1911 edition an effort was made to give proper credit for direct quotations.

[251] Arthur White, Ellen G. White, vol. 3, 213-214. For Ellen G. White's extensive, and often almost verbatim, use of historical sources in GC, see Donald R. McAdams, "Ellen G. White and the Protestant Historians," unpubl. research paper, 1974 (rev. in 1977), 18-19, and passim; Eric Anderson, "Ellen G. White and Reformation Historians," Spectrum, vol. 9, no. 3 (July 1978), 23-26; Jean Zurcher, "A Vindication of Ellen White as Historian," Spectrum, vol. 16, no. 3 (August 1985), 21-31.

Much of the material in the 4th volume of the *Spirit of Prophecy* series was part of a series of *Signs of the Times* articles which had appeared shortly before.[252] The book was published under the subtitle *The Great Controversy* in October 1884.[253] It proved an instant success and sold more than 50,000 copies to Adventists as well as to the general public in the first three years.[254] The 1888 edition provided an extensive revision and was significantly enlarged. Some parts were taken out and some Adventist jargon was eliminated, while a major section on Huss and Jerome was added and the use of sources was extended.[255] This edition has basically become *The Great Controversy Between Christ and Satan*, and has been distributed and translated in scores of languages since. The 1911 edition again contained some changes, but they were far less drastic as those made in 1888. In the present context it is relevant to note that some of the 1911 changes pertained to Ellen White's treatment of Roman Catholicism. Often the word "Romish" would be changed into "Roman" or "Roman Catholic" in order to avoid unnecessary offence, while a few strongly disputed statements regarding the papacy, which were considered difficult to prove from accessible historic sources, were changed in such a way that they would fall within the range of more easily attainable evidence.[256]

Ellen G. White's treatment of the history of the Catholic Church was not essentially different from the approach of other Adventist writers. In chapter 3 of *The*

---

[252] See <u>Signs of the Times</u>, weekly from May 31, 1883 to Sept. 20, 1883 and Oct. 11, 1883 to Nov. 1, 1883.

[253] Ellen G. White, <u>The Spirit of Prophecy</u>, vol. 4: <u>The Great Controversy Between Christ and Satan</u> (Oakland, Cal.: Pacific Press, 1884; facsimile reproduction: Washington DC: RHPA, 1969).

[254] Arthur L. White, <u>Ellen G. White</u>, vol. 3: <u>The Lonely Years - 1876-1891</u>, 249. For the background to the writing of the book, 211-215; 240-249.

[255] Ibid., 436-431.

[256] Arthur L. White, <u>Ellen G. White</u>, vol. 6: <u>The Later Elmshaven Years - 1905-1915</u> (Washington, DC: RHPA), 322-337.

Great Controversy (1884 edition[257]) all the usual elements of Adventist historiography with regard to "The Roman Church"[258] are present: the rise of apostasy in the early church; the gradual increase in heretical beliefs and practices; the suppression of the Bible; the disregard for the second commandment; the substitution of the Sunday for the Sabbath; the establishment of the papacy; the dark ages of superstition and iniquity; the inquisition; the papal claims of supremacy over rulers and the claim of infallibility.[259]

Initially Ellen G. White's view on Babylon did not fully conform to contemporary Adventist thinking, as she applied the term in 1884 exclusively to fallen Protestantism:

> The message announcing the fall of Babylon must apply to some religious body that was once pure, and has become corrupt. It cannot be the Romish Church which is here meant; for that church has been in a fallen condition for many centuries. But how appropriate [is] the figure as applied to the Protestant churches....[260]

The 1911 edition brought her into line with other contemporary Adventist authors by adding just one word: "Therefore it [Babylon] cannot refer to the Roman Church *alone*."[261]

Ellen White's treatment of Revelation 13 followed

---

[257] Since the 1884 ed. in <u>Spirit of Prophecy</u> was the first systematic treatment by Ellen G, White of the subject, we will mainly refer to this edition.

[258] This was the title of the chapter; cf. "The Apostasy" as the title of this chapter in the 1911 ed.

[259] Ibid., 51-65. With regard to the inquisition Ellen G. White notes "there were massacres on a scale that will never be known to mortals" (<u>GC</u>, 1884, 385).

[260] <u>GC</u>, 1884 ed., 232-233. Her arguments for the fall of Babylon emphasized the same aspects--worldliness and doctrinal errors--as contemporary Adventists did.

[261] <u>GC</u>, 1911 ed., 383.

the established pattern.[262] The papacy is said to have suffered its deadly wound in 1798, but there is no speculation as to whether the healing had already occurred, was in process, or yet fully future.[263] Neither does she offer any explanation for the cryptic number 666.

Special attention must be paid to two key chapters toward the end of the book. In the chapter "Character and Aims of the Papacy"[264] we detect the same insistence as we find in publications by other representative Adventist authors that Catholicism will never change, and that one should not be fooled by "the fair front" it now presents to the world. "Every principle of popery that existed in ages past exists today."[265] Ellen G. White was, however, careful to distinguish between the Catholic Church as a system and the individual believers, of whom many are "real Christians." But "Romanism as a system is no more in harmony with the gospel of Christ now than at any former period in her history."[266] "Let the restraints now imposed by secular governments be removed, and Rome be re-instated in her former power, and there would speedily be a revival of her tyranny and persecution."[267]

---

[262] GC, 1884 ed., 276-286.

[263] In spite of her voluminous writing, Ellen G. White did not attempt to settle differences of opinion on doctrinal matters or interpretations of prophecy. She usually maintains silence on disputed issues. A case in point is her almost total silence on the interpretation of Daniel 11.

[264] GC, 1884 ed., 380-397; the chapter was reprinted in the American Sentinel under the same title - AS (Apr. 19, 1894), 121-123; (Apr. 26, 1894), 129-131.

[265] GC, 1884 ed., 387.

[266] Ibid., 381.

[267] Ibid.

One aspect not particularly stressed by other Adventist authors, is E.G. White's attention to Catholic ritual, which--though based upon deception--she found "most impressive"; these could not "fail to impress the

Ellen White shared the concern about the specific interest of the Roman Catholic Church in America, and about the desire of the Protestants for closer co-operation with Rome and their combined moves toward the enforcement of Sunday observance.[268]

The language Ellen G. White uses to describe the pernicious attempts of Catholicism to put everything in place for its future ends is strongly reminiscent of that used by fellow-Adventist writers of her days:

> She is silently growing in power.... Throughout the lands she is piling up her lofty and massive structures, in the secret recesses of which her former persecutions will be repeated. She is stealthily and unsuspectedly strengthening her forces to further her own ends when the time shall come for her to strike....[269]

In the following chapter, "The Coming Conflict", this scenario is further extended into the future.[270] There, in a few sentences, Ellen G. White, summarizes what has continued to be the outline of her (and Adventism's) eschatology:

> Protestantism will yet stretch her hand across the gulf to grasp the hand of Spiritualism; she will reach over the abyss to clasp hands with the Roman power; and under the influence of this threefold union, our country will follow in the steps of Rome in trampling upon the rights of conscience.[271]

That picture, though the later editions of *The Great Controversy* are somewhat less specific about

---

mind with awe and reverence" (GC, 1884 ed., 382-383). Her two-year stay in Europe, during which time she visited several famous cathedrals, strengthened that feeling. See D.A. Delafield, Ellen G. White in Europe, 1885-1887 (Washington, DC: RHPA, 1975), 235.

[268] GC, 1884 ed., 390.

[269] Ibid., 397.

[270] Ibid., 398-410.

[271] Ibid., 405.

developments in America,[272] has remained the core of traditional Adventist eschatological expectations.[273]

Comparing Ellen G. White's statements about Roman Catholicism with those of other Adventist writers, the similarity both in content and tone is striking. But, on the other hand, Ellen White was probably more concerned about reaching Roman Catholics with the Adventist version of Christianity than were most of her contemporaries. Repeatedly she emphasized that there are many conscientious Christians in the Roman Catholic communion,[274] and that "a great number will be saved from among Catholics."[275] She felt very strongly that Adventists should avoid giving the impression that they are the avowed enemies of Roman Catholics, "and should not create a prejudice in their minds unnecessarily by making a raid upon them."[276] There is also the danger, she said, "that our ministers will say too much against the Catholics and provoke against themselves the

---

[272] Cf. 1884 ed., 410 with 1911 ed., 592. Sections in Testimonies for the Church, vol. V (Mountain View, Cal.: PPPA, 1948; first published in 1882) are probably most specific about the threat of national Sunday legislation and the involvement of Catholicism, and organizations as the National Reform Movement (449-454; 711-718).

[273] For other statements of Ellen G. White on the importance of Sunday legislation in the endtime drama, see "The Approaching Crisis," RH Extra (Dec. 11, 1888), 4-5; "David's Prayer," RH (Dec. 18, 1888), 785-787; "An Address in Regard to the Sunday Movement," RH Extra (Dec. 24, 1889), 2-3; Testimonies to the Church, vol. V, 712.

[274] GC, 1884 ed., 381; Ellen G. White, Testimonies to the Church, vol. 9, 241, 243-244; Ellen G. White, "In the Spirit and Power of Elias," concl., RH (Nov. 20, 1913), 3-4; Ellen G. White, "The False and the True," Bible Training School (Feb. 1, 1913), 146; Ellen G. White, Evangelism (Washington, DC: RHPA, 1946), 234.

[275] Written in 1887; see Ellen G. White, Evangelism, 574.

[276] Ibid.

strongest prejudices of that church."[277] Furthermore, she
urged "those who write for our papers" not to "make
unkind thrusts and allusions" that will impede the task
of reaching "all classes, the Catholics included."[278] And
she encouraged the Adventist publishing houses "to keep
out of the books illustrations of auto-da-fé's, Catholic
pictures of persecution and burning," since it was not
necessary to bring "these wicked deeds ... in all their
terrible details" before the eyes of the readers.[279]

VIII Institution vs. Individuals

As time went by Adventists began to distinguish more
clearly between the Roman Catholic Church or the papacy
as an institution and individual Catholics. More and
more it was the papal *system* they denounced. At times
they would even acknowledge that the spirit of the
papacy—of exalting oneself above God—was not confined
to the Vatican or the Roman Catholic Church, but that
"there are [also] followers of the papacy in the true
Church of Christ."[280]
    Adventists had no doubt whatsoever: Roman
Catholicism "as a system of doctrine is a deception and
a delusion, and ... the Pope is the man of sin and the
Antichrist of the Scriptures."[281] An honest effort had to

---

[277] Ellen G. White, <u>Evangelism</u>, 574 (from a letter
written in 1887).

[278] Ellen G. White, <u>Testimonies to the Church</u>, vol.
9, 241; see also Ellen G. White, <u>Counsels to Writers and
Editors</u> (Nashville, Tenn.: SPA, 1947), 64-65, where
material is quoted that was written in 1896, which
expresses the same sentiment.

[279] Ibid., 172; from a letter written in 1897.   In
an other letter, also written in 1897, she recounts
seeing the illustrations in Fox's Book of Martyrs and
the nightmares these caused her. See Ellen G. White, <u>The
Publishing Ministry</u> (Washington, DC: RHPA, 1983), 217.

[280] L.A. Smith, "The Papacy," <u>RH</u> (Nov. 5, 1901),
720.

[281] Editorial, <u>PM</u>, vol. 3, no. 4 (4th quarter,
1911), 194.

be made to represent these [Catholic] teachings fairly, using only "reliable testimony and sound argument when dealing with them."[282]

The language of Adventist publications was not to be unnecessarily antagonistic. This was of special concern to the pioneers of Adventism in Europe, where in some countries more than ninety percent of the people were Catholics; it would be a "questionable policy to speak of the Catholics in a manner that will be sure to antagonize them, before they have heard the truth."[283]

But this in no way diminished the fact that the Roman Catholic system was "inherently and morally wrong" and must be identified as Antichrist.[284] Its errors demanded "uncompromising opposition."[285] "As a system, Romanism is no more in harmony with the principles of the gospel of Christ than it has ever been."[286] Judged by its true nature and its fruits, one cannot fail to see the "dark and dismal cloud," which covers the whole system. Not only is the system corrupted by false doctrines, but it also maintains principles which are diametrically opposed to the ideals of religious liberty and democracy.[287] No one who studies the Scriptures can question that the Catholic Church

> ... as a body was morally fallen, long ages since. Their heathen corruptions in doctrine, worship of images, pride, persecutions, Jesuitical hypocrisy, oppression, blasphemous assumptions, and a vast horde of practices condemned by Scripture, demonstrate the truthfulness of the scriptural

---

[282] Editorial, PM, vol. 3, no. 1 (1st quarter, 1911), 2.

[283] Letter of William C. White to J.H. Waggoner (Apr. 2, 1889; Gen. Conf. Arch.).

[284] Uriah Smith, "Our Attitude Toward Roman Catholicism," RH (June 11, 1901), 379.

[285] Ibid.

[286] R. Weatherby, "No Antagonism to Rome," RH (March 22, 1887), 179.

[287] W.W. Prescott, "The Religio-Political Principles of the Papacy," RH (Dec. 3, 1908), 4.

title given: "the mother of harlots and abominations of the earth."[288]

Unfortunately, there is no hope for the restoration of "modern Babylon."[289] The denominational journal quoted with approval from a speech given by "father" Gavazzi--a former priest--about the "present unreformable condition" of the Church of Rome:

Now, after its multifarious councils, and especially after the last sacrilegious and blasphemous council held under Pius IX, the church is in error from beginning to end, from head to foot....[290]

Consequently, it would be wrong to consider the Catholic Church a Christian church! Dudley M. Canright, in 1872, estimated that among the world's 1.3 billion people, 314 million claimed to be Christians. Among these 314 million Christians he finds 66 million who belong to the "old Greek Church." They must be counted out, because they have so far apostatized from true Christianity, that they are "little better than heathens." In addition to these, Canright estimates, there are 160 million Roman Catholics. They, he says, are only Christians in name. Most Protestants "regard them as the worst enemies of the cross of Christ, and so they are. Hence, they must also be thrown out as not really being Christians."[291] What the Roman Catholic Church teaches is so contrary to the teachings of Christ, that "it cannot be recognized by any true

---

[288] George I. Butler, "Has There Been a Moral Fall of the Churches?" RH, cont. (Dec. 22, 1891), 792.

[289] W.W. Prescott, "The Empty Boast of the Roman Catholic Church," RH (Jan. 25, 1912), 10.

[290] "Rome as It is," RH (March 1, 1881), 141.

[291] D.M. Canright, "Present Condition of the World," RH (April 16, 1872), 143-144. In this article the author further mentions 88 million Protestants, the majority of which he discounts are merely "nominal". This leaves him with "probably no more than ca. 8 million real Christians" in the world.

195

believer as a Christian Church."[292] "That one should laud [the Catholic Church] as a Christian Church," Uriah Smith adds, "shows how far he has departed from Christianity; for from this system Christ is so fully divorced that not a particle of Christianity can be found in it."[293]

Yet, it is within "the fold of this great Babylon that many of the people of God are to be found."[294] Seventh-day Adventists have never believed, Butler affirms, that "our little church comprehends all the Christians in the world."[295] Adventist authors increasingly stressed their conviction that, in spite of the wicked system to which they belong, many "sincere Roman Catholics...are living up to all the light they have, and are therefore Christians."[296] Rays of light will yet, in the future, penetrate the darkness in which they are, and many will yet take their stand with the people of God.[297] With a proper effort multitudes of the Roman Catholic laity could be reached with the message of the Bible and be persuaded to exchange tradition for "the whole truth."[298] And since there are so "many good Christians...in the communion of Rome...it is not against any, as individuals, that opposition is to be raised."[299]

---

[292] Uriah Smith, "Our Attitude Toward Roman Catholicism," RH (June 11, 1901), 379.

[293] Ibid.

[294] R.M. Kilmore, "Babylon," RH (Sept. 17, 1895), 595.

[295] George I. Butler, "Fall of Babylon," RH, extra issue (Nov. 22, 1887), 9.

[296] Editorial, PM, vol. 3, no. 4 (4th quarter, 1911), 194.

[297] R. Weatherby, "No Antagonism to Rome," RH (March 22, 1887), 179.

[298] Uriah Smith, "A Timely Truth," RH (Jan. 2, 1894), 8.

[299] Editorial note, RH (Apr. 30, 1895), 288.

The fundamental premise which precluded any re-
assessment of the Roman Catholic "system" was the oft-
repeated dictum that "Rome never changes."[300] This is,
what Catholicism itself claimed, and the fact was
articulated in an unparalleled fashion in the dogma of
papal infallibility.

Adventists noted that "many Protestants seem to be
foolishly beguiling themselves with the idea that the
Roman Church is not what it used to be," and that it has
truly been remolded by the enlightenment and progress of
the nineteenth century.[301] These Protestants believed
Rome was changing in spite of the fact that Rome itself
claims it never changes. It was admitted that some
individuals might be influenced by "the free spirit of
this age and this land," but the Church as such and its
hierarchy was in no way affected by it.[302] Pope Pius X
(1903-1914) was admired by many as a profoundly
religious man, a reformer of church music and a defender
of civil marriage, but he was not really any more
liberal than his predecessors and his teachings were no
more evangelical than those of the Council of Trent.[303]

If Rome *seemed* to be different from what it had
earlier been, it was simply a matter a expediency.[304]
Rome's more conciliatory attitude did not reflect a
changed spirit, but rather a diminished strength; "if it
had the power, it would be quick to reproduce its former

---

[300] "Temporal Power of the Pope," RH, July 28,
1868), 94; G.W. Morse, "Rome Never Changes," RH (Nov. 2,
1886), 679; "The Romanism of Today," RH (Oct. 18, 1887),
656; L.A. Smith, "Pope Leo's Encyclical," RH (June 30,
1891), 416.

[301] Uriah Smith, "Romanism and Progress," RH (Feb.
8, 1887), 89; George E. Fifield, "Sad Apostasy," RH
(Jan. 21, 1890), 35.

[302] Uriah Smith, "Showing Her Colors," RH (May 3,
1887), 280.

[303] Walter G. Bond, "Rome Never Changes," RH (Oct.
18, 1906), 13.

[304] Uriah Smith, "A Sly Word for Americans," RH
(Apr. 23, 1895), 266.

scenes of torture and blood...."[305] The underlying
ambition of the Catholic Church remained to regain its
full former power. The policy shift of the Vatican with
regard to France in suddenly supporting the republic,
where it had unfailingly advocated the return of the
monarchy, was one of many examples of political
manoeuvres to reach its ultimate goals.[306]

Most importantly, American Protestants should not
be fooled by "the smooth talk of priests in America."
The fact that in the United States Catholicism presented
itself as more accommodating was only due to its
inability to put the real Roman Catholic theory of
church and state into practice.[307] Catholics might appear
to be loyal to the American institutions, but underneath
lay the "settled determination to wipe them out with
fire and sword the first moment they are able to do
it."[308] Had they the power, they would immediately close
every public school and every place of worship in the
country.[309] When that fatal time would arrive, the Roman
Church could count on the unquestioning obedience of the
members of the many religious orders, particularly the
Jesuits, who will do whatever they are told to do.[310] As
soon as Rome would have control of the American
institutions, it would gladly do for America what it had
done for those countries where the Roman Catholic Church
has undisputed authority.[311]

---

[305] "Rome Unchanged," RH (July 21, 1874), 43.

[306] M.E. Kellogg, "The Changed Attitude of the
Catholic Church in France Toward the Republic," RH (Jan.
19, 1892), 37.

[307] W.W. Prescott, "The Pope's Authority over
Rulers," RH (July 9, 1908), 4.

[308] Uriah Smith, "Feel my paw," RH (Nov. 26, 1889),
744.

[309] Ibid. See also W. Covert, "Romanism as it is,"
RH (Apr. 8, 1884), 228.

[310] M.E. Kellogg, "The Catholic Church vs. Secret
Societies," RH (May 3, 1893), 288.

[311] W.W. Prescott, "Romanism in America and Rome,"
RH (Dec. 15, 1904), 6.

If there are any changes in Rome, Adventists maintained, these are temporary, compelled by circumstances, but not by principle. If the Catholic Church underlines that the USA should have no fear of Catholic aspirations, since Catholics in America will work within the democratic American framework, this merely shows a position based on expediency.[312] As part of a long-term strategy the Catholics want to win the sympathy of the Protestants, so that, in the final conflict, "Rome and Romanized Protestantism" can be arrayed against the Sabbath keeping remnant.[313] "Intelligent Protestants," however, should "not be misled by such sophistry."[314] They should realize, before it is too late, that "the Catholic power is far-reaching in her purposes, that she lays her plans in secret, patiently biding the time when coming events shall warrant her in bringing her plans to light."[315]

Only very occasionally would Adventist authors have a word of praise for Catholics. They recognized that many individual Catholics did not want any union of church and state, but were peace-loving, patriotic people, who wanted to take their religion but not their politics from Rome.[316] They admitted that sometimes even a Catholic historian could write without undue bias.[317] And, perhaps more surprisingly, at one time the *Review and Herald* spoke of Archbishop John Ireland, as one of "the friends of humanity," who deserved credit for

---

[312] W.W. Prescott, "The Relation Between the Church and the State: the Roman Catholic Doctrine," RH (Feb. 18, 1909), 3-4.

[313] M.E. Kellogg, "Patting Rome on the Back," RH (Dec. 22, 1891), 800.

[314] Edit. note, RH (Apr. 23, 1895), 272.

[315] R. Weatherby, "No Antagonism to Rome," RH (March 22, 1887), 179.

[316] L.A. Smith, The United States in Prophecy, 152.

[317] W.W. Prescott gave a positive review of Dr. F.X. Funk, Manual of Church History (London, 1910) in "Candid Admissions by a Roman Catholic Historian," RH (Dec. 7, 1911), 6-7.

preserving and manifesting "the true principles of a broad Christian philanthropy."[318] But the fact that "there are many earnest, self-sacrificing members of the Catholic Church, who give evidence of willing to bear burdens, and even lay down their lives, for others," should not mislead us. "These things do not make Christianity."[319]

> Our attitude toward Roman Catholics, then, in a word, is this: Uncompromising opposition to the errors, the workings, and the tendency of that system of religion, but recognition of every good quality in individual members, and a desire to do them good, and to persuade them to better things.[320]

IX Conclusion

In the period 1863-1915 Seventh-day Adventists were not more vehemently anti-Catholic than many other Protestant denominations. They were a good deal less militant than organizations such as the American Protective Association which was backed by a broad spectrum of concerned Protestants. In comparison with many other Protestants, they were not excessive in their anti-Catholic statements. It would seem that the Baptists, for instance, were more involved with anti-Catholic organizations and shared the nativistic worry about massive Catholic immigration to a greater extent than did the Seventh-day Adventists.[321]

---

[318] G.C. Tenney, "A Liberal Catholic," RH (Oct. 15, 1895), 661.

[319] Uriah Smith, "Our Attitude Toward Roman Catholics," RH (June 11, 1901), 379.

[320] Ibid.

[321] For Baptist concerns about large-scale immigration of Catholics in the 1880s and 1890s and involvement in anti-Catholic activities, see Lawrence B. Davis, Immigrants, Baptists and the Protestant Mind in America (Urbana, Ill.: Univ. of Illinois Press, 1973), 63-96; see also Vacua A. Crumpton, "An Analysis of Southern Baptist Response to Diplomatic Relations Between the United States and the Vatican," (Ph.D.

Methodists in the 19th century were regularly involved in anti-Catholic polemics. Like Adventists, they saw between Catholics and Adventists "a chasm which refuses to be bridged."[322] And in their criticism of Roman Catholic doctrines and in expressing their fears of the growth of Roman Catholic strength, they used many similar arguments.[323]

The attitude of Seventh-day Adventists toward Roman Catholicism during this period was conditioned by their interpretations of the prophecies in Daniel and the Revelation, for which they believed they found ample support in history, relying heavily as they did on contemporary Protestant church histories in which Catholicism was the villain. Adventist criticisms of Catholicism continued to focus on the papacy as a power structure, and the Adventist attitude was in fact more anti-papal than just anti-Catholic. It continued to a large extent to be determined by three basic eschatological premises:

(1) The Sabbath-Sunday issue is going to play a decisive role in the endtime conflict.

(2) The two major players in the endtime drama will be apostate Protestantism and the antichristian beast, alias the little horn, alias the whore of Revelation 17: Roman Catholicism.

(3) The United States will play a key role in the endtime drama and will somehow be involved in enforcing the mark of the beast, i.e. obligatory Sunday worship.

A number of events, notably in the 1880s and early 1890s appeared to fit into that framework and provided strong confirmation in the Adventist mind of the correctness of these views.

In commenting on trends and events in Catholicism, Adventists made an eclectic use of available sources, selecting those items which further confirmed their views, without attempts at any in-depth analysis of what

---

diss., Southwestern Baptist Theol. Sem., 1988), 108-113.

[322] Henry King Carroll, "The Catholic Dogma of Church Authority," Methodist Quarterly Review, (Oct. 1884), 719.

[323] Ibid., 719-736. See also Charles Yriogen, jr., "Methodists and Roman Catholics in 19th Century America," Methodist History, vol. 28, no. 3 (Apr. 1990), 172-186.

was really happening,[324] and hardly paying attention to some major problems affecting the American Catholic Church.[325] Operating with the conviction that "Rome never changes," there could be no openness for real dialogue. It was unthinkable even to suggest that there could possibly be some change for the better in Catholicism. As a result everything done by the "Romanists" had to be part of a shrewd masterplan in which the extinction of the Sabbath keeping remnant was the ultimate goal.

Ellen G. White was very much part of this mode of thinking and most of what she wrote about Catholicism originated in the period in which external events on the American scene happened to corroborate earlier predictions.[326] It can be endlessly debated whether her views were largely shaped by the general climate of thought which she shared with other Adventist leaders, or whether that climate was, at least partly, created by her writings. But whichever position is taken, it cannot be denied that Ellen G. White's increasing authority within the Seventh-day Adventist Church greatly contributed to the continued general acceptance of an eschatological scenario which received its more or less final formulation in this peculiar historical late 19th century American setting. And this increased authority of her writings, in its turn, prevented Adventists from taking a good, second, look at contemporary Catholicism when other Protestants were increasingly prepared to do so.

Nonetheless, Adventists became more prepared to acknowledge that many individual Roman Catholics were genuine Christians and would be honest enough to accept "the truth" if it were carefully presented to them.

---

[324] As an example: Adventist made much of the loss of the pope's temporal power, but seemed almost blind to the concurrent ultramontanist trend.

[325] Such as the "Americanist heresy", which did not directly relate to areas of Adventist concern.

[326] For an insightful study of Ellen G. White's relationship with Protestant America in the final decades of the 19th century, see Jonathan Butler, "The World of E.G. White and the End of the World," Spectrum, Vol. 10, no. 2 (Aug. 1979), 2-13.

CHAPTER FIVE

ADVENTISTS AND CATHOLICS
1915-1965

I Adventism Comes of Age

By 1915 the contours of modern Adventism were clearly visible. The church had acquired its organizational and institutional infrastructure that has basically remained unchanged until the present.[1] The "pioneers," and Ellen G. White--who died in 1915--in particular, had left their indelible stamp on Adventist theology and practice.

In spite of the restraints caused by the two World Wars, the church continued to expand, both in the United States of America and in other parts of the world. Adventism continued to be a highly institutionalized movement: educational, medical and publishing facilities increased in number as the church further expanded. Although the church in most ways remained very American --in its outlook, methods, and certainly its leadership --the growth rate outside of North America soon exceeded that in North America itself. In 1915 world membership stood at 136,907, of whom 77,805--still a majority-- lived in North America. In 1926 the point was reached that non-American membership equalled that in North America. Soon North American membership accounted for only a modest percentage of total membership. The following figures show a clear trend:

	North America	world
1915	77,805	136,907
1940	185,788	504,472

---

[1] For a survey of the history of Seventh-day Adventism during the period 1915-1965, see Gary Land, "Shaping the Modern Church; 1906-1930," chap. in: Land, ed., Adventism in America, 139-169; Keld J. Reynolds, "The Church under Stress, 1931-1960," chap. in: Gary Land, ed., Adventism in America, 170-207; R.W. Schwarz, Light Bearers to the Remnant, 354-627.

| 1955 | 293,448 | 1,006,218 |
| 1965 | 380,855 | 1,578,504[2] |

The American context continued very largely to determine the Adventist response to issues of the times. An Adventist War Service Commission was organized during the First World War, mainly to assist Adventists who were conscripted to serve in the US army and faced difficulties in practicing their religion. At the time of World War II the formation of a Medical Cadet Corps represented a conscious effort on the part of the church to help provide Adventism with a type of military service its members could conscientiously perform, while at the same time offering a meaningful contribution to the defence of the United States and its allies.

Apart from the war-related issues, of all social concerns the temperance cause, no doubt, received most attention. Adventists joined many others in promoting a "dry" lifestyle and were staunch supporters of the Eighteenth Amendment which--for a period of 14 years, from 1919 until it was repealed in 1933--made America a nation where alcohol was officially banned. Another phenomenon Adventism had to deal with, was the resurgence of the trade union movement in the 1930s. The anti-labour union position of the Adventist church caused hardship for many of its members. Some more or less successful accommodations were worked out during the late 1940s and 1950s, but the issue was never satisfactorily resolved.

Sunday legislation remained a matter of grave concern to Adventists, although the excitement did not run as high as in the final decades of the previous century. Other church-state issues, such as government aid to parochial schools eclipsed to a considerable extent the fear for universal Sunday laws with inevitable persecutions of Sabbath keepers. But fears that Sabbath keeping might become difficult, if not impossible, never fully subsided and were in particular kept alive by concerns about the strong lobby that worked for the introduction of a new calendar with "blank" days, which would upset the weekly cycle and cause major problems for Sabbath keepers (and some groups of Sunday observers as well). In all areas of real or potential conflict between government and religion, Roman Catholicism was usually seen as a major factor, as this chapter will illustrate.

---

[2] See General Conference of Seventh-day Adventists, (annual) Statistical Reports, 1915-1965.

The most remarkable facet of Adventism in the 1915–1965 period was--certainly in the context of this study--its ability to strengthen its internal unity. Although there were from time to time dissenters, major splits in the denomination did not occur. Throughout the period under review in this chapter the theological climate remained rather calm. Care was taken to remove the remaining traces of Arian and anti-Trinitarian views, which necessitated some revisions in such Adventist classics as Uriah Smith's *Daniel and the Revelation* and *Bible Readings for the Home Circle*.[3] A new emphasis on righteousness by faith and on the dangers of legalism was evident in a number of influential books.[4] Nevertheless, non-essentials proved at times to be divisive, as the bitter controversy over the "daily" of Daniel 8 demonstrated.[5]

Apart from a strong emphasis on the development of a professional ministry--the establishing of a graduate theological school in 1934 was a decisive step in that direction--a few theological study conferences and a number of publications were important factors in the ironing out of differences of opinion and in maintaining doctrinal unity. Relatively little was known about the Bible and Teachers' Conference of 1919 (July 1 to August 11), until in 1974 transcripts were found of the proceedings of most of its sessions.[6] The information presently available reveals an openness and depth of debate that has seldom, if ever, been paralleled in similar Adventist gatherings. It dealt, among many other things, with questions regarding the nature of the writings of Mrs. Ellen G. White in a way that has a

---

[3] See LeRoy E. Froom, <u>Movement of Destiny</u>, 422–428; cf. above, p. 127.

[4] E.g. W.W. Prescott, <u>The Doctrine of Christ</u> (Washington, DC: RHPA, ca. 1920); A.G. Daniells, <u>Christ Our Righteousness</u> (Washington, DC: Ministerial Association, 1926). See also Leroy E. Froom, <u>Movement of Destiny</u>, 377–391; 400–401.

[5] See below, pp. 220–222.

[6] See 1919 Bible Conference transcripts. Copies of these transcripts are in the Heritage Room of the James White Library at Andrews University (Berrien Springs, MI).

distinctly modern ring and resembles discussions of later decades.[7] The 1952 Bible Conference (September 1-13) was a much more international meeting where many of the distinctive features of Adventist theology were restudied and re-affirmed.[8]

A unifying influence was undeniably exerted by the 1931 *Statement of Belief*, which summarized the most important Adventist doctrines in 22 short paragraphs, and by the *Church Manual*, which appeared in 1932. The standardization of the baptismal vow, in 1941, also contributed to further unity.

The seven-volume *Seventh-day Adventist Bible Commentary*, written by 37 contributors--mostly trained scholars--and published between 1953 and 1957, was not intended to furnish an official Adventist view, but was soon widely accepted and did much to strengthen Adventist consensus.[9] The publication of *Seventh-day Adventists Answer Questions on Doctrine*[10] resulted from extensive discussions with a few evangelical leaders and was a studied attempt to clarify aspects of Adventist theology that were causing misunderstandings and were often referred to by others as proof for Adventism's sub-christian theology. The book certainly helped in that respect, though it has since been criticized by many Adventists because of its Christology.[11]

---

[7] Bert Haloviak, In the Shadow of the 'Daily': Background and Aftermath of the 1919 Bible and History Teachers' Conference (Washington, DC: Office of Archives and Statistics, Gen. Conf. of SDA, n.d.), 44-59.

[8] The papers delivered and discussed during this conference were subsequently published in: Our Firm Foundation, 2 vols. (Washington, DC: RHPA), 1953; further referred to as OFF.

[9] Raymond F. Cottrell, "The Untold Story of the Bible Commentary," Spectrum, vol. 16, no. 3 (Aug. 1985), 35-51.

[10] Seventh-day Adventists Answer Questions on Doctrine (Washington, DC: RHPA, 1957); further referred to as QOD.

[11] See Keld J. Reynolds, "The Church under Stress, 1931-1960, 185-188; R.W. Schwarz, Light Bearers to the Remnant, 542-546.

Adventist attitudes toward other Christians remained tense. This chapter will show that, although
their views regarding Catholicism underwent some developments, Adventists remained committed to their anti-
Catholic stance and continued to view Catholicism as a
present threat and a future source of even greater
trouble. With regard to Adventist attitudes toward other
Protestant Christians, a clear ambiguity became more and
more visible. Though not fully aligning themselves with
the fundamentalist movement, Adventists made no secret
of their appreciation for the fundamentalist stand on a
number of common issues.[12] And, while not refraining from
criticizing Protestants, the anti-Protestant polemic was
considerably softened and, in spite of the eschatological belief in a mighty conspiracy of Catholics,
Protestants and secular powers, Adventist publications
showed increasing respect for what they saw as the noble
intent of Protestant leaders in the national and
international ecumenical movement.[13]

II Developments in American Catholicism

In many ways the 1915-1965 period was a turbulent period
for the Roman Catholic Church.[14] The church grew in
numbers and strength, in part due to its strong
missionary program, and certainly due to strong and
capable leadership at the top.
    The pontificate of Benedict XV, an accomplished
career diplomat before he was elected pope, was marked
by the First World War. He remained strictly neutral
during the war, but worked with great zeal for a just
peace. Although he was not able to solve the "Roman
Question," he paved the way for his successor, Pius XI
(pope from 1922 to 1939) to come to (rather favourable)
terms with the Italian authorities. In the Lateran
Treaty and Concordat with the Vatican in 1929 dictator
Mussolini granted the pope complete sovereignty over a
Vatican State and recognized Catholicism's privileged

---

[12] See George McCready Price, <u>Back to the Bible</u>
(Washington, DC: RHPA, 1917).

[13] See below, pp. 267-269.

[14] For a survey of the history of Catholicism in
this period, see Thomas S. Bokenkotter, <u>A Concise
History of the Catholic Church</u>, 344-355.

status in Italy. Pius XI continued the policy of Benedict of concluding concordats with many nations, with the intent of obtaining advantages for Catholics where possible. Pius' concordat with Hitler's Germany in 1933 evoked heavy criticisms. But Pius XI did perceive the grave dangers of Nazism, as is evident from his many notes of protest against the Nazi government and his encyclical *Mit brennender Sorge*, in which he denounced Nazism as fundamentally antichristian.

Pius XII (pope from 1939 to 1958), was the Vatican's Secretary of State before he became pope on the eve of the Second World War. His peace efforts remained unsuccessful. Although it is recognized that he did much to help the victims of the war, he has often been criticized for failing to speak out more strongly against the Nazi atrocities.

During and after the war the papal prestige continued to increase, as was in particular evident from the number of foreign diplomats accredited with the Holy See. The appointment of Myron C. Taylor as President Roosevelt's personal representative at the Vatican in 1940 was a case in point.

The era of excessive authoritarianism and isolationism, which had characterized the rule of both Pius XI and Pius XII, came to an end when John XXIII, who was supposed to be only a care-taker pope, began his pontificate in 1958. He surprised the church with his decision to convene a general church council that was to bring a--by many long awaited--*aggiornamento* to the church. Among other things, Protestant-Catholic relationships were immediately positively affected.

In 1908 American Catholicism exchanged its missionary status for a full recognition as a branch of the church in complete equality with the church in Europe.[15] By 1915 Roman Catholicism was well established in the United States with an ever-growing constituency of multinational origin. But the church's period of growth by immigration effectively came to an end with the outbreak of World War I. Post-war immigration was soon severely restricted by the passing of the Johnson-Reed Immigration Act of 1924, which established a quota system based on race and ethnicity.

---

[15] For a survey of the history of American Catholicism during the 1915-1965 period, see James J. Hennessey, <u>American Catholics</u>, 219-306; J.P. Dolan, <u>The American Catholic Experience</u>, 349-427; Winthrop S. Hudson, <u>Religion in America</u>, 360-373.

In the ensuing decades momentous changes were to take place: American Catholicism rapidly changed--in spite of persistent anti-intellectualist and isolationist tendencies--into a much more Americanized, nonimmigrant, largely middle-class pluralistic community. Although its growth rate decreased, its rate of gain in its membership was still astounding. By 1920 the official, though probably underreported, membership was 17.9 million. By 1930 it stood at 20.2 million, and in 1940 at 21.3 million. By 1950 and 1960 these numbers had increased to 26.6 and 42.1 million respectively.[16]

American Catholicism not only gained in numerical strength, but also in cohesiveness. The National Catholic War Council, organized in 1917 to coordinate the efforts of Catholic agencies involved in war-related activities, continued in the post-war period as the National Catholic Welfare Council (NCWC), which after a somewhat rocky start, developed into a much needed national church structure.

Although the "Bishops' Program of Social Reconstruction," a detailed social action plan policy statement by the NCWC, indicated Catholic willingness to get involved in the social challenges of the times, it was only in the 1930s that Catholic social contributions, notably through its comprehensive Catholic Action program, began to have a major impact. The papal encyclical *Quadragesimo Anno* (1931) provided a vital source of inspiration.

There was strong Catholic support for Roosevelt's New Deal, as many of his programs coincided with Catholic social ideals. Among these ideals those linked to labour issues were emphasized most strongly. Trade unionism in particular received strong Catholic endorsement. Prohibition was never a dominant Catholic concern, while the problem of race discrimination did not appear on the Catholic social agenda until the 1950s.

Throughout the 1915-1965 period, but perhaps most notably in the post-World War I decade, American Catholicism pursued a strong "brick-and-mortar" program of institutional development, especially in the area of education. Though the ideal--every Catholic child educated in a Catholic school--was never fully attained, significant progress was made at all levels. In 1920, 35 percent of Catholic parishes had schools--about the same as in the last two decades of the nineteenth century; by

---

[16] Winthrop S. Hudson, <u>Religion in America</u>, 362.

1959 this percentage had increased to 59.[17] The growth was particularly strong on the secondary level, but the number of Catholic colleges and universities also increased: from 130 in 1921 to 163 by 1928. They enrolled about two-thirds of all Catholic college-age students, compared to only one-third in 1921.[18]

The material resources of American Catholics became more and more important in the financing of the global church. This was particularly the case with the global missionary outreach of Roman Catholics, in which American Catholic mission societies and missionaries played an increasing role. But the strong institutional development at home provided a formidable challenge. Not surprising therefore was the renewed Catholic claim that it ought to profit from public funds for the operating of its parochial school system. This Catholic insistence on federal aid and related benefits was probably the single most important target for the anti-Catholic polemics in this period of American history.

III Continued Anti-Catholicism

Anti-Catholicism was never absent from American society, but a few waves of particularly vivid anti-Catholic sentiments are particularly important.[19] After a period of fierce anti-Catholic bigotry before World War I, it declined significantly during the war. However, growing nativism in the post-war period and the renewed widespread fear of growing Catholicism led to a period of open, and often ugly conflict after the war, which was mainly political rather than doctrinal in orientation. The Ku-Klux-Klan, first founded in 1866 in Tennessee with the aim of terrorizing blacks into submission, was recreated in 1915 as a movement that was

---

[17] James J. Hennesey, <u>American Catholics</u>, 397, 275-276.

[18] Ibid., 237.

[19] For a survey of anti-Catholicism in the United States during the 1915-1965 period, see Lerond Curry, <u>Protestant-Catholic Relations in America</u> (Lexington: The University of Kentucky Press, 1972), 1-79; Clifton E. Olmstead, <u>History of Religion in the United States</u>, 434-435; 558-560; 586-589; Gustavus Myers, <u>History of Bigotry</u>, 211-276.

not only anti-black, but also anti-Semitic, and strongly anti-foreign born, thus: anti-Catholic. The KKK enjoyed strong support from many Baptists and Methodists in the South, and was at least partly responsible for blocking the presidential nomination of Alfred E. Smith (the Roman Catholic governor of New York) at the Democratic national convention in 1924. The KKK had its peak in 1925, when it boasted almost 9 million members, but soon after this it began to decline.

The KKK still played a role in the 1928 anti-Smith campaign, but the anti-Catholic sentiment at that time also found a vociferous expression in journals as the *New Menace* and *The Protestant*. There was also a widespread use of Baptist, Methodist and Presbyterian pulpits for political use.[20] Whether Smith lost his bid for the presidency because he was a Catholic remains a much disputed point. Many, no doubt, voted against him because of his religious conviction, but this was undoubtedly also the reason why many voted for him! Lerond Curry may well be right in his conclusion that in 1928 there were still "too many Americans in whose minds an unwritten law barred a Catholic from the White House and to whom Roman Catholicism still appeared as an alien force to the American way of life."[21]

A period of relative calm in Protestant-Catholic relationships--based more on a successful emphasis on brotherhood and good will than on any increased theological understanding--began soon after the Smith episode and lasted until 1939. When in March 1939 President Roosevelt sent J.P. Kennedy to Rome to represent the USA at the coronation of Pius XII, there was widespread uneasiness about the fact that by doing so he "bestowed new dignity and significance upon the Catholic church in America."[22] But the suspicion and dormant hostility burst into open conflict later that year when the president announced the appointment of Myron C. Taylor as ambassador without portfolio to the Vatican. Scores of Protestant denominations and other organizations joined in sharp protest.

In April 1945, just after the Second World War, anti-Catholic feelings were further fuelled as a result

---

[20] Gustavus Myers, History of Bigotry, 261-263.

[21] Lerond Curry, Protestant-Catholic Relations in America, 19.

[22] Ibid., 36.

of Taylor's reconfirmation by President Truman. When Taylor resigned in 1950, and in 1951 General Mark W. Clark was nominated to take the post of full-ranking ambassador to the Vatican, the vehement protests finally caused Clark to ask Truman for the withdrawal of his name. (In 1970 Henry Cabot Lodge was asked by President Nixon to make periodic visits to the Vatican for talks on international and humanitarian topics; it was not until 1983, under Ronald Reagan, that full diplomatic relations were established with the Holy See.)

Underlying much of the animosity of the 1940s and 1950s was the fundamental issue of separation between church and state. Many felt that the Catholic efforts to secure public money for their parochial school system were a clear breach of this principle. Statements by John A. Ryan and Moorhouse I.X. Millar, in their book *The State and the Church*, first published in 1922, and in a later book *Catholic Principles of Politics*, co-authored by John A. Ryan and F.J. Bolland, continued to cause fears that the rights of non-Catholic Americans would not be safe if Catholics were ever to be become the majority.[23] Such fears were also forcefully expressed in Paul Blanshard's book *America and Catholic Power*[24] which went through numerous printings. A less venomous, but very influential voice in the anti-Catholic clamour during the 1950s (and beyond) was a new organization which called itself "Protestants and Other Americans United for the Separation of Church and State." It was founded in 1947 and soon enjoyed widespread support.

Anti-Catholic sentiments gradually subsided toward the end of the 1950s as a result of concerted efforts of both Catholics and Protestants to improve mutual understanding. When John F. Kennedy in 1960 made his bid for the presidency, the issue of his Catholic affiliation was far less important than it had been for Smith in 1928. Now protests came mainly from smaller, ultraconservative bodies, which did not represent mainstream Protestantism.[25] But nothing in the late 1950s

---

[23] John A. Ryan and Moorhouse I. Millar, <u>The State and the Church</u> (New York: The Macmillan Co, 1922; and John A. Ryan and Francis J. Bolland, <u>Catholic Principles of Politics</u> (New York: The Macmillan Co., 1948).

[24] Boston: Beacon Press, 1949.

[25] Lerond Curry, <u>Protestant-Catholic Relations in America</u>, 72.

and 1960s did more to stimulate interfaith dialogue and understanding, and to diminish anti-Catholic tensions, than Pope John's initiative in calling an ecumenical council.

IV Reconfirming the Prophetic Framework

Adventists seldom sought to justify their method of prophetic interpretation to the uninitiated. This was not only true in the 19th century, when biblicism and millennialism were pervasive elements in much of American Protestantism,[26] but remained so until recently. Although some Adventist publications on prophetic topics in the 1915-1965 period show an increasing awareness of historical critical issues,[27] the basic validity of the method of continuous historical interpretation of apocalyptic prophecy was always tacitly assumed.

The traditional Adventist interpretation of the prophecies in Daniel and the Revelation, as embodied in Uriah Smith's classics *Thoughts on Daniel* and *Thoughts on the Revelation* (often published in one volume as *Daniel and the Revelation*) continued to be the basis for all further denominational prophetic literature. The high regard in which Smith's books were held and the tight control of Adventist leaders over all new publications left little room for innovative views. Against the background of the events surrounding World War I Smith's view of the "Eastern Question," with its prominent role for Turkey in the end-time scenario, was firmly supported by Adventist writers of that period.[28]

---

[26] Jonathan Butler, "When Prophecy Fails: The Validity of Apocalypticism," <u>Spectrum</u>, vol. 8, no. 1 (Sept. 1976), 11.

[27] See e.g. George McCready Price, <u>The Greatest of the Prophets</u> (Mountain View, Cal.: PPPA, 1955); F.D. Nichol, ed., <u>The Seventh-day Adventist Bible Commentary</u>, vol. 4 (Washington, DC: RHPA, 1955), 39-78; 743-744 (further referred to as <u>SDABC</u>).

[28] <u>The World in Crisis</u> (Nashville, Tenn.: SPA, 1915); A.G. Daniells, <u>The World War: Its Relationship to the Eastern Question and Armageddon</u> (Mountain View, Cal.: PPPA, 1917); A.G. Daniells, <u>The World in Perplexity</u> (Washington, DC: RHPA, 1918); <u>World Peace in the Light of Bible Prophecy</u> (Washington, DC: RHPA, 1919).

But Smith remained *the* authority on other aspects of prophecy as well.[29] And even when, in later years, some of his views (in particular about the "Eastern Question") were heavily criticized, and *Daniel and the Revelation* was largely discarded by Adventist colporteurs, this book continued to be used as a textbook in denominational schools.

In 1940 the Autumn Council (the annual meeting of the Executive Committee of the General Conference) voted to appoint a committee to investigate the feasibility of adapting Smith's book "to the needs of this fast-moving age." A year later it was reported that the book could, in the opinion of the committee, be adapted and modernized. Representatives of the three American denominational publishing houses, with the input of many others, were responsible for the 1944 revised edition. Some stylistic improvements were made, and it was also decided to soften or eliminate expressions that the modern reader might take as "unnecessary aspersion upon his religion or his church, or a reflection upon his country."[30] Some sources of questionable authority were replaced by others. The only theological change was the removal of a few lines in which the eternity of Christ was denied. But it was felt that the prophetic interpretations could remain untouched, even though on some points alternative views had arisen.[31] The abiding value of Smith's work was beyond doubt:

> [Smith's] interpretations of prophecy ... have borne the test of time and of diligent scrutiny by Bible students. Indeed, they have borne the test so well that they are the more worthy of being perpetuated in a revised edition, and in the new setting of our own times....[32]

---

[29] Cf. e.g. W.A. Spicer, <u>Our Day in the Light of Prophecy</u> (Washington, DC: RHPA, 1918).

[30] W.E. Howell, "New Edition of 'Daniel and the Revelation'," <u>RH</u> (Oct. 29, 1942), 20; Mervin R. Thurber, "New Edition of 'Daniel and the Revelation'," <u>Min</u>, vol. 18, no. 5 (Apr. 1945), 13–15.

[31] W.E. Howell, "New Edition of 'Daniel and the Revelation'," <u>RH</u> (Oct. 29, 1942), 21.

[32] Preface in U. Smith, <u>The Prophecies of Daniel and the Revelation</u>, I (Washington, DC: RHPA, 1944 ed.), 12.

It should, therefore, not surprise us to find the same approach to prophecy and essentially the same interpretation of specific prophetic Bible chapters (including those applied to Roman Catholicism) in other, more recent, prominent Adventist commentaries on the books of Daniel and the Revelation,[33] and in a number of authoritative doctrinal publications. Among these authoritative works three deserve special mention as they contain major sections on the place of Catholicism in Adventist prophetic interpretation. *Our Firm Foundation* is a two-volume collection of papers read during a Bible Conference for Adventist thought leaders in 1952,[34] some of which dealt with eschatology.[35] The *Seventh-day Adventist Bible Commentary* (7 volumes), the first attempt of the church to deal with the entire Bible in a systematic, expository way, was published between 1953 and 1957. Although the Review and Herald Publishing Association, and not the General Conference, bore the responsibility both for the financing and the theological content, it would be fair to say that this commentary represented Adventist theological consensus.[36] The third work, *Seventh-day Adventists Answer Questions on Doctrine*,[37] was prepared by a representative group of leaders, teachers and editors, and constituted the

---

[33] George McCready Price, <u>The Greatest of the Prophets</u>; Roy Allan Anderson, <u>Unfolding the Revelation</u> (Mountain View, Cal.: PPPA, 1953). Both books were listed as "Representative Adventist Doctrinal Literature" in <u>QOD</u>, 629-637. See also Arthur E. Lickey, <u>God Speaks to Modern Man</u> (Washington, DC: RHPA, 1952; this popular book was sold in large quantities to the public by Adventist colporteurs and heavily emphasized the Adventist views on key prophecies in Daniel and the Revelation (195-299; 361-401).

[34] See note 8; also Keld J. Reynolds, "The Church under Stress - 1931-1960," 182.

[35] F.D. Nichol, "The Increasing Timeliness of the Threefold Message," chap. in: <u>OFF</u>, vol. 1, 543-622; Frank H. Yost, "Antichrist in History and Prophecy," chap. in: <u>OFF</u>, vol. 1, 623-713.

[36] Raymond F. Cottrell, "The Untold Story of the Bible Commentary," 35-51.

[37] See above, p. 206.

Adventist response to a long list of questions posed by
an evangelical author who was preparing a book on
Adventism.[38] The book, which deals with a number of
issues relevant to our discussion, can, according to its
Introduction, "be viewed as truly representative of the
faith and beliefs of the Seventh-day Adventist Church."[39]
Apart from some refinements and minor alterations - to
which we shall return below - all these publications re-
affirm the traditional 19th century Adventist prophetic
views, including the interpretation of those chapters in
the Bible books of Daniel and the Revelation which were
applied to Roman Catholicism.

This is not to say that there was never any
discussion about or disagreement over traditional
positions. But these did not concern the basic
presupposition that Rome was the Antichrist, and that
Babylon stood for the great endtime coalition of
spiritual forces led by Roman Catholicism and
Protestantism. Debates on prophetic issues focused
rather on such details as the identity of the ten kings
in Daniel 7--one of the items on the agenda of the 1919
Bible Conference (July 1 - August 11).[40]

---

[38] The discussions with a group of Adventists led
W.R. Martin, a contributing editor of Eternity Magazine,
to conclude that Adventists were to be regarded as
genuine evangelical Christians. This he expressed in his
book The Truth About Seventh-day Adventism (London:
Marshall Morgan and Scott Ltd, 1960). See Keld J.
Reynolds, "The Church under Stress, 1931-1960, 185; R.W.
Schwarz, Light Bearers to the Remnant, 543-546; T.E.
Unruh, "The Seventh-day Adventist Evangelical
Conferences of 1955-1956," AH, vol. IV (Winter 1977),
35-46; L.E. Froom, Movement of Destiny, 465-492.

[39] QOD, 9; The book caused considerable doctrinal
discussion within the Adventist church, which initially
centered on its views of the atonement and more recently
on its Christology. Church authorities advised against
reprinting the book. See Minutes of the President's Executive Advisory, Sept. 24, 1974 and March 25, 1975
(Arch. of the Gen. Conf. of SDA, Silver Spring, MD). Its
treatment of eschatology has, however, not shared in
these controversies.

[40] A.G. Daniells, "The Bible Conference," RH (Aug.
21, 1919), 3-4. On July 3 C.P. Bollman read a paper on
the identity of the ten kings.

216

More directly related to the Adventist prophetic
views concerning the Catholic Church was the heated
debate about the "daily" in Daniel 8 and the continuing
discussion about the cryptic number of the beast, to
which we shall turn shortly.[41]

More serene were the discussions by the members of
the Bible Research Fellowship, an un-official organization mainly consisting of Adventist teachers, editors
and ministers, which existed from 1943 to 1952 and was
devoted to co-operative Bible study on the research
level.[42] A considerable number of the approximately 190
research papers prepared by the members of the
Fellowship--256 at its peak in 1952[43]--were devoted to
prophetic issues, such as the daily[44] and, in particular,
the interpretation of Daniel 11.[45]

The preparation of *The Seventh-day Adventist Bible
Commentary* naturally occasioned considerable discussion
among its contributors and editors. In dealing with the
books of Daniel and the Revelation every attempt was
made to represent historic Adventist positions fairly.
In some cases two or more options were presented, while
in other instances one particular interpretation was
favoured "where informed consensus had crys-tallized."[46]
One fundamental issue created disagreement between F.D.

---

[41] See below, pp. 226-231.

[42] Raymond F. Cottrell, "The Bible Research
Fellowship," AH, vol. 5, no. 1 (Summer 1978), 39-52.

[43] Ibid., 41.

[44] Leroy E. Froom, "Historical Setting and Background of the Term 'Daily'," research paper presented to
the Biblical Research Fellowship, no. 5, 1951; Alonzo J.
Wearner, "The Daily," research paper presented to the
Biblical Research Fellowship, n.d.

[45] Research papers presented to the Bible Research
Fellowship: Robert M. Eldridge, "A Comparison of
Positions on Daniel 11," n.d.; Jean Vuilleumier, "The
King of the North - Daniel 11:40-45," 1950; Raymond F.
Cottrell, "Pioneer Views on Daniel Eleven and Arma-
geddon," rev. ed, 1951.

[46] Raymond F. Cottrell, "The Untold Story of the
Bible Commentary," 39-40.

Nichol, the general editor, and associate editors R.F. Cottrell and Don. F. Neufeld, who were convinced that all prophecy, Daniel and the Revelation included, is conditional. Pastoral concern led Nichol to override this view.[47] Recounting the story of the creation of the SDA Bible Commentary, Cottrell also referred to the uneasiness on the part of some Adventist scholars with the approach of the Bible Commentary:

> "What should an editor do with "proof texts" that inherently do not prove what is traditionally attributed to them--as, for example, Numbers 14:34 and Ezekiel 4:6 [the basis for the year-day principle] ...? In most of these and a number of other passages, pastoral concern led us to conclude that the Commentary was not the place to make an issue of the Bible versus the traditional interpretation, much as this disappointed us as scholars and would be a disappointment to our scholarly friends who know better.[48]

L. E. Froom[49] defined the framework within which the contributors to the sections of the Bible Commentary dealing with the prophecies of Daniel and the Revelation had to work:

> The interpretations of 25 centuries show that our role, as Seventh-day Adventists, is that of recoverers and continuators of honored and orthodox prophetic expositions of the centuries, cumulatively developed and now restored, and perfected in the light of these latter times....[50]

---

[47] Ibid., 42.

[48] Ibid., 43-44. Elsewhere Cottrell himself, however, follows the Adventist practice of using Numbers 14:34 and Ezekiel 4:6 as proof for the "day-year" principle; see Raymond F. Cottrell, Beyond Tomorrow (Nashville, Tenn.: SPA, 1963) 167, 304-307.

[49] The articles in the SDABC are unsigned. Cottrell provides a list of the specific assignments of introductory articles and commentaries on Bible books; see "The Untold Story of the Bible Commentary," 48-51.

[50] L.E. Froom, "History of the Interpretation of Daniel," chap. in: SDABC, vol. 4, 43.

1. *Points of Discussion in Daniel*

The traditional view of the papacy as the little horn, both in Daniel 7 and 8, remained the official and widely accepted position among Adventists throughout the period under discussion in this chapter. As before, the emphasis in the exposition of Daniel 7 was on the four main characteristics of the little horn: his "great words"; the "wearing out of the saints;" his attempts to "change times and laws"; and his prominence during 3 1/2 prophetic "times," equalling 1260 prophetic days or as many literal years.[51] The "great words" were invariably interpreted in terms of the historic papal claims about the pope's super-human status, while the "wearing out of the saints" continued to be explained as a reference to persecutions instigated or carried out by the Church of Rome. Seldom, however, would specific numbers of victims be given, as had been done earlier.[52] The change of "times and laws," was, as before, interpreted in terms of the dis-regard for the second and in particular the fourth commandment. A.D. 538 and A.D. 1798 continued to be highlighted as the dates for the beginning and the end of the period of supremacy of the Roman Catholic Church.

---

[51] See e.g. W.A. Spicer, "The Prophecy of Daniel 7," RH (Sept. 23, 1915), 4-5; RH (Sept. 30, 1915), 4-5; RH (Oct. 7, 1915), 4-5; RH (Oct. 14, 1915), 4-5; S.M. Butler, "The Little Horn of the Fourth Beast of Daniel 7," RH (March 22, 1917), 6-8; Jesse C. Stevens, The Papacy in Bible Prophecy (Washington, DC: RHPA, 1928), 7-46; Arthur S. Maxwell, Power and Prophecy (Mountain View, Cal.: PPPA, 1940), 46-64; Christian Edwardson, Facts of Faith (Nashville, Tenn.: SPA, 1943), 34-69. Uriah Smith, Daniel (1944 ed.), 119-147; George McCready Price, The Greatest of the Prophets, 138-157; SDABC, vol. 4, 826-838.

[52] For an exception, see C.P. Bollman, "Studies in the Book of Daniel: The Fourth Beast," RH (June 23, 1927), 5. Bollman, in line with earlier Adventist interpreters estimated the number of people executed by Rome at 50 million or "even double that figure." Alonzo J. Wearner quotes a source which also mentions the 50 million figure: Fundamentals of Bible Doctrines (Washington, DC: RHPA, 1935), 134. Mary E. Walsh puts the number at between 50 and 75 million; see The Wine of Roman Babylon (Nashville, Tenn.: SPA, 1945), 210-211.

One aspect of the prophecy of Daniel 8 became the subject of bitter controversy. Early Adventism had explained the "taking away" of the daily in Daniel 8:11 as the replacement of paganism by papal Rome. Proponents of the "new view" interpreted this phrase as the taking away of the knowledge of Christ's priestly mediation in the heavenly sanctuary by Rome, replacing it with a false system.[53] The "new view" had been held by L.R. Conradi as early as 1898, while W.W. Prescott already in 1907 had stated his conviction that this "new" approach established a much more vital connection between Daniel 8 and the heart of the Adventist message.[54]

Although the item was not on the official agenda of the 1919 Bible Conference, considerable time was devoted to the issue. As has repeatedly happened in Adventist doctrinal controversies, the debate reached extraordinary proportions because it was intimately connected with the question of the inspiration of Mrs. E.G. White. The advocates of the "old view" (S.N. Haskell, G.I. Butler, G. Irwin, et al.) based their convictions on a statement made by Ellen White in 1850,[55] whereas the "new view" champions (A.G. Daniells, W.W. Prescott, W.A. Spicer, et al.) emphasized the broader context of that particular statement and pointed to Ellen G. White's refusal to decide the issue.[56]

Although the traditional view continued to be held

_____

[53] For a survey of the "daily"-controversy, see Bert Haloviak's "In the Shadow of the 'Daily': Background and Aftermath of the 1919 Bible and History Teachers' Conference;" also "The Daily," in SDAE, 319-323; and Bert Haloviak and Gary Land, "Ellen G. White and Doctrinal Conflict: Context of the 1919 Bible Conference," Spectrum, vol. 12, no. 4 (June 1982), 25-27.

[54] Bert Haloviak, "In the Shadow of 'the Daily'," 35-37; Gilbert M. Valentine, The Shaping of Adventism: The Case of W.W. Prescott (Berrien Springs, MI: Andrews Univ. Press, 1992), 185-190.

[55] Ellen G. White, Early Writings (Washington, DC: RHPA, 1945), 74-75.

[56] Bert Haloviak, "In the Shadow of the 'the Daily'," 44-59. Cf. E.G. White's chapter "Our Attitude Toward Doctrinal Controversy," in Selected Messages, vol. 1 (Washington, DC: RHPA, 1958), 164-168.

by some, after the 1919 Bible Conference the "new view" seemed to have won majority support. Alonzo L. Baker, in his important book *The Pope King Again*, succinctly expressed what increasingly became the majority position:

> Type met antitype and shadow met substance when Christ was crucified. From that moment the earthly Levitical system of mediation and priesthood was superseded by Christ Himself, 'the Prince of the host.' But the Roman Catholic Church has stepped in and has declared its priests the successors of the Levitical system, and its sacrament of the Mass a continuation of the offerings made in the tabernacle in the wilderness. Thus, no room is left for Christ's mediation and priesthood, which are cardinal and absolutely requisite features of the work of Christ in the new dispensation.[57]

Shortly before Jesse C. Stevens had emphasized the same point:

> ... the Papacy has a sanctuary of its own, which it claims as the antitype of the earthly. It has a priesthood of its own, a chain of mediators of its own, a confessional of its own, a repentance (penance) of its own, a sacrifice of its own, the mass; and thus has the heavenly sanctuary been counterfeited and desolated; for man has been directed away from the heavenly to an earthly system, and in that way the heavenly has been desolated and trodden underfoot.[58]

Although in the revised edition of Smith's commentary on Daniel and the Revelation the "old view" continued to be heard,[59] few Adventist writers and teachers from the 1920s onward adhered to it. McCready Price stated in 1955 that he knew of no Adventist college in America "which now teaches the view that the

---

[57] Alonzo L. Baker, The Pope King Again: Is the 'Deadly Wound' Healing? (Mountain View, Cal.: PPPA, 1929), 93.

[58] Jesse C. Stevens, The Papacy in Bible Prophecy, 56.

[59] Uriah Smith, Daniel (1944 ed.), 164-165.

term 'daily' means paganism."[60] *Questions on Doctrine* supports the "new view" without reference to any other position held by Adventists in the past.[61] The *Bible Commentary* leaves it to the reader to make a choice between the two views. It suggests Daniel 8:11 may be one of the passages of Scriptures "on which we must wait until a better day for a final answer."[62] It further assures the reader that "our salvation is not dependent upon our understanding fully the meaning of Dan. 8:11."[63] Few Adventists in recent decades would doubt this last statement. But this does not detract from the importance of this text, which, in its new interpretation, provided an additional weapon in the Adventist arsenal against Catholicism.

Daniel 11 also provided a battlefield for Adventist expositors. In the post-World War I period the view which identified Turkey as a phase of the "king of the North" (vs. 40-45)[64] was more and more criticized, while the identification of "the king" in vs. 36-39 as France in the age of its revolution also lost much of its support.[65] M.C. Wilcox, for more than a quarter of a century the editor of *Signs of the Times*, was an early critic of the traditional explanation of Turkey as the king of the North and was convinced of the correctness of James White's view that Daniel 11 parallels the prophecies of chapters 2, 7, and 8, and thus likewise culminates in a symbolical presentation of the papacy.[66]

---

[60] George McCready Price, <u>The Greatest of the Prophets</u>, note on p. 174.

[61] <u>QOD</u>, 256-257.

[62] <u>SDABC</u>, vol. 4, 843.

[63] Ibid.

[64] Uriah Smith, <u>Daniel</u> (1944 ed.), 294-299.

[65] Ibid., 280-289.

[66] M.C. Wilcox, <u>The King of the North: A Suggestive Outline Study of Daniel 11</u> (published by the author, 1910). Wilcox wanted to submit his ideas to his fellow ministers before publishing them in the <u>Signs of the Times</u>, the journal of which he was the editor-in-chief.

As already indicated, the 1919 Bible Conference devoted considerable attention to the "Eastern Question" in relationship to Daniel 11.[67] George McCready Price, though unsure of the exact meaning of many details of the last ten verses of Daniel 11, had no doubt that they refer to the papacy.[68] In its treatment of Daniel 11:36-39 the *Bible Commentary* presents the view which points to France as well as the other theory which looks to the papacy, and once again leaves it to the reader to make his choice. With respect to Daniel 11:40-45, virtually no explanation is given other than that the fulfillment of that passage is yet future.[69]

In summary we may conclude that as time passed Adventist interpreters were more and more inclined to assign a greater role to Catholicism in their interpretations of Daniel 11.

2. Points of Discussion in Revelation

Some aspects of the Adventist interpretation of the Revelation, such as the meaning of Armageddon, fuelled discussions among Adventist leaders, teachers and editors, but few impacted in any significant way on their understanding of the role of Catholicism in history and of future events as outlined in Revelation 12-14, 17 and 18.[70] Three elements did, however, remain subjects for debate and thus deserve to be singled out for some further discussion: the healing of the deadly wound; the number of the beast; and the Babylon concept.

a. The healing of the deadly wound

From the 1880s onward Adventists had stressed the evidences of the healing of the deadly wound (the loss

---

[67] R.W. Schwarz, Light Bearers to the Remnant, 400-402.

[68] George McCready Price, The Greatest of the Prophets, 307-323.

[69] SDABC, vol. 4, 875-877.

[70] See Uriah Smith, Revelation (1944 ed.), 549-679; 707-729; Roy Allen Anderson, Unfolding the Revelation (Mountain View, Cal.: PPPA, 1953), 112-158; 170-182; SDABC, vol. 7, 806-835; 848-869.

of prestige and temporal power from the time of the French Revolution to the loss of the Papal States) of the papacy. From the early decades of the 20th century onward, Adventists became more and more convinced that a healing (a new period of prestige and power) was taking place.[71] One author, in 1916, affirmed that the war-related diplomatic activities of the Vatican gave the interpreters of prophecy ample reason to believe that the healing of "the deadly wound received by the papal symbolic beast ... is nearer than we realize,"[72] while another believed, "that the healing process is going on before [our] own eyes."[73] The increased evidence "of events of a trend Romeward" on the ecumenical scene further fulfilled, it was argued, the prophecy that the whole world would be "wondering after the beast."[74] A complete fulfillment of the prophecy predicting papal resurgence was, however, still considered future. It would come when full papal control over all civil government was established, at the time when Europe and the United States would be of one mind to restore universal papal dominion.[75] As one author of a *Review and Herald* article put it:

When will the time come when all the world will wonder after this power? When will the Papal wound be fully healed? When not alone the Catholic powers of Europe, but the great Protestant power of America, will pay tribute to the power on the Tiber.[76]

---

[71] See e.g. W. A. Spicer, "The Prophecy of Daniel 7," part 4, RH (Sept. 30, 1915), 5.

[72] L.L. Caviness, "The Papacy and the War," RH (Dec. 19, 1918), 3.

[73] W.W. Prescott, "The Church Question in Politics," RH (Dec. 14, 1916), 2.

[74] L.L. Caviness, "Roman Catholic Plans," RH (Jan. 25, 1917), 4.

[75] "The Beast Power of the Revelation," paper read by M.C. Wilcox during the 1919 Bible Conference, 6, 10-12.

[76] "The Rush of Civil Governments to Rome," RH (Feb. 2, 1922), 6.

This future aspect, however, did not diminish the importance of contemporary signs of fulfillment. The fact that an increasing number of states exchanged ambassadors with the Vatican was a significant aspect of the healing process.[77] The enormous publicity given to the 1926 Eucharistic Congress in Chicago was another evidence of how the world was "wondering" after the Catholic power and of how far "the final movements" had advanced.[78] Two years later the associate editor of the *Review and Herald* warned his readers, "Unquestionably we are today witnessing the final and complete healing of the deadly wound."[79]

When in 1929 the "Roman Question" was resolved and the temporal domain of the pope was restored, Adventists immediately remembered the prophecy of the healing of the deadly wound. The papacy now had "more power and prestige throughout the world than at any time since the Protestant Reformation."[80] As a result of the wounds inflicted on the papal patient, the pope had been confined to his private quarters for nearly sixty years. But the wounds had gradually healed; "the climax came February 11, 1929, when responsible authorities publicly declared the wound healed and the patient discharged from seclusion."[81]

Most later Adventist writers, however, continued to see the healing as a gradual, still ongoing process, extending into the future. The 1940 appointment of an

---

[77] G.W. Reaser, "The Deadly Wound Was Healed," RH (Feb. 5, 1925), 5-6.

[78] C.A. Holt, "The Eucharistic Congress--Its Meaning and Significance," RH (Aug. 12, 1926), 4-5; Arthur S. Maxwell also referred to the frequent Eucharistic Congresses as indications "that the deadly wound is almost completely healed" - Power and Prophecy: Who Shall Rule the World?, 66.

[79] F.D. Nichol, "The Trend Toward Rome," part III, RH (March 29, 1928), 13.

[80] Alonzo L. Baker, The Pope King Again, 11-24; 99-109. See also F.M. Wilcox, "Papal Sovereignty Restored," RH (Feb. 28, 1929), 3-10.

[81] Andrew C. Gilbert, "The Roman Question," RH (June 27, 1929), 3.

American envoy to the Vatican was regarded in this light.[82] Other events further confirmed that the final steps in the restoration of papal power will be rapid ones.[83] But, once it had been fully restored, it would be short-lived:

> Popery has come back and will yet commit its final acts in the great apostasy. But, thank God, its final resurgence will be of but brief duration before the termination of its course in the final crisis of history.[84]

b. The number of the beast

The explanation first given by Uriah Smith in 1866 that one of the pope's titles, *Vicarius Filii Dei*, had a numerical value in Latin of 666, and thus constituted the number of the beast of Revelation 13,[85] went virtually unchallenged until the late 1930s.[86] Additional support for this view was found in a statement by the editor of *Our Sunday Visitor*, a Catholic journal, in answer to a question of a reader about "the letters supposed to be in the Pope's crown." His response was, "The letters inscribed in the Pope's miter are these: *Vicarius Filii Dei*, which is the Latin for 'Vicar of the

---

[82] W.R. Beach, "The Healing of the Papal Wound," RH (May 30, 1940), 7. For a discussion of the issue of an American ambassador to the Vatican, see below, pp. 252-258.

[83] C.S. Longacre, "Shall the Church Sit at the Peace Table?" RH (Feb. 1, 1945), 11.

[84] W.L. Emmerson, "The Resurgence of Rome," RH (Feb. 13, 1947), 11.

[85] See above, pp. 143ff.

[86] See C.P. Bollman, "The Number of the Beast," RH (Nov. 17, 1921), 6-7; [reprinted in RH (Aug. 1, 1929), 14-15]; Jesse C. Stevens, The Papacy in Bible Prophecy, 63-64; W.A. Spicer, Beacon Lights of Prophecy (Washington, DC: RHPA. 1935), 311; Frank A. Coffin, "The Number of a Man," Watchman Magazine (March 1937), 12, 17.

Son of God,'[87] while the same journal had earlier admitted that the Roman numerals did add up to 666.[88]

While he was the editor of *The Protestant Magazine*, W.W. Prescott had, in the course of his research on Catholic issues, become convinced that the traditional Adventist application of the number 666 to the title *Vicarious Filii Dei* could not be substantiated. He had at one time asked the English evangelist Chas. T. Everson to visit the Lateran Museum in Rome and photograph the papal tiara. Everson sent some pictures and reported that nowhere on any papal crown had he seen the title *Vicarius Filii Dei*. Prescott used the pictures in his journal and later lent the plates to the Southern Publishing House where Leon A. Smith was preparing a new edition of his father's commentary on Daniel and the Revelation. To Prescott's dismay he subsequently discovered that Smith had ordered an artist to add the words *Vicarius Filii Dei* to the picture of the tiara. Prescott informed the General Conference, which immediately ordered the removal of the fraudulent picture from the new edition of Uriah Smith's book.[89]

The matter came up again in 1935 when *The Sunday Visitor* challenged the Adventist claim that *Vicarius Filii Dei* was one of the pope's official titles, and insisted that this interpretation was based on biased and dishonest use of Catholic sources.[90] Adventist leaders enlisted the help of Prescott to search for Catholic sources that would support the Adventist interpretation. Prescott reported his findings in a contribution to the *Ministry*, the journal of the

---

[87] Our Sunday Visitor (Apr. 18, 1915), 3. The same journal later denied that such words were in fact on the papal mitre or tiara. See Our Sunday Visitor (Aug. 3, 1941), 7.

[88] Our Sunday Visitor (Nov. 15, 1914), 3.

[89] See Transcript of interview with W.W. Prescott in the office of the General Conference president (1936) at Prescott's request; besides Prescott and President Watson seven other leaders and prominent editors were present (Gen. Conf. Arch., RG 261, Book Editorial Files, Number of the Beast Committee 1943). See also Gilbert M. Valentine, The Shaping of Adventism, 273-274.

[90] Our Sunday Visitor (Dec. 1, 1935), 9; Gilbert M. Valentine, The Shaping of Adventism, 274.

Adventist clergy, which created considerable disturbance among Adventist teachers and ministers. His conclusions were that there was ample historical evidence, not for *Vicarius Filii Dei*, but rather for *Vicarius Christi* as an official title for the pope.[91] This conviction was also the major thrust of a document Prescott later prepared for the General Conference committee.[92] He felt especially troubled by the dubious nature of the only source for the *Vicarius Filii Dei* title: the *Donation of Constantine*. He stated this already in 1936 to a committee called at his request:

> What troubles me is that ... we in the twentieth century find it necessary to defend the Donation of Constantine, to use it to establish our theology. If you brethren think that is wise dealing with history and with facts, all right; but I do not.[93]

In order to defend the traditional Adventist view, several prominent authors were requested by the General Conference Secretariat to gather evidence in various libraries around the world. One of them, Leroy E. Froom, reported from London that his efforts had remained fruitless:

> In the hundreds and hundreds (literally!) of papal documents and pictures of tiaras and other papal implements which I have examined I have never found an authentic use [of the title *Vicarius Filii Dei*] by a papal leader, save in the forged Donation of Constantine in the decretum of Gratian.
> I have studied coins and medallions and pictures and documents in Rome, and Vienna, Geneva, Paris, London, Berlin, and I have had the assistance of skilful men in these different places, not only Adventist experts in Latin, but I have appealed to

---

[91] W.W. Prescott, "The Official Title of the Pope," <u>Min</u>, vol. 12, no. 3 (March 1939), 17-19, 26, 46.

[92] W.W. Prescott, "The Interpretation of the Number of the Beast" (unpublished paper; Gen. Conf. Arch., RG 261, Book Editorial Files, Number of the Beast Committee 1943).

[93] Transcript of interview with W.W. Prescott, 3.

the finest experts in those institutions without any result.[94]

All evidence gathered pointed in the same direction: The title *Vicarius Filii Dei* was only used in the *Donation of Constantine*, a forgery dating from the eighth century, fabricated in support of the temporal claims of the papacy, and later incorporated in the "Decretum Gratiani," a collection of canon law that, although never officially approved, acquired considerable authority. Frank H. Yost, one of the researchers, in a letter to the secretary of the General Conference expressed his opinion that it would be "worthwhile to try to find this very expression [*Vicarius Filii Dei*] in an unimpeachable source as a definite papal claim," and hoped that "we would find it unnecessary to make use of the material from the *Donations*.[95]

On August 30, 1939 J.L. McElhany, recently elected president of the General Conference, called a special committee in his office "to hear a classified digest of evidence that had been gathered from many quarters" (a 42-page document, prepared by General Conference secretary W.E. Howell). After a long discussion a small committee was appointed to do further research and "to prepare something for publication."[96] This committee met several times and eventually concluded that *Vicarius Filii Dei* could indeed be considered as one of the official titles of the pope. Although its origin was in the fraudulent *Donation of Constantine*, the very fact that it was incorporated in such a prestigious source as Gratian's *Decretum*, to which pope after pope appealed, justified the conclusion that "the practice of the Roman Catholic Church ... affords a substantial basis for our

---

[94] Letter Leroy E. Froom to W.E. Howell, Aug. 29, 1938 (Gen. Conf. Arch., RG 261, Book Editorial Files, Number of the Beast Committee 1943).

[95] Letter Frank H. Yost to W.E. Howell, Oct. 18, 1938 (Gen. Conf. Arch., RG 261, Book Editorial Files, Number of the Beast Committee 1943).

[96] Minutes of "Hearing on 666," Aug. 30, 1939 (Gen. Conf. Arch., RG 261, Book Editorial Files, Number of the Beast Committee, 1943).

interpretation of 666 as the number of the beast."[97]

It seems that the commotion of the late 1930s and early 1940s about the validity of the Adventist position of 666 was soon forgotten. In public evangelism the "*Vicarius Filii Dei* = 666" theme remained immensely popular, and it continued to appear in the publications of the church. Christian Edwardson, writing in 1943, asserted that the *Vicarius Filii Dei* title is "used officially in Roman Catholic canon law, from medieval times down to the present."[98] The authority of Gratian's *Decretum* in which the title is found is substantiated by a long series of quotations from Catholic sources.[99] The April 18, 1915 article in *Our Sunday Visitor*, which affirmed that *Vicarius Filii Dei* was one of the official titles of the pope, was not invalidated by later statements in the same journal. These later statements, it was alleged, were the result of pressure from the Catholic hierarchy after they had discovered to what anti-Catholic use this earlier article had been put.[100] Edwardson then quoted several letters of individuals who claimed to have seen the title on a papal tiara.[101]

Further research suggested that greater prudence was needed in claims about the *Vicarius Filii Dei* title on the papal tiara.[102] Most more recent publications were indeed more careful in their wording, but they continued to defend the traditional Adventist viewpoint. The topic

---

[97] Minutes of the "Committee on 666," Jan. 17, 1943 (Gen. Conf. Arch., RG 261, Book Editorial Files, Number of the Beast Committee 1943).

[98] Christian Edwardson, <u>Facts of Faith</u>, 219.

[99] Ibid., 219-222.

[100] Ibid., 224.

[101] Ibid., 227-229; two of the three witnesses were referred to in the Dec. 20, 1906 issue of the <u>RH</u>. See above, pp. 146-147.

[102] See Leroy E. Froom, "Dubious Pictures of the Tiara," <u>Min</u>, vol. 21, no. 11 (Nov. 24, 1948), 35; and Clyde Dale Vineyard, "The Origin, Development and Significance of the Roman Catholic Papal Tiara" (Unpubl. M.A. thesis, SDA Theol. Sem., Washington, DC, 1951), 26-33.

was discussed in a paper read to the delegates to the 1952 Bible Conference.[103] The original source for the *Vicarius Filii Dei* title was duly recognized as the spurious *Donation of Constantine*, but its incorporation in Gratian's *Decretum* granted it a status equal to that of an official document. Repeated use of the English equivalent *Vicar of the Son of God* by Cardinal Henry Manning was regarded as giving extra credence to the view that this is indeed one of the titles Catholics attribute to the pope.[104]

Roy Allen Anderson in his 1953 commentary on the Revelation tried to establish a link between the use of the number 666 in ancient Babylonian religion and Roman religion on the one hand and its appearance in the papal title of *Vicarius Filii Dei* on the other hand.[105] The *Bible Commentary* points to precedents for the Adventist interpretation among post-Reformation exponents of the same view, but is careful not to make dogmatic statements. It recognizes that "there may be more implied in the cryptogram than this interpretation provides" and suggests that it is "besides the point" whether the inscription *Vicarius Filii Dei* actually appears on any crown or mitre. "The title is admittedly applied to the pope, and that is sufficient for the purposes of prophecy."[106]

c. Babylon

In the period under review in this chapter the question "What is Babylon?" continued to receive essentially the same answer as before. Babylon "primarily ... refers to the Church of Rome," but also includes "the great religious organizations which ... are following in the

---

[103] Frank H. Yost, "Antichrist in History and Prophecy," 623-713.

[104] Henry Manning, <u>The Temporal Power of the Vicar of Jesus Christ</u> (London: J.H. Parker, 1862), 140-141.

[105] Roy Allen Anderson, <u>Unfolding the Revelation</u>, 125-134.

[106] <u>SDABC</u>, vol. 4, 823-824.

footsteps of the Roman Catholic Church."[107] At times the full emphasis was on Catholicism,[108] while at other times Protestantism received most of the prophetic blame. The "daughters" of the Babylonian power have "the same corrupt blood" in their veins as their parent.[109] The Protestant apostasy is apparent in such teachings as the doctrine of eternal torment, the sprinkling of infants, and, of course, the observance of Sunday.[110]

Some voices pleaded for a more moderate use of words in descriptions of the Protestant component of Babylon. A.G. Daniells wondered during one of the sessions of the 1919 Bible Conference whether the term "apostate Protestantism" was not too harsh an epithet to use. Several alternatives were suggested: "neo-Protestantism," "lapsed Protestantism," "modern Protestantism," or "backslidden Protestantism."[111] Most authors apparently shared Daniells' sentiment and began to show greater reticence in accusations of sin and corruption,[112] but the message remained the same. The progres-

---

[107] F.M. Wilcox, "'The Remnant Church' Not Babylon," RH (March 16, 1916), 3.

[108] See e.g. L.L. Caviness, "Babylon in the New Testament," RH (Jan. 17, 1918), 4.
Hislop's book The Two Babylons (see above, p. 148) continued to be quoted by Adventist authors, particularly in the 1910s and 1920s. See e.g. Charles M. Snow, "Rome Never Changes, no. 13: Relic Worship," RH (Feb. 18, 1915), 7; and "Rome Never Changes, no. 15: Celibacy," RH (March 4, 1915), 8; [W.W. Prescott], Handbook for Bible Students (Washington, DC: RHPA, 1922), 33, 89, 145, 161, 250-252, 444, 484-485; Jesse C. Stevens, The Papacy in Bible Prophecy, 31-33.

[109] C.A. Holt, "Comments on Current Events," RH (Jan. 31, 1924), 2.

[110] Carlyle B. Haynes, "Protestantism--Its Impending Doom," RH (Dec. 27, 1934), 3.

[111] Transcript of 1919 Bible Conference, July 17, 37.

[112] See e.g. the series of 7 articles of F.D. Nichol, "A Latter-Day Sign--Babylon is Fallen," RH (March 6, 1930 - April 17, 1930) which deals with the

sive fall of Protestantism was not only evident in its shift toward liberalism; fundamentalism with its "false and destructive theories of dispensationalism and the rapture" also deserved strong condemnation.[113] And the spirit of Babylon might manifest itself even closer to home. Adventists are not saved simply because they are Adventists.[114] It is possible for Adventists to be "tinctured with this spirit of Babylon," and to be simultaneously "numbered among those who are looking for the coming of the Lord, and yet be a partaker of the sins of Babylon."[115] But although the Seventh-day Adventist Church may have its problems, yet it will never become Babylon.[116]

The *Bible Commentary* uses *Babylon* as a comprehensive term for all religious bodies and movements, of all ages, that "have fallen away from the truth." Babylon's fall is progressive and cumulative and the message, first preached by the Millerites, when they saw their message rejected by Protestantism, will increase in relevancy as the end draws near.[117] However, it leaves the user in no doubt that "Babylon the great" is the term "by which Inspiration refers [in particular] to the great threefold religious union of the papacy, apostate Protestantism, and spiritism." It immediately adds,

---

dangers of modernism and liberalism in Protestantism. Another example is: Eric Beaven, "The Spirit of Babylon," ST (Feb. 26, 1935), 7, 14-15), which points at the illicit union with civil government as the main characteristic of Babylon, without directly identifying any church organizations.

[113] Rose Boose, "Know Your Bible Better: The Fall of Babylon," Concl., RH (Sept. 24, 1953), 8-9.

[114] Wilcox, "Come Out of Her, My People," RH (May 11, 1922), 8.

[115] O. Montgomery, "Come Out of Babylon," RH (Oct. 4, 1917), 9.

[116] D.E. Robinson, "Has the Seventh-day Adventist Church Become Babylon?" RH (May 22, 1930), 8-12; F.M. Wilcox, "Come Out of Her, My People," RH (May 11, 1922), 8.

[117] SDABC, vol. 7, 828-830.

however, that the term does not refer to the members of these organizations, but to the organizations themselves and their leaders.[118]

Questions on Doctrine expresses itself much in the same way. It refers to the use of Babylon as a symbol for the Catholic Church by medieval believers, Protestant reformers and post-Reformation writers. It was only natural that the Millerites and early Adventists would subsequently use the term for those whom they felt had rejected light and truth.[119] And Adventists are justified in continuing this application to the papacy and its Protestant "daughters," for

> ... wherever there are individuals, that hold to and advocate the unchristian doctrines, practices and procedures of the papal church, such may justifiably be dominated 'Babylon'--hence part of the great apostasy. Wherever such conditions obtain, Adventists, with others, believe that the guilty organizations may rightly be denominated 'Babylon.'[120]

This does not mean that all members of these churches are condemned. It is a "caricature of our preaching" to suggest that only Adventists will be saved.[121] "A host of true followers of Christ are scattered all through the various churches of Christendom, including the Roman communion," which God "clearly recognizes as his own."[122] *Questions on Doctrine* insists that the Adventist convictions about Babylon "do not have the defamatory character that some would impute" to them. "They are uttered in sorrow, not for invidious comparisons."[123]

---

[118] Ibid., 852.

[119] QOD, 197-201.

[120] Ibid., 202.

[121] F.D. Nichol, "Will Adventists Alone Be Saved?" RH (Jan. 10, 1935), 5.

[122] QOD, 197.

[123] Ibid., 202.

V Catholic Doctrine: Rome Never Changes

The general title--"Rome Never Changes"--of a 1914-1915 series of articles by Charles M. Snow succinctly characterizes Adventist criticism of Catholic doctrine in the 1915-1965 period.[124] The themes and general approach of this extended exposé of Catholic errors closely resembled *The Wine of Roman Babylon*, written by Mary E. Walsh, a former Catholic, and published thirty years later,[125] and Frank H. Yost's 1952 summary of Catholic apostasy.[126]

All specifically Catholic teachings came under regular Adventist criticism: infant baptism, auricular confession, celibacy of the clergy, the emphasis on tradition, the worship of idols and relics, etc.[127] But most Adventist condemnations focused in particular on just a few issues: (1) Sabbath vs. Sunday; (2) the immortality of the soul and related questions; (3) the veneration of saints and Mary; (4) the status of the pope; and (5) the Catholic view of salvation. In general Adventist criticism resembled that of earlier times. The only major development was the greater attention for the Mass and all that it, from an Adventist point of view, involves.

---

[124] Charles M. Snow, "Rome Never Changes," series of 15 articles, RH (Nov. 5, 1914 - March 4, 1915).

[125] See above, note 52.

[126] Frank H. Yost, "Antichrist in History and Prophecy," 639-652; 678-691.

[127] The [W.W. Prescott], Source Book for Bible Students (Washington, DC: RHPA), 1919, contains an enormous amount of material related to--and critical of --Catholic doctrine. This also applies to its companion, the Handbook for Bible Students; see esp. 126-127. See also Robert M. Eldridge, "Test by Comparison," RH (March 8, 1945), 8-10, 23; and "The Reply of Seventh-day Adventists to the Pope's Encyclical 'Lux Veritatis'," which was voted by the Executive Committee of the General Conference of Seventh-day Adventists on March 3, 1932, and lists 12 major dogmatic differences with the Roman Catholic Church (RH, March 31, 1932, 3-4).

The extensive work done by Andrews and Conradi on the history of Sabbath and Sunday remained the standard; it had once and for all set the pattern for Adventist publications on the subject. Their conclusions about the major role of the Church of Rome and of the Roman pontiffs were followed by later Adventist authors on this topic, though--with Conradi--they usually laid greater stress on the pagan roots of Sunday worship than Andrews had done.[128] The statements from Catholic sources about the change from Sabbath to Sunday, which had become standard elements in Adventist apologetics,[129] continued to appear in almost every discussion of Daniel 7:25 or other exposés about the establishment of Sunday observance to the detriment of Sabbath keeping.[130]

---

[128] See Jesse C. Stevens, The Papacy in Bible Prophecy, 28-36; Carlyle B. Haynes, From Sabbath to Sunday (Washington, DC: RHPA, 1928), 31-44; C.P. Bollman, "The Greek Church and the Change of the Sabbath," RH (Nov. 8, 1923), 6-9; Walter E. Straw, Origin of Sunday Observance (Washington, DC: RHPA, 1939), passim; Christian Edwardson, Facts of Faith, 70-117; Robert L. Odom, Sunday in Pagan Romanism (Washington, DC: RHPA, 1944), passim. Frank H. Yost, The Early Christian Sabbath (Mountain View, Cal.: PPPA, 1947), 36-85; QOD, 166-176.

[129] Dr. James Butler's Catechism; Henry Tuberville's Abridgment of Catholic Doctrine; Richard Challoner's The Catholic Christian Instructed; Stephen Keenan's Doctrinal Catechism; Cardinal Gibbons' Faith of Our Fathers; the 1893 article in the Catholic Mirror. For full bibliographical details see above, pp. 108-109. Added to these was Peter Geiermann, Converts Catechism of Catholic Doctrine (St. Louis, MO: B. Herder, 1911).
W.W. Prescott argued (ca. 1915) that both Keenan's and Geiermann's catechisms should not be used in this way, since they could not, in his opinion, be regarded as authoritative pronouncements of the Catholic Church. C.S. Longacre produced a lengthy document, "A Review of Professor Prescott's Points and Positions," to counter his arguments (Gen. Conf. Arch., RG 52; Religious Liberty Dep. - C.S. Longacre Ref. Files, n.d.).

[130] See e.g. W.A. Spicer, "The Prophecy of Daniel 7," part 5, RH (Oct. 14, 1915), 5; Frederick Griggs, "The Change of the Sabbath," RH (Oct. 31, 1918), 5-6; [W.W. Prescott], Source Book for Bible Students, 475-

The Catholic view of the immortal soul continued to be seen as a key error with many fateful consequences - "a fountain of deadly error,"[131] from which flow "an endless horde of false theories."[132] Among these is the belief in saints and their ability to intercede for the living,[133] and, in particular, the worship of Mary.[134] In

---

476; Charles Thompson, "Who Changed the Sabbath?" RH (Nov. 24, 1921), 5; The Bible Made Plain (Washington, DC: RHPA, 1922), 68; Titus Kurtichanov, "A Divine Forecast of World History: Imminence of God's Kingdom Indicated in the Prophecies of Daniel 2 and 7," RH (Feb. 26, 1925), 9-10; N.S. Ashton, "A General Review of the Sabbath Controversy," RH (May 28, 1925), 10-11; Carlyle B. Haynes, "How, Why, and by Whom Was the Sabbath Change Effected?" RH (Apr. 26, 1928), 4-5; "Four Beasts and the Little Horn," Present Truth (Apr. 1, 1929), 3; Carlyle B. Haynes, The Christian Sabbath (Nashville, Tenn.: SPA, n.d.), 73-78. Carlyle B. Haynes, From Sabbath to Sunday, 44-46; Jesse C. Stevens, The Papacy in Bible Prophecy, 16-21; F.M. Wilcox, "The Author of the First-Day Sabbath," RH (Dec. 10, 1936), 2; F.M. Wilcox, "Who Changed the Sabbath?" RH (June 29, 1944), 2. Christian Edwardson, Facts of Faith, 288-301; Uriah Smith, Revelation (1944 ed.), 608-611; Arthur E. Lickey, God Speaks to Modern Man, 297; QOD, 179-182; Richard Lewis, The Protestant Dilemma (Mountain View, Cal.: PPPA, 1961), 78-79.

[131] As reads the title of chapter 12 of Carlyle B. Haynes' Life, Death, and Immortality (Nashville, Ten.: SPA, 1952); see also "Varner J. Johns, "False Ideas of the Antichrist," RH (Dec. 11, 1941), 5.

[132] Carlyle B. Haynes, Life, Death, and Immortality, 105.

[133] S.M. Butler, "The Little Horn and the Fourth Beast of Daniel 7," RH (March 22, 1917), 7-8; T.M. French, "Catholics and the Spirit World," RH (Aug. 20, 1936), 7; Mary E. Walsh, The Wine of Babylon, 146-173; F. Lee, "New Catholic Saint Canonized, RH (Aug. 1, 1946), 3-4.

contrast to earlier times the doctrine of the Immaculate
Conception was now often singled out for special
attack.[135] In the "dark" Middle Ages the idea developed
that Mary shared in the redemptive and mediatorial work
of Christ. The pagan roots of the "Mother of God"
concept were obvious to Adventist critics.[136] Purgatory
was another by-product of the erroneous view of death.[137]

Naturally, the doctrine of papal infallibility
continued to come under attack.[138] But the origin of the
papacy was also further scrutinized. Peter was not the
first pope; he was not *the* Rock, but *a* rock![139] Christ is
the Rock![140] Peter's biography shows he was not the
greatest of the apostles; nor did he have any special
powers the other apostles did not have.[141] James, rather

---

[134] Charles M. Snow, "Rome Never Changes," no. 2, RH
(Nov. 19, 1914), 7-8; Jesse C. Stevens, The Papacy in
Bible Prophecy, 78-80; D.A. Delafield, "Miracles
Ascribed to the Roman Pontiff," RH (Dec. 20, 1951), 12;
"Rome Exalts the Virgin Mary," RH (May 13, 1954), 10.

[135] Charles M. Snow, "Rome Never Changes," no. 4, RH
(Dec. 4, 1914), 8-10; Mary E. Walsh, The Wine of Roman
Babylon, 128-145; Frank H. Yost, "Antichrist in History
and Prophecy," 678- 679.

[136] Charles M. Snow, "Rome Never Changes," no. 4, RH
(Dec. 4, 1914), 9.

[137] Charles M. Snow, "Rome Never Changes, no. 5: The
Doctrine of Purgatory," RH (Dec. 10, 1914), 6-8; Mary E.
Walsh, The Wine of Roman Babylon, 78-88.

[138] Charles M. Snow, "Rome Never Changes," no. 1, RH
(Nov. 5, 1914), 7-8; Varner J. Johns, "False Ideas of
the Antichrist," RH (Dec. 11, 1941), 5.

[139] Mary E. Walsh, The Wine of Roman Babylon, 89-99;
L.L. Caviness, "Is Peter *the* Rock or a Rock?" RH (Aug.
10, 1950), 10-11; Max Trummer, "Do Scriptures Teach the
Primacy of Peter?" RH (March 5, 1953), 3-4.

[140] J.C. Stevens, Was Peter the First Pope?
(Washington, DC: RHPA, ca. 1925), 11-13.

[141] Mary E. Walsh, The Wine of Roman Babylon, 100-
127.

than Peter, was the first general leader of the church; the primacy of Peter is not supported by Scripture, but was conceived only centuries after Peter's death.[142] And Paul soon "eclipsed" all apostles, Peter included. Yet the New Testament does not allow for any apostle to have authority over another. And there is no indication whatsoever in the New Testament that Peter ever was the bishop of Rome.[143]

More than in earlier times Adventist authors focused on the Mass in their condemnation of Catholic doctrines and practices. This new emphasis was closely linked to the "new view" of the "daily" in Daniel 8, which claimed that the true sanctuary service in heaven, with Christ as the only true Mediator, had been "taken away" and been replaced by a false system of intercession. Works and acts of penance had taken the place of total reliance on the sacrifice of Christ.[144] The Catholic way of dealing with sin was based on "external rites," and was not "heart religion." Repentance took the form of selfish fear rather than of "godly sorrow," and all emphasis on the need of a sanctified character was missing.[145]

When Christ died the Old Testament system of mediation and priesthood was superseded by Christ Himself. But

> ... the Roman Catholic Church stepped in and has declared its priests the successor of the Levitical system, and its sacrament of the Mass a continuation of the offerings made in the tabernacle in the wilderness. Thus, no room is left for Christ's mediation and priesthood, which are cardinal and absolutely requisite features of the work of Christ in the new dispensation.[146]

---

[142] Max Trummer, "Do Scriptures Teach the Primacy of Peter?" concl., RH (March 12, 1953), 4-5.

[143] J.C. Stevens, Was Peter the First Pope?, 1-19.

[144] Charles M. Snow, "Rome Never Changes, no. 6: Another Sacrifice--Another Savior," RH (Dec. 17, 1914), 6-8.

[145] Ernest Lloyd, "Catholic Doctrine--A Comparison," Present Truth (July 1, 1930), 3-4.

[146] Alonzo L. Baker, The Pope King Again, 93.

While the Bible teaches that Christ died "once for all," Christ is offered daily in Catholic worship. The only conclusion can be that "Rome counterfeits Calvary."[147] "Beneath a mass of priestly interposition and interference" the "beautiful simplicity of the gospel" is lost.[148] In the ceremony of the Mass "the Roman priest attempts to rob Christ of His continual mediation," as he "presumes to fill the offices Christ can only occupy.[149] The "absurd" dogma of transubstantiation, not officially adopted until 1215 during the Fourth Lateran Council, is a "contradiction and a perversion of Scripture,"[150] while the medieval practice of restricting the use of the communion wine to the priest is further proof of Rome's disregard for God's Word.[151] In Adventist opinion "the Roman Catholic Mass is nothing more than idolatry of a wafer!"[152]

VI Adventism and Anti-Catholicism

Before discussing the Adventist reaction to some of the specific issues which kept Catholic-Protestant tensions alive in the 1915-1965 period, some preliminary remarks about the Adventist involvement in the anti-Catholic

---

[147] Ibid.; Charles M. Snow, "Rome Never Changes, no. 9: The Sacrifice of the Mass," RH (Jan. 14, 1915), 6-8; Charles M. Snow, "Rome Never Changes, no. 10: The Sacrifice of the Mass," RH (Jan. 21, 1915), 7-8; George McCready Price, The Greatest of the Prophets, 175; QOD, 257-258.

[148] Alonzo L. Baker, The Pope King Again, 98.

[149] Ibid.

[150] Charles M. Snow, "Rome Never Changes, no. 7: The Doctrine of Transubstantiation," RH (Dec. 24, 1914), 6-7; Mary E. Walsh, The Wine of Roman Babylon, 63-68.

[151] Mary E. Walsh, Ibid., 74-77.

[152] Alonzo L. Baker, The Pope King Again, 96.

debate seem in order.[153] We will notice in this section of this chapter that Adventists shared the concerns of many other Protestants who were perturbed by the rapid growth of Catholicism, in particular in the United States of America. But although at times Adventists were prepared to use language many today would find abusive, they were determined to stay away from the tactics of such fiercely anti-Catholic organizations as the Ku Klux Klan and to avoid the approach of such hate-filled journals as *The Menace*.[154] As time went by this resolve to combat Catholicism with dignity rather than "to line up with anti-Catholic organizations or imbibe their hatred" was further strengthened.[155] F.D. Nichol, while leaving no doubt about the prophetic picture of Catholic power, was convinced that Adventists should not "rail at the Catholic Church," nor stoop to the various kinds of attacks "that have so often characterized certain Protestant zealots in their misguided endeavors to turn men from the errors of Rome." He added that some methods are "not only ineffective ... but also unchristian."[156] Though not always living up to his own credo, Frederick Lee, throughout his long editorial career one of the most outspoken Adventist critics of Catholicism, stated that Adventists should "never distort or exaggerate views of others" and only use reliable sources, in "a spirit of Christian fairness and integrity."[157] Earlier W.W. Prescott had consistently appealed for greater care in accusations of Rome.[158]

---

[153] For a survey of anti-Catholicism during this period, see above, pp. 209-213.

[154] C.P. Bollman, "'The Menace' Dynamited," Lib, vol. 11, no. 6 (4th quarter, 1916), 223.

[155] George A. Campbell, "Roman Catholics and the Advent Message," RH (Apr. 21, 1932), 5.

[156] F.D. Nichol, "Seventh-day Adventist Teachings an Answer to Catholicism and Modernism," RH (Feb. 1, 1934), 4.

[157] F. Lee, "Beliefs and Practices of Roman Catholics," RH (July 9, 1953), 13.

[158] Gilbert M. Valentine, The Shaping of Adventism, 222.

The only Adventist journal exclusively devoted to anti-Catholic propaganda that ever existed ceased publication in 1915 after only six years.[159] What caused *The Protestant Magazine* to fold after just a few years? It met with Catholic resistance, and in 1915 the Federation of Catholic Societies even tried to prevent its further circulation.[160] Editors of Catholic journals complained that every article in *The Protestant Magazine* misrepresented the aims and purposes of the Catholics.[161] Although the journal was faced with continuing circulation problems and editor Prescott's subtle introduction of his convictions about the "daily" was a further complicating factor,[162] Catholic objections may well have played a role in the final decision to abandon this project. A special committee appointed by the publishing house advised the members of the board of trustees to stop advertising the journal in "sensational anti-Catholic periodicals," and in its editorial

---

[159] See above, p. 174.

[160] This organization had been working since 1911 toward securing legislation that would forbid sending publications containing "scurrilous and slanderous attacks on our faith" through the US Mail. In 1915 two bills providing such restrictions were presented to Congress. See Gilbert M. Valentine, "William Warren Prescott: Seventh-day Adventist Educator," 458. Adventists strongly protested these bills which reminded them of "Roman decretals which were in full force in the Middle Ages"; see C.S. Longacre, "Great Things Are Happening," RH (Apr. 15, 1915), 19.

[161] Letter of C.F. Thomas (editor of the Baltimore Catholic Review) to W.W. Prescott, June 8, 1914 (Gen. Conf. Arch., PC 21, W.W. Prescott, Protestant Magazine Ref. Files, ca. 1909-1916: Personal); see also: "Catholic Reactions to 'The Protestant Magazine'," Lib, vol. 11, no. 2 (1st quarter 1916, extra), 56; and the editorial in The Truth (Aug. 15, 1915), which listed *The Protestant Magazine* among regularly published anti-Catholic journals. The *Review and Herald* was listed in the category of journals which are "bitterly anti-Catholic in tendency, though not professedly published for the purpose of combating Catholicity."

[162] Gilbert M. Valentine, "Warren Prescott: Seventh-day Adventist Educator," 461.

policies to "avoid the methods of the sensational anti-Catholic papers, and all scandals and partisan issues."[163] A few months later the same board voted to reassign Prescott to other duties and to "suspend" the publication of *The Protestant Magazine*. The reason for this decision was recorded in the board minutes as follows:

> ... Whereas, the view is entertained by some of the responsible men in the field that the publication of a magazine devoted especially to the Roman question may cause an embarrassment to this movement, and possibly precipitate a crisis before it is due, therefore
> Resolved, that the publication of the "Protestant Magazine" be suspended for the present...[164]

Later attempts to resurrect the magazine were unsuccessful.

It would seem that Adventists in general did not get involved with anti-Catholic societies, although there may have been exceptions to that rule.[165] But Adventists did have a close relationship with "Protestants and Other Americans United for the Separation of Church and State" (POAU), an organization created in 1948, not so much intended to combat Catholic dogma, but rather to protest against Catholic efforts to encroach on the principle of strict separation between church and state. Several articles in the *Review and Herald* lauded this Protestant attempt to develop a well-outlined and well-crystallized plan for meeting the steady encroachments

---

[163] Minutes of the Board of Trustees of the Review and Herald Publishing Association, April 22, 1915 (Gen. Conf. Arch.).

[164] Minutes Board of Trustees of the RHPA, Nov. 30, 1915 (Gen. Conf. Arch.).

[165] During its meeting of April 8, 1915 the Board of Trustees of the Review and Herald Publishing Association considered at length the question of employees "being members of local Patriotic and Anti-Catholic societies," without, however, taking any action. (Minutes Apr. 8, 1915; Gen. Conf. Arch.)

of Rome.[166] On several church-state related issues POAU and Adventists were to join forces,[167] while Frank H. Yost, a prominent Adventist theology teacher and religious liberty leader, became a member of the POAU executive committee and co-authored *Separation of Church and State in the United States*[168] with another POAU leader.[169]

One further note should be added to these preliminary remarks. While most anti-Catholic propaganda considered unrestricted immigration a major threat, Adventist publications remained largely silent on this topic. The widespread fear of strong Catholic growth as a result of unrestricted immigration was only occasionally echoed by Adventists.[170] Statements by Mrs. E.G. White about God's providence in bringing people from all nations to the United States reminded them that the presence of so many immigrants presented not only problems but also limitless evangelistic opportunities.[171] In the divine order of things "a little portion of each of these

[166] F.D. Nichol, "Protestants Organize Against Catholic Legislative Campaign," <u>RH</u> (Apr. 1, 1948), 3-4; F.D. Nichol, "Catholic Reactions to Protestants United," <u>RH</u> (Apr. 8, 1948), 4-5; F.D. Nichol, "The Catholic Bridge Between Church and State," <u>RH</u> (May 20, 1948), 5-6.

[167] See Eric Syme, <u>A History of Church-State Relations in the United States</u>, passim; R.W. Schwarz, <u>Light Bearers to the Remnant</u>, 537.

[168] Alvin W. Johnson, and Frank H. Yost, <u>Separation of Church and State in the United States</u> (Minneapolis: University of Minnesota Press, 1948).

[169] R.W. Schwarz, <u>Light Bearers to the Remnant</u>, 536-537.

[170] C.A. Holt, "Immigration and the Catholic Influence in the United States," <u>RH</u> (March 30, 1922), 8.

[171] Ellen G. White, <u>Testimonies to the Church</u>, vol. 8 (Mountain View, Cal.: PPPA, 1948 ed.), 35-36; Ellen G. White, "Mission Fields at Home," <u>Pacific Union Recorder</u> (Apr. 21, 1910), 1-2.

[mission] fields has been brought to our very doors."[172] Moreover, most immigrants seemed to assimilate the American ideas and became a loyal and stable part of the population. There was therefore no reason to cherish "a spirit of suspicion against those foreign-born, but loyal, citizens."[173]

VII Adventist Reactions to Specific Issues

The growing strength of Catholicism, worldwide as well as in the United States of America, remained a major concern for Adventists throughout the 1915-1965 period. Ellen G. White's description in chapter 35 of *The Great Controversy* of the growing power of Roman Catholicism and the true character and aims of the papacy, remained the blueprint for Adventist interpretations of developments in Catholicism.[174]

In the post World War I era the rise and development of Bolshevism made the papacy a welcome ally for those who were worried about this phenomenon.[175] It was felt that the Roman Catholic Church "was the only power that came out of the war with its political prestige enhanced.[176] Rome's stature was greatly strengthened by

---

[172] B.P. Hoffmann, "Foreign Missions at Home," RH (Jan. 31, 1924), 10-12.

[173] F.M. Wilcox, "Love Versus Hate," RH (Jan. 22., 1942), 2.

[174] Numerous times this chapter was quoted, in part or even in its entirety, in Adventist publications. When in 1927 the *Present Truth* devoted three full, consecutive issues to Catholicism, this section from the *Great Controversy* was printed as a general introduction. See "Roman Catholicism--Its Growing Power: The Character and Aims of the Papacy," PT (Feb. 15, 1927), 1-3; also "The Papacy--Its Aims and Character," PT (July 1, 1930), 1-3.

[175] C.P. Bolland, "Rome's Opportunity," RH (June 24, 1920), 4.

[176] L.H. Christian, "The Other Side of Europe," RH (May 21, 1936), 5-6. See also C.A. Holt, "The Vatican and Russia," RH (July 27, 1922), 9; L.H. Christian, Facing the Crisis in the Light of Bible Prophecy

royal visits to the pope,[177] and by the exchange of diplomats with scores of nations, and concordats with different countries.[178] The tendency away from democratic rule in Europe in the mid 1920s was also considered as playing into the hands of the papacy.[179] One European Adventist leader reported that "the Papacy is growing everywhere. We meet it on every hand."[180] The restoration of the temporal power of the Vatican in 1929 was the crowning event in this development.[181] We shall return in more detail to these significant events, and to the political strategies of the popes before, during and after World War II.[182] In the post-World War II developments Adventists continued to see numerous proofs of the growing influence of Catholicism.[183]

(Washington, DC: RHPA, 1937), 226-232.

[177] The audience granted to the English King George and Queen Mary on May 9, 1923 was described as a historic occasion; C.A. Holt, "Comments on Current Events," RH (May 31, 1923), 2.

[178] L.H. Christian, "Europe in 1925," RH (May 14, 1925), 2; Alonzo L. Baker, The Pope King Again, 99-109; F.D. Nichol, "Is Rome Growing Stronger?" RH (Jan. 7, 1937), 4-6; F. Lee, "The Road Ahead: A Challenge to our Faith," part 2, RH (March 4, 1943), 5-7; F. Lee, "Re-vival of Papal Power," RH (July 13, 1944), 7-8; W.L. Emmerson, "The Resurgence of Rome," RH (Feb. 13, 1947), 1, 10-11.

[179] L.H. Christian, "Political and Economic Conditions in Europe," no. 1, RH (Jan. 10, 1924), 3-4.

[180] L.H. Christian, "Conditions in the European Division," RH (Nov. 29, 1923), 3-6.

[181] See below, pp. 250-251; An immediate Adventist reaction to the settlement of the "Roman Question" was Alonzo L. Baker's book, The Pope King Again - Is the "deadly wound" healing?, published in the same year.

[182] See below, pp. 248-250.

[183] W.L. Emmerson, "The Resurgence of Rome," RH (Feb. 13, 1947), 10-11; Raymond F. Cottrell, "The Resurgence of Catholic Power," RH (May 21, 1959), 16-17, 23-24.

The phenomenal growth of the Catholic Church in the
United States remained a matter of grave concern. In
spite of sharply decreased immigration in the World War
I era, the number of American Catholics rose nonetheless
by fourteen percent during 1915-1920.[184] Describing
American Catholicism in the 1930s, F.D. Nichol pointed
to the success of the Catholic Action, and at Catholic
social influence and political pressure.[185] The *Review
and Herald* regarded the official attention given to the
death of Pope Pius XI in 1939 as rather ominous. "Why,"
the article asked, "did Congress adjourn out of respect
to the death of the head of one religious organization
while it utterly disregards similar events when the
heads of other religious organizations die?"[186] A "rapid
slide" was noted toward pro-Roman policies under
President Roosevelt, the appointment of Myron C. Taylor
as his personal envoy to the Vatican being the prime
example.[187]

Rome's determination to make America Catholic
continued. In many of the large cities Catholicism had
become the dominant religion. "Now it is the studied
effort of the church leadership to win rural America."[188]
The Jesuits gradually became less prominent in Adventist
literature, but they were still there and their
influence in the extensive educational Catholic program
was not to be lost sight off.[189] Neither must the
Catholic attempts at gaining control of organized labour

---

[184] C.A. Holt, "Immigration and the Catholic
Influence in the United States," RH (March 30, 1922), 8.

[185] F.D. Nichol, The Answer to Modern Religious
Thinking (Washington, DC: RHPA, 1936), 169-194; F.D.
Nichol, "Rome's Gains and Losses," RH (Jan. 14, 1937),
5-6; F.D. Nichol, "Rome's Power Revealed in Many Ways,"
RH (Jan. 21, 1937), 9-10.

[186] C.S. Longacre, "The Papacy in Prophecy," RH
(Apr. 20, 1939), 19.

[187] W.L. Emmerson, "America and World History," RH
(Feb. 27, 1947), 8-10.

[188] F.M. Wilcox, "The Seal of the Living God," RH
(Oct. 11, 1945), 8.

[189] Christian Edwardson, Facts of Faith, 273-287.

be underestimated.[190] Considering these and other factors, one Adventist writer concluded:

> We are entitled to ask, therefore, whether any such profound change in the spiritual climate of the United States has occurred during the past century and a half, and whether today Roman Catholic pressure from within is directing this great last-day power along the road delineated in the prophetic picture.[191]

1. Papacy and Peace

Although Pope Benedict XV (1914-1922) never unequivocally condemned World War I and remained strictly neutral (since to do otherwise would have posed a terrible dilemma for Catholics on both sides), his opposition to war was absolute, and unswervingly he pursued peace and reconciliation from the first moment of his pontificate.[192] Adventists soon recognized Benedict's desire for peace, but were also quick to attribute some ulterior motives to his peace efforts. They pointed to the view expressed by several Catholic writers and also by Benedict in his first encyclical "Ad Beatissimi" (1 Nov. 1914), that the war was the result of the renunciation of Christian principles by the countries of Europe, and that a return to these principles was a prerequisite for peace. This return to Christian principles would mean an increase in papal power, it was argued.[193] With concern it was noted that not only Catholic but also some Protestant voices were raised suggesting that the pope would be the best

---

[190] Carlyle B. Haynes, "Growing Catholic Control," RH (Feb. 9, 1950), 12-13.

[191] W.L. Emmerson, "The Growth of Catholic Influence in America," RH (July 12, 1951), 4.

[192] Thomas Bokenkotter, A Concise History of the Catholic Church, 345.

[193] W.W. Prescott, "The Papacy and the War: The Chastisement of the Nations for their Disloyalty to the Catholic Church," RH (Jan. 21, 1915), 4-6; see also Percy T. Magan, The Vatican and the War (Nashville, Ten.: SPA, 1915), 121-127.

arbiter for peace.[194] More alarming was the idea that, if the pope were to be successful in restoring worldly peace, he might also be successful in bringing unity to Christendom.[195] If Rome were to be successful in her diplomacy for peace, it would thereby "have cleared for herself the path to that high pinnacle of fame and power to which she longs to exalt herself."[196]

The fact that at one point even the American Jewish Committee decided to call on Benedict XV, requesting him to intercede on behalf of the Polish Jews, was found almost unbelievable. "Were it not that the Bible said that the world would wonder after the beast, it would seem hard to believe such a thing possible."[197]

When after the war plans were laid for a League of Nations, any mention of a possible papal involvement invariably aroused Adventist fears that religion would be injected into this institution.[198] Such a League of Nations might be a positive thing, but it might also be extremely dangerous, since "in these peace movements religio-political reformers are quick to recognize opportunities and avenues whereby their propaganda may be advanced and their ideals realized."[199]

When World War II broke out, once again it was feared that the pope wanted a role in the peace making process

---

[194] W.W. Prescott, "The Papacy and the War: Some of the Benefits Likely to Accrue to the Holy See as the Result of this Great Struggle," RH (Jan. 28, 1915), 3-4; L.L. Caviness, "The Papacy and the War," RH (Dec. 19, 1918), 3.

[195] F.M. Wilcox, "The Pope as Peacemaker," RH (May 4, 1916), 2, 5.

[196] Percy T. Magan, The Vatican and the War, 127.

[197] F.C. Gilbert, "All the World Wondered after the Beast," RH (Sept. 14, 1916), 10.

[198] L.L. Caviness, "The Pope in the League of Nations," RH (Jan. 29, 1920), 5.

[199] F.M. Wilcox, "The Glorious Consummation," no. 7, RH (Apr. 15, 1920), 4; See also F.M. Wilcox, "The Peace of the World: Belligerent Nations Arrange Armistice," RH (Nov. 28, 1918), 1-3.

to further his own long-term objectives. Taking history
as a guide for the future, the Adventist church paper
expressed the concern that Pope Pius, even though he
possessed "many admirable traits," would work for the
kind of peace that would be "to the distinct advantage
of the papal hierarchy."[200] The Vatican was utilizing the
conflict to its own advantage and its willingness to act
as peacemaker was primarily an attempt to build its
public image.[201] Opposition to the possible role of the
pope in the peace process was not to be construed as
manifesting an attitude of bigotry. It was only the
political ambition of Rome that was condemned.[202]

2. The Events of 1929

By withdrawing Vatican support from the Catholic Popular
Party, Pope Pius XI helped Mussolini in his attempts to
gain power over Italy. The pope reaped his reward in
1929 when Mussolini signed the Lateran Concordat and the
Vatican Treaty. The treaty granted the pope a sizable
sum of money, but more importantly, complete sovereignty
over Vatican City, thus restoring temporal power to the
pope. The concordat accorded the Catholic religion a
privileged status in Italy, notably in the domain of
education.[203]

For many years Adventists had predicted a
restoration of temporal power for the pope--the healing
of the deadly wound--and immediately emphasized how

----

[200] F.M. Wilcox, "Pope Pius as Peacemaker," RH (Oct.
30, 1941), 2, 12. For other statements about the
probability that the pope would play a major role in the
post-war peace process, see F. Lee, "Peace and the
Papacy," RH (Sept. 2, 1943), 10; Carlyle B. Haynes, "The
Pope at the Peace Table," RH (Nov. 11, 1943), 19-20;
Carlyle B. Haynes, "Who Shall Shape the Peace - Church
or State?" RH (Dec. 2, 1943), 7-8.

[201] Arthur S. Maxwell, Power and Prophecy: Who Shall
Rule the World?, 42-43.

[202] C.S. Longacre, "Shall the Church Sit at the
Peace Table?" RH (Feb. 1, 1945), 10-11.

[203] Thomas Bokenkotter, A Concise History of the
Catholic Church, 347-348.

prophecy had been fulfilled in the agreements between Mussolini, "one of the strongest civil dictators in the world today," and Pius XI, the "skillful diplomat."[204] "Since the beginning of our history as a denomination," the *Review and Herald* stated, "an occurrence more meaningful to us as a denomination has not taken place."[205]

Alonzo L. Baker's book, *The Pope King Again* (1929), after sketching the background of the "Roman Question," was quick to interpret the agreements between Mussolini and the Vatican as an example of the aims of the Catholic Church "in every nation where it has numbers and power sufficient to carry out its program."[206] The solution to the "Roman Question" was no occasion for optimism; it "turns the clock back to medieval ages, when union of church and state was the well-nigh universal rule."[207] But Roman Catholicism benefitted immensely. The prestige of the pope, the wealth of the church, as well as "the cunning of the Jesuits and the courage of the priests" were manifested by this event.[208] For Adventists this posed a further all-important question: What will happen next?

> Will this be confined to Italy? Not if the Catholic Church can win from the powers the homage which she claims is her due. For while the Roman See does not seek territory or subjects, it does seek the obeisance of kings and kingdoms....[209]

---

[204] Andrew C. Gilbert, "The Roman Question, RH (June 27, 1929), 3.

[205] Ibid.; the same sentiment is expressed by F.D. Nichol, "Notable Happenings of 1929," RH (Jan. 23, 1930), 3.

[206] Alonzo L. Baker, The Pope King Again, 21.

[207] Ibid., 19.

[208] L.H. Christian, Facing the Crisis in the Light of Bible Prophecy, 230.

[209] F.A. Coffin, "All the World Wondered," PT (Apr. 10, 1929), 1.

3. An Ambassador to the Vatican

The increasing number of ambassadors accredited to the Holy See was constantly referred to in Adventist publications as a sign of the ever growing political importance of the Vatican. In 1915 it was noted that England now had a representative at the Vatican, while the pope was trying to force new ties with France and Italy.[210] By 1920 the number of nations with accredited ambassadors at the Vatican had risen to 22.[211] The renewal of diplomatic ties between France and the Holy See in 1920 meant a further reinforcement of papal prestige.[212] More countries followed suit. In 1929 the number of accredited diplomats at the Vatican stood at more than 30, the United States and Russia being the "only two major powers not yet represented."[213] By 1943 the number had further risen to 39.[214] From 1940, when President Roosevelt appointed Myron C. Taylor as his personal representative to the Vatican, an American envoy was included in that number.

Not since 1848, when President James K. Polk (1845-1849) had sent an American consular representative to the Papal States, had there been any direct American diplomatic relationship with the Vatican. The diplomatic mission was closed in 1867, when the Papal States were reduced to the city of Rome and it no longer had seaports which justified American consular representation.[215]

-----

[210] Percy T. Magan, The Vatican and the War, 115; see also "The Rush of Civil Governments to Rome," (Feb. 2, 1922), 5-6.

[211] L.L. Caviness, "The Rising Prestige of the Vatican," RH (May 20, 1920), 4.

[212] W.A. Spicer, "The Papal Power of Rome," RH (Dec. 30, 1920), 2.

[213] Alonzo L. Baker, The Pope King Again, 23-24.

[214] F. Lee, The Road Ahead: A Challenge to our Faith," part 2, RH (March 4, 1943), 5.

[215] For a short survey of American-Vatican Diplomatic Relations, see Anson Phelps Stokes and Leo Pfeffer, Church and State in the United States, 273-280;

As early as 1915 voices were heard suggesting that the United States follow Britain's example in establishing diplomatic ties with the Vatican. But Adventists considered such a move a great danger: "The less business of any kind that this nation has with Rome, the better off our country will be. The avowed business of Catholics is to make America Catholic."[216] When the issue came up again at the time President W.G. Harding (1921-1923) was about to assume office, the *Review and Herald* stated it had too much confidence in President-elect Harding to think "that he wants to be part of this Roman Catholic scheme." But at the same time the fear was expressed that "this long-desired hope of Roman Catholics may sometime be realized. It will be in direct line with the re-establishment of the papal power, which we believe the prophecies of Scripture clearly forecast."[217] The editor of the same journal acknowledged in 1939 that so far no diplomatic ties had been established, but that it would be impossible to predict what would happen. It would be in line with Revelation 13 to think that "the time will come when such ties will be established."[218] When in that same year the American Cardinal Mundelein visited Rome, he was treated by the American embassy in Rome and other officials with unprecedented honors--a clear signal, it was believed--that diplomatic relations between the USA and the Vatican might be established in the near future.[219] When the United States sent an official representative to attend the coronation of Pius XII, the new pope, it seemed "evident, that the American

---

V. Norskov Olsen, <u>Papal Supremacy and Democracy</u> (Loma Linda, Cal.: Loma Linda Univ. Press, 1987), 61-66. For an earlier Adventist comment, see C.E. Holmes, "America's Representative to the Papal States," <u>RH</u> (March 5, 1914), 5-7.

[216] Claude E. Holmes, "Relation of the United States Government to the Vatican," <u>RH</u> (Apr. 1, 1915), 20.

[217] "Papal Representative to the American Government," <u>RH</u> (Feb. 17, 1921), 8.

[218] F.D. Nichol, "Diplomatic Relations with Vatican," <u>RH</u> (Jan. 6, 1939), 2.

[219] C.S. Longacre, "The Papacy in Prophecy," <u>RH</u> (Apr. 20, 1939), 19.

government is drifting away from original moorings in its attitude toward politico-ecclesiastical Romanism."[220]

When late in 1939 President Roosevelt announced the appointment of Myron C. Taylor as his personal representative to the Vatican, with the rank but not the status of ambassador, Adventists denounced this as "another of his dramatic and unexpected moves."[221]

J.L. McElhany, the president of the General Conference, wrote an official letter of protest to the White House, hand delivered by himself and C.S. Longacre, one of the church's prominent religious liberty leaders. Pledging support to the president's "earnest and diligent efforts to preserve peace in our own country and to help restore it in other lands," McElhany felt nevertheless compelled to point out

> ...a danger which we believe threatens certain fundamental American principles. This danger arises in connection with the appointment of a repre- sentative to the Vatican in an endeavor to coordinate your efforts with those of the Pope in working for world peace.[222]

After offering an explanation of the Adventists view on the relationship between church and state, and warning about the dangers to which this unfortunate act might lead, the letter rejected the concept of a "personal representative," since representatives appointed by the Chief Executive of the country would automatically become "the representatives of every citizen."[223] The letter ended with a direct appeal:

> We know. Mr. President, that there are many of your fellow citizens who, while recognizing the Pope and the Roman Catholic Church as a great religious force in the world, do not, on principle, believe

---

[220] Ibid., 20.

[221] F. Lee, "United States Representative at the Vatican," RH (Jan. 14, 1940), 10.

[222] Letter of J.L. McElhany to President Roosevelt, Dec. 29, 1939; published under the title "The United States and the Vatican" in RH (Jan. 11, 1940), 4.

[223] Ibid., 5.

that the United States should be represented at the
Vatican.... On behalf of the Seventh-day Adventist
Church, I therefore appeal to you to withdraw the
appointment of a personal representative to the
Vatican, and thereby safeguard the principles of
separation of church and state.[224]

On January 9, together with representatives of the
Baptist and Lutheran churches--who had also criticized
the Taylor appointment--president J.L. McElhany and
secretary E.D. Dick were invited to the White House,
with an hour's notice, for a conference with President
Roosevelt.[225] In a press conference later that day
Roosevelt stated that he had outlined his peace
objectives to leaders of the Baptist, Lutheran and
Adventist churches under a pledge of secrecy. The matter
of the appointment of Taylor had also been discussed.
The President stated that his visitors had told him that
"some of the protests they came to make had been based
on misinformation." Dr. Weaver, a Baptist, who acted as
the spokesman for the group, afterwards told the press,
he did not know whether the respective delegations had
changed their minds, but added, that they had been
"informed much more fully than we had expected as to the
policy of the President in naming Mr. Taylor his
personal representative to the Vatican."[226]

The next day, when informing the General Conference
Committee, McElhany stated that the press statement by

---

[224] Ibid.

[225] President Roosevelt had earlier, on December 27,
1939--a few days after the official announcement of the
Taylor appointment--discussed the issue with the
president of the Federal Council of the Churches of
Christ and the president of the Jewish Theological
Seminary of America. Afterwards these men said that they
were "all in agreement" with the plans of President
Roosevelt. ("Dr. Buttrick and Adler Call on President;
Two Peace Leaders See 'All in Agreement'," New York
Times, Dec. 27, 1939, 1, 3.) The Federal Council later
went on record that it only favoured the appointment of
Taylor as long as it stayed a temporary post.
("Churchmen Back Taylor Peace Task," New York Times,
Jan. 27, 1940, 4.)

[226] "President Sets Up Peace Objectives and Bides
his Time," New York Times (Jan. 10, 1940), 1, 6.

Roosevelt had unfortunately given the wrong impression. He and the other invitees had not been convinced by Roosevelt's arguments.[227] In a sermon which he preached a few days later McElhany described the White House conference in some detail. He did not reveal the peace plans Roosevelt had shared with the three delegations, but indicated that they sounded much like proposals which had already been publicly expressed by Cardinal Spellman. Roosevelt had done most of the talking and "the thing we all felt was vital" [presumably the principle of church-state separation] was not touched upon."[228] Some weeks later McElhany wrote to Dr. Weaver, one of the Baptist delegates at the White House meeting, that he had left the Oval Office with "a feeling of deep disappointment." He could not recall "what seemed ... one valid reason" as to why the Taylor appointment was necessary.[229]

Adventist publications repeatedly discussed the appointment of Taylor, but never was there any reference to the visit of the two Adventist leaders to the White House. Apparently it was not considered an unqualified success. F. Lee did mention Roosevelt's meeting with Dr. Buttrick of the Federal Council of the Churches of Christ and Rabbi Addler of the Jewish Seminary, but he remained silent about the meeting attended by McElhany and Dick.[230]

In spite of Roosevelt's explanations, Adventists continued to see "cause for alarm," and pointed to the prophecy of Revelation 13 as the context within which the Taylor appointment should be viewed. Roosevelt was not charged with ulterior motives, but fear was expressed that "he does not see the end to which his

---

[227] Minutes General Conference Committee, Jan. 10, 1940 (Gen. Conf. Arch.).

[228] Sermon by J.L. McElhany in the Takoma Park Church, Jan. 13, 1940 (Gen. Conf. Arch., RG 11 Presidential, General Files, 140).

[229] Letter of J.L. McElhany to Dr. Rufus W. Weaver, March 4, 1940 (Gen. Conf. Arch., RG 11, Presidential, General Files, 140).

[230] F. Lee, "United States Representative at the Vatican," RH (Jan. 14, 1940), 10.

action will logically lead."[231] It was also quickly pointed out that, when Taylor was officially presented to the pope, the ceremony did not differ in outward form from the way regular ambassadors are usually presented.[232] And fears that the appointment of a "personal representative" would soon lead to full diplomatic relationships persisted.[233]

During its Spring Meeting of 1940 the General Conference Committee went on record that it was convinced that recent events--such as the "sending of an ambassadorial representative to the Vatican by the President of the United States--called for a renewed emphasis on the prophecies of Revelation 13. It was decided to prepare a tract with the Adventist views on this issue and distribute at least 2 million copies.[234] The excitement about the Taylor appointment in Protestant circles in general was short-lived. In 1943 the *Liberty* editor wondered why Protestant America had ceased to protest.[235]

Myron C. Taylor continued to serve as President Truman's personal representative, until he retired in 1949, at which time this unique United States-Vatican relationship came to an end.[236] The issue flared up again two years later when President Truman nominated General Mark W. Clark to be an American ambassador at the Vatican. Adventists reacted immediately. They disagreed with

---

[231] F.M. Wilcox, "Restoration of Papal Sovereignty," RH (March 7, 1940), 11; see also W.A. Spicer, "President Sends Ambassador to Pope," PT (June 1, 1940), 1-3.

[232] F. Lee, "Special Envoy at the Vatican," RH (March 14, 1940), 10.

[233] Robert L. Odom, "Those Diplomatic Relations With the Vatican - Are They Dangerous?" The Watchman Magazine (March 1945), 4-5, 13-14.

[234] E.D. Dick, "Spring Meeting, General Conference Committee," RH (May 16, 1940), 13.

[235] H.H. Votaw, "Are Americans Indifferent?" Lib, vol. 38, no. 1 (1st quarter 1943), 28.

[236] V. Norskov Olsen, Papal Supremacy and American Democracy, 62.

those--many Protestants among them--who said that protesting Clark's nomination was "a revival of anti-
Catholic bigotry, which plagues the country perio-
dically."[237]

> Let no one be deceived. The ambassador to the
> Vatican, if ever confirmed, will mean that the
> United States has linked itself diplomatically with
> the Papacy--The Roman Catholic Church--and not
> merely with 'the scrap of real estate called Vati-
> can City.'[238]

During the first business meeting of the 1951
Autumn Council (October 21), the General Conference
Committee passed a resolution of protest against the
appointment of an American embassador to the Vatican. It
considered such an appointment a gross violation of the
principle of separation between church and state.[239] A
day later, a more far-reaching appeal was launched:
Church institutions and members were urged to deluge
their senators with letters of protest.[240]

In spite of strong opposition from many sides--
practically every major Protestant organization and publication protested[241]--Truman submitted Clark's name to
the Senate for confirmation. A few months later,
however, Clark requested that his name be withdrawn.
Although Truman said he would suggest another name, he
left office without doing so. Plans for sending an envoy
to the Vatican remained dormant in the 1950s and 1960s,
but whenever the possibility was mentioned Adventist
protests followed.[242]

---

[237] F. Lee, "Ambassador to the Roman Catholic
Church," RH (Jan. 17, 1952), 13.

[238] Ibid., 13.

[239] Edit. note, RH (1 Nov. 1951), 24.

[240] Alvin W. Johnson, "The Appointment of an Amba-
sador to the Vatican", part 2, RH (Dec. 13, 1951), 6-7.

[241] A.W. Johnson, "Opposition to the Vatican Grows,"
RH (March 27, 1952), 7-8.

[242] See "Vatican Envoy" folder in Gen. Conf. Arch.,
RG 52, Rel. Lib. Files R. 762.

4. Catholic Presidential Candidates

While Adventists vigorously protested the sending of an American ambassador to the Vatican, they were far less vocal in their opposition to Catholic presidential candidates. Governor Alfred E. Smith, a Roman Catholic, lost the Democratic presidential nomination in 1924, but, in spite of heavy opposition from the Ku Klux Klan and other anti-Catholic organizations--and in particular from the Southern Baptists--he was nominated presidential candidate by an overwhelming majority at the Democratic convention of 1928. For many Protestants, notably the Methodists, Smith's anti-prohibition stand, was highly controversial.

Many Adventists naturally wondered how they should vote in this election, but their leaders were not prepared to give any direct guidelines, whether to vote at all, or how to vote. The readers of the *Review and Herald* were urged to keep all discussion of political questions out of the church.[243] There was a subtle pressure on Adventist church members not to vote for Smith, but this was never directly linked to his religious affiliation. Although Adventists were told they were perfectly free to cast their vote as they wanted,[244] they were reminded that they could use the power of their vote in favour of temperance.[245] The Catholic presidential candidate happened to be against prohibition! It was not accidental that both the *Review and Herald* and the *Present Truth* carried many articles about the value of temperance and the need for prohibition during the months of August and September 1928, just prior to the election.

In 1960 the issue of a Catholic president once again came to the forefront, when John F. Kennedy won the presidential nomination for the Democratic Party. From

---

[243] F.M. Wilcox, "The Church and Politics," RH (Sept. 13, 1928), 3.

[244] F.M. Wilcox, "Temperance and Prohibition: The Coming Presidential Election," RH (Aug. 2, 1928), 3.

[245] F.M. Wilcox, "Politics and Prohibition," RH (Sept. 27, 1928), 3-4; F.M. Wilcox, "Temperance and Prohibition: The Coming Presidential Election," RH (Aug. 2, 1928), 3.

the beginning Kennedy's campaign was plagued by a
gigantic outpouring of anti-Catholic propaganda. The
U.S. Justice Department identified 144 producers of
anti-Catholic literature, most of them representing an
extremely conservative Protestant orientation.[246]
Not surprisingly, Adventists were quite uneasy
about the prospect of having a Roman Catholic in the
White House. A *Review and Herald* editorial argued that
protesting against a candidate who belongs to a church,
which is in official policy and practice opposed to the
traditional American principles of religious liberty and
the separation of church and state, should not be regarded as bigotry.[247] The same author further commented:

> The consistent pattern of clerical oppression and
> persecution of predominantly Catholic lands provi-
> des American Protestants with a valid and cogent
> reason for looking with misgivings and foreboding
> upon an adherent of that faith becoming President
> of this country.[248]

Several *Review and Herald* editorials recommended
the Adventist readers to shun party politics. If they
were to vote at all, they were advised to vote
intelligently, for candidates of known integrity. But no
overt attempt was made to dissuade Adventists from
voting for Kennedy. Although the readers were warned
that "Rome's intentions" were unchanged, they were also
urged not to participate in circulating biased anti-
Catholic propaganda.[249] The moderate tone of the comments
in the church journal caused some Adventists to worry
whether their paper had "established a new policy of
silence concerning Rome."[250] But this moderation did not

---

[246] Michael Schwartz, <u>Anti-Catholicism in America</u>
(Huntington, IN: Our Sunday Visitor, Inc., 1984), 118.

[247] Raymond F. Cottrell, "What is Bigotry?" <u>RH</u>
(March 31, 1960), 4.

[248] Raymond F. Cottrell, "Catholic Bishop
Corroborates Baptist President," <u>RH</u> (March 3, 1960), 6.

[249] K.H. Wood, "The Fake Oath," <u>RH</u> (Sept. 15, 1960), 5.

[250] F.D. Nichol, "From the Editor's Mailbag," <u>RH</u>
(Oct. 20, 1960), 4.

preclude editorial anxiety about whether a Catholic president would be able to ignore traditional Catholic standpoints and policies.[251]

Kennedy's victory was regarded as having "signicance when viewed in the light of Bible prophecy." But once the election had taken place, Adventists were advised to pray for the President-elect, and to give the new president their loyal support:[252]

> It is not necessary to approve of all his acts, but it is important to guard against imputing sinister motives to the President every time he takes a step that looks dangerous, as viewed from the Adventist prophetic frame of reference. To develop an attitude of constant suspicion is inimical to one's spiritual health, and is, at the same time, grossly unfair to the nation's Chief Executive.[253]

5. Education-related Issues

From the beginning the Roman Catholic Church in the United States placed a strong emphasis on the education of Catholic children in parochial school. Adventists likewise were strongly convinced of the desirability of a system of denominational schools. By 1915 Adventists were financing more than 1,000 elementary schools besides a number of secondary schools and colleges. Half a century later this number had more than quadrupled. With their commitment to a strong denominational school programme Adventists naturally closely watched developments in Catholic parochial education.

Never did Adventists question the right of Catholics to have their own schools. When in 1922 the State of Oregon proposed a statute requiring all children between the ages of 8 and 16 to attend public

---

[251] See Walter C. Utt, "Quanta Cura and the Syllabus of Errors," <u>Lib</u>, vol. 55, no. 6 (Nov./Dec. 1960), 12-13; 32-35; K.H. Wood, "The Vatican Newspaper Editorial," <u>RH</u> (June 30, 1960), 4; Raymond F. Cottrell, "The Religious Issue and the New Administration," <u>RH</u> (Dec. 22, 1960), 5.

[252] K.H. Wood, "The President-elect," <u>RH</u> (Dec. 8, 1960), 3.

[253] Ibid.

school in the district where they lived, Adventists denounced this as antichristian, un-American, autocratic, unjust, and paternalistic.[254] Every "patriotic citizen of Oregon" was asked to vote "no" on the proposed amendment.

> It is vicious legislation, because it is conceived and born in bigotry ... While we do not agree with many of the doctrines of the Catholic Church, against which in particular this drastic measure seems to be aimed, yet under our Constitution that church is entitled to the same rights and privileges as any other church.[255]

Adventists applauded the 1925 Supreme Court decision, which upheld the challenge brought to the Oregon law by an order of nuns which operated parochial schools and by the owner of a secular private school.[256] In the "Pierce vs. Society of Sisters" case the Supreme Court ruled that the Oregon law unreasonably interfered with the liberty of parents and guardians to direct the upbringing and education of children under their control.[257]

But although Adventists supported the Catholic right to have a parochial school system, they fiercely denounced every attempt of the Roman Catholic Church to receive government funds for the operating of their schools.[258]

---

[254] C.S. Longacre, "Reasons Why the Proposed Oregon Anti-Parochial School Amendment is Wrong," _Lib_, vol. 17, no. 5 (4th quarter 1922), 119-122; see also L.P. Jorgenson, "The Oregon School Law of 1922," _Catholic Historical Review_, vol. 54, no. 3 (Oct. 1968), 455-466.

[255] Ibid., 120.

[256] "The Supreme Court Decision on the Oregon School Law," _Lib_, vol. 20, no. 4 (4th quarter 1925), 111-114.

[257] Anson Phelps Stokes and Leo Pfeffer, _Church and State in the United States_, 116.

[258] _Ibid._, 433-446; Eric E. Syme, _A History of Church-state Relationships_, 120-127; C. Stanley Lowell, "Shall the State Subsidize Church Schools?" _Lib_, vol. 55, no. 5 (Sept./Oct. 1960), 11-15.

They did not accept the Catholic argument that it was unreasonable to expect them to support both the public schools and their own schools.[259] Catholics, they said, wanted no interference in their educational system. "The Catholic Church here claims a monopoly on everything in education, except in the payment of bills!"[260] When an attempt was made to get funds from the Ohio state government for Catholic schools, *Liberty* magazine warned, that

> The Catholics in Ohio are playing with political and religious dynamite, and courting trouble. They must not be surprised when anti-catholic organizations spring up like mushrooms in the night to oppose their raids upon the State funds....[261]

In response to the Catholic charge that refusing aid to parochial schools was discriminatory, the same journal insisted that no injustice is done to Catholics when such aid is refused. The Catholic schools exist solely and entirely as an agency of the church, "for the purpose of enabling the church to direct the minds of its youth into channels favorable for the church." Therefore even the smallest amount of financial assistance from the state would be unjustified.[262] But Adventists doubted the Catholic hierarchy would listen to Protestant protests: "We can be sure of one thing, and that is, Catholicism will grow more and more demanding."[263]

Until the end of World War II the issue of *Federal* aid to church operated schools remained more or less dormant. But expected pressures on the educational

---

[259] C.S. Longacre, "Imposition of Double Taxation," <u>Lib</u>, vol. 45, no. 2 (2nd quarter 1950), 28-29.

[260] Alonzo L. Baker, <u>The Pope King Again</u>, 61.

[261] C.S. Longacre, "Protestants Oppose Parochial Aid From Public Funds," <u>Lib</u>, vol. 30, no. 3 (3rd quarter 1935), 26.

[262] Herbert H. Votaw, "No Discrimination Against Catholics," <u>Lib</u>, vol. 31, no. 3 (3rd quarter 1936), 32.

[263] F. Lee, "Catholic Schools in America," <u>RH</u> (Apr. 25, 1940), 17.

system after the end of the war led to several proposals to inject federal funds into the educational programme, which normally depended for its funds on the individual states. Catholics felt that they should share in any federal money for education.[264] The debate became extremely vigorous when Representative Graham A. Barden of North Carolina introduced a law that would make 300 million dollars of federal funds available to public schools.[265] He specifically excluded the possibility that part of that money would benefit parochial schools. This evoked a strong protest from Cardinal Spellman who declared the bill "un-American" and "unconstitutional." The discussion became even more passionate when Mrs. Eleanor Roosevelt in her column in a New York newspaper took issue with the cardinal and emphasized the importance of total separation between church and state. Spellman then accused the first lady of bigotry and anti-Catholic feelings. *Liberty* magazine and the *Protestants and Other Americans United* led the campaign to support Barden and expressed strong agreement with Mrs. Roosevelt.[266] Even though Adventists stood to gain just as much from legislation approving federal aid to denominational schools as the Catholics, they continued to condemn direct federal funding for any aspect of a parochial school system.[267]

The Adventist opposition to Catholic attempts to get government money for parochial schools also extended to such fringe issues as subsidies for text books and free transportation, and the use of public school buildings for the teaching of religion.[268] An issue to

---

[264] F. Lee, "Beacon Lights," RH (March 22, 1945), 5.

[265] See Anson Phelps Stokes and Leo Pfeffer, Church and State in the United States, 435-440; R.W. Schwarz, Light Bearers to the Remnant, 537.

[266] See Frank H. Yost, "The Press Comments on the Roosevelt-Spellman Dispute," Lib, vol. 44, no. 4 (4th quarter 1949), 13-28.

[267] Frank H. Yost, "On the Religious Front," RH (Nov. 3, 1949), 19.

[268] In one Supreme Court case about the issue of teaching religion in a public school, the General Conference directed its attorneys to submit an *Amicus Curiae* Brief in support of a Mrs. Vashti McCollum, who

draw much attention was the use of public money to provide free transportation to Catholic school children in New Jersey. One tax payer complained. The State Court upheld him, but the New Jersey Court of Appeal reversed the decision. The Supreme Court decision in "Everson vs. Board of Education of the Township of Ewing" of Feb. 10, 1947 rendered a 5-4 decision against the tax payer. Legal opinion may have been divided about the propriety of letting Catholic children ride free on public school buses, but Adventist opinion was not.[269] During the 1947 Spring Council of the General Conference it was recommended that Adventists should not follow the Catholic example and refrain from using busses that were operated at public expense.[270] Two years later a *Review and Herald* article underlined the same principle:

> This denomination has taken a position officially against the use of public funds for free transportation and textbooks for church school children and for maintenance and teachers' salaries in church schools.[271]

6. Bible Reading

When Cardinal Gibbons in one of his sermons emphasized the power of the Bible to impress and change human hearts, this was considered sufficiently newsworthy to be noted in the columns of the *Review and Herald*. But this was immediately followed by the comment that the

---

objected that her son was obliged to follow religious instruction. The boy was excused, but Mrs. McCollum then argued that the matter caused her son embarrassment. See Clifton E. Olmstead, History of Religion in the United States, 123-124; "On the Religious Liberty Front," RH (Jan. 1, 1948), 10.

[269] F.D. Nichol, "What Do Jurists Say of Catholic Legislative Activity?" RH (Apr. 15, 1948), 4-5.

[270] J.I. Robinson, "Spring Council Proceedings, Los Angeles," RH (May 29, 1947), 14. See also Norman W. Dunn, "Autumn Council Proceedings," RH (Dec. 2, 1948), 7-8.

[271] Frank H. Yost, "On the Religious Liberty Front," RH (Nov. 3, 1949), 19.

Catholic laity could, of course, only read an approved version with Catholic explanatory notes.[272]

Adventists were told not to accept the erroneous view held by many Protestants that the reading of the Bible was forbidden to members of the Catholic Church.[273] But the refusal of the Church in centuries past to give its members a Bible in the vernacular, its Bible burnings, and its extolling of tradition above Scripture were not to be forgotten. The change with regard to Bible reading was seen as largely forced upon the Catholic Church, because of the influence of Bible distribution by the Protestants. And the subject of Bible reading was approached by Catholics with so much warning and caution, that "the Bible is still a little known book in Catholic lands today."[274] Furthermore, it was argued, the Douay version, for which the Jesuits were responsible, was far from perfect. It was not by chance that in Revelation 22:14 this version had opted for the variant "wash their robes," rather than for the reading in other manuscripts: "keep the commandments!"[275]

In spite of the change in the Catholic attitude toward Bible reading since the 19th century, Roman Catholics were perceived as remaining rather indifferent toward the reading of the Scriptures. Tradition continued in actual practice to be more important: "Converts to Catholicism are not made through reading the Scriptures."[276] The Catholic accusation that a multiplicity of versions in Protestantism had only resulted in confusion, was brushed aside with the remark that greater danger lay in "one authoritative interpretation that is wrong and that is imposed upon all men."[277] Bible

---

[272] "Cardinal Gibbons Praises the Bible," RH (Dec. 2, 1915), 2.

[273] George A. Campbell, "Roman Catholics and the Advent Message," RH (Apr. 21, 1932), 5.

[274] W.A. Spicer, "The Catholic Church and the Bible," RH (Aug. 27, 1936), 10.

[275] Christian Edwardson, Facts of Faith, 25.

[276] F. Lee, "World Trends," RH (Apr. 4, 1946), 5.

[277] F. Lee, "Roman Catholics and the Bible," RH (Feb. 15, 1951), 14.

reading was not going to bring about major changes in Catholicism:

> ... when the Roman Catholic Church encourages its members to read the Bible, it does not mean the same as when Protestant churches encourage their members to read the Bible. Members of Protestant churches are not hedged in by walls of interpretation or given certain colored glasses through which they must read the Bible.[278]

7. Rome and Christian Unity

For decades prior to 1915 Adventists had discerned ominous signs of Protestant-Catholic cooperation and had predicted further ecumenical developments that would set the stage for the endtime drama in which a small commandment keeping minority would be persecuted by a religio-political alliance of Protestantism, Catholicism, and Spiritism, with the United States as the prime facilitator of its global ambitions. This view persisted throughout the period under review in this chapter, but a major shift occurred, not only in tone, but also in emphasis.

For some time the emphasis remained on Protestant initiatives, in particular from Anglican leaders, in seeking rapprochement with the Roman Catholic Church.[279] Instances were noted of proposals to organize a league of churches, patterned after the League of Nations, in which the pope would play an important role.[280]

But gradually, as Adventist condemnations of other

---

[278] F. Lee, "Roman Catholic Bishop Encourages Bible Reading," RH (May 24, 1956), 9.

[279] F.M. Wilcox, "The Peace of the World," part 4, RH (Dec. 19, 1918), 5; Alfred L. Rowell, "The Road to Rome," RH (May 18, 1922), 9; C.A. Holt, "Comment on Current Events," RH (Jan. 31, 1924), 2; F.D. Nichol, "Conversions to Rome," RH (Jan. 28, 1937), 9.

[280] L.L. Caviness, "Will the Pope Unite All the Churches? RH (March 27, 1919), 5.

Protestants softened,[281] a more friendly approach to ecumenical trends emerged. The General Conference Autumn Council of 1926 adopted a "Statement of Relationships to Other Societies" manifesting a remarkable openness toward other Christians:

> We recognize every agency that lifts up Christ before men as part of the divine plan for the evangelization of the world, and we hold in high esteem the Christian men and women in other communions who are engaged in winning souls to Christ.[282]

Adventists insisted they had a unique mission and could not be restricted in their evangelistic activities to certain geographical areas; they feared that increased interchurch unity might bring certain pressures to curtail the freedom of individual churches. But nevertheless, they expressed the highest regards for the "promoters of this great movement," who "stand high in the religious world, and are entitled to respect and honor for the achievement for the cause of their Master."[283] When Adventist editors wrote about the ecumenical conferences which they had attended, warnings about possible future dangers and doubts about whether real unity would be possible--considering the immense doctrinal differences--were usually accompanied by words of appreciation for the lofty motives of the participants. Arthur S. Maxwell, after attending the 1927 World Conference on Faith and Order, admitted he had expected a conference "steeped in higher criticism; yet so far as our observations have gone, the emphasis

---

[281] Jesse C. Stevens, for example, devoted less than one page to the "daughters of Babylon" (The Papacy in Bible Prophecy, 84-85); W.C. Spicer in his Beacon Lights of Prophecy is also sparingly in his criticism of Protestantism.

[282] Quoted from QOD, 625-626. The 1926 statement underwent through the years some editorial changes; it is presently incorporated in the General Conference Working Policy, as Policy O 75 ([Hagerstown, MD: RHPA, 1992], 380-381).

[283] F.M. Wilcox, "The Interchurch World Movement," RH (June 3, 1920), 11.

has been on the side of evangelism."[284] F.D. Nichol commented on the 1937 meetings in Oxford (Life and Work) and Edinburgh (Faith and Order): "One cannot read the report of these two great meetings without being conscious that profound convictions stirred the souls of the speakers."[285] When the World Council of Churches was founded in Amsterdam in 1948, W.L. Emmerson, covering the meetings for the *Review and Herald*, concluded, "Much is being said that reveals genuine spiritual concern and even alarm over the state of the church and the world."[286] And D.A. Delafield, in 1949, while expressing doubts as to whether the Federal Council of Churches in the United States would be able to establish true spiritual union, credited its leaders with "worthy and commendable" objectives.[287] Many similar positive statements about the intentions of ecumenical initiatives could be added.[288]

But with the attention to Protestant ecumenical initiatives, the role of Catholicism was never forgotten. It was duly noted that Protestant leaders expressed regrets about the absence of the Roman

---

[284] Arthur S. Maxwell, "A Movement to Secure Christian Unity: The World Conference on Faith and Order," part 5, RH (Nov. 3, 1927), 15.

[285] F.D. Nichol, "Comments on Oxford and Edinburgh," RH (Nov. 11, 1937), 10.

[286] W.L. Emmerson, "Spotlight on Amsterdam: Protestant Leaders Discuss Church's Relation to the World," RH (Sept. 30, 1948), 11.

[287] D.A. Delafield, "The Federal Council After Forty Years," RH (Jan. 6, 1949), 7.

[288] E.g. F.D. Nichol, "A World Council of Churches," RH (Aug. 11, 1938), 3-4; R.A. Anderson, "International Congress on Prophecy," RH (Jan. 8, 1953), 6-7; D.E. Rebok, "National Council of Churches Meets in Denver," RH (Jan. 29, 1953), 6-7; A series of 4 articles on the 1954 Evanston meeting of the WCC by F.D. Nichol and W. L. Emmerson ("World Council of Churches Convenes," RH, Aug. 26, 1954, 4-6; Sept. 2, 1954, 3-5, 20-21; Sept. 9, 1954, 3-5, 20-21); F.D. Nichol, "Comments on the World Council of Churches," RH (Sept. 23, 1954), 14-15.

Catholic Church during ecumenical conferences.[289] And
Adventists did not for a moment think that the
ecumenical tide would halt before the gates of Rome. The
Catholic Church, however, would want to dictate the
terms for unity.[290] Compromise would have to come from
the Protestants, because it would not come from Rome.[291]
Expectations about an ecumenical "breakthrough" during
and as a result of Vaticanum II[292] were viewed by
Adventists with grave suspicion, as no alteration of
fundamental doctrines was expected.[293] And papal
initiatives such as Pope Paul VI's Jerusalem meeting
with Patriarch Athenagoras of Constantinople in 1964,[294]
and his visit to the United Nations in New York one year
later, were clear signals of the pope's enhanced status
as a leader in Christendom and in the world at large.[295]

---

[289] F.D. Nichol, "A Notable Conference at Oxford,"
RH (Oct. 14, 1937), 11; F.D. Nichol, "Comments on Oxford
and Edinburgh," RH (Nov. 11, 1937), 10.

[290] F. Lee, "Why Roman Catholics Stand Apart," RH
(Dec. 2, 1954), 13.

[291] F. Lee, "Rome Waits for Wandering Sheep," RH
(July 28, 1955), 9.

[292] For the Adventist evaluation of Vaticanum II,
see below, pp. 282-291.

[293] W.L. Emmerson, "That They All May Be One," Lib,
vol. 58, no. 2 (March/Apr., 1963), 12-15; B.B. Beach,
"Obstacles to Unity," Lib, vol. 58, no. 2 (March/Apr.,
1963), 16-17, 28-29; see also H. Ward Hill, "Montreal:
The Fourth World Conference on Faith and Order -
Failure?" Lib, vol. 58, no. 6 (Nov./Dec., 1963), 23.

[294] Roland R. Hegstad, "Summit Conference of Pope
and Patriarch," RH (Jan. 23, 1964), 1; Kenneth H. Wood,
"More on Pope Paul's Journey," RH (Feb. 13, 1964), 12-
13.

[295] F.D. Nichol, "Pope Paul Addresses the United
Nations," RH (Oct. 21, 1965), 1, 8-9; Roy Allan
Anderson. "The Pope and World Peace," Min, vol. 38, no.
8 (Sept. 1965), 24-27, 36-37.

8. Sunday Laws

The Religious Liberty Department of the Adventist Church closely monitored all attempts at Sunday legislation.[296] But, contrary to Adventist fears, there was hardly any expansion of Sunday "blue" laws or persecution of their violators in the first half of the twentieth century.[297] The movement for Calendar Reform, with its greatest momentum in the 1920s and 1930s, seemed a new threat for Sabbath keepers. Various proposals had one thing in common: they would disrupt the weekly cycle by inserting one or two "blank days." Adoption of such plans would cause immense problems for Sabbath keepers.[298] In general no strong Catholic influence was detected in the movement for Calendar Reform. Occasionally some Catholic support was noted,[299] but Arthur S. Maxwell reported from Rome, after discussions with prominent Catholic spokesmen, that the Catholic Church was opposed to any "blank-day" calendar plan.[300]

In the Adventist eschatological scheme the Sabbath-Sunday issue and Rome's role therein continued to figure prominently. The time would come when Protestants would carry out the proposals of the Vatican. Protestants

---

[296] "Report of the Religious Liberty Department," RH (May 16, 1918), 11-15; F.M. Wilcox, "Gathering Clouds," RH (Aug. 18, 1921), 7.

[297] R.W. Schwarz, Light Bearers to the Remnant, 531-535.

[298] For a survey of the Calendar Reform movement, see art. "Calendar Reform," in: SDAE, 183-186; R.W. Schwarz, Light Bearers to the Remnant, 517-520. See also the extra issue of Liberty, vol. 23, no. 2 (1st quarter 1929), 33-46.

[299] E.g. Frank A. Coffin, "Revision of the Weekly Calendar," RH (May 5, 1921), 9; F.D. Nichol, "Shall We Have a Wandering Sabbath?, part 13, RH (Apr. 25, 1929), 5.

[300] Arthur S. Maxwell, "Calendar Reform: Recent Investigations in Geneva, Rome and London," RH (Dec. 17, 1936), 3-5; see also Carlyle B. Haynes, "Roman Catholics Oppose Calendar Revision," RH (May 8, 1947), 8-9.

would do much of the talking, but the Catholics would be the real power behind the scenes.[301] Catholics would co-operate with Protestants in every project from which common benefit might be expected.[302] Sunday laws would certainly fall into that category.[303]

A new wave of Sunday legislation during the 1950s was largely in defense of businesses which were likely to suffer from the competition of large "discount stores" with their additional opening hours. Adventists were once again extremely active in their protests; they insisted that these Sunday laws were primarily religiously motivated, although this time they were dressed up as social or economic measures.[304] And they did not fail to notice that, as time went by, "the Catholic hierarchy and the Catholic legislators" were giving more support to this new Sunday law movement.[305]

9. *Future Developments*

However seriously this wave of Sunday legislation in the 1950s was taken, a nation-wide or world-wide legally enforced worship on the first day of the week was no onger regarded as an immediate danger, as it had been, for instance, in the 1880s and 1890s. But the traditional endtime scenario was, nonetheless, still very much alive. One writer, in 1919, had little doubt there would soon be some kind of world federation that would establish a world religion; and with the Catholic Church gaining so much in influence, it was clear in

---

[301] F. Lee, "Roman Catholics and Church Unity," RH (June 29, 1944, 4.

[302] F. Lee, "Catholics Pray for Unity of Christendom," RH (March 8, 1956), 10.

[303] F. Lee, "The Road Ahead: A Challenge to our Faith," part 2, RH (March 4, 1943), 6; F. Lee, "Protestants and Catholics Support Sunday Sacredness," RH (Sept. 16, 1954), 12.

[304] Many articles on this subject may be found in the Liberty issues of the 1950s.

[305] C.S. Longacre, "Catholics, Protestants, Soon to Work Together," RH (May 26, 1955), 7.

what direction that world religion would lean.[306] Another author continued to stress the role of "political Protestantism" as the dominant force in the eschatological drama.[307]

Some Adventist authors used the same strong language that had also been employed by a previous generation:

> Rome is planning her cathedrals, churches, and cloisters in all lands, but especially in Protestant countries like Germany, England, the United States and Scandinavia. She will yet have power to persecute the saints of God. But this last period of her glory will be brief.[308]

Or, to quote another example:

> Standing as we are today in the shadow of these two gigantic religio-political powers—Romanism triumphant in the Old World, apostate Protestantism organized and dictatorial in the New—we are foolish virgins if we do not understand that we have come to a late hour, and it is time to wake out of our sleep.[309]

"Popery has come back," another Adventist writer affirmed, "and it will yet commit its final acts in the great apostasy."[310] Frederick Lee fully concurred:

---

[306] Charles B. Haynes, "The Last Hope of the World," RH (Apr. 24, 1919), 10. See also F.M. Wilcox, "The Glorious Consummation," no. 11, RH (May 13, 1920), 2, 5-6.

[307] I.A Crane, "Not Catholicism, but Political Protestantism to Rule America," Lib, vol. 19, no. 1 (1st quarter 1924), 20-21.

[308] L.H. Christian, Facing the Crisis in the Light of Bible Prophecy, 232.

[309] C.A. Holt, "Romanism in the Old World, Apostate Protestantism in the New," RH (Apr. 28, 1927), 4.

[310] W.L. Emmerson, "The Resurgence of Rome," RH (Feb. 13, 1947), 11.

... Roman Catholics have one great objective held before them and that is the restoration of the medieval glory of the church when the Christian world was as one man subject to the Roman See in both spiritual and secular matters.[311]

But as time went by such specific statements became less frequent, and many Adventists preferred to say that though ominous developments are taking place, they are "still vague and shadowy."[312]

VIII Prospects for Evangelization

As Adventists in thought, and especially in action, began to allow for a longer interim period between the present and the eschatological finale, global evangelism was increasingly emphasized. The task of preaching the Adventist message to all the world would have to be accomplished before the end would come. And Roman Catholics were more and more explicitly included among those who had to be reached.

Although previously Adventists had often, with Ellen G. White, affirmed that there are many sincere Christians in the Roman Catholic Church, this was now emphasized in a much more consistent way. Alonzo L. Baker wanted to avoid the impression that his book about the renewed "kingship" of the pope, was seen as "an attack on Roman Catholics":

We have no quarrel with individual Catholics and no allegations to make against them. Personally we are acquainted with many members of the Roman Catholic Church whose deep piety and upright character we respect.[313]

Arthur S. Maxwell stressed the same point. His interpretation of Bible prophecy was no "prejudiced attack on the Roman Catholic Church." He felt no personal antagonism toward Catholics. On the contrary,

---

[311] F. Lee, "Catholics Pray for Unity of Christendom," RH (March 8, 1956), 10.

[312] Arthur S. Maxwell, Power and Prophecy: Who Shall Rule the World?, 75.

[313] Alonzo L. Baker, The Pope King Again, 9.

274

he remembered "pleasant personal visits with high digni-
taries in Rome." When he mentioned the papacy in his
book, he was thinking of an "ecclesiastical system, not
of individuals."[314]

Adventists insisted they differentiated between the
Roman hierarchy and "individual adherents of Romanism."
Few positive things could be said about the hierarchy,
but among the "adherents of this false system" are
"Christian men and women possessing qualities we must
recognize." For that reason "the abusive epithets by
which some writers and speakers characterize everything
Roman Catholic" must be condemned.[315] The same author
took this point even a little further: "Had we ... been
born and bred in the Catholic faith, we would
undoubtedly see as Catholics see, and do as they do."[316]

At times very positive remarks were made about specific
Roman Catholics. As early as 1915 Percy T. Magan in his
book *The Vatican and the War* described Pope Pius X as "a
God-fearing, kind-hearted priest."[317] George McCready
Price, one of the foremost Adventist authors in the
field of creationism, lauded the stand of Pius XII in
his encyclical "Humani Generis" in defense of the
historicity of the Genesis account.[318] The associate
editor of the *Review and Herald* wrote in extremely

---

[314] Arthur S. Maxwell, <u>Power and Prophecy: Who Shall
Rule the World?</u>, 55. The same sentiment is expressed by
C.P. Bollman, "1260 Years of Papal Supremacy," <u>RH</u> (Dec.
29, 1921), 6.

[315] F.M. Wilcox, "The Papacy in Prophecy," <u>RH</u> (Apr.
11, 1929), 3-4; F.M. Wilcox, "The Papacy in Prophecy,"
<u>RH</u> (Feb. 29, 1940), 2, 10. See also F.M. Wilcox,
"Catholics and Protestants Possess Equal Rights," <u>Lib</u>,
vol. 8, no. 4 (4th quarter, 1913), 153.

[316] F.M. Wilcox, "About Catholics," part 2, <u>RH</u> (July
14, 1949), 12.

[317] Percy T. Magan, <u>The Vatican and the War</u>, 111.

[318] George McCready Price, "The Pope Comes to the
Defense of Genesis," <u>RH</u> (Apr. 12, 1951), 3; he does,
however, emphasize the Jesuit background of the pope,
and places the encyclical in a broader, less reassuring
context.

positive terms about Catholic theologian Hans Küng,
after he had heard him speak on the topic of religious
liberty.[319] Dr. Jean Nüssbaum, one of Adventism's
foremost "diplomats," often entrusted with sensitive
missions, in a personal letter to the president of the
General Conference mentioned his constructive visits
with several cardinals, two of whom he had known for
over 20 years.[320] Another church leader mentioned several
things Adventist ministers could learn from the monks in
the Carthusian monastery he had visited in Spain.[321]

Individual Catholics were candidates for membership in
the Seventh-day Adventist Church like anyone else! Many
are among "God's people" who must be called out of
Babylon.[322] But even though Adventists were able to
welcome some converts from Catholicism, the challenge
remained enormous.[323] It was even more formidable in
other parts of the world, such as South America,[324] and
Southern Europe.[325]
    Working for Catholics could be very fruitful, it
was argued by one writer. "For Catholicism is not
contaminated with Modernism, higher criticism, and the
infidelity" that is so rampant in Protestant churches.
Catholics at least still believe in the virgin birth and

---

[319] Raymond F. Cottrell, "The Church and Freedom,"
RH (May 30, 1963), 15.

[320] Letter J. Nüssbaum to R.R. Figuhr, Nov. 27, 1961
(Gen. Conf. Arch.).

[321] J.R. Spangler, "Lessons From a Carthusian
Monastery," Min, vol. 38, no. 8 (Sept., 1965), 26-28,
32.

[322] Alonzo L. Baker, The Pope King Again, 123-127.

[323] F.D. Nichol, "Catholic Conversions," RH (Aug.
25, 1955), 10.

[324] C.K. Meyers, "In the Grip of Catholicism," RH
(May 29, 1930), 11: Orley Ford, "Approach to Catholics
in Latin America," Min, vol. 18, no. 5 (Apr. 1945), 11-
12.

[325] L.H. Christian, "The Mission Needs of Europe,"
RH (Feb. 17, 1927), 12-13.

the miracles of Christ, and still have a reverence for the supernatural.[326] The attitude that all is wrong in Catholicism must be avoided. "We must give credit where we can." Tact is of utmost importance. Catholics may have been told all kinds of things about Protestants. The approach must be absolutely free from all contempt, bigotry, and bitterness.[327]

"Reckless assertions" based on dubious sources will justifiably give offense.[328] The secret of success with Catholics was to make them read their Bible, to find areas of agreement and then to move from there to other topics.[329] It was, of course, a prerequisite to know the basic tenets of Catholicism and to be well prepared to meet "the persuasive arguments of Rome."[330] In discussions with Catholics "a few of our distinctive doctrines" must be emphasized: the Adventist understanding of prophecy; the nature of man, because of its relevancy for such subjects as purgatory, Mary, and the saints; the sanctuary service, because of the contrast it offers with the Mass and priestly intercession; and the Sabbath.[331]

In a series of four *Review and Herald* articles Mary E. Walsh, once herself a Roman Catholic, offered more detailed advice about ways to reach Roman Catholics. Not only must they be brought to the point where they are prepared to read their Bible, but care must also be exercised to use Catholic instead of Protestant

---

[326] George A, Campbell, "Roman Catholics and the Advent Message, RH (Apr. 21, 1932), 4.

[327] Doreen Fox, "Winsome Ways With Roman Catholics," Min, vol. 37, no. 5 (May 1964), 37-38.

[328] Mary E. Walsh, "Approaching the Intelligent Catholic," Min, vol. 9, no. 4 (Apr. 1936), 5-6.

[329] George A. Campbell, "Roman Catholics and the Advent Message, RH (Apr. 21, 1932), 5.

[330] F.D. Nichol, "Our Answer to the Challenge of Rome's Revival," RH (Feb. 4, 1937), 7.

[331] F.D. Nichol, "Seventh-day Adventist Teachings an Answer to Catholicism and Modernism," RH (Feb. 1, 1934), 3.

terminology.[332] Since Catholics will not readily attend Protestant meetings, they must be approached in personal contacts. During these conversations in subtle ways questions must be raised in their minds about their own religion.[333] A special effort must be made to show how the apocryphal books are inconsistent with the 66 canonical books. In the process a number of Catholic doctrines can be touched upon that find support only in the Apocrypha.[334] Finally, the order in which the doctrines are studied must be carefully thought through.[335] To assist those who wanted to evangelize Catholics, Mary Walsh developed a series of 12 detailed "Bible Lessons for Catholics."[336]

A few popular novel-like books were also intended to draw Catholic interest. G.A. Campbell wrote a story about a poor, but virtuous and proud Irish American girl who found a job as a maid for an Adventist pastor. When she tried to convert the pastor to her views, she was in for a few shocks. She had to admit that the Adventist views are biblical and that she had been in error.[337] Another example of this genre is *A Brand from the Burning*.[338] It is, according to the title page, "a true story of the life of a Roman Catholic priest and of his conversion to the Seventh-day Adventist Church, where he

---

[332] Mary E. Walsh, "How Shall We Reach Roman Catholics?" RH (Oct. 5, 1961), 1, 4-5; see also Niels Wensell, "How to Approach Catholics," Min, vol. 23, no. 7 (July 1950), 6.

[333] Mary E. Walsh, "Reaching the Catholic Mind," RH (Oct. 19, 1961), 3-4.

[334] Mary E. Walsh, "Meeting Catholic Dogma," RH (Oct. 26, 1961), 6-7.

[335] Mary E. Walsh, "Important Questions Answered on How to Work for Catholics," RH (Nov. 2, 1961), 7-8.

[336] Mary E. Walsh, Bible Lessons for Catholics (Nashville, Tenn.: SPA, 1967).

[337] G.A. Campbell, Mary Kennedy's Victory (Mountain View, Cal.: PPPA, 1953).

[338] Alcyon Ruth Heck, A Brand from the Burning (Mountain View, Cal.: PPPA, 1960).

is now a minister." Posted to China after his seminary
training, this priest soon discovered many parallels
between the heathen religion in the region where he
worked and his own. In later years his doubts became
stronger. Working in Guatemala, he came into contact
with Adventists who pointed him to the Bible and gave
him Adventist literature. After intense self-examination
he finally made his decision to leave Catholicism and
convert to "the truth."

The desire to win Catholics to Adventism was a major
factor in the effort of church leaders to keep Adventist
literature, destined for the public at large, free from
expressions Roman Catholics might find offensive.
Stylistic changes were made in such classics as Uriah
Smith's commentaries on Daniel and the Revelation.[339]
The, largely negative, Catholic focus of "source books"
for "Bible Students" diminished considerably.[340] In 1930
a council of Adventist editors concluded that "dangers
are to be avoided" in the presentation of sensitive
topics, such as the role the papacy is expected to play
in future events.[341] The editors spent most of their time
on problems related to reaching Catholics. It was
pointed out that Adventist literature contained much
that warns non-Catholics against Catholics, "but very
little that is intended primarily to convert Catholics
themselves." And further, that courtesy was needed in
the treatment of "subjects offensive to Catholics, and
that abuse and derision have no place in Seventh-day
Adventist literature."[342]

When Miss Walsh had prepared a new manuscript,
entitled "Corruption of the Catholic Church," the
Southern Publishing Association first sought the counsel

---

[339] See above, pp. 213-214.

[340] 516, or 35,7 %, of the 1442 entries in the 1919
edition of the Source Book for Bible Students deal with
Catholicism; in the 1962 Seventh-day Adventist Bible
Student's Source Book (Don F. Neuffeld and Julia
Neuffer, eds.; Washington, DC: RHPA, 1962) 399 out of a
total of 1815 entries, or only 22%, focus on Catholicism.

[341] Alonzo L. Baker, "The Editor's Council," RH
(Sept. 18, 1930), 25.

[342] Ibid.

of the General Conference to determine whether the approach of the book was deemed acceptable.[343] The General Conference leaders were also asked for their guidance with respect to a manuscript by Walter Schubert about methods in working for Roman Catholics.[344]

IX Does Catholicism Change?

1. *No Signs of Real Change*

Adventists remained convinced that Catholicism never changes. The chapter in Ellen G. White's *Great Controversy* about the character and ultimate aims of the papacy continued to express the Adventist belief that prophecy unequivocally indicates that Roman Catholicism will not basically alter its doctrines, nor its craving for universal power.[345]

The emphasis on the unchanging character of the Roman Catholic Church may have been somewhat less prominent than in the previous period, but the conviction had by no means disappeared. On fundamental doctrinal and social issues Catholic thinking had not altered.[346] Commenting on the Encyclical "Humani Generis" of August 21, 1950, the *Review and Herald* pointed out how this papal document took strong issue with all who wanted to minimize or undermine Catholic doctrine and how it affirmed its stand on traditional Catholic doctrine.[347] In a later comment the same journal emphasized that the ideas expressed in earlier Catholic pronouncements, in particular in the "Syllabus Errorum"

---

[343] Minutes of the Meeting of General Conference Officers, Sept. 23, 1942 (Gen. Conf. Arch.).

[344] Minutes Meeting General Conference Officers, Feb. 11, 1953 (Gen. Conf. Arch.).

[345] See note 174.

[346] F.D. Nichol, The Answer to Modern Religious Thinking, 183-186.

[347] F. Lee, "Rome Never Changes," RH (Nov. 16, 1950), 4-5.

of 1864, had never been withdrawn.[348]

Adventist fears about the unchanging character of Catholicism were especially concentrated on Catholic intolerance for non-Catholics. Percy T. Magan, in 1915, predicted that a restoration of temporal power to the papacy would bring renewed persecution.[349] He found support for his gloomy forecast in statements of Ellen G. White in her *Great Controversy*.[350] Thirty years later these same fears were still present in Adventist minds:

> [The Catholic Church] is still fearful of democracy and would rather find shelter under autocratic power, which she can control, than to dwell where freedom of religion, freedom of the press, and freedom of speech are the ruling features of government.[351]

The Catholic Church intends to undo what the Reformation did and to regain its former power.[352] Its view of a perfect society still harks back to the Middle Ages: "one society controlled by the pope and his representatives."[353] That is why, toward the end of World War II, it was considered so dangerous to allow the pope a major role in peace negotiations.[354] Roman Catholicism, it was stressed, differs from other religious organizations. It is more than a church; it is also a political entity, "purporting to have divine sanction

---

[348] F.D. Nichol, "Catholic Authorities on Church-State Relationships, RH (May 13, 1947), 3-4.

[349] Percy T. Magan, The Vatican and the War, 29; also 65.

[350] Ibid., 46.

[351] F. Lee, "The Papacy Unchanged," RH (July 20, 1944), 7.

[352] L.L. Caviness, "Roman Catholic Plans," RH (Jan. 25, 1917), 3.

[353] F. Lee, "A Perfect Society on Earth: A Catholic View," RH (Aug. 10, 1944), 5.

[354] C.S. Longacre, "Shall the Church Sit at the Peace Table?" RH (Feb. 1, 1945), 10.

over all kings, rulers, and people," in secular as well as spiritual matters.[355]

Adventists warned American Protestants not to believe naïvely that the more tolerant attitude of American Catholicism was a sign of change. It was simply part of the over-all Catholic strategy to be tolerant where the Catholic Church is in the minority.[356] The face of American Catholicism does not truly represent the Catholic spirit. Catholicism has two faces, one that it shows in such countries as Spain and Colombia, and the more pleasant one it turns toward America.[357] But Rome is much older than Washington, "and Catholicism had a very clearly fixed policy long before America was discovered."[358] Rome cannot yet do in the United States what it can do in other lands and has therefore temporarily adapted to the American situation. That should, however, not be mistaken for real change.[359]

2. *Vaticanum II*

A discussion of the Adventist reactions to the Second Vatican Council fits most naturally in this section about the Adventist perception of change, or rather of the absence thereof, in Catholicism. Practically all Adventist evaluations of the council were focused on whether it produced any real change in the Roman Catholic Church.

When John XXIII was elected pope at the age of

---

[355] C.S. Longacre, "Roman Catholic Attitude Toward Protestants," RH (Nov. 7, 1946), 8.

[356] C.S. Longacre, "Roman Catholic Attitude Toward Protestants," RH (Nov. 7, 1946), 7; F. Lee, "When and Where Are Roman Catholics Tolerant?", part 1, RH (July 17, 1952), 11.

[357] F. Lee, "Roman Catholics Seeking Friends and Converts," RH (July 10, 1952), 13.

[358] F.D. Nichol, "The Pope and Liberty," RH (June 18, 1931), 11.

[359] F.D. Nichol, "Attitude Toward Catholics," RH (July 4, 1929), 13-14.

almost 77, he surprised his church and the world by calling a general church council, the first after the Vatican Council of 1869-1870. He not only hoped a council could be a major step on the way toward reunion with the Eastern Churches and the "separated brethren" in Protestant communions, but that it would also result in a general *aggiornamento* (bringing up to date) of the Roman Catholic Church.

Naturally the *Review and Herald* soon commented on the papal plans. It highlighted the ecumenical intentions of the pope, who from the beginning of his pontificate seemed to be especially interested in unity. The council would no doubt be used to develop a strategy for the eventual reunion of non-Roman Christendom with the mother-church.[360] The cautious optimism of many Protestants suggested that the time was near when Ellen G. White's predictions in the book *The Great Controversy* --about Protestantism "stretching her hand across the gulf to grasp the hand of Roman power"--would be fulfilled.[361] Other articles in subsequent issues of the church paper provided further support for this conviction by underlining the growing power of Catholicism, in the world at large, but in particular in the United States.[362]

When in 1962 the council was about to begin its first session, Adventist leadership decided to arrange for in-depth reporting of this event in the denominational journals, in particular in *Liberty* and in the *Review and Herald*. Several editors and religious liberty leaders stayed in Rome for a number of weeks during one or more of the four sessions of the Council: R.F. Cottrell, M.E. Loewen, W.L. Emmerson, and Dr. J. Rossi. The services of Dr. B.B. Beach, an American serving the church in Europe as coordinator of its educational programme, were also requested; his academic background as a historian, his knowledge of Europe and his linguistic skills, seemed to

---

[360] Raymond F. Cottrell, "Pope John Lays Plans to Reunite Christendom," RH (May 7, 1959), 14, 16-17.

[361] Raymond F. Cottrell, "The Protestant Reaction," RH (May 14, 1959), 7-9.

[362] Raymond F. Cottrell, "The Resurgence of Catholic Power," RH (May 21, 1959), 16-17, 23-24; Raymond F. Cottrell, "The Roman Catholic Church Comes of Age in the United States," RH (May 28, 1959), 16-19.

provide the prerequisites for a critical evaluation of council events. Dr. Beach spent considerable time in Rome during all four sessions and became the chief reporter for the *Review and Herald*.[363] He, like the other reporters, provided professional journalistic coverage in a mostly dignified and sympathetic tone.

In this reporting, in particular of the first two sessions, background information was provided about the inner workings of the council. Considerable attention was given to the conflicts between the conservative council fathers and their progressive colleagues.[364] But most attention was concentrated on following the various schemata on their, often eventful, way through the process of composition, discussion, rewriting, renewed debate, etc., and finally the voting and official promulgation.[365]

During the first session (October 11 to December 8, 1962) consideration was given to five schemata, but real progress was only made on the schema of the "sacred liturgy" and that of the "means of social communication." Tangible results were meager, but a very evident result of the first phase of the council was the growing world stature of the pope. "The very calling of the council was a masterpiece of political timing, which has paid inestimable dividends to the Papacy."[366]

---

[363] His book <u>Vatican II--Bridging the Abyss</u> (Washington, DC: RHPA, 1968) was a more systematic evaluation of the Second Vatican Council from an Adventist perspective; the author draws from his articles in the *Review and Herald* at the time of the Council.

[364] B.B. Beach, "Report from Rome," <u>RH</u> (Nov. 1, 1962), 1, 8-9; B.B. Beach, "The Second Vatican Council Opens With Medieval Splendor and Pageantry," <u>RH</u> (Nov. 8, 1962), 5, 8-9; B.B. Beach, "When the Machine is Being Put Together," <u>RH</u> (Nov. 15, 1962), 1, 8-9; Raymond F. Cottrell, "On the Eve of the Council," <u>RH</u> (Jan. 10, 1963), 13; B.B. Beach, "Days of Drama and Delay," <u>RH</u> (Jan. 16, 1964), 10-11.

[365] For the final version of all Council documents, see Austin Flannery, O.P., ed., <u>Vatican Council II: The Conciliar and Post Conciliar Documents</u> (Northport, N.Y.: Costello Publishing Company, 1987).

[366] B.B. Beach, "Looking Back on the First Session of Vatican Council II," <u>RH</u> (Feb. 14, 1963), 9.

Evaluating the first session, the associate editor of the *Review and Herald* did not share the "wait-and-see" attitude that seemed to characterize Beach's reports. He acknowledged that a historic change was taking place in the Catholic Church; that the advocates of reform and renewal were clearly in the ascendancy, but contended that the change would merely be one of "appearance."[367] One week later, in another editorial, he rather bluntly stated that

> ... Vatican Council II is the adroitly staged first act in a play whose plot is intended to reach a climax in the submission of all Christendom to the authority of Rome.... Vatican Council II will provide the final therapy needed for the complete healing of the grievous "wound" the Papacy has been nursing since reformation times....[368]

The opening address of the second session (September 29 to December 4, 1963) by Pope John Paul VI--he had been elected during the nine month recess between the first and second session to succeed Pope John XXIII, who had died in June 1963--received close scrutiny to detect whether the new pope would continue the strategy of his predecessor.[369] This inaugural address was a "program speech," both for the council and his pontificate. It was noted with satisfaction that the pope strongly emphasized the person of Christ and that "his talk was less steeped in 'Marian piety'" than Pope John's address had been one year before, but there was criticism for his merging of christology with ecclesiology in his identification of the Catholic Church with Christ.[370] Further criticism concerned the pope's use of the term "renewal" rather than the term "reform" in describing his aims for the council, and his refusal to apply the word "churches" to the communions of the "separated

---

[367] Raymond F. Cottrell, "Peter's Bark Changes Course," RH (Jan. 31, 1963), 13.

[368] Raymond F. Cottrell, "The Import of Vatican Council II for Adventists," RH (Feb. 7, 1963), 13.

[369] B.B. Beach, "The Roman Church - Whither Bound?" RH (Dec. 19, 1963), 2-3, 8-9.

[370] Ibid., 2.

brethren."[371]

The second session voted on the "Constitution of Liturgical Reform," which, together with a papal *motu proprio*, brought a great number of changes in the Mass. But these changes were mainly concerned with outward ritual, Beach commented, "and it is very obvious that essentially 'there is nothing new' and Catholic worship remains fundamentally what it has been since the Reformation era."[372]

Attached to this schema was a short declaration on the "revision of the calendar." It dealt with two matters: (1) a possible fixation of the Easter date, and (2) a perpetual calendar. With regard to this second point the council went on record that it did not oppose "efforts designed to introduce a perpetual calendar into civil society," but that it would oppose any system that would endanger the seven-day week, "unless in the judgment of the Apostolic See there are extremely weighty reasons to the contrary."[373] Although this declaration was a minor item on the council agenda, Adventists paid close attention and noted that there was no immediate danger of Catholic support for a new calendar that would upset the weekly cycle with "blank" days, but that, on the other hand, Catholic opposition to such a scheme was not absolute.[374] One area of great interest to all Protestants, and thus naturally also to Adventists, was that of the church and related subjects. Debates on these topics occupied much time of the council fathers during the second and the third session (September 14 to November 21, 1964). Dogmatic changes were not expected and a new role for the bishops would leave the primacy of the pope intact.[375]

---

[371] Ibid., 3, 8.

[372] B.B. Beach, "Vatican Council II--Retrospect and Prospect," RH (Feb. 6, 1964), 11.

[373] Austin Flannery, Vatican Council II, 37.

[374] B.B. Beach, "Calendar Reform and the Catholic Church," RH (Jan. 2, 1964), 9-11.

[375] B.B. Beach, "The Relation of Vatican II to Collegiality," RH (Dec, 26, 1963), 5-7; B.B. Beach, "Collegiality," RH (Dec. 3, 1964), 2-5; B.B. Beach, "The Bishops and Their Work," RH (Dec. 10, 1964), 7-9.

Collegiality is probably a step forward, but in the last analysis it does not make a great deal of difference to Protestants, for collegiality is in no way a rejection of the papal infallibility doctrine; it is only an affirmation that such doctrine includes the solidarity of pope and bishops.[376]

Progress was reported with respect to the Catholic view of the laity. For the first time, Beach noted, on a conciliar level, the Catholic understanding of the reality of the priesthood of the laity was spelled out.[377] But after much debate and extensive rewording of the part of the schema on the church which deals with the laity, it was to be acknowledged that "the role of the Catholic layman seems hardly destined to become that of his Protestant counterpart" and that it seemed "very doubtful that any real policy-making authority would be granted them."[378]

The last chapter of the Constitution on the Church dealt with Mary. Beach noted with satisfaction that Vatican II was not expected to add new Mariological doctrines, although he, of course, registered his protest against the title of 'Mediatrix' attributed to Mary.[379] He believed that the practical result of the chapter on Mary would be to slow down the independent development of Mariological doctrine that had been gaining momentum during the last century and "would put the brakes on the onward march of Marian dogma toward 'Coredemptrix'."[380]

But even more important than the authority of the bishops, the role of the laity and the status of Mary, was the new Catholic emphasis on ecumenism. Reporting on the Decree on Ecumenism, Beach pointed out in several

---

[376] B.B. Beach, "Collegiality," RH (Dec. 26, 1963), 7.

[377] B.B. Beach, "The Council Fathers Debate the Role of the Laity," RH (Jan. 14, 1965), 4.

[378] Ibid., 5.

[379] B.B. Beach, "Rome Takes a Look at Eschatology and Mariology," RH (Nov. 26, 1964), 6.

[380] Ibid.

articles, that for the Catholic Church unity meant a return of non-Catholics to Rome. In final analysis the pope wanted to see other Christians return to Rome and submit to his authority.[381] Some of the main obstacles for true Protestants--besides the papacy and its Petrine claims--remained the Catholic view of tradition and its sacrifice of the Mass.[382] But Beach also pointed out that the final version of the document on ecumenism for the first time applied the word *churches* to Protestant communions, which could be used by God as means of salvation, albeit in a limited way.[383]

A revised text of the Constitution on Divine Revelation was also among the schemata debated during the third session. On a positive note, Beach remarked that Catholic theology was shifting toward "a more open, more ecumenical, more patristic, and even more 'Biblical' theology".[384] But although he saw a new emphasis on the Bible, he also noted, that the Catholic Church stayed with a "church-interpreted Scripture, understood through tradition".[385] The Bible was raised to a higher level, but it was still far from supreme in determining dogma.[386]

Adventist comments on the fourth and final session (September 14 to December 8, 1965) included remarks on the last schema (no. 13), dealing with "the church and the modern world." This schema provided Rome with "a program of dialogue and action in various sectors of social, scientific, cultural, and political endeavor."[387]

---

[381] B.B. Beach. "What Kind of Unity?" RH (Dec. 6, 1962), 13-14, 21.

[382] B.B. Beach, "Obstacles to Unity," RH (Nov. 29, 1962), 8.

[383] B.B. Beach, "Ecumenism," RH (Dec. 31, 1964), 6.

[384] B.B. Beach, "Divine Revelation," RH (Dec. 24, 1964), 5.

[385] Ibid., 6.

[386] B.B. Beach, "Vatican II: Retrospect and Prospect," RH (March 31, 1966), 2.

[387] Ibid., 3.

Cottrell suggested that this schema went "far toward casting the church in the role of the moral leader of mankind," and that it represented a major step toward the further restoration of the former prestige and power of the papacy.[388]

But the one subject on which most Adventist attention was focused was no doubt that of religious liberty. As with many other Protestants, Adventist fears and hopes alternated as the various versions of a document on this topic were hotly debated by the council fathers, and caused serious controversy between conservatives and progressives. At first *Liberty* correspondent W.L. Emmerson did not expect the council to approve a text incorporating a definition of religious freedom that would be acceptable to Protestants. He feared that basic rights, such as the freedom of religious education and evangelistic witness, and the right of an individual to change his religious affiliation would be omitted, and that the privileged position of Roman Catholicism (in predominantly Catholic countries, such as Spain) would be maintained.[389] Beach believed the council would adopt a new, though defective, view of religious freedom, but wondered how Catholic leaders could maintain that there was no basic contradiction between what the church was presently proposing and its intolerant attitude of the past. He was quite sure, that whatever pronouncement was finally made, it would be interpreted in a way that would allow for concordats and for a privileged position of the Catholic Church in countries with a predominantly Catholic tradition.[390] When, at last, the final version of the Declaration on Religious Liberty was voted, Emmerson was not totally negative in his appraisal, but concluded that it had some fatal flaws. Under certain conditions, the church could, by virtue of its divine authorization, instruct the state on what would be

---

[388] Raymond F. Cottrell, "The Church Faces Up to the Modern World," RH (Nov. 11, 1965), 8.

[389] W.L. Emmerson, "Rome and Religious Liberty," Lib, vol. 59, no. 2 (March/Apr., 1964), 20-24; W.L. Emmerson, "What Will Vatican II Say About Freedom?" Lib, vol. 59, no. 5 (Sept./Oct., 1964), 20-23.

[390] B.B. Beach, "Religious Liberty," RH (Dec. 17, 1964), 6-9; B.B. Beach, "Catholicism and Liberty," Lib, vol. 60, no. 5 (Sept./Oct. 1965), 23-25; 32-34.

advisable for the common good.[391] "The document," he said, "is typical of the age-old casuistry of Rome and between the lines we can still read its historic dictum *semper eadem*."[392] Cottrell also saw some loopholes, but he believed, nonetheless, that it represented "so vast a forward step in the official attitude of the church that we should doubtless accept it with joy and expect the church to live up to it."[393] Writing just after the historic vote on the Declaration, he commented, "Today the church visibly laid aside the sword of intolerance with which it has confronted the world for the past fifteen centuries."[394] But a week later he added that this change unfortunately was one of expediency rather than of principle.[395]

Did Vaticanum II bring real change? It did, Cottrell asserted, but only in externals.[396] There is a new atmosphere, but the changes are "procedural and not substantive.... The ultimate objective of the church has not altered one iota, but only the methods by which it proposes to reach that objective."[397] Beach was more positive in his appraisal of the accomplishments of the council. Although, when "weighed in the gospel's doctrinal balance, it is found sadly wanting," he believed the council "performed rather better than might have been feared."[398] Beach saw a number of important

---

[391] W.L. Emmerson, "Rome Speaks on Religious Liberty," Lib, vol. 60, no. 6 (Nov./Dec., 1965), 7-10.

[392] Ibid., 10.

[393] Raymond F. Cottrell, "The Declaration on Religious Liberty," RH (Oct. 21, 1965), 5.

[394] Ibid., 2.

[395] Raymond F. Cottrell, "Saint Peter's Bark Tacks About," RH (Oct. 28, 1965), 5.

[396] Raymond F. Cottrell, "Vatican II and the Future," RH (Nov. 18, 1965), 9-11.

[397] Ibid., 11.

[398] B.B. Beach, "Success of Failure?" RH (Apr. 14, 1966), 9.

changes in Catholicism as a result of the council in:
(1) its self-definition; (2) its attitude toward the
outside world; (3) its attitude toward non-Catholics;
its view of religious liberty; (4)many liturgical
practices; (5) methods and tactics; and (6) its attitude
toward the Bible.[399] He felt that "there is no denying
that considerable self-criticism and genuine effort to
reform have taken place," and that observers in Rome
could not help but noticing "a sincere concern for
renewal and considerable desire for reform."[400] But any
reform or renewal was always "within the strict limits
of doctrinal continuity and the Catholic past."[401] A
certain reinterpretation of Catholic dogma might be
taking place, making it possible to look at certain
former dogmatic pronouncements in a relative way, but
"there is no factual evidence indicating that Rome is
giving up--officially at least--a single dogmatic
iota."[402]

> The music has changed. The road on which mankind is
> invited to proceed is smoother and more pleasing.
> But the destination of Catholic roads has not
> changed. They all lead to the same well-known
> destination--Rome.[403]

X Conclusion

During the 1915-1965 period Seventh-day Adventists
maintained their strong anti-Catholic attitude. The
theological presuppositions on which their negative
evaluation of Catholicism was based--developed in the
nineteenth century--remained largely unchanged. The
historicist approach to apocalyptic prophecy was
maintained and the interpretations of those Bible
chapters that had traditionally been applied to Roman

---

[399] B.B. Beach, "Change in the Church of Rome," RH
(Apr. 21, 1966), 4.

[400] Ibid., 5.

[401] Ibid.

[402] Ibid.

[403] Ibid.

Catholicism since the beginnings of Adventism underwent but little change. Some aspects of Uriah Smith's prophetic scheme were criticized, but his interpretations remained the basis for practically all Adventist exegesis of Daniel and the Revelation. Ellen G. White's endorsement of the late 19th century application of specific apocalyptic Bible passages to contemporary or imminent events was no doubt a primary factor in ensuring the absence of innovative views.

Although Catholic doctrine received a little more attention than in the past, the threat of a restoration of medieval papal power, which would show the same intolerance it had manifested in centuries past, remained Adventism's primary fear. Most of the criticism of the Roman Catholic Church focused on real or supposed evidence that "Rome" was regaining its former power and was, in particular, strengthening its position in the United States.

Even though Adventists as a rule denounced violent anti-Catholic organizations and extreme anti-Catholic publications, increased anti-Catholic sentiment in Adventist publications parallelled periods in which such organizations were most active and popular anti-Catholicism was at its peak (notably toward the end of the 1920s and around 1939). When anti-Catholicism in general subsided, Adventist expressions of their anti-Catholic views also became more restrained (as was, for instance, evident at the time of Kennedy's election).

During the period under review many Protestant denominations, like the Adventist Church, continued to manifest anti-Catholic sentiments. This, for instance, was quite evident in the 1928 presidential elections,[404]

---

[404] Both Methodists and Baptists, like Adventists, did not stress the fact that Smith was a Catholic, but rather emphasized the "wet" or "dry" issue. For some Methodist comments, see "Wet or Dry," Zions Herald (Aug. 8, 1928), 1020-1021, 1028; "Governor Smith Accepts," Zions Herald (Aug. 29, 1928), 1104-1105; "Recruit the Voters!" Zions Herald (Oct. 17, 1928), 1327-1328. For a similar position held by the Baptists, see "What Governor Smith Wants to Change," The Baptist (Sept. 18, 1928). See also James J. Thompson, jr, "Southern Baptists and Anti-Catholicism in the 1920's," Mississippi Quarterly, vol. 32, no. 4 (Fall 1979), 611-625.

but also in the ensuing decades.[405] Gradually, however, most Protestant denominations became less judgmental and more open toward Catholics, while Adventists, though more careful in their public pronouncements, remained unchanged in their conviction concerning the fundamental anti-christian character of Catholicism as an ecclesiastical system.

Increasingly the Adventist condemnation of Catholicism, however, emphasized the hierarchical system of past and present, rather than the Catholic Church as a communion of believers or the believers as individuals. This movement from anti-Catholicism toward anti-papism (in a broad sense, including the complete hierarchy), already present in the previous period, became marked. Individual Catholics were more and more regarded as suitable candidates for Adventist recruitment activities and special techniques were designed to make such recruiting attempts successful.

Adventists did not relinquish their view of the "Protestant component" of "Babylon," but their criticism of contemporary Protestantism softened remarkably as time went by. When evaluating the "Roman component" of "Babylon," however, the terminology might become less harsh, but earlier arguments were maintained and a total condemnation of the Roman Catholic Church as an apostate system of belief and religio-political power with sinister aims remained the rule.

One development in the eschatological understanding of the menace of Catholicism should be mentioned. The complex of endtime events, in which the Roman Catholic Church and the United States would co-operate in a universal Sunday legislation and persecution of a remnant of dissenters, continued to be emphasized. However, the focus shifted from the present to the near future. Present events indicated that final events were imminent, but they had not yet arrived. This state of

---

[405] Some Protestant denominations in the United States remained as least as anti-Catholic as the Adventists. For a survey of anti-Catholic sentiments among Southern Baptists (which in many ways closely resembles this study), see Ira V. Birdwhistell, "Southern Baptist Perceptions of and Responses to Roman Catholics, 1917-1972," Ph.D. diss., The Southern Baptist Theological Seminary, 1975). The Taylor ambassadorship to the Vatican and various church-state related issues, which figured prominently in Adventist criticisms of Roman Catholicism, were at least as prominent in the Southern Baptist response to Roman Catholicism.

affairs allowed for a more positive view of the present role of some of the endtime players (Protestantism and the United States), and, to a much more limited extent, for a less derogatory assessment of trends in modern Catholicism. But basically "Rome" had not changed and would not change. Any signs in that direction were merely cosmetic and any seemingly positive steps were invariably seen as rooted in ulterior motives.

CONCLUSIONS

I Origin of Anti-Catholicism
in Seventh-day Adventism

Anti-Catholicism was part of Adventism from its inception. A number of factors played an important role:

1. Strong anti-Catholic sentiments, imported to North America in the colonial period, were widespread among the Protestant denominations from which the Millerites drew their support. Adventists inherited--through the Millerites--the Puritan anti-Catholic tradition and its apocalyptic interpretations which identified the pope as the antichrist.

2. The Millerites--and those who formed the nucleus of Sabbatarian Adventism after the 1844 disillusion--were subject to and influenced by the general anti-Catholic climate which prevailed in the United States in the 1830s through the 1850s.

3. The Millerite movement developed in a historical, geographical and religious context in which millenarian views, with detailed endtime scenarios, could flourish. Early Adventism further shaped the teachings it inherited from Millerism largely within this same setting.

4. William Miller's hermeneutical method in dealing with apocalyptic Bible prophecy, and many of his interpretations of specific prophetic Bible passages, were rather uncritically adopted by early Adventist thought leaders.

5. Millerite convictions about the historical role of Roman Catholicism (or, more specifically, of the papacy), and 1798 as the date of its prophesied demise, were from the start adopted by Adventist exegetes.

6. The interpretation of "Babylon" as a symbol for both Roman Catholicism and "apostate Protestantism," which became prominent in the last phase of the Millerite movement, was to play a vital role in the Adventist self-understanding and in Adventist views on endtime developments.

II Unique Adventist Features

1. The adoption of the seventh-day Sabbath set Adventists apart as no other feature of their theology would. The observance of Sabbath was understood as God's "seal" on the "remnant", while the keeping of Sunday was declared to be the "mark" of the antichristian "beast" of Revelation 13. The Sabbath-Sunday controversy was thus accorded the most prominent role in the imminent, dramatic events that were to precede the second coming of Christ.

2. Roman Catholicism was identified as the major agent in the change from Sabbath to Sunday. This change, Adventists argued, was a deliberate attempt to put church tradition above the precepts of Scripture.

3. The development of the doctrine of the heavenly sanctuary added a new element to the anti-Catholic position of Adventists. The Catholic priesthood and its ceremonies were seen as a willful substitute for the high-priestly ministry of Christ in the heavenly sanctuary.

4. With the further development of the interpretation of "Babylon" as consisting of a Protestant and a Catholic component, and with the attribution of a major role to the United States in the endtime drama, the scene was set for a final conflict--during which loyalty to God's commandments would be tested. In this crisis the American state, having forsaken its heritage of separation between church and state, would facilitate a coalition led by Protestant and Catholic forces against a faithful "remnant".

III Factors Explaining Sustained Anti-Catholicism among Adventists

1. Recurring waves of anti-Catholic agitation continued to influence Adventism, as was the case with most other Protestant denominations in the United States.

2. The hermeneutics and prophetic interpretations, inherited by early Adventism from Millerism, were further refined, but remained basically unchanged. This is especially true with regard to those prophecies that were applied to Roman Catholicism.

3. For decades the role of "Rome" in the history of Sabbath and Sunday remained one of the most important foci of Adventist historical research.

4. A number of events in the United States in the 1880s and 1890s in the domain of religion and politics,

most notably concerning Sunday legislation, were interpreted by Adventists as convincing evidence of the correctness of their eschatological views, in which Roman Catholicism played a vital role.

5. The worldwide resurgence of Roman Catholicism in the late 19th and 20th century and the phenomenal development of the Roman Catholic Church in the United States were interpreted as further irrefutable evidence of the accuracy of Adventist prophetic views.

5. The major writings of Ellen G. White about Roman Catholicism date from the 1880s. They originated in this climate of Adventist confidence about the reality of the Catholic threat and the imminence of events they had been predicting for decades. Once Ellen G. White had codified these views, it became virtually impossible to re-evaluate them critically, without questioning her prophetic authority.

IV Characteristics of Adventist Anti-Catholic Views

Throughout the period under review in this study, Seventh-day Adventist views about Roman Catholicism manifested a number of characteristics:

1. Adventist criticism was increasingly anti-papal rather than anti-Catholic, even though this distinction was not usually explicitly made by Adventist authors.

2. Emphasis was usually on the history of the Roman Catholic Church, and, more specifically, on the historical role of the papacy and the hierarchy. In their study of history, Adventists mostly relied on 19th century church histories by Protestant authors, who showed a strong anti-Catholic bias. For the more recent past Adventist interest centered on perceived or real displays of Catholic power and Catholic politics.

3. Adventist sources show a pre-occupation with the Sabbath-Sunday topic, but also a limited, though gradually increasing, attention to other doctrinal aspects, in particular the immortality of the soul and papal infallibility.

4. The main purpose in studying Catholicism was to find further support for positions early Adventism had adopted. Adventists usually did not look for positive things in the Catholic past, but were focused on elements that would further strengthen their viewpoints. Some citations from Catholics sources became standard ammunition. The basic premise remained that Roman Catholicism would never change. Any signs to the

contrary were to be mistrusted. If there appeared to be some positive development, there must be an ulterior motive.

5. The present and future role of the Roman Catholic Church in the United States remained a constant concern.

6. Sensationalism and convent horror stories did not figure prominently in Adventist literature, but some instances occurred and conspiracy theories did at times find acceptance.

7. While much anti-Catholicism in the United States was related to concern over the large numbers of (mostly Catholic) immigrants, this aspect does not seem to have worried Adventists to any great extent. In fact, the presence of large numbers of immigrants was often seen as providential; it facilitated the spreading of the Adventist message to other "nations and tongues."

8. Adventist interest in current developments in Catholicism focused to a large extent on issues directly related to Adventist eschatological expectations about the growing influence of Catholicism worldwide and particularly in the United States; its alleged disregard for the principle of separation between church and state (notably in the area of education); its perceived role in Sunday legislation; and the increased co-operation between Catholics and Protestants.

9. Adventist anti-Catholicism did not find expression in, nor encouraged support for political anti-Catholic movements.

10. Although Adventist anti-Catholicism sometimes tended to become more pronounced when waves of anti-Catholic sentiment engulfed the United States, its consistency and permanency are more striking than any occasional escalation.

V Developments in Adventist Anti-Catholicism

At most only limited change could be expected in Adventist attitudes toward Catholicism, considering the general unwillingness to re-evaluate or re-consider the doctrinal consensus of the "pioneers"--including those elements on which the condemnation of Catholicism was based--which had received Ellen G. White's approval. Some changes are, however, clearly noticeable.

1. As time went by the language used to describe the Catholic Church and its institutions and teachings became less harsh and--in general--the arguments became more sophisticated.

2. In its criticism of Catholicism the emphasis

remained on its historical role, its power structure, and its present threat, but the various Catholic doctrines--in particular the theology of the Mass--gradually began to receive more attention.

3. The earlier tension between the conviction that the Roman power had received a fatal blow at the time of the French Revolution and the expectation that only a limited and shortlived resurgence of the papacy could be expected, gave place to strong emphasis on the "healing of the deadly wound"--interpreted as a period of unparallelled strength of Roman Catholicism, clear indications of which were abounding.

4. After the 1890s the eschatological finale, with persecutions of a Sabbath-keeping minority by a coalition of Catholics and Protestants in an America that would do the bidding of these forces, was no longer felt to be as imminent as had been the case earlier. The development of the antichristian potential of Protestantism and the United States of America gradually shifted toward the future.

5. At the same time a clearer distinction was made between Catholicism as an institution and Catholic individuals. Whereas the institution was antichristian, many of its adherents were now believed to be true Christians who lived in accordance with "the light they possessed," and were targeted as candidates for Adventist recruitment.

VI Protestants vs. Catholics

In recent decades Adventism has been more conciliatory toward other Protestants than before. The changes in the Adventist attitude toward other Protestants have been much more pronounced than any such changes in the attitude toward Roman Catholics. A few factors help to explain this difference:

1. In spite of Adventism's traditional condemnation of Protestantism as "apostate," its theology was always much closer to conservative Protestantism than to Catholicism. As Adventism matured, it corrected its earlier Arian and anti-trinitarian positions and became more outspoken on the Protestant principle of justification by faith alone.

2. In spite of their heavy criticism of other Protestants, Adventists saw their roots in the Reformation and understood themselves as Protestants *par excellence*.

3. Although objecting to many features of fundamentalism, Adventism shared many fundamentalist

299

convictions.

4. When Adventists participated (usually as observers) in (ecumenical) Protestant events, such encounters with other Protestant Christians helped to dispel stereotypical attitudes.

5. Adventism opted for an educated ministry. It is impossible to determine how this stimulated the ministry, and by extension the church, toward a less sectarian, more Protestant, self-understanding. As Adventism grew, it clearly developed a need for acceptance by conservative Protestantism, and a desire to be regarded as a genuine part of Protestantism rather than a sect or a cult. Dialogues with other Protestants often led to a reduced emphasis on doctrinal differences and stress on points of doctrinal agreement.

6. While Adventists always distinguished two components in "Babylon"--Protestantism and Roman Catholicism--a subtle shift in emphasis occurred. In early Adventism the Protestant component was heavily stressed. The emphasis gradually shifted toward the Catholic Church. "Babylon's fall", moreover, was increasingly seen as progressive, and thus in part still future. This perspective enabled Adventists to maintain their prophetic views and eschatology, while maintaining more cordial relations with other Protestants in the present.

7. There was no similar need for Adventists to adjust their attitudes toward Roman Catholics. In the United States Adventism developed mainly in areas with low concentrations of Catholics. For their information about Roman Catholicism, Adventists largely continued to rely on 19th century sources and Protestant materials with a familiar anti-Catholic bias, rather than on first-hand encounters. The sending of Adventist observers to the Second Vatican Council was the first significant deviation from that pattern.

8. At no time was there a significant dialogue between the Seventh-day Adventist Church and the Roman Catholic Church. Adventism seems to have been virtually ignored by the Catholic Church. The long Adventist tradition of unbending anti-Catholicism prevented any unprejudiced re-evaluation of its basic premises.

POSTCRIPT

This study has attempted to chronicle Seventh-day Adventist attitudes toward Roman Catholicism until the year 1965. Almost thirty years have transpired since then. At some future time I intend to do further research on how Adventist views on Catholicism have developed in the last three decades, with some critical evaluations and suggestions for the future.

As an active member of the Seventh-day Adventist church during all of this period and as a minister, educator and administrator in this church since the late 1960s (in various parts of the world) I believe I have a fair idea about trends in recent Adventism. Since 1965, official Adventist prophetic interpretation has not undergone any dramatic change. As a result the Adventist understanding of the historical role of Roman Catholicism and of the endtime drama, with Catholicism as one of the key-players, has remained basically unaltered. The traditional arguments for the anti-christian nature of Roman Catholicism continue to be heard, even though they are often more carefully worded.

The rapidly-growing church is still remarkedly united, both organizationally and theologically, but it manifests an increasing pluralism. Unfortunately, this seems to lead to a significant degree of polarization. Where one current seeks to find ways of making Adventism more relevant to this generation, others insist that "the old landmarks" of the Adventist faith must be zealously guarded and are unwilling to re-think or modify traditional views. These more conservative Adventists insist that Adventism must continue to subscribe to its traditional interpretations of prophecy, with the corresponding condemnation of Roman Catholicism and other Christian churches. The more "progressively" inclined are increasingly open to emphasizing the common bond with other Christians and tend to feel uncomfortable with traditional attitudes. Considerable research is needed, however, to get a precise picture of the situation.

It seems to me that Adventists must enter into some sort of dialogue with Roman Catholics, both on the individual and corporate level, if they want to arrive at a fair appraisal of present-day Roman Catholicism. Many--possibly even most--Adventists still look at late 20th century Catholicism through 19th century eyes. Many are unable, or unwilling, to see the many different faces of Catholicism in different parts of the world, or to recognize the tremendous changes and developments that have taken place within Catholicism. I hope this study (and further work I intend to do in this area) will help some of my fellow-Adventists to realize how the traditional Adventist position developed in a particular historical context, and to understand the need for a fresh approach that will re-evaluate the traditional Adventist views in the context of our time.

BIBLIOGRAPHY

I Primary Sources

1. Books

Anderson, Roy A., <u>Unfolding the Revelation</u>. Mountain View, Cal.: PPPA, 1953.

Andrews, J.N., <u>The Complete Testimony of the Fathers of the First Three Centuries Concerning the Sabbath and First Day</u>. Battle Creek, MI: Steam Press of the SDA Publ. Ass., 1876.

_____ and Conradi, L.R., <u>Die Geschichte des Sabbats und des Ersten Wochentages</u>. Basel: Internationale Tratat-Gesellschaft, 1891.

_____. <u>History of the Sabbath and the First Day of the Week, Showing the Bible Record of the Sabbath, also the Manner in which it has been Supplanted by the Heathen Festival of the Sun</u>. Battle Creek, MI: Steam Press of the SDA Publ. Ass., 1862.

_____. <u>History of the Sabbath and First Day of the Week</u>. Battle Creek, MI: Steam Press of the SDA Publ. Ass., 1873.

_____. <u>History of the Sabbath and First Day of the Week</u>. Battle Creek, MI: RHPA, 1887.

_____ and Conradi, L.R., <u>History of the Sabbath and First day of the Week</u>. Washington, DC: RHPA, 1912.

_____. <u>The Three Angels of Rev. 14:6-12: particularly, The Third Angel's Message, and the Two-Horned Beast</u>. Rochester, N.Y.: Advent Review Office, 1855.

_____. <u>The Three Messages of Revelation XIV, 6-12</u>. Battle Creek, MI: Steam Press of the SDA Publ. Ass., 1864.

Armstrong, Amzi, A Syllabus of Lectures on the Visions
of the Revelation. Morris-town, N.J.: P.A. Johnson,
1815.

Baker, Alonzo L., The Pope King Again: Is the 'Deadly
Wound' Healing? Mountain View, Cal.: PPPA, 1929.

Beach, B.B., Vatican II--Bridging the Aby. Washington,
DC: RHPA, 1968.

Beecher, Lyman, A Plea for the West. Cincinnati, 1835.

Bell, Godloe H., Progressive Bible Lessons for Youth; to
be Used in Sabbath Schools, Bible Classes, and
Families. Battle Creek: Steam Press of the SDA
Publ. Ass., 1877.

The Bible Made Plain. Washington, DC: RHPA, 1922.

Bible Readings for the Home Circle. Battle Creek, MI:
Review and Herald Publishing Co., 1891.

Bible Readings for the Home Circle. Washington, DC:
RHPA, 1914.

Blakely, William A., American State Papers, Bearing on
Sunday Legislation. Washington, DC: The Religious
Liberty Association, 1911.

Bliss, Sylvester, Memoirs of William Miller, Generally
Known as a Lecturer on the Prophecies, and the
Second Coming of Christ. Boston: Joshua V. Himes,
1853.

Bush, George, Reasons for Rejecting Mr. Miller's Views
on the Advent; with Mr. Miller's Reply. Boston:
Joshua V. Himes, 1844.

Butler, George I., The Change of the Sabbath: Was It by
Divine or Human Authority? Battle Creek, MI: Review
and Herald Publishing Co., 1889.

Butler, James, The Most Rev. Dr. James Butler's
Catechism, Revised, Enlarged, Approved, and
Recommended by the Four Roman Catholic Archbishops
of Ireland as a General Catechism for the Kingdom.
To Which is Added the Scriptural Catechesis of Rt.
Rev. Dr. Milner. 1827.

Campbell, G.A., <u>Mary Kennedy's Victory</u>. Mountain View, PPPA, 1953.

Canright, Dudley M., <u>History of the Doctrine of the Immortality of the Soul</u>. Battle Creek, MI: Steam Press of the SDA Publ. Ass., 1871.

Challoner, Rt. Rev. Dr. Richard, <u>The Catholic Christian Instructed in the Sacraments, Sacrifice, Ceremonies, and Observances of the Church. By Way of Question and Answer</u>. 1786.

Christian, L.H., <u>Facing the Crisis in the Light of Bible Prophecy</u>. Washington, DC: RHPA, 1937.

Conradi, Louis R., <u>Die Offenbarung Jesu Christi</u>. Hamburg: Internationale Traktatgesellschaft, 1903.

_____. <u>Der Seher von Patmos</u>. Hamburg: Internationale Traktatgesellschaft, 1906.

_____. <u>Die Weissagung Daniels</u>. Hamburg: Internationale Traktatgesellschaft, 1901.

Cornell, M.E., <u>Facts for the Times - Extracts from the Writings of Eminent Authors, Ancient and Modern</u>. Battle Creek: publ. by the author, 1858.

A Cosmopolite (pseud.), <u>Miller Overthrown, or the False Prophet Confounded</u>. Boston: A. Thompkins, 1840.

Cottrell, Raymond F., <u>Beyond Tomorrow</u>. Nashville, Tenn.: SPA, 1963.

Cramp, John Mockett, <u>The Reformation in Europe</u>. New York: American Tract Society, ca. 1840.

Croly, George, <u>The Apocalypse of St. John</u>. Philadelphia: E. Littell, 1827.

Cunninghame, William, <u>The Political Destiny of the Earth, as Revealed in the Bible</u>. Philadelphia: Orrin Rogers, 1840.

Czeckowski, M.B., <u>Thrilling and Instructive Developments: an Experience of Fifteen Years as Roman Clergyman and Priest</u>. Boston: Publ. by the author, 1862.

Daniells, Arthur G., _Christ Our Righteousness_. Washington, DC: Ministerial Association of SDA, 1926.

_____. _The World in Perplexity_. Washington, DC: RHPA, 1918.

_____. _The World War: Its Relationship to the Eastern Question and Armageddon_. Mountain View, Cal.: PPPA, 1917.

Dowling, John, _An Exposition of the Prophecies Supposed by William Miller to Predict the Second Coming of Christ in 1843, With a Supplementary Chapter Upon the True Scriptural Doctrine of the Millennium Prior to the Judgment_. New York: J.R. Bigelow, 1842.

_____. _The History of Romanism: From the Earliest Corruptions of Christianity to the Present Time_. New York: Edward Walker, 1848.

Edwardson, Christian, _Facts of Faith_. Nashville, Tenn.: SPA, 1943.

Fitch, Charles, _Come Out of Her, My People, A Sermon_. Rochester, N.Y.: Joshua V. Himes, 1843.

Froom, LeRoy E., _Movement of Destiny_. Washington, DC: RHPA, 1971.

Galusha, Elon, _Address of Elder Elon Galusha, with Reasons for Believing Christ's Second Coming at Hand_. Rochester, N.Y., 1844.

Geiermann, Peter, _The Convert's Catechism of Catholic Doctrine_. St. Louis, MO: B. Herder, 1911.

Gibbon, Edward, _The History of the Decline and Fall of the Roman Empire_. 5 vols. London: W. Strahan and T. Cadell, 1776-1788; recent repr.: Hutchins, Robert M., _Great Books of the Western World_, vols. 40, 41. Chicago: Encyclopedia Brittanica, 1952.

Gibbons, James, _Faith of our Fathers_. Baltimore: John Murphy & Company, 1885, 1896.

Hale, Apollos, <u>Second Advent Manual in which the Objections to Calculating Prophetic Times are Considered; the Difficulties Connected with the Calculation Explained; and the Facts and Arguments on which Mr. Miller's Calculations Rest, are Briefly Stated and Sustained</u>. Boston: Joshua V. Himes, 1843

Hall, D.P., <u>Man not Immortal, the Only Shield against the Seductions of Modern Spiritualists</u>. Rochester, N.Y.: Advent Review Office, 1855.

Haskell, Stephen N., <u>The Story of Daniel the Prophet</u>. Nashville, Tenn: SPA, 1903.

_____. <u>The Story of the Seer of Patmos</u>. Nashville, Tenn.: SPA, 1905 (1977 facs. reprod.).

Hastings, H.L., <u>The Signs of the Times; or, a Glance at Christendom as it is</u>. Boston: H.L. Hastings, 1862.

Haven, Kettridge, <u>The World Reprieved: Being a Critical Examination of William Miller's Theory</u>. Woodstock, Vt.: Haskell and Palmer, 1839.

Haynes, Carlyle B., <u>The Christian Sabbath</u>. Nashville, Tenn.: SPA, n.d.

_____. <u>Life, Death, and Immortality</u>. Nashville, Ten.: SPA, 1952.

_____. <u>From Sabbath to Sunday</u>. Washington, DC: RHPA, 1928.

Heck, Alcyon Ruth, <u>A Brand from the Burning</u>. Mountain View, Cal.: PPPA, 1960.

Himes, Joshua V., ed., <u>Statement of Facts Demonstrating the Rapid and Universal Spread and Triumph of Roman Catholicism</u>. Boston: Joshua V. Himes, 1847.

_____. <u>Views of the Prophecies and Chronology Selected from the Manuscripts of William Miller</u>. Boston: M.A. Dow, 1841.

Hislop, Alexander, <u>The Two Babylons, or the Papal Worship Proved to Be the Worship of Nimrod and his Wife</u>. First publ. in 1858; recent photostatic edition: Neptune, N.J.: Loizeau Brothers, Inc., 1959.

Huit, Ephraim, <u>The Whole Prophecie of Daniel Explained.</u> <u>By a Paraphrase, Analysis and Briefe Comment:</u> <u>Wherein the Severall Visions Shewed to a Prophet</u> <u>Are Clearly Interpreted, and the Application</u> <u>Thereof Vindicated Against Dissenting Opinions</u>. London: Henry Overton, 1644.

Hull, Moses, <u>The Bible from Heaven: or a Dissertation on</u> <u>the Evidences of Christianity</u>. Battle Creek: Steam Press of the SDA Publ. Ass., 1863.

_____. <u>The Transgressor's Fate, or A Short Argument</u> <u>on the First and Second Deaths</u>. Battle Creek: Steam Press of the Review and Herald Office, 1861.

Jones, A.T., <u>The Two Republics: Rome and the United</u> <u>States of America</u>. Battle Creek, MI: Review and Herald Publishing Co., 1891.

Jones, Henry, <u>Principles of Interpreting the Prophecies;</u> <u>briefly illustrated and applied with Notes</u>. Andover: Gould and Newman, 1837.

Keenan, Stephen, <u>A Doctrinal Catechism; wherein divers</u> <u>points of Catholic Faith and Practice Assailed by</u> <u>Modern Heretics are Sustained by an Appeal to the</u> <u>Holy Scriptures, the Testimonies of the Ancient</u> <u>Fathers, and the Dictates of Reason on the Basis of</u> <u>Scheffmacher's Catechism</u>. 3rd American edition. New York: P.J. Kennedy and Sons, 1846.

<u>Key to the Prophetic Chart</u>. Battle Creek: Steam Press of the SDA Publ. Ass., 1864.

King, Edward, <u>Remarks on the Signs of the Times</u>. Philadelphia: Jas. Humphreys, 1800.

Lewis, Richard, <u>The Protestant Dilemma</u>. Mountain View, Cal.: PPPA, 1961.

Lickey, Arthur E., <u>God Speaks to Modern Man</u>. Washington, DC: RHPA, 1952.

Litch, Josiah, <u>An Address to the Public and especially</u> <u>the Clergy on the Near Approach of the Glorious,</u> <u>Everlasting Kingdom of God on Earth, as Indicated</u> <u>by the Word of God, the History of the World, and</u> <u>Signs of the Present Times</u>. Boston: Joshua V. Himes, 1842.

Littlejohn, W.H., <u>The Coming Conflict: Or, The United States Becoming a Persecuting Power</u>. Battle Creek, MI: Review and Herald Publishing House, 1883.

_____. <u>Rome in Prophecy</u>. Battle Creek: Review and Herald Publishing Co., 1898.

Magan, Percy T., <u>The Vatican and the War</u>. Nashville, Tenn.: SPA, 1915.

Maxwell, Arthur S., <u>Power and Prophecy: Who Shall Rule the World?</u> Mountain View, Cal.: PPPA, 1940.

<u>The Metropolitan Catholic Almanac and Laity's Directory for the year 1844</u>. Baltimore: Fielding Lucas, jr., ca. 1845.

Miller, William, <u>Apology and Defence</u>. Boston: Joshua V. Himes, 1845.

_____. <u>Dissertations on the True Inheritance of the Saints, and the Twelve Hundred and Sixty Days of Daniel and John, with an Address to the Conference of Believers in the Near Advent</u>. Boston: Joshua V. Himes, 1842.

_____. <u>Evidence from Scirpture [sic] and History of the Second Coming of Christ about the Year 1843: Exhibited in a Course of Lectures</u>. Troy, N.Y.: Kemple & Hooper, 1836.

_____. <u>Evidence from Scripture and History of the Second Coming of Christ about the Year 1843: Exhibited in a Course of Lectures</u>. Troy, N.Y.: Elias Gates, 1838.

_____. <u>Evidence from Scripture and History of the Second Coming of Christ about the Year 1843: Exhibited in a Course of Lectures</u>. Boston, B.B. Mussey, 1840.

_____. <u>Evidence from Scripture and History of the Second Coming of Christ about the Year 1843: Exhibited in a Course of Lectures</u>. Boston, J.V. Himes, 1842.

Miller, William, "Explanation of Prophetic Figures," in: Joshua V. Himes, ed., Views of the Prophecies and Prophetic Chronology, Selected from Manuscripts of William Miller, with a Memoir of his Life. Boston: Moses A. Dow, 1841.

_____. A Familiar Exposition of the Twenty-Fourth Chapter of Matthew and the Fifth and Sixth Chapters of Hosea. To which are Added an Address to the General Conference on the Advent and A Scene of the Last Days. Boston: Joshua V. Himes, 1842.

_____. Remarks on Revelation Thirteenth, Seventeenth and Eighteenth. Boston: Joshua V. Himes, 1844.

_____. Synopsis of Miller's Views. Boston: Joshua V. Himes, 1842.

Milner, John, The End of Religious Controversy, in a Friendly Correspondence between a Religious Society of Protestants and a Roman Catholic Divine. New York, P.J. Kennedy, Catholic Publishing House, 1802.

Monk, Maria, Awful Disclosures of the Hotel Dieu Nunnery of Montreal. New York: Howe & Bates, 1836; reprint New York: Arno Press, 1977.

Morse, Samuel F.B., Foreign Conspiracy Against the Liberties of the United States. New York, 1841.

Neufeld, Don. F. and Julia Neuffer, SDA Bible Student's Source Book. Washington, DC: RHPA, 1962.

Nichol, F.D., The Answer to Modern Religious Thinking. Washington, DC: RHPA, 1936.

_____. "The Increasing Timeliness of the Threefold Message." Chap. in: Our Firm Foundation, vol. 1, 543-622. Washington, DC: RHPA, 1953.

_____, ed., The Seventh-day Adventist Bible Commentary, 7 vols. Washington, DC: RHPA, 1953-1957.

Noel, Gerard T., A Brief Enquiry into the Prospects of the Church, in Connexion with the Second Advent of Our Lord Jesus Christ. Philadelphia: Orrin Rogers, 1840.

Norris, Sylvester, <u>An Antidote of Treatise of Thirty Controversies: With a large Discourse of the Church, in which the Souvereigne Truth of Catholike doctrine, is faythfully deliuevered: against the pestiferous writings of all English Sectaryes ...</u>, 1622. Reprinted in D.M. Rogers, ed., <u>English Recusant Literature: 1558-1640</u>, vol. 185. London: The Scholars Press, 1974.

Odom, Robert L., <u>Sunday in Pagan Romanism</u>. Washington, DC: RHPA, 1944.

<u>Our Firm Foundation</u>. 2 vols. Washington, DC: RHPA, 1953.

Parker, Thomas, <u>The Visions and Prophecies of Daniel Expounded: Wherein the Mistakes of Former Interpreters Are Modestly Discovered</u>. London: Edmund Paxton, 1646.

[W.W. Prescott], <u>Handbook for Bible Students</u>. Washington, DC: RHPA, 1922.

_____. <u>The Doctrine of Christ</u>. Washington, DC: RHPA, 1920.
_____. <u>Source Book for Bible Students</u>. Washington, DC: RHPA, 1919.

Price, George McCready, <u>Back to the Bible</u>. Washington, DC: RHPA, 1917.

_____. <u>The Greatest of the Prophets</u>. Mountain View, Cal.: PPPA, 1955.

<u>Prophetic Conjectures on the French Revolution</u>, originally published in 1747 and reprinted in part in Philadelphia: William Young, 1794.

Reed, Rebecca, <u>Six Months in a Convent</u>. Boston: Russel, Odiorne & Metcalf, 1835.

<u>Report of the General Conference of Christians expecting the advent of our Lord Jesus Christ, held in Boston, Oct. 14, 15, 1840</u>. Boston: Joshua V. Himes, 1841.

Rupp, I. Daniel, comp., <u>HE PASA EKKLESIA: An Original History of the Religious Denominations at present existing in the United States</u>. Philadelphia: J.Y. Humphrey, 1840.

Seventh-day Adventists Answer Questions on Doctrine.
Washington, DC: RHPA, 1957.

Shimeall, Richard, Age of the World. New York: Swords,
Stanford & Co, 1842.

Skinner, Otis A., Miller's Theory Utterly Exploded.
Boston: T. Whittemore, 1840.

Smith, L.A., The United States in Prophecy; Our Country:
Its Past, Present, and Future, and What the
Scriptures Say of It. Nashville, Tenn.: SPA, 1914.

Smith, Uriah, Daniel and the Revelation; The Response of
History to the Voice of Prophecy. Battle Creek, MI:
Review and Herald Publishing Company, 1897.

_____. Here and Hereafter, or, Man in Life and Death.
Battle Creek, MI: RHPA, 1897.

_____. The Marvel of Nations – Our Country: Its Past,
Present, and Future, and What the Scriptures Say of
It. Battle Creek, MI: Review and Herald Publishers,
1886.

_____. The Prophecies of Daniel and the Revelation.
2 vols., rev. ed.. Washington, DC: RHPA, 1944.

_____. Synopsis of the Present Truth: A Brief
Exposition of the Views of S.D. Adventists. Battle
Creek, MI: SDA Publ. Ass., 1884.

_____. Thoughts, Critical and Practical on the Book
of Daniel. Battle Creek, MI: Steam Press of the SDA
Church, 1873.

_____. Thoughts, Critical and Practical on the Book
of Daniel. Battle Creek, MI: Steam Press of the SDA
Church, second, enlarged and revised edition, 1881.

_____. Thoughts Critical and Practical on the
Revelation. Battle Creek, MI: Steam Press of the
SDA Publ. Ass., 1865.

_____. Thoughts Critical and Practical on the Book
of the Revelation. Battle Creek, MI: Steam Press of
the SDA Publ. Ass., 1873.

Smith, Uriah, <u>The United States in the Light of Prophecy, or, An Exposition of Revelation 13:11-17</u>. Battle Creek, MI: Steam Press of the SDA Publ. Ass., 1876.

_____. <u>Which? Mortal or Immortal? or An Inquiry into the Present Constitution of Man</u>. Battle Creek: Steam Press of the Review and Herald Office, 1859.

Snook, B.F., <u>The Nature, Subject and Design of Christian Baptism</u>. Battle Creek, MI: Steam Press of the Review and Herald Office, 1861.

Spicer, W.A., <u>Beacon Lights of Prophecy</u>. Washington, DC: RHPA, 1935.

_____. <u>The Gospel in All the World</u>. Washington, DC: RHPA, 1926.

_____. <u>Our Day in the Light of Prophecy</u>. Washington, DC: RHPA, 1918.

Stevens, Jesse C., <u>The Papacy in Bible Prophecy</u>. Mountain View, Cal.: PPPA, 1928.

Straw, Walter E., <u>Origin of Sunday Observance</u>. Washington, DC: RHPA, 1939.

Stuart, Moses, <u>Hints on the Interpretation of Prophecy</u>. Andover: Allen, Morrill & Wardwell, 1842.

Tuberville, Henry, <u>Douay Catechism or An Abridgment of the Christian Doctrine. With Proof for Points Controverted by Way of Question and Answer. Composed in 1649 by Rev. Henry Tuberville of the English College of Douay. Now Approved and Recommended for His Diocese by the Right Rev. Benedict [Fenwick], Bishop of Boston</u>. New York: P.J. Kennedy, Excelsior Publishing House, 1833.

Waggoner, E.J., <u>Fathers of the Catholic Church: A Brief Examination of the "Falling Away" of the Church in the First three Centuries</u>. Oakland, Cal.: Pacific Press Publishing Company, 1888.

Waggoner, J.H., <u>The Nature and Tendency of Modern Spiritualism</u>. Battle Creek, MI: Steam Press of the Review and Herald Office, 1860.

Waggoner, J.H., _Prophetic Lights: Some of the Prominent rophecies of the Old and New Testaments, Interpreted by the Bible and History_. Oakland, Cal.: PPPA, 1888.

Walsh, Mary E., _Bible Lessons for Catholics_. Nashville, Tenn.: SPA, 1967.

_____. _The Wine of Roman Babylon_. Nashville, Tenn.: SPA, 1945.

Wearner, Alonzo J., _Fundamentals of Bible Doctrines_. Washington, DC: RHPA, 1935.

White, Ellen G., _Colporteur Ministry_. Mountain View, Cal.: PPPA, 1953.

_____. _Counsels to Writers and Editors_. Nashville, Tenn.: SPA, 1947.

_____. _Early Writings_. Washington, DC: RHPA, 1945.

_____. _Evangelism_. Washington, DC: RHPA, 1946.

_____. _The Great Controversy between Christ and Satan_. Mountain View, Cal.: PPPA, 1911.

_____. _The Publishing Ministry_. Washington, DC: RHPA, 1983.

_____. _Selected Messages_, vol. 1. Washington, DC: RHPA, 1958.

_____. _Spirit of Prophecy_, vol. 4: _The Great Controversy between Christ and Satan_. Oakland, Cal.: Pacific Press; Battle Creek: Review and Herald, 1884; Washington, DC: RHPA, 1969 facsimile ed.

_____. _Spiritual Gifts_, vol. 1: _The Great Controversy_. Battle Creek, MI: James White, 1858.

_____. _Testimonies for the Church_. 9 vols. Mountain View, Cal.: PPPA, 1948.

White, James, _Sketches of the Life and Public Labors of William Miller_. Battle Creek, Mich.: Steam Press of the SDA Publ. Ass., 1875.

White, James, <u>The Sounding of the Seven Trumpets of Rev.8 and 9</u>. Battle Creek, MI: Steam Press of the Review and Herald Office, 1859.

<u>The World in Crisis</u>. Nashville, Tenn.: SPA, 1915.

<u>World Peace in the Light of Bible Prophecy</u>. Washington, DC: RHPA, 1919.

Yost, Frank H., "Antichrist in History and Prophecy." Chap. in: <u>Our Firm Foundation</u>, vol. 1, 623-713. Washington, DC: RHPA, 1953.

_____. <u>The Early Christian Sabbath</u>. Mountain View, Cal.: PPPA, 1947.

2. Pamphlets

Andrews, John N., <u>Advent and Sabbath Tracts</u>, No. 1-4. Rochester, N.Y., n.d.

Bates, Joseph, <u>A Seal of the Living God. A Hundred Forty-Four Thousand of the Servants of God Being Sealed</u>. New Bedford: Press of Benjamin Lindsey, 1849.

_____. <u>Second Advent Way Marks and High Heaps, or a Connected View, of the Fulfillment of Prophecy, by God's Peculiar People, From the Year 1840 to 1847</u>. New Bedford: Press of Benjamin Lindsey, 1847.

_____. <u>The Seventh Day Sabbath, a Perpetual Sign, From the Beginning, to the Entering into the Gates of the Holy City, According to the Commandment</u>. New Bedford: Press of Benjamin Lindsey, 1846.

_____. <u>The Seventh Day Sabbath, a Perpetual Sign, From the Beginning, to the Entering into the Gates of the Holy City, According to the Commandment</u>. Revised and enlarged ed. New Bedford: Press of Benjamin Lindsey, 1846.

Bollman, C.P., <u>Papacy and Persecution, or Did the Roman Catholic Church Ever Persecute?</u> Battle Creek, MI: IRLA, 1895.

Bollman, C.P., <u>The Prohibition Party and Freedom of Conscience</u>. Oakland, Cal.: Pacific Press Publishing Co., 1891.

Cottrell, R.F., <u>Mark of the Beast, and Seal of the Living God</u>. Battle Creek, n.d.

<u>A Declaration of the Fundamental Principles Taught and Practiced by the Seventh-day Adventists</u>. Battle Creek, MI: SDA Publ. Ass., 1872.

Flower, B.O., <u>Religious Intolerance in the Republic: Christians Persecuting Christians in Tennessee</u>. Battle Creek, MI: IRLA, 1892.

Gaussen, [L.], <u>The German Rebuke of American Neology, A Discourse at the Opening of the Course in Oct. last, entitled: Popery, an Argument for the Truth by its Fulfilment of Scripture Prophecies</u>. Boston: Joshua V. Himes, 1844.

Jones, A.T., <u>The American Papacy--The Outcome of National Reform Religion</u>. Oakland, Cal.: Pacific Press Publishing Co., 1889.

_____. <u>Appeal from the U.S. Supreme Court Decision Making this "a Christian Nation."</u> Battle Creek, MI, IRLA, 1893.

_____. <u>The Captivity of the Republic: A Report of the Hearing by the House Committee on the Columbian Exposition, Jan. 10-13, 1893, and the Present Status and Effect of the Legislation on Sunday Closing of the World's Fair</u>. Washington, DC: IRLA, 1893.

Kennedy, J.J., <u>Catholic Doctrine: How I Found the Faith</u>. Oakland, Cal.: Pacific Press Publishing Co., 1902.

<u>Lessons on the Great Threefold Message of Revelation Fourteen, senior division, 1st quarter 1896</u>. Oakland, Cal.: PPPA, 1896.

Lewis, Abraham H., <u>The Catholization of Protestantism on the Sabbath Question or Sunday-Observance Non-Protestant</u>. Plainfield, N.J.: American Sabbath Tract Society, 1897.

Lewis, Abraham H., The Sabbath Question from the Roman Catholic Standpoint as Stated by the "Catholic Mirror," together with Introduction and Remarks. New York: American Sabbath Tract Society, 1894.

Loughborough, J.N., The Two-Horned Beast. Rochester, N.Y., ca. 1854.

_____. The Two-Horned Beast of Rev. 13, a Symbol of the United States. Battle Creek, MI: The Review and Herald Office, 1857.

Morton, J.W., Vindication of the True Sabbath; in Two Parts. Battle Creek, MI: Steam Press of the SDA Publ. Ass., 1876.

Preble, T.M., Tract, Showing that the Seventh Day Sabbath Should Be Observed as the Sabbath, Instead of the First Day; According to the Commandment. Nashua: Printed by Murray & Kimhall, 1845.

Prescott, W.W., Seventh-day Adventists and the Roman Peril. Washington, DC: Religious Liberty Association, 1912.

Rome's Challenge: Why Do Protestants Keep Sunday? Battle Creek, MI: IRLA, n.d.

Sabbath School Lessons on the Coming of the Lord, senior division, 2nd quarter 1893. Oakland, Cal.: PPPA, 1893.

Smith, Uriah, The Prophecy of Daniel: the Four Kingdoms, the Sanctuary, and the Twenty-three Hundred Days. Battle Creek: Steam Press of the SDA Publ. Ass., 1863.

Stevens, Jesse C., Was Peter the First Pope? Washington, DC: RHPA, ca. 1925.

Waggoner, E.J., The Blair Sunday-Rest Bill. Its Nature and History. Oakland, Cal.: Pacific Press Publishing Co., 1889.

White, James, The Signs of the Times, showing that the Second Coming of Christ is at the Doors. Spirit Manifestations, a Foretold Sign that the Day of God's Wrath Hasteth Greatly. Rochester, N.Y.: The Review Office, 1853.

White, James, <u>A Word to the Little Flock</u>. May, 1847.

<u>Who Changed the Sabbath?</u> Battle Creek, MI, ca. 1854.

<u>Why Don't You Keep the Sabbath?</u> Rochester, N.Y.: The Advent Review Office, 1854.

Wilcox, M.C., <u>The King of the North: A Suggestive Outline Study of Daniel 11</u>. Publ. by the author, 1910.

3. Articles

a. Author not mentioned

"Ancient and Modern Idolatry," <u>RH</u>, Oct. 21, 1902, 24.

"Another Blow at the Papacy," <u>RH</u>, Dec. 1, 1868, 262-263.

"The Bible in Rome," <u>RH</u>, Jan. 31, 1871, 49.

"The Bible in Rome," <u>RH</u>, Sept. 26, 1871, 115.

"Bismarck and the Pope," <u>RH</u>, March 10, 1874, 99.

"Book Notice," <u>RH</u>, May 6, 1862, 184.

"Bower's Escape from Inquisition," <u>RH</u>, Aug. 13, 1867, 134-135; Aug. 20, 1867, 150-151.

"Cardinal Gibbons Praises the Bible," <u>RH</u>, Dec. 2, 1915, 2.

"Catholic Reactions to 'The Protestant Magazine'," <u>Lib</u>, vol. 11, no. 2 (1st quarter 1916, extra), 56.

"Catholic Schemes," <u>MC</u>, Nov. 25, 1842, 1.

"Catholic Total Abstinence Union," <u>RH</u>, June 14, 1887, 384.

"Charity Run Wild," <u>RH</u>, Apr. 22, 1880, 265.

"The Christian Sabbath," <u>AS</u> (Sept. 21, 1893), 291; Sept. 28, 1893, 298-299; Oct. 12, 1893, 308-309; Oct. 12, 1893, 316-317.

"The Christian Sabbath," <u>The Catholic Mirror</u>, Sept. 2,
    1893, 8; Sept. 9, 1893, 8; Sept. 16, 1893, 8;
    Sept. 23, 1893, 8-9.

"Churchmen Back Taylor Peace Task," <u>New York Times</u>, Jan.
    27, 1940, 4.

"Collisions of Protestantism and Popery," <u>ST</u>, March 1,
    1841, 182.

"Come out of Babylon," extracted from "The Voice of
    Truth," <u>RH</u>, Dec. 9, 1851, 58-59.

"Convent Tragedy," <u>PM</u>, vol. 5, no. 3 (March 1913), 102-
    111; vol. 5, no. 4 (Apr. 1913), 150-163; vol. 5,
    no. 5 (May 1913), 203-217; vol. 5, no. 6 (June
    1913), 258-266.

"Convocation of a General Council at Rome," <u>RH</u>, Jan. 2,
    1867, 81.

"Course of Study for Ministers," <u>RH</u>, May 10, 1870, 164.

"A Cutting Reproof; Extracts from Milner's End of
    Controversy, a Catholic work, pages 89, 90," <u>RH</u>,
    Jan. 20, 1853, 139.

"Daniel Chapters VIII and IX," <u>RH</u>, Nov. 21, 1854, 116-
    117.

"Daniel's Vision of the Four Beasts," <u>MC</u>, Aug. 10, 1843,
    196.

"The Deadly Wound - When was it Healed?" <u>RH</u>, June 30,
    1885, 408.

"Decline of the Romish Church in Europe," <u>RH</u>, June 6,
    1871, 198.

"Decretalia," <u>RH</u>, July 9, 1867, 55.

"Destruction of the Wicked," extracted from: "Bible vs.
    Tradition," <u>RH</u>, Oct. 24, 1854, 82-83.

"The Downward Tendency of Man," <u>RH</u>, Feb. 21, 1854, 35.

"The Dragon Voice," <u>RH</u>, Feb. 5, 1857, 106.

"Dr. Buttrick and Adler Call on President; Two Peace Leaders See 'All in Agreement'," <u>New York Times</u>, Dec. 27, 1939, 1, 3.

"Efforts and Aims of Romanism," <u>RH</u>, July 26, 1870, 48.

"Ending of the 1260 Years," <u>RH</u>, June 18, 1867, 6-7; June 25, 1867, 22,23; July 2, 1867, 38-39; July 9, 1867, 54-55.

"Extract From the 'Catholic Herald'," <u>MC</u>, Aug. 3, 1843, 191.

"Facts for Everybody," <u>RH</u>, Sept. 10, 1861, 115.

"The Fall of Popery, Events of 1798," <u>MC</u>, Nov. 25, 1842, 2.

"Four Beasts and the Little Horn," <u>PT</u>, Apr. 1, 1929, 3.

"French Mission," <u>RH</u>, May 5, 1859, 188-189.

"The General Councils of the Romish Church," <u>RH</u>, Oct. 1, 1867, 246-247.

"The Glory of God in the Earth," <u>MC</u>, Nov. 28, 1842, 4.

"Governor Smith Accepts," <u>Zions Herald</u>, Aug. 29, 1928, 1104-1105

"The Great Speech in the Vatican," <u>RH</u>, June 13, 1871, 202-203.

"The Great Speech in the Vatican," <u>RH</u>, June 27, 1871, 10.

"Has the Pope's Dominion Been Taken Away?" <u>MC</u>, Nov. 9, 1842, 2-3.

"History of the Society of Jesuits," cont., <u>ST</u>, Apr. 27, 1842, 26-27.

"The Infallibility of the Pope," <u>PM</u>, vol. 5, no. 9 (Sept. 1913), 395-401.

"The Inquisition," <u>RH</u>, March 19, 1867, 172.

"Inside the Nunnery," <u>RH</u>, Nov. 4, 1890, 679.

"An Interesting Relic," <u>MC</u>, Aug. 10, 1843, 193.

"Is America to Become Roman Catholic?" PM, vol. 4, no. 2 (2nd quarter 1912), 112-114.

"Is Antioch Epiphanes the Hero of Daniel's Prophecy?" ST, Dec. 28, 1842, 113-114.

"The Land of Promise," PM, vol. 5, no. 10 (Oct. 1913), 438-447.

"The Last Form of Papacy," ST, June 8, 1842, 76.

"The Little Horn--The Pope," ST, Feb. 15, 1841, 169-171.

"The Little Horn Prevailing," ST, Aug. 2, 1843, 174.

"The Little Horn Prevailing," cont., ST, Apr. 26, 1843, 62-63.

"The Little Horn Prevailing," ST, Oct. 11, 1843, 61.

"Methods of the Romish Church," RH, Sept. 18, 1867, 198.

"Miracle of the Romish Church," RH, Nov. 20, 1868, 199.

"The Mystery of Iniquity," RH, May 24, 1870, 182-183.

"The National Sunday Bill," AS, Oct. 1888, 73-74.

"The New York Observer," MC, March 10, 1843, 45.

"Not As It Once Was," RH, Nov. 17, 1891, 712.

"The Office," RH, Feb. 20, 1855, 182-183.

"On the Religious Liberty Front," RH, Jan. 1, 1948, 10.

"Origin of Popish Errors," RH, Sept. 11, 1856, 147.

"Our Course," ST, Nov. 15, 1840, 126.

"Papal Expectations," ST, June 15, 1842, 95.

"Papal Infallibility," RH, March 12, 1872, 100.

"Papal Infallibility and Mariolatry," RH, Aug. 29, 1871, 82.

"Papal Representative to the American Government," RH, Feb. 17, 1921, 8.

"The Papal Syllabus of Errors," PM, vol. 4, no. 1 (1st quarter 1911), 35-63.

"A Paraphrase on the 11th Chapter of Daniel," MC, Aug. 10, 1843, 198-199.

"Persecution," RH, Jan. 7, 1868, 54-55.

"Philadelphia Riots," MC, July 11, 1844, 413.

"Plans of the Catholics," RH, Jan. 21, 1868, 90.

"The Plans of the Papacy," AS, March 28, 1895, 97-98.

"The Pope and the Bible," MC, July 18, 1844, 6-7.

"The Pope and the Bible," AHSTR, July 31, 1844, 201-202.

"The Pope and Europe," RH, Apr. 9, 1872.

"The Pope and the Roman Catholic Monarchs," RH, Nov. 5, 1867, 326.

"The Pope in America," MC, May 4, 1843, 63.

"The Pope in Extremis," RH, Sept. 6, 1870, 91.

"The Pope Speaks Again," RH, July 23, 1895, 471.

"The Pope's Lamentations," RH, Nov. 26, 1867, 382.

"The Pope's Perplexity," RH, July 23, 1861, 59.

"The Pope's Troubles," RH, Aug. 26, 1862, 99.

"The Pope's Troubles," RH, Nov. 10, 1868, 238-239.

"The Popedom," RH, July 29, 1862, 67.

"Popery," MC, Nov. 22, 1842, 3.

"Popery," MC, Aug. 3, 1843, 191.

"Popery and the Schools," RH, July 7, 1885, 421-422.

"Popery Prevailing by Craft," MC, July 11, 1844, 414.

"Popery vs. the Bible," MC, May 8, 1844, 343.

"Popish Falsehood," MC, July 18, 1844, 406.

"Popish Tyranny in America," MC, July 18, 1844, 4.

"President Beecher, Jacksonville," ST, Jan. 1, 1842, 149.

"President Sets Up Peace Objectives and Bides his Time," New York Times, Jan. 10, 1940, 1, 6.

"Primitive Christianity in England - An Incident of Romish Aggression," RH, Oct. 15, 1867, 278.

"Progress of Popery," ST, Oct. 25, 1843, 77-78.

"Protest Ambassador to Vatican," RH, Nov. 1, 1951, 24.

"Protestant and Romish Nations," RH, June 30, 1863, 34.

"Protestantism and Catholicism Joining Hands," RH, May 16, 1871, 171.

"Puseyism," ST, March 8, 1843, 5.

"Puseyism, a Sign of the Times," MC, Jan. 25, 1844, 215.

"Puseyism and Neology," ST, Aug. 23, 1843, 4, 6.

"Reasons for Believing the Second Coming of Christ in 1843," MC, Nov. 23, 1842, 3-4.

"Recruit the Voters!" Zions Herald, Oct. 17, 1928, 1327-1328.

"Religion in the United States," extracted from: "London Christian Times," RH, Feb. 14, 1856, 159-160.

"Religious Excitement in Philadelphia," ST, Apr. 1, 1841, 7.

"Remarkable Events During the Past Nine Years," RH, Feb. 15, 1870, 63.

"The Reply of Seventh-day Adventists to the Pope's Encyclical 'Lux Veritatis'," RH, March 31, 1932, 3-4.

"Report of the Religious Liberty Department," RH, May 16, 1918, 11-15.

"Revelation XII and XIII," RH, May 29, 1860, 4.

"Riots in Philadelphia," MC, May 16, 1844, 348.

"The Rise and Progress of Adventism," The Advent Shield and Review, May 1844, 90.

"Roman Catholic Claims," RH, Apr. 10, 1894, 240.

"Roman Catholic Inquisition," RH, May 2, 1871, 159.

"Roman Catholic Protracted Meeting," MC, Dec. 6, 1842, 1.

"The Romanism of Today," RH, Oct. 18, 1887, 656.

"Rome as It is," RH, March 1, 1881, 141.

"Rome Exalts the Virgin Mary," RH, May 13, 1954, 10.

"Rome Takes a New Departure," RH, Jan. 7, 1890, 7.

"Rome Unchanged," RH, July 21, 1874, 43.

"The Rush of Civil Governments to Rome," RH, Feb. 2, 1922, 5-6.

"Scoffing in High Places," ST, March 8, 1843, 5.

"Significant," RH, Feb. 14, 1888, 112.

"The Signs of the Times," MC, Nov. 30, 1843, 132-133.

"The So-called Encyclical," AS, June 29, 1893, 206.

"Something About Catholics," RH, Feb. 10, 1874, 67.

"Something for Protestants," ST, Nov. 30, 1843, 134.

"The Sounding of the Seven Trumpets," RH, July 8, 1858, 57-59; July 22, 1858, 73-75; July 29, 1858, 82-84; Aug. 5, 1858, 89-90.

"The Supreme Court Decision on the Oregon School Law," Lib, vol. 20, no. 4 (4th quarter 1925), 111-114.

"Temporal Power of the Pope," RH, July 28, 1868, 94.

"To the Conference," AHSTR, Feb. 10, 1844, 8-9.

"Triumph of the Jesuits in New York," ST, Apr. 20, 1842, 21.

"The Triple Crown," _PM_, vol. 2, no. 1 (1st quarter 1910), 3-4.

"Two Hundred Men Wanted," _RH_, Sept. 20, 1870, 112.

"The Vision of the Ram and the He-Goat," _MC_, Aug. 10, 1843, 196-198.

"The Visions - Objections Answered," _RH_, July 31, 1866, 65.

"Wet or Dry?" _Zions Herald_ (Aug. 8, 1928), 1020-1021, 1028.

"What Governor Smith Wants to Change," _The Baptist_, Sept. 18, 928.

"Where Sunday Laws Hit," _AS_, Apr. 17, 1889, 100-101.

"Works of Darkness," _RH_, July 11, 1893, 448.

"The Worship of the Virgin," _RH_, Feb. 28, 1871, 81.

Editorial, _PM_, vol. 1, no. 1 (2nd quarter 1909), 1.

Editorial, _PM_, vol. 3, no. 1 (1st quarter, 1911), 1-5.

Editorial, _PM_, vol. 3, no. 4 (4th quarter, 1911), 193-195.

Editorial, _The Truth_, Aug. 15, 1915

Editorial note, _RH_, March 7, 1854, 56.

Editorial note, _RH_, Dec. 18, 1856, 3.

Editorial note, _RH_, June 5, 1888, 368.

Editorial note, _RH_, Apr. 27, 1891, 224.

Editorial note, _AS_, Jan. 3, 1895, 1.

Editorial note, _RH_, Apr. 23, 1895, 272.

Editorial note, _RH_, Apr. 30, 1895, 288.

Editorial note, _RH_, Oct. 17, 1907, 6.

Editorial note, _RH_, Nov. 1, 1951, 24.

Our Sunday Visitor, Nov. 15, 1914, 3.

Our Sunday Visitor, Apr. 18, 1915, 3.

Our Sunday Visitor, Dec. 1, 1935, 9.

Our Sunday Visitor, Aug. 3, 1941, 7.

2. Author indicated

A., G.W., "Evidences of the End," RH, Nov. 20, 1860, 5-6.

Anderson, Roy A., "International Congress on Prophecy," RH, Jan. 8, 1953, 6-7.

Anderson, Roy A., "The Pope and World Peace," Min, vol. 38, no. 8 (Sept. 1965), 24-27, 36-37.

Andrews, John N., "The Angels of Revelation 14," RH, Aug. 19, 1851, 12-13; Sept. 2, 1851, 20-21; Dec. 9, 1851, 63-64; Dec. 23, 1851, 69-72.

_____. "Causes Which Elevated the Sunday," RH, Feb. 3, 1874, 60.

_____. "History of the Sabbath," series, RH, Apr. 14 - May 12, 1853.

_____. "History of the Sabbath," series, RH, Dec. 3, 1861 - May 27, 1862.

_____. "History of the Sabbath and the First Day of the Week," series, RH, July 14, 1859 - Aug. 4, 1859.

_____. "Is the First Day of the Week the Sabbath?" RH, March 31, 1853, 178-180.

_____. "The Sanctuary," RH, Jan. 6, 1853, 129-133; Feb. 3, 1853, 145-149.

_____. "Things to be Considered," RH, Jan. 31, 1854, 9-10.

Andrews, John N., "Thoughts on Revelation XIII and XIV," RH, May 19, 1851, 81-86.

_____. "The Three Angels of Revelation XIV:6-12," RH, Jan. 23, 1855, 161-163; Feb. 6, 1855, 169-171; Feb. 20, 1855, 177-178; March 6, 1855, 185-187; March 20, 1855, 193-196; Apr. 3, 1855, 201-205; Apr. 17, 1855, 209-212; May 1, 1855, 217-218.

_____. "Tradition," RH, Oct. 10, 1854, 69-70.

_____. "What is Babylon?" RH, Feb. 21, 1854, 36-37.

Ashton, N.S., "A General Review of the Sabbath Controversy," RH, May 28, 1925, 5-11.

Baker, Alonzo L., "The Editor's Council," RH, Sept. 18, 1930, 25.

Bates, Joseph, "The Beast with Seven Heads," RH, Aug. 5, 1851, 3-4.

_____. "Church Order," RH, Aug. 29, 1854, 22-23.

Beach, B.B., "The Bishops and Their Work," RH, Dec. 10, 1964, 7-9.

Beach, B.B., "Calendar Reform and the Catholic Church," RH, Jan. 2, 1964, 9-11.

_____. "Catholicism and Liberty," Lib, vol. 60, no. 5 (Sept.-Oct. 1965), 23-25; 32-34.

_____. "Change in the Church of Rome," RH, Apr. 21, 1966, 4-5.

_____. "Collegiality," RH, Dec. 3, 1964, 2-5.

_____. "The Council Fathers Debate the Role of the Laity," RH, Jan. 14, 1965, 2-5.

_____. "Days of Drama and Delay," RH, Jan. 16, 1964, 10-11.

_____. "Divine Revelation," RH, Dec. 24, 1964, 4-6.

_____. "Ecumenism," RH, Dec. 31, 1964, 4-6.

_____. "Looking Back on the First Session of Vatican Council II," RH, Feb. 14, 1963, 1, 8-9.

Beach, B.B., "Obstacles to Unity," <u>RH</u>, Nov. 29, 1962, 6-8.

_____. "Obstacles to Unity," <u>Lib</u>, vol. 58, no. 2 (March/Apr., 1963), 16-17, 28-29.

_____. "The Relation of Vatican II to Collegiality," <u>RH</u>, Dec. 26, 1963, 5-7.

_____. "Religious Liberty," <u>RH</u>, Dec. 17, 1964, 6-9.

_____. "Report from Rome," <u>RH</u>, Nov. 1, 1962, 1, 8-9.

_____. "The Roman Church - Whither Bound?" <u>RH</u>, Dec. 19, 1963, 2-3, 8-9.

_____. "Rome Takes a Look at Eschatology and Mariology," <u>RH</u>, Nov. 26, 1964, 4-6.

_____. "The Second Vatican Council Opens With Medieval Splendor and Pageantry," <u>RH</u>, Nov. 8, 1962, 5, 8-9.

_____. "Success or Failure?" <u>RH</u>, Apr. 14, 1966, 1, 8-9.

_____. "Vatican II: Retrospect and Prospect," <u>RH</u>, March 31, 1966, 2-3.

_____. "Vatican Council II--Retrospect and Prospect," <u>RH</u>, Feb. 6, 1964, 10-12.

_____. "What Kind of Unity?" <u>RH</u>, Dec. 6, 1962, 13-14, 21.

_____. "When the Machine is Being Put Together," <u>RH</u>, Nov. 15, 1962, 1, 8-9.

Beach, W.R., "The Healing of the Papal Wound," <u>RH</u>, May 30, 1940, 4-7.

Beard, J.O., "The Last Move," <u>RH</u>, May 1, 1894, 278-279.

Beaven, Eric, "The Spirit of Babylon," <u>ST</u>, Feb. 26, 1935, 7, 14-15.

Bliss, Sylvester, "The Downfall of Babylon," <u>Advent Shield</u>, May, 1844, 112-120.

Bollman, C.P., "The A.P.A. and the Papists," <u>AS</u>, Sept. 28, 1893, 299.

_____. "The Greek Church and the Change of the Sabbath," <u>RH</u>, Nov. 8, 1923, 6-9.

_____. "'The Menace' Dynamited," <u>Lib</u>, vol. 11, no. 6 (4th quarter, 1916), 223.

_____. "The Number of the Beast," <u>RH</u>, Nov. 17, 1921, 6-7.

_____. "The Number of the Beast," <u>RH</u>, Aug. 1, 1929, 14-15.

_____. "Rome's Opportunity," <u>RH</u>, June 24, 1920, 4.

_____. "Seventh-day Adventists in the Chain-Gang, <u>AS</u>, Aug. 18, 1892, 251.

_____. "Studies in the Book of Daniel: The Fourth Beast," <u>RH</u>, June 23, 1927, 5-6.

_____. "1260 Years of Papal Supremacy," <u>RH</u>, Dec. 29, 1921, 6-7.

_____. editorial, <u>AS</u>, March 15, 1894, 81-82.

Bond, Walter G., "Rome Never Changes," <u>RH</u>, Oct. 18, 1906, 13-14.

Boose, Rose, "Know Your Bible Better: The Fall of Babylon," concl., <u>RH</u>, Sept. 24, 1953, 8-9.

Bourdeau, D.T., "How the Sabbath was Changed," <u>RH</u>, June 10, 1873, 201-202.

Butler, E.P, "Letter to James and Ellen White," <u>RH</u>, Jan., 1851, 30.

Butler, George I., "Babylon and Its Fall," <u>RH</u>, Feb. 11, 1909, 9-10.

_____. "The Causes Which Led to the Fall of Babylon," <u>RH</u>, March 4, 1909, 9-10.

_____. "Fall of Babylon," <u>RH</u>, extra issue, Nov. 22, 1887, 9-10.

Butler, George I., "Has There Been a Moral Fall of the Churches?" _RH_, Dec. 15, 1891, 776-779; Dec. 22, 1891, 792-793.

_____. "Interesting Facts Concerning Babylon's Fall," _RH_, Apr. 1, 1909, 9-10

Butler, S.M., "The Little Horn and the Fourth Beast of Daniel 7," _RH_, March 22, 1917, 6-8.

C.S.M., "Philadelphia Riots," _AHSTR_, May 29, 1844, 133.

Cage, W.C., "His Deadly Wound Was Healed," _RH_, Dec. 5, 1882, 762.

Calendar Reform, Extra issue, _Lib_, vol. 23, no. 2 (1st quarter 1929).

Campbell, George A., "Roman Catholics and the Advent Message," _RH_, Apr. 21, 1932, 4-6.

Canright, Dudley M. "Are the Roman Catholics United?" _RH_, May 31, 1870, 189.

_____. "Episcopalians Returning to Rome," _RH_, Nov. 17, 1874, 165.

_____. "Men and Things," _RH_, Feb. 27, 1872, 85.

_____. "Origin of the Doctrine of the Immortality of the Soul and Eternal Misery," _RH_, Dec. 8, 1863, 9-10; Dec. 15, 1863, 21-22.

_____. "Present Condition of the World," _RH_, Apr. 16, 1872, 143-144.

Caviness, L.L., "Babylon in the New Testament," _RH_, Jan. 17, 1918, 4.

_____. "Is Peter _the_ Rock or _a_ Rock?" _RH_, Aug. 10, 1950, 10-11.

_____. "The Papacy and the War," _RH_, Dec. 19, 1918, 3.

_____. "The Pope in the League of Nations," _RH_, Jan. 29, 1920, 5.

_____. "The Rising Prestige of the Vatican," _RH_, May 20, 1920, 4.

Caviness, L.L., "Roman Catholic Plans," RH, Jan. 25, 1917, 3-4.

_____. "Will the Pope Unite All the Churches? RH, March 27, 1919, 5-6.

Christian, L.H., "Conditions in the European Division," RH, Nov. 29, 1923, 3-6.

_____. "Europe in 1925," RH, May 14, 1925, 2, 14.

_____. "The Mission Needs of Europe," RH, Feb. 17, 1927, 12-13.

_____. "The Other Side of Europe," RH, May 21, 1936, 5-6.

_____. "Political and Economic Conditions in Europe," no. 1, RH, Jan. 10, 1924, 3-4.

Coffin, Frank A., "All the World Wondered," RH, Apr. 10, 1929, 1.

_____. "The Number of a Man," Watchman Magazine, March 1937, 12, 17.

_____. "Revision of the Weekly Calendar," RH, May 5, 1921, 9.

Colcord, W.A., "Making America Catholic," RH, Nov. 26, 1889, 752.

_____. "The 'Secret Recesses' of Rome," RH, Aug. 23, 1906, 19-20.

_____. "Unbecoming Selfpity," RH, Dec. 3, 1889, 768.

Conradi, Louis R., "The World Turning Toward Rome," RH, Feb. 11, 1896, 89.

Cornell, M.E., "The Cause in Marion, Iowa," RH, May 10, 1860, 193.

_____. "Meetings in Anamosa, Iowa," RH, Feb. 23, 1860, 109.

_____. "Meetings in Chesaning, Mich." RH, Feb. 26, 1861, 116-117.

_____. "The Power of Satolli," RH, May 9, 1893, 295.

Cornell, M.E., "They Will Make an Image to the Beast,"
    RH, Sept. 19, 1854, 42-43.

_____. "Ye Know Not What Manner of Spirit Ye Are Of,"
    RH, Jan. 2, 1894, 7.

Cottrell, R.F. "The Approaching Conflict," RH, July 15,
    1864, 457.

_____. "Blasphemy," RH, Jan. 31, 1854, 13-14.

_____. "Breaking the Law of the Land," RH, Feb. 9,
    1860, 92-93.

_____. "The Doctrine of the Trinity," RH, June 1,
    1869, 180-181.

_____. "How Shall I Vote?" RH, Oct. 30, 1856, 205.

_____. "Keep Your Eyes Turned Toward Rome!" RH, July
    23, 1895, 472-473.

_____. "Mark of the Beast," RH, Aug. 6, 1857, 109.

_____. "Mark of the Beast and Seal of the Living
    God," RH, July 28, 1859, 77-78.

_____. "The Popes of the Tenth Century," RH, Feb. 27,
    1872, 87.

_____. "A Prophecy Being Fulfilled," RH, June 11,
    1889, 370.

_____. "Speaking of the Image," RH, Dec. 12, 1854,
    134.

_____. "What Will Cause the Image?" RH, Nov. 14,
    1854, 110.

Cottrell, Raymond F., "Catholic Bishop Corroborates
    Baptist President," RH, March 3, 1960, 3.

_____. "The Church and Freedom," RH, May 30, 1963,
    15.

_____. "The Church Faces Up to the Modern World," RH,
    Nov. 11, 1965, 6-8.

_____. "The Declaration on Religious Liberty," RH,
    Oct. 21, 1965, 2-5.

Cottrell, Raymond F., "The Import of Vatican Council II for Adventists," <u>RH</u>, Feb. 7, 1963, 13.

_____. "On the Eve of the Council," <u>RH</u>, Jan. 10, 1963, 13.

_____. "Peter's Bark Changes Course," <u>RH</u>, Jan. 31, 1963, 13.

_____. "Pope John Lays Plans to Reunite Christendom," <u>RH</u>, May 7, 1959, 16-17, 14.

_____. "The Protestant Reaction," <u>RH</u>, May 14, 1959, 7-9.

_____. "The Religious Issue and the New Administration," <u>RH</u>, Dec. 22, 1960, 5.

_____. "The Resurgence of Catholic Power," <u>RH</u>, May 21, 1959, 16-17, 23-24.

_____. "The Roman Catholic Church Comes of Age in the United States," <u>RH</u>, May 28, 1959, 16-19.

_____. "Saint Peter's Bark Tacks About," <u>RH</u>, Oct. 28, 1965, 5-6.

_____. "Vatican II and the Future," <u>RH</u>, Nov. 18, 1965, 9-11.

_____. "What is Bigotry?" <u>RH</u>, March 31, 1960, 4-5.

W. Covert, W., "Romanism as it is," <u>RH</u>, Apr. 8, 1884, 228.

Crane, I.A., "Not Catholicism, but Political Protestantism to Rule America," <u>Lib</u>, vol. 19, no. 1 (1st quarter 1924), 20-21.

Crozier, O.R.L., "The Law of Moses," <u>The Day-Star Extra</u>, Feb. 7, 1846, 37-44.

Daniells, Arthur G., "The Bible Conference," <u>RH</u>, Aug. 21, 1919, 3-4.

Delafield, D.A., "The Federal Council After Forty Years," <u>RH</u>, Jan. 6, 1949, 6-7.

_____. "Miracles Ascribed to the Roman Pontiff," <u>RH</u>, Dec. 20, 1951, 12.

Dick, E.D., "Spring Meeting, General Conference Committee," <u>RH</u>, May 16, 1940, 13.

Duffie, David, "Advent Hope Proclaimed to World Conference," <u>RH</u>, Apr. 7, 1949, 8-9.

Dunn, Norman W., "Autumn Council Proceedings," <u>RH</u>, Dec. 2, 1948, 3-11.

Durland, J.H., "England and Catholicism," <u>RH</u>, Jan. 21, 1890, 34; Jan. 28, 1890, 50; Feb. 4, 1890, 67.

_____. "The Coming Struggle for Supremacy," <u>RH</u>, Dec. 14, 1886, 770; Dec. 21, 1886, 786.

Edson, Hiram, "The Commandments of God, and the Mark of the Beast brought to view by the Third Angel of Rev. XIV, considered in connection with the Angel of Chap. VII, having the Seal of the Living God," <u>RH</u>, Sept. 2, 1852; Sept. 16, 1852, 73-75; Sept. 30, 1852, 81-84.

_____. "The Two Laws," <u>RH</u>, Oct. 7, 1851, 36-40.

Eldridge, Robert M., "Test by Comparison," <u>RH</u>, March 8, 1945, 8-10, 23.

Emmerson, W.L., "America and World History," <u>RH</u>, Feb. 27, 1947, 8-10.

_____. "The Growth of Catholic Influence in America," <u>RH</u>, July 12, 1951, 4-6.

_____. "The Resurgence of Rome," <u>RH</u>, Feb. 13, 1947, 1, 10-11.

_____. "Rome and Religious Liberty," <u>Lib</u>, vol. 59, no. 2 (March/Apr., 1964), 20-24.

_____. "Rome Speaks on Religious Liberty," <u>Lib</u>, vol. 60, no. 6 (Nov./Dec., 1965), 7-10.

_____. "Spotlight on Amsterdam: Protestant Leaders Discuss Church's Relation to the World," <u>RH</u>, Sept. 30, 1948, 9-11.

_____. "That They All May Be One," <u>Lib</u>, vol. 58, no. 2, (March/Apr., 1963), 12-15.

Emmerson, W.L., "What Will Vatican II Say About Freedom?" <u>Lib</u>, vol. 59, no. 5 (Sept./Oct., 1964), 20-23.

_____. "World Council of Churches Convenes," <u>RH</u>, Sept. 16, 1954, 3-5.

Evan, N.Y., "The Catholics in New Orleans," <u>AHSTR</u>, May 15, 1844, 118-119.

Everson, Chas. T., "The Inscription on the Pope's Tiara," <u>RH</u>, July 27, 1905, 10-11.

Fifield, George E., "Sad Apostasy," <u>RH</u>, Jan. 21, 1890, 35.

Fitch, Charles, "Come Out of Her, My People," <u>Second Advent of Christ</u>, July 26, 1843.

_____. "Come Out of Her, My People," <u>MC</u>, Sept. 21, 1843, 33-36.

_____. "What is it for God's People to Come out of Babylon?" <u>ST</u>, Sept. 13, 1843, 27.

Fleming, Lorenzo D., "A Chapter on Popery," <u>MC</u>, March 21, 1844, 276-277.

Ford, Orley, "Approach to Catholics in Latin America," <u>Min</u>, vol. 18, no. 5 (Apr. 1945), 11-12.

Fox, Doreen, "Winsome Ways With Roman Catholics," <u>Min</u>, vol. 37, no. 5 (May 1964), 37-38.

French, T.M., "Catholics and the Spirit World," <u>RH</u>, Aug. 20, 1936, 7-8.

Froom, Leroy E., "Dubious Pictures of the Tiara," <u>Min</u>, vol. 21, no. 11 (Nov. 1948), 35.

[Gaussen, Prof. L.], "Popery, an Argument for the Truth, by its Fulfillment of Scripture Prophecies," <u>AHSTR</u>, July 3, 1844, 169-171; July 10, 1844, 177-178.

_____. "A Voice from Geneva," <u>MC</u>, July 11, 1844, 409-411.

Gilbert, Andrew C., "The Roman Question," <u>RH</u>, June 27, 1929, 3, 11.

Gilbert, F.C., "All the World Wondered after the Beast," _RH_, Sept. 14, 1916, 10-11.

Dr. [?] Goodman, "Possessing the Land," _RH_, Aug. 30, 1881, 148.

Griggs, Frederick, "The Change of the Sabbath," _RH_, Oct. 31, 1918, 5-6.

H.J., "Popery, Where Unsuspected," _MC_, Aug. 22, 1844, 50-51.

Hale, Apollos, and Joseph Turner, "Has Not the Savior Come as the Bridegroom?" _Advent Mirror_, Jan. 1845, 1-4.

Haskell, S.N., "Penance," _RH_, Aug. 20, 1895, 538.

Haynes, Carlyle B., "Growing Catholic Control," _RH_, Feb. 9, 1950, 12-13.

_____. "How, Why, and by Whom Was the Sabbath Change Effected?" _RH_, Apr. 26, 1928, 4-5.

_____. "The Last Hope of the World," _RH_, Apr. 24, 1919, 7-10.

_____. "The Pope at the Peace Table," _RH_, Nov. 11, 1943, 19-20.

_____. "Protestantism--Its Impending Doom," _RH_, Dec. 27, 1934, 3-5.

_____. "Roman Catholics Oppose Calendar Revision," _RH_, May 8, 1947, 8-9.

_____. "Who Shall Shape the Peace--Church or State?" _RH_, Dec. 2, 1943, 7-8.

Hawley, S., "The Doctrine of the Second Advent sustained by the Voice of the Church--Extract of a Sermon preached at the Dedication of the Tabernacle, May 4th, 1843, by Rev. S. Hawley," _ST_, June 7, 1843, 110-111.

Hegstad, Roland R., "Summit Conference of Pope and Patriarch," _RH_, Jan. 23, 1964, 1.

Hildreth, D., "Babylon is Fallen," _RH_, June 30, 1863, 35.

Hill, H. Ward, "Montreal: The Fourth World Conference on Faith and Order--Failure?" Lib, vol. 58, no. 6 (Nov./Dec., 1963), 20-23.

Himes, Joshua V., "Operations of Popery," ST, Nov. 1, 1843, 81-83.

Hoffmann, B.P., "Foreign Missions at Home," RH, Jan. 31, 1924, 10-12.

Holmes, Claude E., "America's Representative to the Papal States," RH, March 5, 1914, 5-7.

_____. "Relation of the United States Government to the Vatican," RH, Apr. 1, 1915, 19-20.

Holser, H., "Papists and Protestants in Europe," RH, Sept. 2, 1890.

Holt, C.A., "Comments on Current Events," RH, May 31, 1923, 2.

_____. "Comments on Current Events," RH, Jan. 31, 1924, 2.

_____. "The Eucharistic Congress--Its Meaning and Significance," RH, Aug. 12, 1926, 3-5.

_____. "Immigration and the Catholic Influence in the United States," RH, March 30, 1922, 7-8.

_____. "Romanism in the Old World, Apostate Protestantism in the New," RH, Apr. 28, 1927, 3-4.

_____. "The Vatican and Russia," RH, July 27, 1922, 9.

Howell, W.E., "New Edition of 'Daniel and the Revelation'," RH, Oct. 29, 1942, 20-21.

Hull, D.W., "Bible Doctrine of the Divinity of Christ," RH, Nov. 10, 1859, 193, 195.

Hull, Moses, "The Mark of the Beast, and the Seal of the Living God," RH, Sept. 29, 1863, 137-138.

Johns, Varner J., "False Ideas of the Antichrist," RH, Dec. 11, 1941, 4-6.

Johnson, Alvin W., "The Appointment of an Ambassador to the Vatican", part 2, RH, Dec. 13,1951, 5-7.

_____. "Opposition to the Vatican Grows," RH, March 27, 1952, 7-8.

Jones, A.T., "The American Papacy," AS, Dec. 1886, 93-94.
_____. The Breckinridge Sunday Bill," AS, Jan. 23, 1890, 25-27.

_____. "Catholic Federation," RH, Dec. 18, 1900, 808.

_____. "The Image of the Papacy," AS, March 1887, 19-20.

_____. "The Keeping of the Commandments--The Second Commandment," RH, Apr. 2, 1990, 216; Apr. 9, 1890, 232; Apr. 16, 1890, 249-250; Apr. 23, 1890, 265-266.

_____. "The New Blair Sunday Law," AS, Jan. 9, 1890, 9-11.

_____. "Which is the More So?" RH, Oct. 12, 1897, 647.

_____. Editorial, AS, March 15, 1894, 81-82.

Kellogg, M.E., "The Catholic Church and the A.P.A.," RH, Feb. 19, 1895, 119.

_____. "The Catholic Church vs. Secret Societies," RH, May 3, 1893, 288.

_____. "Catholicism in New England," RH, June 13, 1893, 375.

_____. "Catholics and the Liquor Business," RH, Aug. 21, 1894, 535.

_____. "The Cause of a Nation's Decadence," RH, Jan. 2, 1894, 5-6; Jan. 9, 1894, 21-22.

_____. "The Changed Attitude of the Catholic Church in France Toward the Republic," RH, Jan. 19, 1892, 37.

_____. "Comments on the Papal Encyclical," RH, Feb. 19, 1895, 122-123.

Kellogg, M.E., "Idolatry," RH, June 11, 1901, 377.

_____. "The Meaning of Satolli," RH, Apr. 25, 1893, 263.

_____. "Patting Rome on the Back," RH, Dec. 22, 1891, 800.

_____. "The Pope's Encyclical," RH, July 31, 1894, 486.

_____. "Prayers and Purgatory," RH, May 2, 1893, 279.

_____. "A Reunion of Christendom," RH, July 21, 1896, 453.

_____. "Rome's Character, Fate and Company," RH, Feb. 20, 1894, 120-121.

_____. "Romish Secrets," RH, Feb. 14, 1893, 105-106.

_____. "Salvation by Works," RH, June 8, 1897, 361-362.

Kilgore, R.M., "Babylon," RH, Sept. 17, 1895, 595.

_____. "Paying Penance," RH, Sept. 4, 1895, 612.

Kuntz, A., "Roman Catholic Pilgrim Resort," RH, Sept. 1, 1891, 551.

Kurtichanov, Titus, "A Divine Forecast of World History: Imminence of God's Kingdom Indicated in the Prophecies of Daniel 2 and 7," RH, Feb. 26, 1925, 3-12.

Lee, F., "Ambassador to the Roman Catholic Church," RH, Jan. 17, 1952, 13-14.

_____. "Beacon Lights," RH, March 22, 1945, 5, 19.

_____. "Beliefs and Practices of Roman Catholics," RH, July 9, 1953, 13-14.

_____. "Catholics Pray for Unity of Christendom," RH, March 8, 1956, 10.

_____. "Catholic Schools in America," RH, Apr. 25, 1940, 17.

Lee, F., "New Catholic Saint Canonized," RH, Aug. 1, 1946, 3-4.

_____. "The Papacy Unchanged," RH, July 20, 1944, 6-7.

_____. "Peace and the Papacy," RH, Sept. 2, 1943, 10.

_____. "A Perfect Society on Earth: A Catholic View," RH, Aug. 10, 1944, 3-5.

_____. "Protestants and Catholics Support Sunday Sacredness," RH, Dec. 16, 1954, 12.

_____. "Revival of Papal Power," RH, July 13, 1944, 7-8.

_____. "The Road Ahead: A Challenge to our Faith," part 2, RH, March 4, 1943, 5-7.

_____. "Roman Catholic Bishop Encourages Bible Reading," RH, May 24, 1956, 8-9.

_____. "Roman Catholics and the Bible," RH, Feb. 15, 1951, 13-14.

_____. "Roman Catholics and Church Unity," RH, June 29, 1944, 3-4.

_____. "Roman Catholics Seeking Friends and Converts," RH, July 10, 1952, 13-14.

_____. "Rome Never Changes," RH, Nov. 16, 1950, 4-5.

_____. "Rome Waits for Wandering Sheep," RH, July 28, 1955, 9.

_____. "Special Envoy at the Vatican," RH, March 14, 1940, 10.

_____. "United States Representative at the Vatican," RH, Jan. 14, 1940, 10.

_____ "When and Where Are Roman Catholics Tolerant?" part 1, RH, July 17, 1952, 11.

_____. "Why Roman Catholics Stand Apart," RH, Dec. 2, 1954, 13.

Lee, F., "World Trends," RH, Apr. 4, 1946, 5.

Litch, Josiah, "The Bible its own Interpreter," ST, May 15, 1840, 29.

_____. "The Four Beasts of Daniel VII," RH, June 20, 1854, 161-163.

Littlejohn, W.H., "D'Aubigné's History of the Reformation," RH July 18, 1871, 33.

_____. "The Constitutional Amendment: Or the Sunday, the Sabbath, the Change, and the Restitution," RH, Oct. 22, 1872, 145-146; Oct. 29, 1872, 159; Nov. 5, 1872, 163.

_____. "The Temple in Heaven," RH, March 24, 1885, 167-168.

Lloyd, Ernest, "Catholic Doctrine--A Comparison," PT, July 1, 1930, 3-4.

Longacre, C.S., "Catholics, Protestants, Soon to Work Together," RH, May 26, 1955, 6-7.

_____. "Great Things Are Happening," RH, Apr. 15, 1915, 19.

_____. "Imposition of Double Taxation," Lib, vol. 45, no. 2 (2nd quarter 1950), 28-29.

_____. "The Papacy in Prophecy," RH, Apr. 20, 1939, 19-20.

_____. "Protestants Oppose Parochial Aid From Public Funds," Lib, vol. 30, no. 3 (3rd quarter 1935), 25-26.

_____. "Reasons Why the Proposed Oregon Anti-Parochial School Amendment is Wrong," Lib, vol. 17, no. 5 (4th quarter 1922), 119-122.

_____. "Roman Catholic Attitude Toward Protestants," RH, Nov. 7, 1946, 7-8.

_____. "Shall the Church Sit at the Peace Table?" RH, Feb. 1, 1945, 10-11.

Loughborough, J.N., "The Image of the Beast," RH, Sept. 20, 1853, 85.

Loughborough, J.N., "Inquisition and Papal Intolerance," RH, Sept. 22, 1874, 105-106; Sept. 29, 1874, 105-106.

_____. "Invocation of the Saints and Exaltation of Mary," RH, May 12, 1874, 175.

_____. "A Letter to a Friend on the Seven Churches," RH, March 19, 1857, 153-155.

_____. "Papal and Protestant Bible," RH, Apr. 28, 1874, 159.

_____. "Purgatory and Mass," RH, May 26, 1874, 191; June 2, 1874, 199.

_____. "Similarity of Paganism and Papacy," RH, Apr. 14, 1874, 142-143.

_____. "Temporal Power of the Papacy--Italian and other Testimony," RH, March 24, 1874,

_____. "The Two-Horned Beast," RH, March 21, 1854, 65-67; March 28, 1854, 73-75, 79.

_____. "The Two-Horned Beast of Rev. 13, a Symbol of the United States," RH, June 25, 1857, 57-60; July 2, 1857, 65-68; July 9, 1857, 73-75.

Lowell, C. Stanley, "Shall the State Subsidize Church Schools?" Lib, vol. 55, no. 5 (Sept./Oct. 1960), 11-15.

Maxwell, Arthur S., "Calendar Reform: Recent Investigations in Geneva, Rome and London," RH, Dec. 17, 1936, 3-5.

_____. "A Movement to Secure Christian Unity: The World Conference on Faith and Order," part 5, RH, Nov. 3, 1927, 15-16.

McElhany, J.L., "The United States and the Vatican," RH, Jan. 11, 1940, 4,5.

Meyers, C.K., "In the Grip of Catholicism," RH, May 29, 1930, 11.

Miller, William, "Miller's Letter No. 5--The Bible its own Interpreter," ST, May 15, 1840, 25-26.

Miller, William, "Letter from Bro. Miller," <u>AHSTR</u>, Dec. 18, 1844, 142.

[Millard, D.], "The Inquisition in America," <u>MC</u>, Oct. 19, 1843, 80.

Morton, J.W., "Narrative of Recent Events," <u>RH</u>, Nov. 1, 1853, 129-131.

Montgomery, O., "Come Out of Babylon," <u>RH</u>, Oct. 4, 1917, 9.

Morse, G.W., "Rome Never Changes," <u>RH</u>, Nov. 2, 1886, 679.

Nichol, F.D., "Attitude Toward Catholics," <u>RH</u>, July 4, 1929, 13-14.

_____. "Catholic Authorities on Church-State Relationships," <u>RH</u>, May 13, 1947, 3-4.

_____. "The Catholic Bridge Between Church and State," <u>RH</u>, May 20, 1948, 5-6.

_____. "Catholic Conversions," <u>RH</u>, Aug. 25, 1955, 9-10.

_____. "Catholic Reactions to Protestants United," <u>RH</u>, Apr. 8, 1948, 4-5.

_____. "Comments on Oxford and Edinburgh," <u>RH</u>, Nov. 11, 1937, 9-11.

_____. "Comments on the World Council of Churches," <u>RH</u>, Sept. 23, 1954, 14-15.

_____. "Conversions to Rome," <u>RH</u>, Jan. 28, 1937, 7-9.

_____. "Diplomatic Relations with Vatican," <u>RH</u>, Jan. 6, 1939, 2.

_____. "From the Editor's Mailbag," <u>RH</u>, Oct. 20, 1960, 4-5.

_____. "Is Rome Growing Stronger?" <u>RH</u>, Jan. 7, 1937, 4-6.

_____. "A Latter-Day Sign--Babylon is Fallen," series of 7 articles. <u>RH</u>, March 6, 1930 - Apr. 17, 1930.

Nichol, F.D., "A Notable Conference at Oxford," <u>RH</u>, Oct. 14, 1937, 10-12.

_____. "Notable Happenings of 1929," <u>RH</u>, Jan. 23, 1930, 3-6.

_____. "Our Answer to the Challenge of Rome's Revival," <u>RH</u>, Feb. 4, 1937, 7-8.

_____. "The Pope and Liberty," <u>RH</u>, June 18, 1931, 11.

_____. "Pope Paul Addresses the United Nations," <u>RH</u>, Oct. 21, 1965, 1, 8-9,

_____. "Protestants Organize Against Catholic Legislative Campaign," <u>RH</u>, Apr. 1, 1948, 3-4.

_____. "Rome's Gains and Losses," <u>RH</u>, Jan. 14, 1937, 5-6.

_____. "Rome's Power Revealed in Many Ways," <u>RH</u>, Jan. 21, 9-10.

_____. "Seventh-day Adventist Teachings an Answer to Catholicism and Modernism," <u>RH</u>, Feb. 1, 1934, 3-4.

_____. "Shall We Have a Wandering Sabbath?, part 13, <u>RH</u>, Apr. 25, 1929, 5-6.

_____. "The Trend Toward Rome," part 3, <u>RH</u>, March 29, 1928, 13-14.

_____. "What Do Jurists Say of Catholic Legislative Activity?" <u>RH</u>, Apr. 15, 1948, 4-5.

_____. "Will Adventists Alone Be Saved?" <u>RH</u>, Jan. 10, 1935, 5-6.

_____. "A World Council of Churches," <u>RH</u>, Aug. 11, 1938, 3-4.

_____. "World Council of Churches Convenes," <u>RH</u>, Aug. 26, 1954, 4-6; Sept. 2, 1954, 3-5, 20-21; Sept. 9, 1954, 3-5, 20-21.

Nichols, O., "The Dragon, the Beast, and the False Prophet," <u>RH</u>, March 2, 1852, 98-99.

Odom, Robert L., "Those Diplomatic Relations With the Vatican--Are They Dangerous?" <u>The Watchman Magazine</u>, March 1945, 4-5, 13-14.

Penniman, W., "What Romanism is Doing," <u>RH</u>, May 20, 1880, 322.

Phelps, H.F., "Catholics And Protestants to Elevate the American Sunday," <u>AS</u>, Sept. 7, 1893, 276-277.

_____. "The Present State of Protestantism," <u>RH</u>, Jan. 2, 1900, 2.

Prescott, W.W., "Candid Admissions by a Roman Catholic Historian," <u>RH</u>, Dec. 7, 1911, 6-7.

_____. "The Church Question in Politics," <u>RH</u>, Dec. 14, 1916, 2.

_____. "The Empty Boast of the Roman Catholic Church," <u>RH</u>, Jan. 25, 1912, 9-10.

_____. "Federation Among Catholics," <u>RH</u>, Aug. 23, 1906, 3-4.

_____. "The Official Title of the Pope," <u>Min</u>, vol. 12, no. 3 (March 1939), 17-19,26,46.

_____. "The Papacy and the War: Some of the Benefits Likely to Accrue to the Holy See as the Result of this Great Struggle," <u>RH</u>, Jan. 28, 1915, 3-4.

_____. "The Papacy and the War: The Chastisement of the Nations for their Disloyalty to the Catholic Church," <u>RH</u>, Jan. 21, 1915, 4-6.

_____. "The Pope's Authority over Rulers," <u>RH</u>, July 9, 1908, 3-4.

_____. "The Program of the Papacy," <u>RH</u>, Nov. 30, 1905, 4-5.

_____. "The Relation Between the Church and the State: the Roman Catholic Doctrine," <u>RH</u>, Feb. 18, 1909, 3-4.

_____. "The Religio-Political Principles of the Papacy," <u>RH</u>, Dec. 3, 1908, 4-5.

Prescott, W.W.,"The Roman Catholic Program," RH, Nov. 2, 1911, 7-8.

_____. "Roman Optimism," RH, Feb. 8, 1912, 8.

_____. "Romanism in America and Rome," RH, Dec. 15, 1904, 6.

Price, George McCready, "The Pope Comes to the Defense of Genesis," RH, Apr. 12, 1951, 3-4.

Reaser, G.W., "The Deadly Wound Was Healed," RH, Feb. 5, 1925, 5-6.

Rebok, D.E., "National Council of Churches Meets in Denver," RH, Jan. 22, 1953, 3-4, and Jan. 29, 1953, 6-7.

Roberson, R.W., "The Catholic Party," RH, Oct. 3, 1893, 619.

Robinson, D.E., "Has the Seventh-day Adventist Church Become Babylon?" RH, May 22, 1930, 8-12.

Robinson, J.I., "Spring Council Proceedings, Los Angeles," RH, Apr. 29 1947, 11-15.

Rowell, Alfred L., "The Road to Rome," RH, May 18, 1922, 9.

Sanders, N.G., "Facts vs. Unbelief," RH, Sept. 30, 1858, 150.

Santee, L.D., "The Worship of the Virgin Mary," RH, June 29, 1897, 403.

Scoles, D.E., "The Pope's Crown," RH, Dec. 20, 1906, 10.

Smith, A., "Drunken with the Blood of the Saints," RH, Apr. 3, 1894, 213-214.

_____. "The Ten-Horned Beast of Revelation 13:1-10," RH, Jan. 24, 1888, 51-52.

Smith, L.A., "Babylon's Fall; and the Church's Purification," RH, Nov. 12, 1901, 737.

_____. "The Blair Sunday Bill in Secular Dress," RH, Jan. 7, 1890, 8-9.

Smith, L.A., "The Breckinridge Sunday Bill for the District of Columbia," <u>RH</u>, Jan. 21, 1890, 3.

_____. "The Catholic National Federation," <u>RH</u>, June 30, 1904, 5.

_____. "Dr. McGlynn Excommunicated," <u>RH</u>, July 19, 1887, 454.

_____. "Growth of Papal Prestige," <u>RH</u>, Sept. 18, 1888, 601.

_____. "Increasing Power of the Papacy," <u>RH</u>, March 24, 1903, 5.

_____. "Note and Comment," <u>RH</u>, May 20, 1902, 6.

_____. "The Papacy," <u>RH</u>, Nov. 5, 1901, 720.

_____. "Pope Leo's Encyclical," <u>RH</u>, June 30, 1891, 416.

_____. "The Pope's Jubilee," <u>RH</u>, May 24, 1887, 336.

_____. "The Pope's Jubilee," <u>RH</u>, June 7, 1887, 368.

_____. "Popery in Washington," <u>RH</u>, Feb. 21, 1893, 119.

_____. "The Sabbath and the World's Fair," <u>RH</u>, Sept. 23, 1890, 585.

_____. "Washington in the Lap of Rome," <u>RH</u>, June 5, 1888, 368.

Smith, Uriah, "Catholic Ceremonies of Heathen Origin," <u>RH</u>, Apr. 3, 1888, 216

_____. "Disturbing Voices," <u>RH</u>, Sept. 4, 1888, 568.

_____. "Don't Break the Sabbath," <u>RH</u>, Oct. 24, 1854, 85-87.

_____. "Feel my Paw," <u>RH</u>, Nov. 26, 1889, 744.

_____. "A Good Contest Begun," <u>RH</u>, Jan. 1, 1889, 8.

_____. "In the Question Chair," <u>RH</u>, Jan. 19, 1897, 42.

Smith, Uriah, "In the Question Chair," <u>RH</u>, March 2, 1897, 135.

_____. "In the Question Chair: Motto on the Pope's Tiara," <u>RH</u>, July 23, 1901, 475.

_____. "The Little Horn," <u>RH</u>, Dec. 24, 1857, 52-53.

_____. "The Little Season of Rev. 6:11," <u>RH</u>, Dec. 23, 1873, 9.

_____. "The Message from the Sanctuary," <u>RH</u>, May 20, 1858, 4.

_____. "Our Attitude Toward Roman Catholicism," <u>RH</u>, June 11, 1901, 378-379.

_____. "Politics," <u>RH</u>, Sept. 11, 1856, 152.

_____. "Pope or President," <u>RH</u>, Dec. 1, 1863, 1-2.

_____. "The Pope's Lament," <u>RH</u>, March 24, 1874, 120.

_____. "The Present State of the World," <u>RH</u>, June 20, 1854, 164-165.

_____. "Romanism and Progress," <u>RH</u>, Feb. 8, 1887, 89.

_____. "Rome and the United States," <u>RH</u>, Sept. 22, 1896, 605-606.

_____. "Rome Rules in New York," <u>RH</u>, Jan. 8, 1889, 26.

_____. "The Sanctuary," <u>RH</u>, March 21, 1854, 77-78.

_____. "Showing Her Colors," <u>RH</u>, May 3, 1887, 280.

_____. "A Sly Word for America," <u>RH</u>, Apr. 23, 1895, 265-266.

_____. "The Spirit of Rome," <u>RH</u>, June 12, 1888, 376.

_____. "Sunday Keeping--Is it of Rome?" <u>RH</u>, Sept. 22, 1874, 108.

_____. "Thoughts on Revelation," <u>RH</u>, June 3, 1862, 4-5; July 8, 1862, 44.

Smith, Uriah, "Thoughts on Revelation," RH, Nov. 4, 1862, 180; Nov. 11, 1862, 188; Nov. 18, 1862, 196-197; Dec. 9, 1862, 12; Dec. 16, 1862, 20.

_____. "Thrives on Ignorance," RH, Feb. 23, 1897, 121.

_____. "A Timely Truth," RH, Jan. 2, 1894, 8.

_____. "The Two-Horned Beast--A Review of H.E. Carver," RH, Nov. 20, 1868, 196-197.

_____. "The United States in the Light of Prophecy," RH, Feb. 13, 1872, 68.

_____. "The Vatican and the White House," RH, July 12, 1887, 441.

_____. "Vicarius Filii Dei," RH, May 13, 1875, 157.

_____. "A Voice from the Dark Ages," RH, Sept. 8, 1896, 569.

Snook, B.F., "The Holy Sabbath of the Lord," RH, June 19, 1860, 33-34.

Snow, Charles M., "The American Federation of Catholic Societies," RH, Sept. 12, 1912, 6-8.

_____. "American Federation of Catholic Societies," Lib, vol. 6, no. 4 (4th quarter, 1911), 24-26.

_____. "The Roman Catholic International Eucharistic Congress," RH, Sept. 29, 1910, 12-14; Oct. 6, 1910, 6-8.

_____. "Roman Purpose and American Liberties," RH, June 23, 1910, 10-11.

_____. "Rome Never Changes," series of 15 articles, RH, Nov. 5, 1914 - March 4, 1915.

_____. Rome's Substitute for Christ," PM, vol. 1, no. 1 (2nd quarter, 1909), 36-41.

[Southard, N.J.], "The Home of Wm. Miller," MC, Oct. 26, 1843, 88.

_____. "The Mark of the Beast," MC, Oct. 26, 1843, 84-85.

Spangler, J.R., "Lessons From a Carthusian Monastery," Min, vol. 38, no. 8 (Sept., 1965), 26-28, 32.

Spicer, W.A., "The Catholic Church and the Bible," RH, Aug. 27, 1936, 10-11.

_____. "The Papal Power of Rome," RH, Dec. 30, 1920, 2, 6.

_____. "President Sends Ambassador to Pope," PT, June 1, 1940, 1-3.

_____. "The Prophecy of Daniel 7," RH Sept. 23, 1915, 4-5; Sept. 30, 1915, 4-5; Oct. 7, 1915, 4-5; Oct. 14, 1915, 4-5.

Starr, George B., "Rome's Hold Upon the United States," RH, Feb. 18, 1890, 103.

Stephenson, J.M., "The Number of the Beast," RH, Nov. 29, 1853, 166.

_____. "The Scarlet-colored Beast," RH, Jan. 31, 1854, 14-15.

Stone, Albert, "Authority for Sunday-Keeping," RH, March 10, 1874, 99.

Storrs, George, "Exposition of Daniel 7th Chapter," MC, May 4, 1843, 34-37.

_____. "Exposition of Daniel 7th Chapter, Or, The Vision of the Four Beasts," RH, Feb. 3, 1853, 150-151; Feb. 17, 1853, 153-154.

_____. "Exposition of Daniel VII, Or, The Vision of the Four Beasts," RH, Nov. 14, 1854, 108-110.

_____. "Exposition of Daniel VII, Or, The Vision of the Four Beasts," RH, Apr. 23, 1857, 194-196.

_____. "Exposition of Daniel 8th Chapter," MC, May 4, 1843, 37-44.

_____. "Will The Papacy Have Dominion Again?" MC, Oct. 19, 1843, 79.

Tefft, B.E., "Toward Rome," RH, May 24, 1887, 327.

Tenney, G.C., "A Liberal Catholic," <u>RH</u>, Oct. 15, 1895, 661.

_____. "The Papal Encyclical," <u>RH</u>, Feb. 5, 1895, 86-87.

_____. "Rome is Waking Up," <u>RH</u>, Aug. 27, 1895, 549.

Thompson, Charles, "Who Changed the Sabbath?" <u>RH</u>, Nov. 24, 1921, 3-6.

Trummer, Max, "Do Scriptures Teach the Primacy of Peter?" <u>RH</u>, March 5, 1953, 3-4; March 12, 1953, 4-5.

Utt, Walter C., "Quanta Cura and the Syllabus of Errors," <u>Lib</u>, vol. 55, no. 6 (Nov./Dec. 1960), 12-13; 32-35.

Votaw, H.H., "Are Americans Indifferent?" <u>Lib</u>, vol. 38, no. 1 (1st quarter 1943), 28.

_____. "No Discrimination Against Catholics," <u>Lib</u>, vol. 31, no. 3 (3rd quarter 1936), 32.

Vuilleumier, J., "The Coming Crisis in Europe," <u>RH</u>, July 16, 1889, 450-451; July 23, 1889, 467-468.

Waggoner, J.H., "The American Sentinel, <u>AS</u>, Jan. 1886, 1-2.

_____. "Babylon is Fallen," <u>RH</u>, Sept. 5, 1854, 29-30.

_____. "Policy of Romanism," <u>RH</u>, Oct. 7, 1875, 109.

Walsh, Mary E., "Approaching the Intelligent Catholic," <u>Min</u>, vol. 9, no. 4 (Apr. 1936), 5-6.

_____. "How Shall We Reach Roman Catholics?" <u>RH</u>, Oct. 5, 1961, 1, 4-5.

_____. "Important Questions Answered on How to Work for Catholics," <u>RH</u>, Nov. 2, 1961, 7-8.

_____. "Meeting Catholic Dogma," <u>RH</u>, Oct. 26, 1961, 6-7.

_____. "Reaching the Catholic Mind," <u>RH</u>, Oct. 19, 1961, 3-4.

Ward, Dana, "To the Conference of Christians," <u>ST</u>, Jan. 1, 1842, 146-147.

Weatherby, R., "No Antagonism to Rome," <u>RH</u>, March 22, 1887, 179.

Weeks, A., "The Catholics Preparing," <u>RH</u>, Apr. 29, 1884, 274-275.

Wensell, Niels, "How to Approach Catholics," <u>Min</u>, vol. 23, no. 7 (July 1950), 6.

Westcott, A. Delos, "What Sunday-Keeping Really Means," <u>AS</u>, Sept. 21, 1894, 301-302.

White, Ellen G., "An Address in Regard to the Sunday Movement," <u>RH</u> Extra, Dec. 24, 1889, 2-3.

_____. "The Approaching Crisis," <u>RH</u> Extra, Dec. 11, 1888, 4-5.

_____. "Character and Aims of the Papacy," <u>AS</u>, Apr. 19, 1894, 121-123; Apr. 26, 1894, 129-131.

_____. "David's Prayer," <u>RH</u>, Dec. 18, 1888, 785-787.

_____. "The False and the True," <u>Bible Training School</u> Feb. 1, 1913, 143-144.

_____. "In the Spirit and Power of Elias," concl., <u>RH</u>, Nov. 20, 1913, 3-4.

_____. "Mission Fields at Home," <u>Pacific Union Recorder</u>, Apr. 21, 1910, 1-2.

_____. "The Papacy--Its Character and Aims, <u>PT</u>, July 1, 1930, 1-3.

_____. "Roman Catholicism--Its Growing Power: The Character and Aims of the Papacy," <u>PT</u>, Feb. 15, 1927, 1-3.

White, James, "Babylon," <u>RH</u>, June 10, 1852, 20-24.

_____. "The one hundred and forty-four thousand," <u>RH</u>, May 9, 1854, 123-124.

_____. "Our Faith and Hope; or, Reasons why we Believe as we Do," <u>RH</u>, Feb. 8, 1870, 49-51.

White, James, "The Sabbath," RH, Oct. 30, 1856, 201-204.

_____. "The Seven Churches," RH, Oct. 16, 1856, 188-189, 192.

_____. "The Seven Churches, Seven Seals, and Four Beasts," RH, Feb. 12, 1857, 116-117.

_____. "Signs of the Times," RH, Sept. 8, 1853, 65-67, 70-71.

_____. "The Third Angel's Message," RH, Aug. 14, 1856, 116.

_____. "Thoughts on Revelation," RH, June 3, 1862, 4-5; July 8, 1862, 44.

Wightman, John S., "A Significant Movement--Federation Among the Catholics," RH, Aug. 23, 1906, 9-12.

Wilcox, F.M., "About Catholics," part 2, RH, July 14, 1949, 7, 12.

_____. "The Author of the First-Day Sabbath," RH, Dec. 10, 1936, 2.

_____. "Catholics and Protestants Possess Equal Rights," Lib, vol. 8, no. 4 (4th quarter, 1913), 151-153.

_____. "The Church and Politics," RH, Sept. 13, 1928, 3.

_____. "Come Out of Her, My People," RH, May 11, 1922, 7-8.

_____. "Gathering Clouds," RH, Aug. 18, 1921, 7.

_____. "The Glorious Consummation," no. 7, RH, Apr. 15, 1920, 2-4.

_____. "The Glorious Consummation," no. 11, RH, May 13, 1920, 2, 5-6.

_____. "The Interchurch World Movement," RH, June 3, 1920, 2, 11-12.

_____. "Love Versus Hate," RH, Jan. 22., 1942, 2.

Wilcox, F.M., "The Papacy in Prophecy," RH, Apr. 11, 1929, 3-4.

_____. "The Papacy in Prophecy," RH, Feb. 29, 1940, 2, 10.

_____. "Papal Sovereignty Restored," RH, Feb. 28, 1929, 3-10.

_____. "The Peace of the World: Belligerent Nations Arrange Armistice," RH, Nov. 28, 1918, 1-3.

_____. "The Peace of the World," part 4, RH, Dec. 19, 1918, 3-6.

_____. "Politics and Prohibition," RH, Sept. 27, 1928, 3-4.

_____. "The Pope as Peacemaker," RH, May 4, 1916, 2, 5.

_____. "Pope Pius as Peacemaker," RH, Oct. 30, 1941, 2, 12.

_____. "'The Remnant Church' Not Babylon," RH, March 16, 1916, 3-4.

_____. "Restoration of Papal Sovereignty," RH, March 7, 1940, 2, 11.

_____. "The Roman Catholic Peril," RH, May 9, 1912, 8-10.

_____. "Temperance and Prohibition: The Coming Presidential Election," RH, Aug. 2, 1928, 3.

_____. "The Seal of the Living God," RH, Oct. 11, 1945, 7-9.

_____. "Who Changed the Sabbath?" RH, June 29, 1944, 1-3.

Williamson, T.R., "The First Church--Can the Roman Catholic Church Rightfully Claim that Designation?" RH, Nov. 29, 1887, 743.

Wood, Kenneth H., "The Fake Oath," RH, Sept. 15, 1960, 5.
_____. "More on Pope Paul's Journey," RH, Feb. 13, 1964, 12-13.

Wood, Kenneth H., "The President-elect," <u>RH</u>, Dec. 8, 1960, 3.

_____. "The Vatican Newspaper Editorial," <u>RH</u>, June 30, 1960, 4.

Yost, Frank H., "On the Religious Front," <u>RH</u>, Nov. 3, 1949, 19.

_____. "The Press Comments on the Roosevelt-Spellman Dispute," <u>Lib</u>, vol. 44, no. 4 (4th quarter 1949), 13-28.

4. Unpublished Sources

a. Research papers

Cottrell, Raymond F., "Pioneer Views on Daniel Eleven and Armageddon," rev. ed, 1951. Research paper presented to the Bible Research Fellowship. Heritage Room, Andrews Univ., Berrien Springs, MI.

Eldridge, Robert M., "A Comparison of Positions on Daniel 11", n.d.. Research paper presented to the Bible Research Fellowship. Heritage Room, Andrews Univ., Berrien Springs, MI.

Froom, Leroy E., "Historical Setting and Background of the Term 'Daily'", 1951. Research paper presented to the Bible Research Fellowship. Heritage Room, Andrews Univ., Berrien Springs, MI.

Longacre, C.S., "A Review of Professor Prescott's Points and Positions." Gen. Conf. Arch.: RG 52, Religious Liberty Dep. - Longacre, C.S. Ref. Files.

Peterson, Stanley R., "A Syllabus and Study Guide for a Survey Course in Church History." M.A. thesis, SDA Theol. Sem., 1950.

Prescott, W.W., "The Interpretation of the Number of the Beast." Unpubl. paper. Gen. Conf. Arch.: GC 261, Review and Herald 666 Committee.

Vuilleumier, Jean, "The King of the North--Daniel 11:40-45." Research paper presented to the Bible Research Fellowship. Heritage Room, Andrews Univ., Berrien Springs, MI.

Wilcox, M.C., "The Beast Power of the Revelation." Paper presented during the 1919 Bible Conference. Transcripts of the 1919 Bible Conference, Heritage Room, Andrews Univ., Berrien Springs, MI.

Wearner, Alonzo J., "The Daily," n.d. Research paper presented to the Bible Research Fellowship. Heritage Room, Andrews Univ., Berrien Springs, MI.

b. Minutes, letters, and miscellaneous

General Conference of Seventh-day Adventists annual Statistical Reports, 1915-1965.

General Conference Working Policy. Hagerstown, RHPA, 1992.

Interview with W.W. Prescott in the office of the General Conference president, April 16, 1936. Gen. Conf. Arch.: RG 261, Book Editorial Files, Number of the Beast Committee, 1943.

Letter L.E. Froom to W.E. Howell, Aug. 29, 1938. Gen. Conf. Arch.: RG 261, Book Editorial Files, Number of the Beast Committee 1943.

Letter J.L. McElhany to Dr. Rufus W. Weaver, March 4, 1940. Gen. Conf. Arch.: RG 11, Presidential, General Files, 140.

Letter J. Nüssbaum to R.R. Figuhr, Nov. 27, 1961. Gen. Conf. Arch.

Letter C.F. Thomas (editor of Baltimore Catholic Review) to W.W. Prescott, June 8, 1914. Gen. Conf. Arch.: PC 21, Prescott, W.W., Protestant Magazine Ref. Files, ca. 1909-1916: Personal.

Letter William C. White to J.H. Waggoner, Apr. 2, 1889. Gen. Conf. Arch.

Letter Frank H. Yost to W.E. Howell, Oct. 18, 1938. Gen. Conf. Arch.: RG 261, Book Editorial Files, Number of the Beast Committee 1943.

Minutes Board of Trustees of the RHPA, Apr. 8, 1915. Gen. Conf. Arch.

Minutes Board of Trustees of the RHPA, Apr. 22, 1915. Gen. Conf. Arch.

Minutes Board of Trustees of the RHPA, Nov. 30, 1915. Gen. Conf. Arch.

Minutes of the Committee on 666, Jan. 17, 1943. Gen. Conf. Arch.: RG 261, Book Editorial Files, Number of the Beast Committee 1943.

Minutes General Conference Committee, Jan. 10, 1940. Gen Conf. Arch.

Minutes General Conference Officers Meeting, Sept. 23, 1942. Gen. Conf. Arch.

Minutes General Conference Officers Meeting, Feb. 11, 1953. Gen Conf. Arch.

Minutes of "Hearing on 666", Aug. 30, 1939. Gen Conf. Arch.: RG 261, Book Editorial Files, Number of the Beast Committee, 1943.

Minutes of the President's Executive Advisory, Sept. 24, 1974 and March 25, 1975. Gen. Conf. Arch.

1919 Bible Conference transcripts. Heritage Rooom, Andrews Univ., Berrien Springs, MI.

Sermon by J.L. McElhany in the Takoma Park Church, Jan. 13, 1940. Gen Conf. Arch.: RG 11 Presidential, General Files, 140.

Seventh-day Adventist Yearbook. Silver Spring, MD: GC of SDA, 1990.

"Vatican Envoy" folder in Gen. Conf. Arch.: RG 52, Rel. Lib. Files R. 762.

II Secondary Sources

1. Books

Ahlstrom, Sydney E., <u>A Religious History of the American People</u>. New Haven: Yale University Press, 1972.

Anderson, Godfrey T., "Sectarianism and Organization--1846-1864." Chap. in: Gary Land, ed., <u>Adventism in America, 36-65</u>. Grand Rapids, MI: William B. Eerdmans Publishing Co, 1984.

Anderson, Godfrey T., <u>Outrider of the Apocalypse: Life and Times of Joseph Bates</u>. Mountain View, Cal.: PPPA, 1972.

Anderson, Ruth B., <u>Women and Temperance</u>. Philadelphia: Temple University Press, 1981.

Arthur, David T., "Millerism." Chap. in: Edwin S. Gaustad, ed., <u>The Rise of Adventism: Religion and Society in Mid-Nineteenth Century America</u>, 154-172. New York: Harper and Row Publishers, 1974.

Ball, Bryan W., <u>The English Connection: The Puritan Roots of Seventh-day Adventist Belief</u>. Cambridge: James Clarke, 1981.

_____. <u>The Great Expectation: Eschatological Thought in English Protestantism to 1660</u>. A. Heiko, ed., <u>Studies in the History of Christian Thought</u>, vol. XII. Leiden: E.J. Brill, 1975.

Bauckham, Richard, <u>Tudor Apocalypse</u>. Oxford: The Sutton Courtenay Press, 1978.

Beiser, J. Ryan, <u>The Vatican Council and the American Secular Newspapers, 1869-70</u>. Washington, DC: The Catholic University of America Press, 1941.

Best, G.F.A., "Popular Protestantism in Victorian Britain." Chap. in: R. Robson, ed., <u>Ideas and Institutions of Victorian Britain</u>, 115-142. New York: Barnes & Noble, Inc., 1967.

Billington, Ray Allen, <u>The Protestant Crusade, 1800-1860</u>. New York: Macmillan Co, 1938.

Blanshard, Paul, <u>American Freedom and Catholic Power</u>. Boston: The Beacon Press, 1958, rev. ed.

Blocker Jr., Jack S., <u>American Temperance Movements: Cycles of Reform</u>. Boston: Twayne Publishers, 1989.

Bokenkotter, Thomas S., <u>A Concise History of the Catholic Church</u>. Garden City: Doubleday & Company, 1977.

Brion, David, "Some Themes of Countersubversion: An Analysis of Anti-Masonic, Anti-Catholic and Anti-Mormon Literature." Chap. in: Richard O. Curry and Thomas M. Brown, eds., <u>The Fear of Subversion in American History</u>, 61-77. New York: Holt, Rinehart and Winston, Inc., 1972.

Broderick, John F., <u>Documents of the Vatican Council I, 1869-1870</u>. Collegeville, Minn.: The Liturgical Press, 1971.

Brown, Thomas M., "The Image of the Beast: Anti-Papal Rhetoric in Colonial America." Chap. in: Richard O. Curry and Thomas M. Brown, eds., <u>The Fear of Subversion in American History</u>, 1-20. New York: Holt, Rinehart and Winston, Inc., 1972.

Bull, Malcolm and Keith Lockart, <u>Seeking a Sanctuary: Seventh-day Adventists and the American Dream</u>. San Francisco: Harper & Row, 1989.

Bury, J.B., <u>History of the Papacy in the 19th Century</u>. Augmented ed. New York: Schocken Books, 1964.

Butler, Jonathan M., "Adventism and the American Experience." Chap. in: Edwin S. Gaustad, ed., <u>The Rise of Adventism: Religion and Society in Mid-Nineteenth Century America</u>, 173-206. New York: Harper and Row Publishers, 1974.

Cadwallader, E.M., <u>A History of Seventh-day Adventist Education</u>. Lincoln, Nebr.: Union College Press, 1958.

Canevin, J.F. Regis, <u>An Examination Historical and Statistical into Losses and Gains of the Catholic Church in the United States from 1790-1910</u>. Pitsburgh, 1912.

Canright, Dudley M., <u>Seventh-day Adventism Renounced</u>.
New York: F.H. Revell, 1889.

Capp, B.S., <u>The Fifth Monarchy Men: A Study in
Seventeenth Century Millenarianism</u>. Totowa, N.J.:
Rowman and Littlefield, 1972.

Carlen, Claudia, <u>The Papal Encyclicals: 1740-1878</u>.
Wilington, N.C.: McGrath Pub. Co., 1981.

_____. <u>The Papal Encyclicals: 1878-1903</u>. The Pierian
Press, 1990.

Carlow, George, <u>A Defense of the Sabbath, in Reply to
Ward on the Fourth Commandment</u>. New York: Publ. by
Paul Stillman for the American Tract Society, 1847.

Carner, Vern, Sakae Kubo, and Kurt Rice, "Bibliographical Essay." Chap. in: Edwin S. Gaustad, ed.,
<u>The Rise of Adventism: Religion and Society in Mid-
nineteenth-century America</u>, 207-317. New York:
Harper & Row, 1974.

Chadwick, Owen, <u>The Popes and the European Revolution</u>.
Oxford: Clarendon Press, 1981.

Cohn, Norman C., <u>The Pursuit of the Millennium</u>. Rev. and
exp. ed. New York: Oxford University Press, 1970.

Commager, Henry S., <u>The American Mind--An Interpretation
of American Thought and Character Since the 1880s</u>.
New Haven: Yale University Press, 1950.

Cook, Norman P., <u>A Brief History of William Miller, the
Great Pioneer in the Adventual Faith</u>. Boston:
Advent Christian Publication Society, 1895.

Cottrell, R.F., "The Theologian of the Sabath." Chap.
in: Harry Leonard, ed., <u>J.N. Andrews--The Man and
the Mission</u>, 105-130. Berrien Springs, MI: Andrews
University Press, 1985.

Cross, Whitney R., <u>The Burnt-Over District: The Social
and Intellectual History of Enthusiastic Religion
in Western New York, 1800-1850</u>. Ithaca, N.Y.:
Cornell University Press, 1950.

Curry, Lerond, <u>Protestant-Catholic Relations in America</u>.
Lexington: The University of Kentucky Press, 1972.

Dabrowski, Rajmund L., "M.B. Czechowski--his Early Life until 1851." Chap. in: Rajmund L. Dabrowski and B.B. Beach, eds., <u>Michael Belina Czechowski 1818-1876</u>, 78-99. Warsaw: Znaki Publishing House, 1979.

_____. "The Sojourn of M.B. Czechowski on the American Continent." Chap. in: Rajmund L. Dabrowski and B.B. Beach, eds., <u>Michael Belina Czechowski 1818-1876</u>, 100-159. Warsaw: Znaki Publishing House, 1979.

Damsteegt, P. Gerard, "Among Sabbatarian Adventists." Chap. in Frank B. Holbrook, ed., <u>Doctrine of the Sanctuary--A Historical Survey</u>, 17-56. Silver Spring, MD: Biblical Research Institute, Gen. Conf. of SDA, 1989.

_____. <u>Toward the Theology of Mission of the Seventh-day Advent Church</u>. Grand Rapids, Mich.: Wm. B. Eerdmans Publishing Co., 1977.

Davis, Lawrence B., <u>Immigrants, Baptists and the Protestant Mind in America</u>. Urbana, Ill.: University of Illinois Press, 1973.

Delafield, D.A., <u>Ellen G. White in Europe, 1885-1887</u>. Washington, DC: RHPA, 1975.

Denzinger, H., <u>Enchiridion Symbolorum Definitionum et Declarationum de Rebus Fedei et Morum</u>. Freiburg i.Br., 1952.

Dickinson, J.C., <u>The Later Middle Ages</u>. New York: Barnes & Noble, 1979.

Dolan, Jay P., <u>The American Catholic Experience: A History from Colonial Times to the Present</u>. New York: Doubleday and Co., Inc., 1985.

Durand, Eugene F., <u>Yours in the Blessed Hope</u>. Washington, D.C: RHPA, 1980.

Eberhardt, C.E., <u>A Summary of Catholic History</u>, 2 vols. St. Louis, MO,: Herder, 1961-62.

Ellis, John T., <u>American Catholicism</u>. 2nd. ed. Chicago: University of Chicago Press, 1969.

Feldberg, Michael, <u>The Philadelphia Riots of 1844; A Study of Ethnic Conflict</u>. Westport, Conn.: Greenwood, 1975.

Fell, Marie Leono, <u>The Foundations of Nativism in American Textbooks, 1783-1860</u>. Washington, D.C., 1941.

Flannery, Austin, ed., <u>Vatican Council II: The Conciliar and Post Conciliar Documents</u>, study ed. Northport, N.Y.: Costello Publishing Company, 1987.

Froom, Leroy E., "History of the Interpretation of Daniel." Chap. in: F.D. Nichol, ed., <u>Seventh-day Adventist Bible Commentary</u>, vol. 4, 39-78. Washington, DC: RHPA, 1955.

_____. <u>Movement of Destiny</u>. Washington, DC: RHPA, 1971.

_____. <u>The Prophetic Faith of our Fathers</u>. 4 vols. Washington, DC: RHPA, 1946-1954.

Gale, Robert L., <u>The Urgent Voice</u>. Washington, DC: RHPA, 1975.

Gaustad, Edwin S., <u>Historical Atlas of Religion in America</u>. New York: Harper & Row, Publ., 1962.

Goodspeed, Eric J., <u>The Apostolic Fathers</u>. New York: Harper & Brothers, Publ., 1950.

Gorman, Robert, <u>Catholic Apologetical Literature in the United States--1784-1858</u>. Washington, D.C.: The Catholic University Press, 1939.

Hales, E.E.Y., <u>The Catholic Church in the Modern World</u>. Garden City: Hannover House, 1958.

Handy, Robert T., <u>A Christian America: Protestant Hopes and Historical Realities</u>. New York: Oxford University Press, 2nd ed., 1984.

_____. <u>A History of the Churches in the United States and Canada</u>. New York: Oxford University Press, 1977.

Hall, David D., <u>World of Wonder, Days of Judgement: Popular Beliefs in Early New England</u>. New York: Alfred A. Knopf, 1989.

Hatch, Nathan O., <u>The Democratization of American Christianity</u>. New Haven: Yale University Press, 1989.

Hennesey, James J., <u>American Catholics: A History of the Roman Catholic Community in the United States</u>. New York: Oxford University Press, 1981.

_____. <u>The First Council of the Vatican: The American Experience</u>. New York: Herder and Herder, 1963.

Heylyn, Peter, <u>The History of the Sabbath in Two Books</u>. London, 1636.

Higham, John, <u>Strangers in the Land: Patterns of American Nativism, 1860-1925</u>. New Brunswick, N.J.: Rutgers University Press, 1955.

Hill, Christopher, <u>Antichrist in Seventeenth Century England</u>. Rev. ed. London: Verso, 1990.

Holbrook, Frank B., ed., <u>Doctrine of the Sanctuary--A Historical Survey</u>. Silver Spring, MD: Biblical Research Institute, Gen. Conf. of SDA, 1989.

Hudson, Winthrop S., <u>Religion in America</u>. 4th ed. New York: Macmillan Publishing Company, 1987.

Johns, Warren L., <u>Dateline Sunday, U.S.A.--The Story of Three and a Half Centuries of Sunday-law Battles in America</u>. Mountain View: PPPA, 1967.

Johnson, Alvin W., and Frank H. Yost, <u>Separation of Church and State in the United States</u>. Minneapolis: University of Minnesota Press, 1948.

Johnson, Albert C., <u>Advent Christian History: A Concise Narrative of the Origin and Progress, Doctrine and Work of this Body of Believers</u>. Boston: Advent Christian Publication Society, 1918.

Jordan, Philip D., <u>The Evangelical Alliance for the United States of America, 1847-1900: Ecumenism, Identity and the Religion of the Republic</u>. New York: The Edwin Mellen Press, 1982.

Kellogg, J.H., <u>The Living Temple</u>. Battle Creek, MI: Good Health Publishing Company, 1903.

Kinzer, Donald L., <u>An Episode in Anti-Catholicism: The American Protective Association</u>. Seattle: University of Washington Press, 1964.

Knight, George R., <u>Angry Saints</u>. Hagerstown: RHPA, 1989.

_____. <u>From 1888 to Apostasy - The Case of A.T. Jones</u>. Hagerstown: RHPA, 1987.

Labland, David N., and Dobarah H. Heinbuc, <u>Blue Laws: The History, Economics, and Politics of Sunday-Closing Laws</u>. Lexington, Mass.: Lexington Books, 1987.

Land, Gary, "Coping with Change." Chap. in: Gary Land, ed., <u>Adventism in America</u>, 208-230. Grand Rapids, MI: William B. Eerdmans Publishing Co., 1984.

_____. "Shaping the Modern Church; 1906-1930." Chap. in Gary Land, ed., <u>Adventism in America</u>, 139-169. Grand Rapids, MI: William B. Eerdmans Publishing Co., 1984.

Latreille, A., <u>L'Eglise Catholique et la Révolution Française</u>. 2 vols. Paris: Les Editions du Cerf, 1970.

Leonard, Harry, ed., <u>J.N. Andrews--the Man and the Mission</u>. Berrien Springs: Andrews University Press, 1985.

Lewis, Abraham H., <u>A Critical History of Sunday Legislation from 321 to 1888 A.D.</u>. New York: D. Appleton and Company, 1888.

Lindén, Ingemar, <u>1844 and the Shut Door Problem</u>. Vol. 35 in <u>Acta Universitatis Upsaliensis</u>, 1982.

Loughborough, J.N., <u>Rise and Progress of Seventh-day Adventists</u>. Battle Creek: General Conference of the Seventh-day Adventists, 1892.

Manning, Henry, <u>The Temporal Power of the Vicar of Jesus Christ</u>. London: J.H. Parker, 1862.

Martin, W.R., <u>The Truth About Seventh-day Adventism</u>. London: Marshall Morgan and Scott Ltd, 1960.

Maynard, Theodore, <u>The Story of American Catholicism</u>. New York: The Macmillan Co., 1941.

Maxwell, C. Mervyn, "Joseph Bates and Seventh-day Adventist Theology." Chap. in: Kenneth A. Strand, ed., The Sabbath in Scripture and History, 352-363. Washington, DC: RHPA, 1982.

McAvoy, Thomas T., A History of the Catholic Church in the United States. Notre Dame, Ind.: University of Notre Dame Press, 1969.

McMaster, John Bach, A History of the People of the United States, From the Revolution to the Civil War. 8 vols. New York: D. Appleton and Company, 1883-1913.

Merle d'Aubigné, Histoire de la Réformation du seizième siècle. 5 vols., 1835-1853; publ. in English as History of the Great Reformation of the Sixteenth Century, 1838-1841.

Morill, Milo T., A History of the Christian Denomination in America. Dayton: The Christian Publishing Association, 1912.

Mosheim, Johann L., Institutiones Historiae Ecclesiasticae Antiquae et Recentioris. 6 vols., 1755; English translation: An Ecclesiastical History, Ancient and Modern, from the Birth of Christ to the Beginning of the Eighteenth Century. 6 vols., 1819.

Mourret, Fernand, A History of the Catholic Church, vol. VII: Period of the French Revolution--1775-1823. St. Louis, MO: B. Herder Book Co., 1955.

Mourret, Fernand, A History of the Catholic Church, vol. VIII: Period of the Early Nineteenth Century--1823-1878. St. Louis, MO: B. Herder Book Co., 1957.

Mueller, F.K., "The Architect of Adventist Doctrines." Chap. in: Harry Leonard, ed., J.N. Andrews--The Man and the Mission, 75-104. Berrien Springs, MI: Andrews Univ. Press, 1985.

Mustard, Andrew G., James White and SDA Organization: Historical Development, 1844-1881. Berrien Springs, MI: Andrews University Press, 1987.

Myers, Gustavus, History of Bigotry in the United States. New York: Capricorn Books, 1960.

Neufeld, Don. F., "Biblical Interpretation in the Advent Movement." Chap. in: G. Hyde, ed., <u>Symposium on Biblical Hermeneutics</u>, 109-125. Washington, DC: GC of SDA, 1974.

_____. ed., <u>Seventh-day Adventist Encyclopedia</u>. Washington, DC: RHPA, 1976. s.v.: "Calendar Reform," 183-186; "The Daily," 319-323; "Development of Organization of SDA Church," 1042-1054; "Millerite Movement," 892-898; "William Miller," 889-891.

Nichol, F.D., <u>Ellen G. White and Her Critics</u>. Washington, D.C.: RHPA, 1951.

_____. "The Increasing Timeliness of the Threefold Message." Chap. in: <u>Our Firm Foundation</u>, vol. 1, 543-622. Washington, DC: RHPA, 1953.

_____. <u>The Midnight Cry: A Defense of the Character and Conduct of William Miller and the Millerites, who Mistakenly Believed that the Second Coming of Christ would take place in the year 1844</u>. Washington, DC: RHPA, 1944.

Niebuhr, H. Richard, <u>The Kingdom of God in America</u>. New York: Harper & Row, Publishers, 1937; Torchbook ed., 1959.

Numbers, Ronald L., <u>Prophetess of Health: A Study of Ellen G. White</u>. New York: Harper & Row, 1976. Rev. ed. 1992.

Olbricht, Thomas H., "Biblical Primitiveness in American Scholarship, 1670-1870." Chap. in: Richard T. Hughes, ed., <u>The American Quest for the Primitive Church</u>, 81-98. Urbano: University of Illinois Press, 1988.

Olmstead, Clifton E., <u>History of Religion in the United States</u>. Englewood Cliffs, N.J.: Prentice Hall, Inc., 1960.

Olsen, A.V., <u>Through Crisis to Victory, 1888-1901</u>. Washington, DC: RHPA, 1966.

Olsen, M.E., <u>Origin and Progress of Seventh-day Adventists</u>. Washington, D.C.: RHPA, 1925.

Olsen, V. Norskov, <u>Papal Supremacy and Democracy</u>. Loma Linda, Cal.: Loma Linda University Press, 1987.

Pettibone, Dennis, "The Sunday Law Movement." Chap. in: Gary Land, ed., <u>The World of Ellen G. White</u>, 112-128. Washington: RHPA, 1987.

<u>Progress of the Catholic Church in America and the Great Columbian Catholic Congress of 1893</u>. Chicago: J.S. Hyland & Company, 1897.

Raab, Earl, ed., <u>Religious Conflict in America</u>. Garden City: Doubleday and Comp., Inc., 1964.

Radice, Betty, ed., <u>The Letters of Pliny the Younger</u>. Harmondsworth: Penguin Books, 1975 ed.

Reynolds, Keld J., "The Church under Stress, 1931-1960." Chap in: Gary Land, ed., <u>Adventism in America,</u> 170-207. Grand Rapids, MI: William B. Eerdmans Publ., 1984.

Roberts, Alexander and James Donaldson, eds., <u>The Ante-Nicene Fathers</u>. Edinburgh: T&T Clark; Grand Rapids, MI: Wm. B. Eerdmans Publ. Comp., 1989 reprint.

Robinson, Dores E., <u>The Story of Our Health Message: The Origin, Character and Development of Health Education in the Seventh-day Adventist Church</u>. Nashville, Tenn.: SPA, 1955.

Robinson, Virgil, <u>James White</u>. Washington, D.C.: RHPA, 1976.

Rowe, David L., <u>Thunder and Trumpets: Millerites and Dissenting Religion in Upstate New York</u>. Chico, Cal.: Scholars Press, 1985.

Ryan, John A., and Francis J. Boland, <u>Catholic Principles of Politics</u>. New York: The Macmillan Co, 1948.

_____. and M.I. Millar, <u>The State and the Church</u>. New York: The Macmillen Co., 1922.

Sandeen, Ernest, "Millennialism." Chap. in: Edwin S. Gaustad, ed., <u>The Rise of Adventism: Religion and Society in Mid-Nineteenth Century America</u>, 104-118. New York: Harper & Row, Publishers, 1974.

Sandeen, Ernest, The Roots of Fundamentalism: British and American Millenarianism, 1800-1930. Chicago: University of Chicago Press, 1970.

Sanford, Elias B., Origin and History of the Federal Council of the Churches of Christ in America. Hartford, Conn.: The S.S. Scranton Company, 1916.

Schwartz, Michael, Anti-Catholicism in America. Huntington, IN: Our Sunday Visitor, 1984.

Schwarz, R.W., Light Bearers to the Remnant. Boise, ID.: PPPA, 1979.

Sears, Clara E., Days of Delusion: A Strange Bit of History. Boston: Houghton Mifflin Company, 1924.

Seventh Day Baptists in Europe and America: Historical Papers. 2 vols. Plainfield, N.J.: Seventh Day Baptist General Conference, 1910.

Shepperson, George, "The Comparative Study of Millenarian Movements." Chap. in: Sylvia Thrupp, ed., Millennial Dreams in Action, 44-52. The Hague: Mouton & Co, Publ., 1974.

Smoot, Joseph G., "Andrew's Role in Seventh-day Adventist History." Chap. in: Harry Leonard, ed., J.N. Andrews--The Man and the Mission, 1-13. Berrien Springs, MI: Andrews University Press, 1985.

Spalding, Arthur W., Origin and History of Seventh-day Adventists. 4 vols. Washington, D.C.: RHPA, 1961.

Spicer, William A., Our Story of Missions. Mountain View, Cal.: PPPA, 1921.

Stokes, Anson Phelps and Leo Pfeffer, Church and State in the United States. Westport, Con: Greenwood Press, Publishers, 1975.

Strong, Josiah, Our Country: Its Possible Future and its Present Crisis. New York: The Baker & Taylor Co., 1885.

Syme, Eric D., A History of S.D.A. Church-State Relationships in the United States. Mountain View, Cal.: PPPA, 1973.

368

Thomsen, Russel J., *Seventh-day Baptists--their Legacy to Adventists*. Mountain View, Cal.: PPPA, 1971.

Valentine, Gilbert M., *The Shaping of Adventism: The Case of W.W. Prescott*. Berrien Springs, MI: Andrews University Press, 1992.

VandeVere, Emmett K., "Years of Expansion: 1865-1885." Chap. in: Gary Land, ed., *Adventism in America*, 66-94. Grand Rapids: William B. Eerdmans Publishing Company, 1986.

Walters, Robert G., *American Reformers, 1815-1860*. New York: Hill and Wang, 1978.

Wellcome, Isaac, *History of the Second Advent Message and Mission and People*. Yarmouth: by the author, 1874.

Welter, Barbara, "From Maria Monk to Paul Blanshard: A Century of Protestant Anti-Catholicism." Chap. in: Robert N. Bellah and Frederick E. Greenspahn, eds., *Uncivil Religion: Interreligious Hostility in America*, 43-71. New York: The Crossroad Publ. Comp., 1987.

White, Arthur L., *Ellen G. White*. 6 vols. Washington, D.C.: RHPA, 1982-1986.

Williams, George H., *The Radical Reformation*. Philadelphia: The Westminster Press, 1962.

Wilson, G.T., "The Keys of the Future--Or, the Meaning of the Chicago Catholic Congress and the World's Parliament of Religion." Chap. in: Walter R. Houghton, ed., *The Parliament of Religions and Religious Congresses at the World's Columbian Exposition*. Chicago: F.T. Neely, 1893.

The World's Columbian Catholic Congresses and Educational Exhibit. 2 vols. New York: Arno Press, 1978.

Wylie, J.A., *The History of Protestantism*. 3 vols. London: Cassel Peter & Galpin, n.d.

Wynne, John J., ed., *The Great Encyclical Letters of Pope Leo XIII*. New York: Benziger Brothers, 1903.

2. Articles

Anderson, Eric, "Ellen G. White and Reformation Historians." Spectrum, vol. 9, no. 3 (July 1978), 23-26.

Butler, Jonathan, "The World of E.G. White and the End of the World." Spectrum, vol. 10, no. 2 (Aug. 1979), 2-13.

_____. "When Prophecy Fails: The Validity of Apocalypticism." Spectrum, vol. 8, no. 1 (Sept. 1976), 11.

Carroll, Henry King, "The Catholic Dogma of Church Authority." Methodist Quarterly Review, Oct. 1884, 719-730.

Cottrell, Raymond F., "The Bible Research Fellowship." AH, vol. 5, no. 1 (Summer 1978), 39-52.

_____. "The Untold Story of the Bible Commentary," Spectrum, vol. 16, no. 3 (Aug. 1985), 35-51.

Haloviak, Bert and Gary Land, "Ellen G. White and Doctrinal Conflict: Context of the 1919 Bible Conference," Spectrum, vol. 12, no. 4, (June 1982), 25-27.

Jorgenson, L.P., "The Oregon School Law of 1922." Catholic Historical Review, vol. 54, no. 3 (Oct. 1968), 455-466.

Lake, Peter, "The Significance of the Elizabethan Identification of the Pope as Antichrist." Journal of Ecclesiastical History, vol. 31, no. 2 (Apr. 1980), 161-178.

McArthur, Ben, "The 1893 Chicago World's Fair: An Early Test for Adventist Religious Liberty." AH, vol. 2, no. 2, 23-32.

Olbricht, Thomas H., "Christian Connection and Unitarian Relations," Restoration Quarterly, vol. 9, no. 3 (3rd Quarter 1966), 160-186.

Rowe, David L., "A New Perspective on the Burnt-over District: The Millerites in Upstate New York." Church History, vol. 47, no. 4 (Dec. 1978), 408-420.

Thompson, jr, James J, "Southern Baptists and Anti-Catholicism in the 1920s," _Mississippi Quarterly_, vol. 32, no. 4 (Fall 1979), 611-625.

Thurber, Mervin R., "New Edition of 'Daniel and the Revelation'." _Min_, vol. 18, no. 5 (Apr. 1945), 13-15.

_____. "Uriah Smith and the Charge of Plagiarism." _Min_, vol. 18, no. 7 (June 1945), 15-16.

Unruh, T.E., "The Seventh-day Adventist Evangelical Conferences of 1955-1956." _AH_, vol. IV (Winter 1977), 35-46.

White, Arthur L., "Thoughts on Daniel and the Revelation," _Min_, vol. 18, no. 1 (Jan. 1945), 11-14.

Yrigoyen, Charles, jr., "Methodists and Roman Catholics in the 19th Century." _Methodist History_, vol. 28, no. 3 (Apr. 1990), 172-186.

Zurcher, Jean, "A Vindication of Ellen White as Historian." _Spectrum_, vol. 16, no. 3 (Aug. 1985), 21-31.

3. Unpublished Sources

Arthur, David T., "'Come out of Babylon': A Study of Millerite Separatism and Denominationalism." Ph.D. diss., The University of Rochester, 1970.

Arthur, David T., "Joshua V. Himes and the Cause of Adventism; 1839-1845." M.A. thesis, University of Chicago, 1961.

Balharrie, Gordon, "A Study of the Contributions Made to the Seventh-day Adventist Movement by John Nevins Andrews." M.A. thesis, Andrews University, SDA Theol. Sem., 1949.

Bidwhistell, Ira V., "Southern Baptist Perceptions and Responses to Roman Catholics, 1917-1972." Ph.D. diss., The Southern Baptist Theol. Seminary, 1975.

Carmody, Charles J., "The Roman Catholic Catecheses in the United States 1784-1930: A Study of its Theory, Development and Materials." Ph.D. diss., Loyola University of Chicago, 1975.

Carter, Terry C., "Baptist Participation in Anti-Catholic Sentiment and Activities, 1830-1860." Ph.D. diss., Southwestern Baptist Theol. Sem., 1983.

Crumpton, Vacua A., "An Analysis of Southern Baptist Response to Diplomatic Relations Between the United States and the Vatican." Ph.D. diss., Southwestern Baptist Theol. Sem., 1988.

Dean, David A., "Echoes of the Midnight Cry: The Millerite Heritage in the Apolegetics of the Advent Christian Denomination, 1860-1960. Ph.D. diss., Westminster Theol. Sem., 1976.

Dick, Everett N., "The Adventist Crisis of 1843-1844." Ph.D. diss., University of Wisconsin, 1930.

Dunton, Hugh I., "The Millerite Adventists and other Millenarian Groups in Great Britain, 1830-1860." Ph.D. diss., University of London, 1984.

Gane, E.R., "The Arian or Anti-Trinitarian Views Presented in Seventh-day Adventist Literature and the Ellen G. White Answer." M.A. thesis, Andrews University, 1963.

Gilsdorf, A.J.B., "The Puritan Apocalypse: New England Eschatology in the Seventeenth Century." Ph.D. diss., Yale University, 1965.

Gorman, Sister M. Adele Francis, "Federation of Catholic Societies in the United States - 1870-1920." Ph.D. diss., Notre Dame, Ind., 1962.

Gustavsson, Ulf L., "Aspects of the Development of Prophetic Interpretation within the Seventh-day Adventist Church." M.A. thesis, Andrews University, 1981.

Haloviak, Bert, "In the Shadow of the 'Daily': Background and Aftermath of the 1919 Bible and History Teachers' Conference." Unpublished research paper. Washington, DC: Office of Archives and Statistics, GC of SDA, n.d.

Hueston, Robert F., "The Catholic Press and Nativism--
    1840-1860." Ph.D. diss., University of Notre Dame,
    1972.

McAdams, Donald R., "Ellen G. White and the Protestant
    Historians." Unpubl. research paper. Andrews
    University, 1974, rev. in 1977.

Maxwell, C. Mervyn, "An Exegetical and Historical
    Examination of the Beginning and Ending of the 1260
    Days of Prophecy, with Special Attention Given to
    A.D. 538 and 1798 as Initial and Terminal Dates."
    M.A. thesis, SDA Theol. Sem., Washington, 1951.

Oliver, Barry David, "Principles for Reorganization of
    the Seventh-day Adventist Administrative Structure,
    1888-1903: Indications for an International
    Church." Ph.D. diss., SDA Theol. Sem., Andrews
    Univ., 1989.

Poehler, Rolf J., "And the door was shut: Seventh-day
    Adventists and the shut-door doctrine in the decade
    after the Great Disappointment." Unpubl. paper, SDA
    Theol. Sem., Andrews Univ., 1978.

Rubencamp, C.F.X., "Immortality and Seventh-day Adven-
    tist Eschatology." Ph.D. diss., The Catholic
    University of America, 1968.

Schwarz, Richard W., "John Harvey Kellogg: American
    Health Reformer." Ph.D. diss., University of
    Michigan, 1964.

Syme, Eric D., "Seventh-day Adventist Concepts on Church
    and State." Ph.D. diss., American University, 1969.

Thomas, Nathan G., "The Second Coming in the Third New
    England: The Millennial Impulse in Michigan, 1830-
    1860." Ph.D. diss., Michigan State University,
    1967.

Valentine, Gilbert M., "William Warren Prescott:
    Seventh-day Adventist Educator." Ph.D. diss., An-
    drews University, 1982.

Vineyard, Clyde Dale, "The Origin, Development and
    Significance of the Roman Catholic Papal Tiara."
    M.A. thesis, SDA Theol. Sem., Washington, DC, 1951.

Walter, E.C., "A History of Seventh-day Adventist Higher Education in the United States." Ed.D. diss., University of California, Berkeley, 1966.

White, Arthur L., "Thoughts on Daniel and the Revelation." Mimeographed document, publ. by the Ellen G. White Estate, Washington, DC, n.d.